For more in~~fo~~

on all our products, along with the most up-to-date news on releases, series announcements, and contests, please visit us at:

 SuBLimeManga.com

 twitter.com/**SuBLimeManga**

 facebook.com/**SuBLimeManga**

 instagram.com/**SuBLimeManga**

 SuBLimeManga.tumblr.com

The World's Greatest First Love: The Case of Ritsu Onodera

Volume 12
SuBLime Manga Edition

Story and Art by **Shungiku Nakamura**

Translation—**Adrienne Beck**
Touch-Up Art and Lettering—**Eric Erbes**
Cover and Graphic Design—**Shawn Carrico**
Editor—**Jennifer LeBlanc**

SEKAIICHI HATSUKOI ~ONODERA RITSU NO BAAI~ Volume 12
© Shungiku NAKAMURA 2017
Edited by KADOKAWA SHOTEN
First published in Japan in 2017 by KADOKAWA CORPORATION, Tokyo.
English translation rights arranged with KADOKAWA CORPORATION,
Tokyo.

ASUKA
COMICS
CLX

Printed in the U.S.A.

Published by SuBLime Manga
P.O. Box 77010
San Francisco, CA 94107

10 9 8 7 6 5 4 3 2 1
First printing, April 2019

 PARENTAL ADVISORY
THE WORLD'S GREATEST FIRST LOVE is rated M for Mature and is
recommended for mature readers. This volume contains graphic
MATURE imagery and mature themes.

www.SuBLimeManga.com

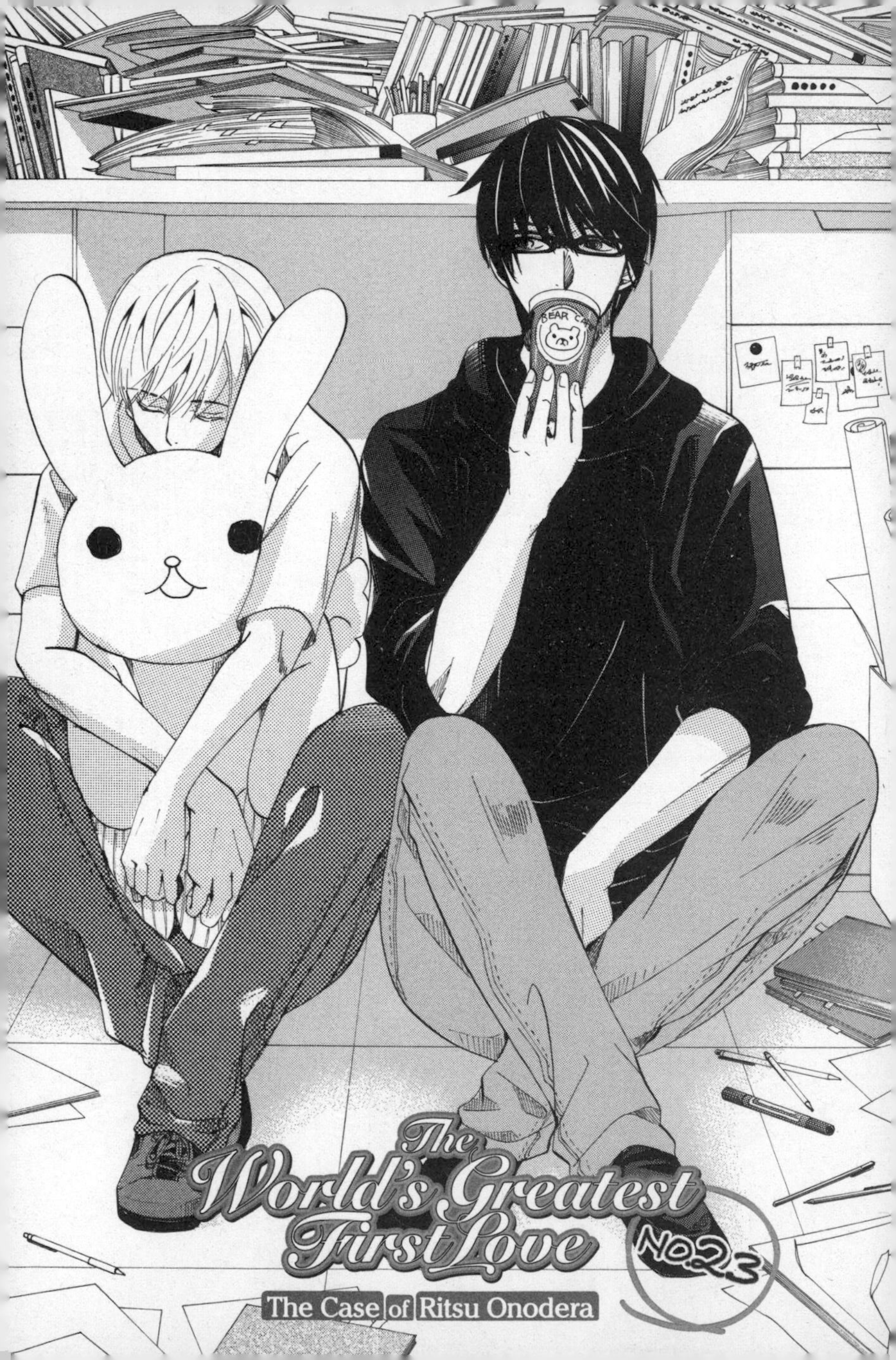
The World's Greatest First Love
No.23
The Case of Ritsu Onodera
BEAR CA

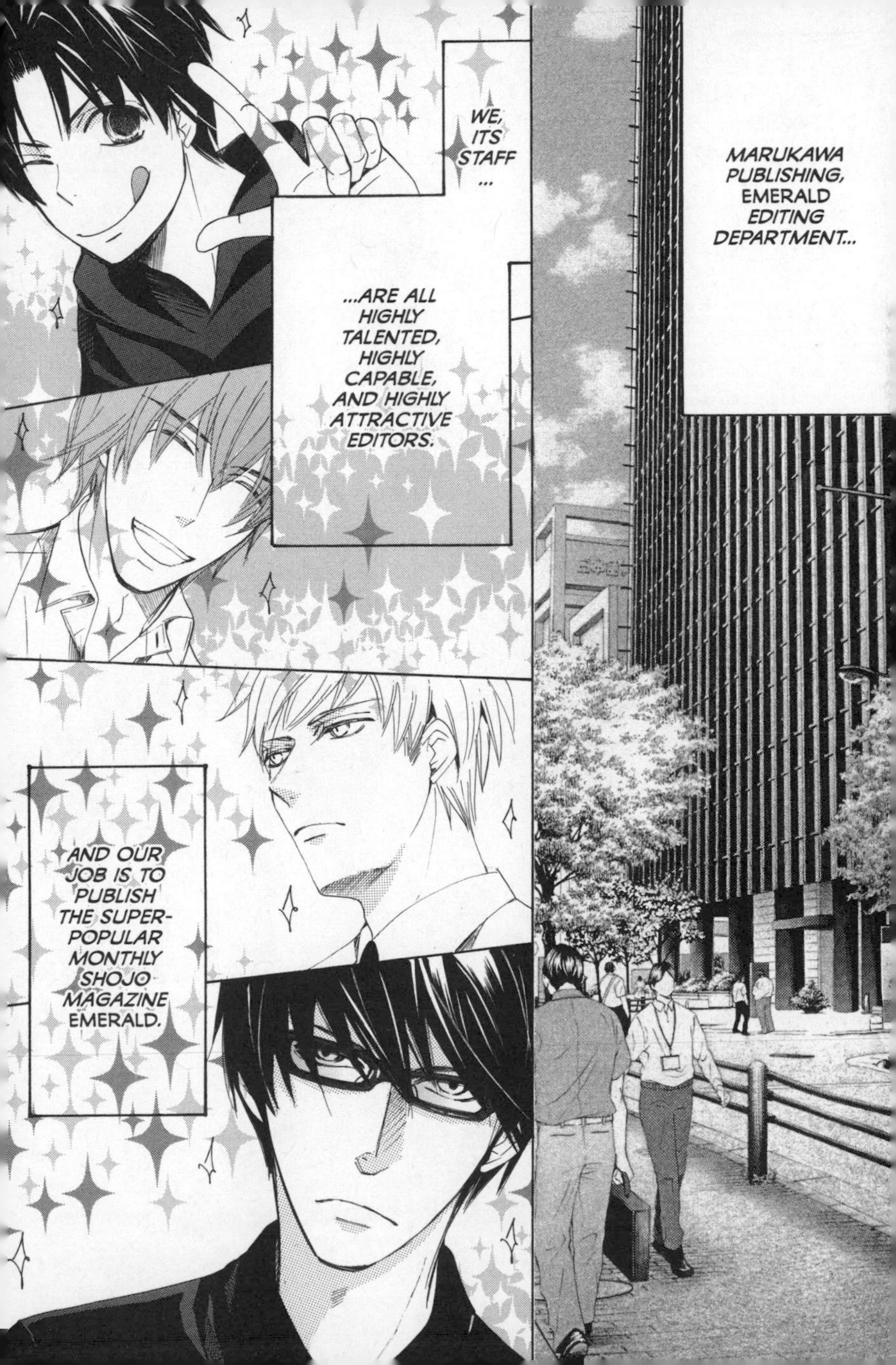
MARUKAWA PUBLISHING, EMERALD EDITING DEPARTMENT...
WE, ITS STAFF...
...ARE ALL HIGHLY TALENTED, HIGHLY CAPABLE, AND HIGHLY ATTRACTIVE EDITORS.
AND OUR JOB IS TO PUBLISH THE SUPER-POPULAR MONTHLY SHOJO MAGAZINE EMERALD.

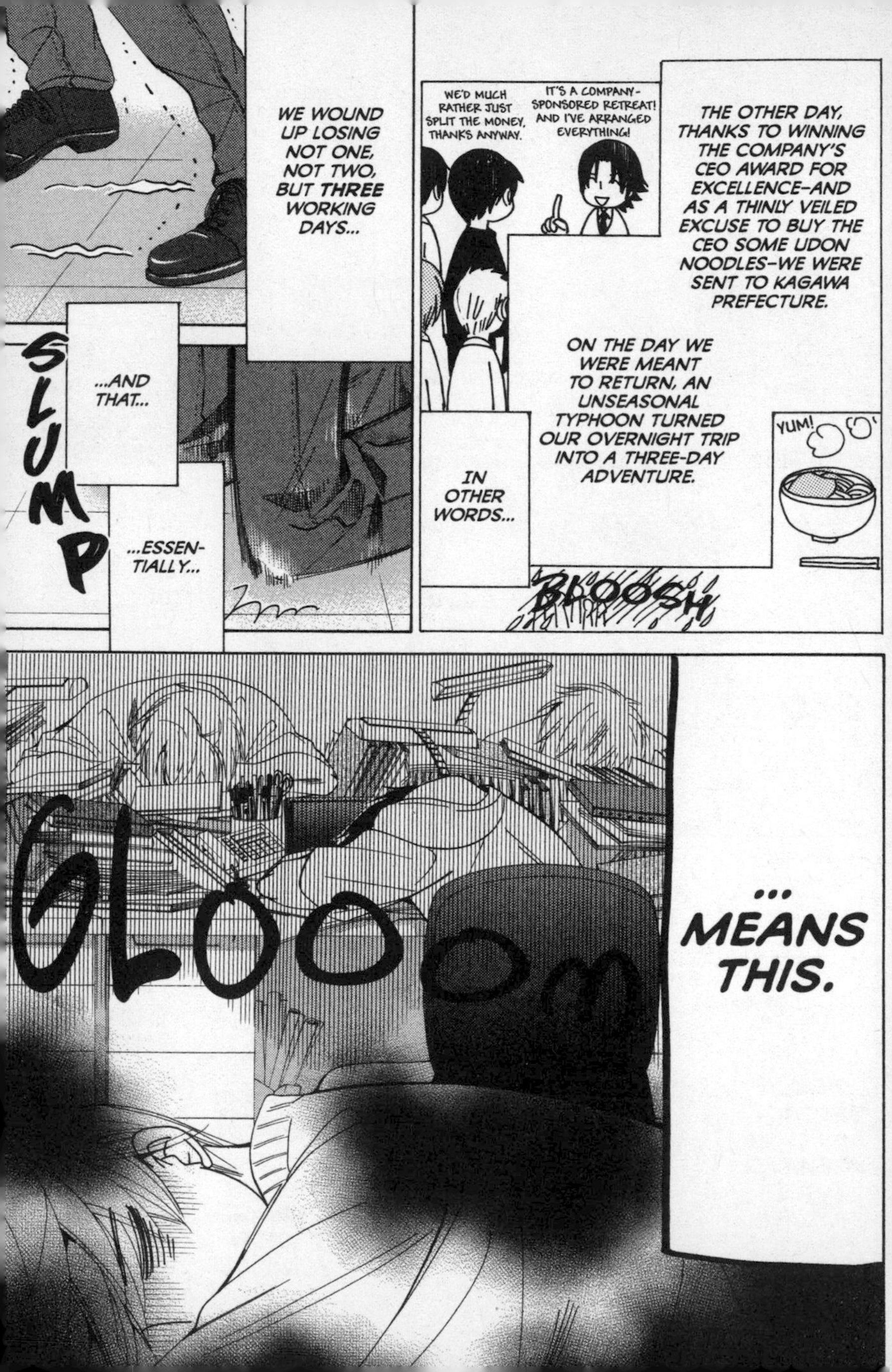
THE OTHER DAY, THANKS TO WINNING THE COMPANY'S CEO AWARD FOR EXCELLENCE–AND AS A THINLY VEILED EXCUSE TO BUY THE CEO SOME UDON NOODLES–WE WERE SENT TO KAGAWA PREFECTURE.
IT'S A COMPANY-SPONSORED RETREAT! AND I'VE ARRANGED EVERYTHING!
WE'D MUCH RATHER JUST SPLIT THE MONEY, THANKS ANYWAY.
YUM!
ON THE DAY WE WERE MEANT TO RETURN, AN UNSEASONAL TYPHOON TURNED OUR OVERNIGHT TRIP INTO A THREE-DAY ADVENTURE.
BLOOSH
IN OTHER WORDS...
WE WOUND UP LOSING NOT ONE, NOT TWO, BUT THREE WORKING DAYS...
...AND THAT...
SLUMP
...ESSEN-TIALLY...
... MEANS THIS.
GLOOOM

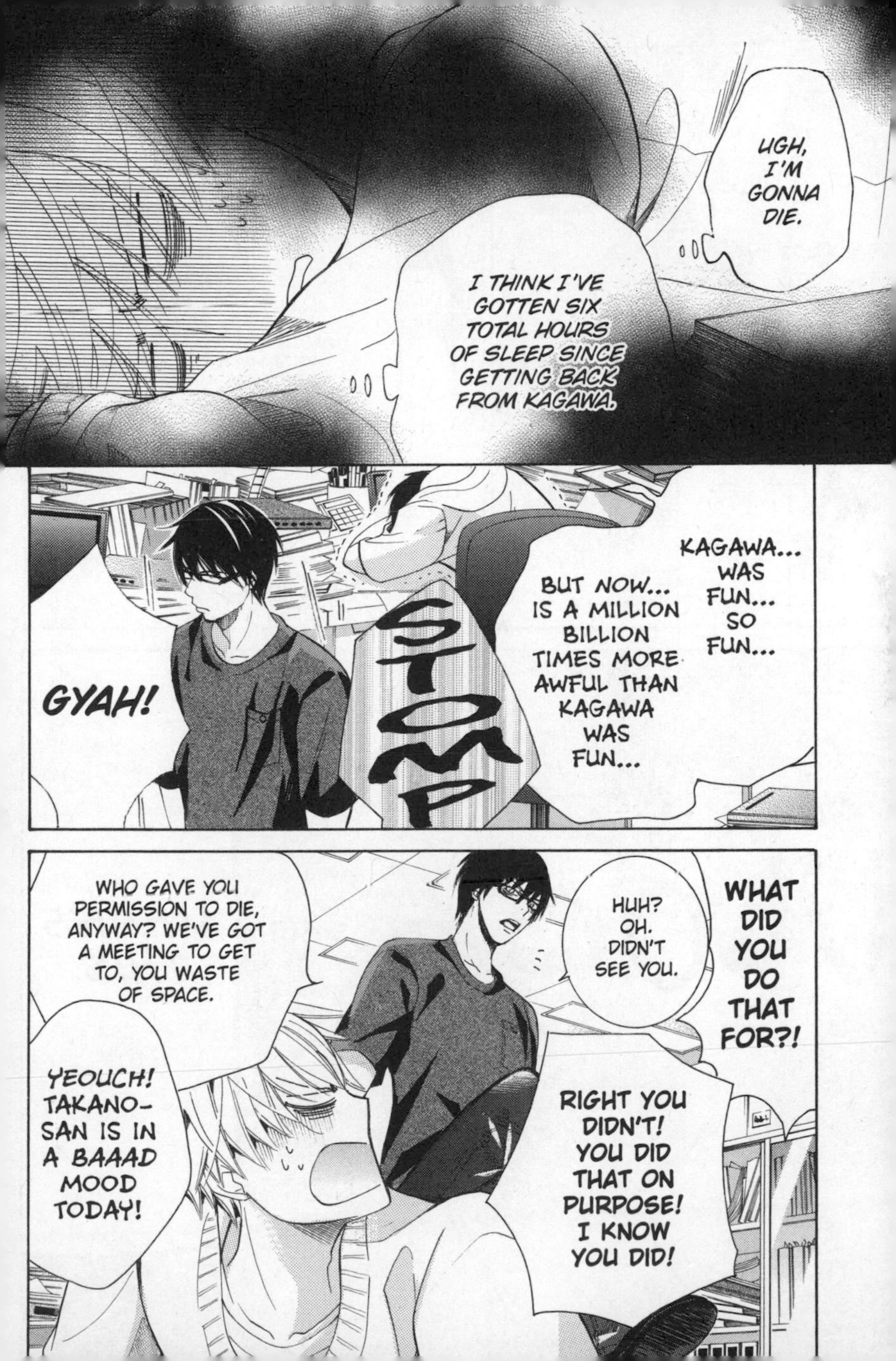
UGH, I'M GONNA DIE.
I THINK I'VE GOTTEN SIX TOTAL HOURS OF SLEEP SINCE GETTING BACK FROM KAGAWA.
KAGAWA... WAS FUN... SO FUN...
BUT NOW... IS A MILLION BILLION TIMES MORE AWFUL THAN KAGAWA WAS FUN...
STOMP
GYAH!
WHAT DID YOU DO THAT FOR?!
HUH? OH. DIDN'T SEE YOU.
RIGHT YOU DIDN'T! YOU DID THAT ON PURPOSE! I KNOW YOU DID!
WHO GAVE YOU PERMISSION TO DIE, ANYWAY? WE'VE GOT A MEETING TO GET TO, YOU WASTE OF SPACE.
YEOUCH! TAKANO-SAN IS IN A BAAAD MOOD TODAY!

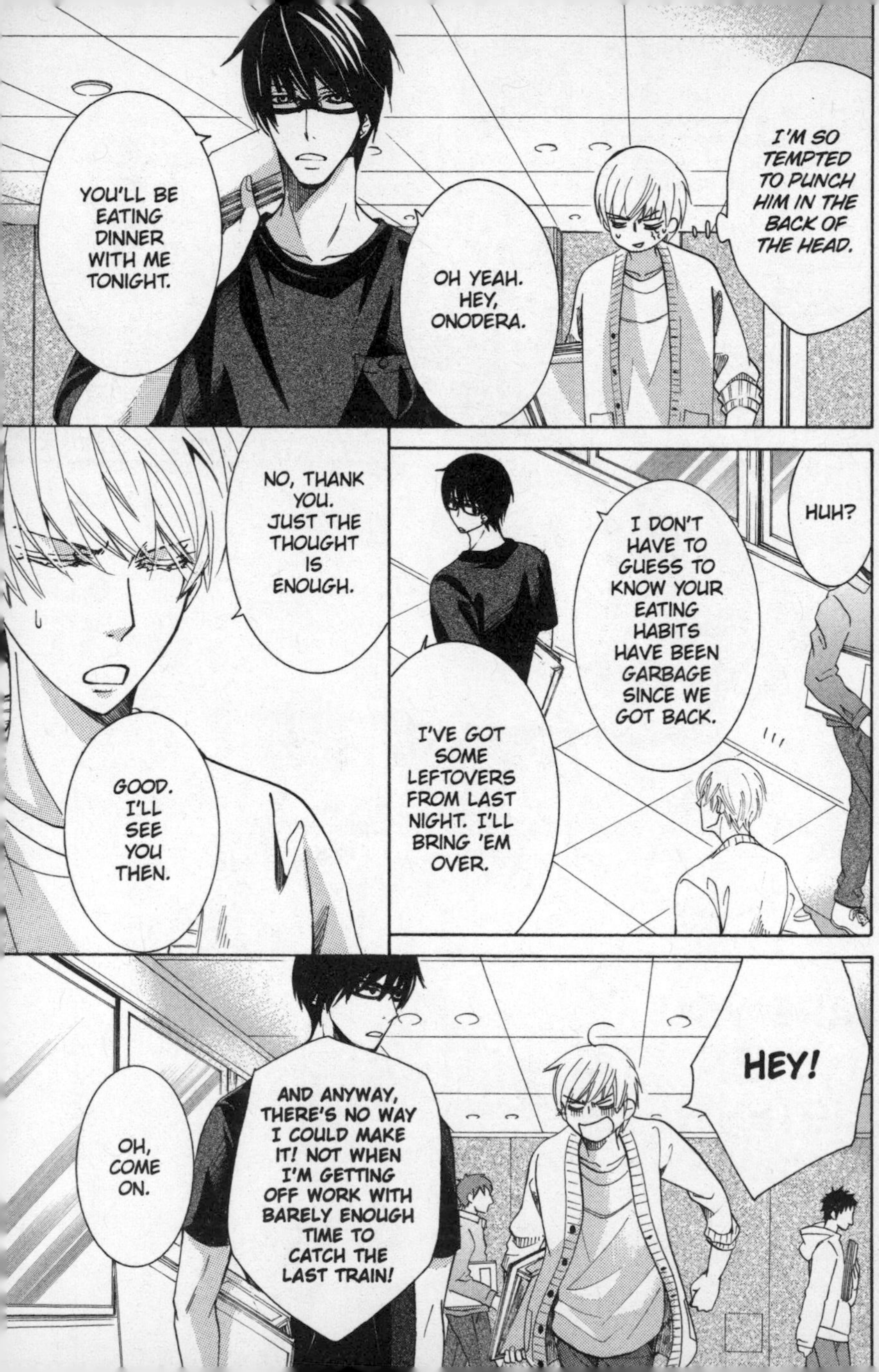
I'M SO TEMPTED TO PUNCH HIM IN THE BACK OF THE HEAD.
OH YEAH. HEY, ONODERA.
YOU'LL BE EATING DINNER WITH ME TONIGHT.
HUH?
I DON'T HAVE TO GUESS TO KNOW YOUR EATING HABITS HAVE BEEN GARBAGE SINCE WE GOT BACK.
I'VE GOT SOME LEFTOVERS FROM LAST NIGHT. I'LL BRING 'EM OVER.
NO, THANK YOU. JUST THE THOUGHT IS ENOUGH.
GOOD. I'LL SEE YOU THEN.
HEY!
AND ANYWAY, THERE'S NO WAY I COULD MAKE IT! NOT WHEN I'M GETTING OFF WORK WITH BARELY ENOUGH TIME TO CATCH THE LAST TRAIN!
OH, COME ON.

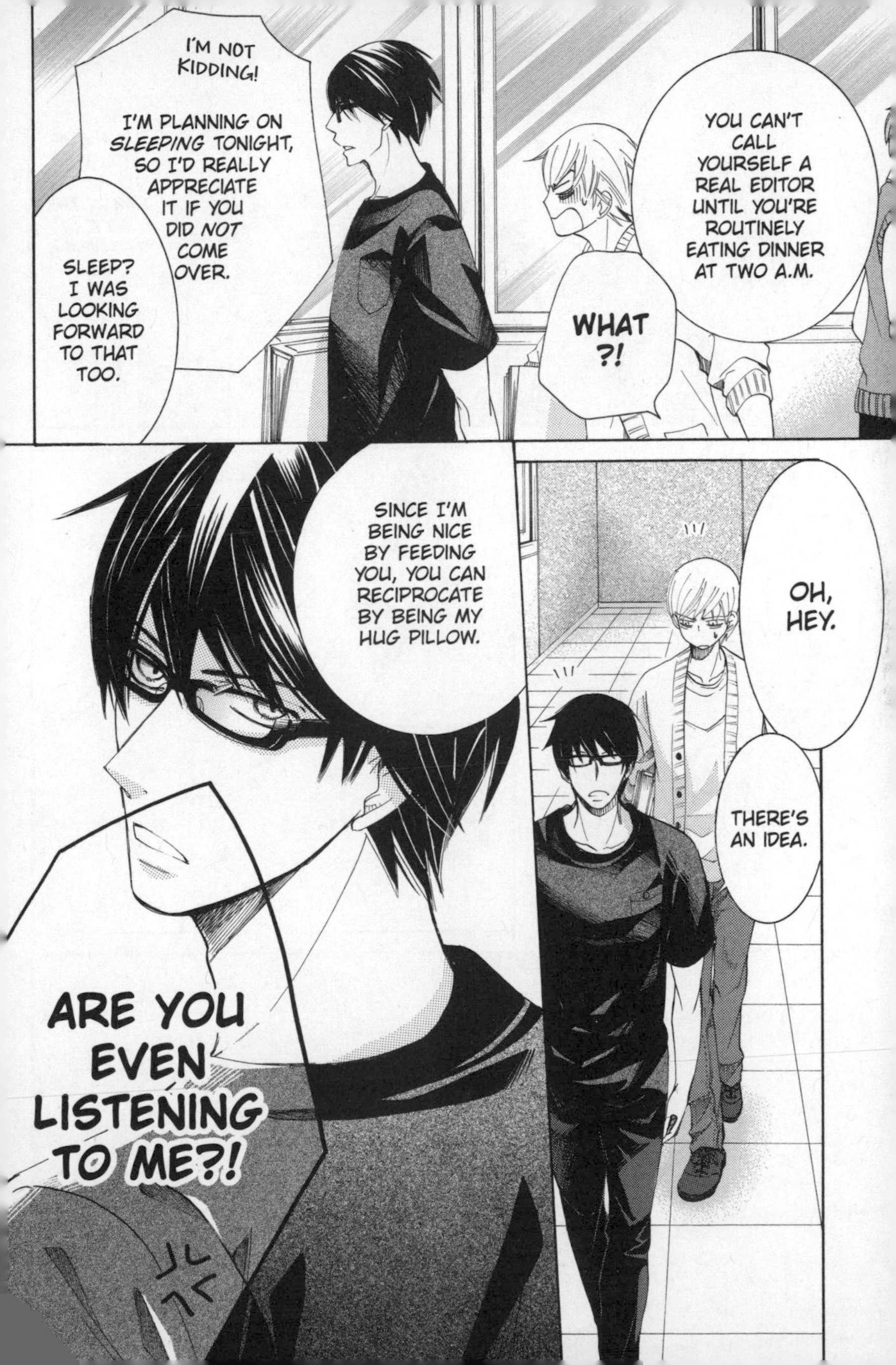

YOU CAN'T CALL YOURSELF A REAL EDITOR UNTIL YOU'RE ROUTINELY EATING DINNER AT TWO A.M.
WHAT?!
I'M NOT KIDDING!
I'M PLANNING ON SLEEPING TONIGHT, SO I'D REALLY APPRECIATE IT IF YOU DID NOT COME OVER.
SLEEP? I WAS LOOKING FORWARD TO THAT TOO.
OH, HEY.
THERE'S AN IDEA.
SINCE I'M BEING NICE BY FEEDING YOU, YOU CAN RECIPROCATE BY BEING MY HUG PILLOW.
ARE YOU EVEN LISTENING TO ME?!

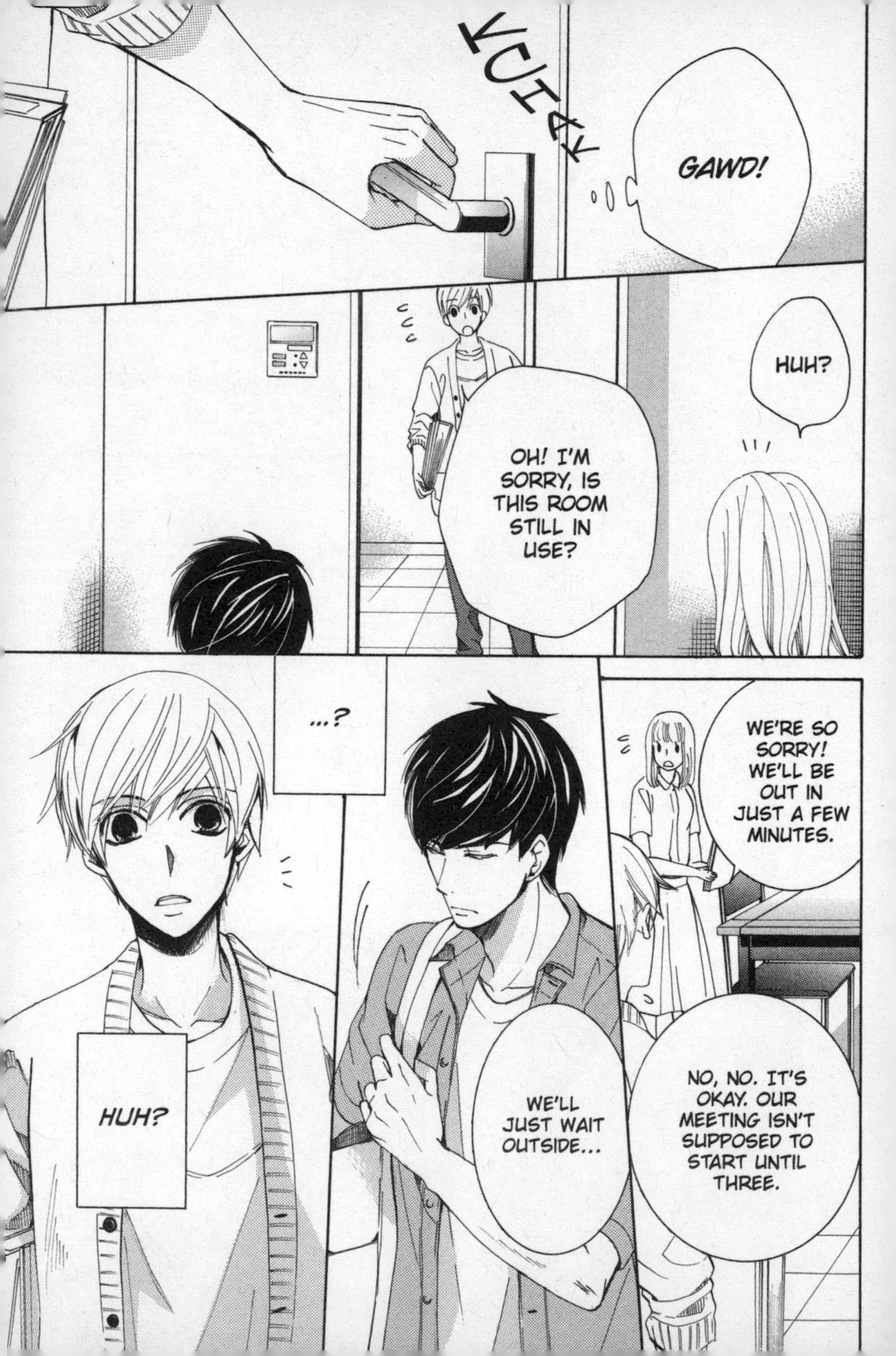
KCHAK
GAWD!
HUH?
OH! I'M SORRY, IS THIS ROOM STILL IN USE?
WE'RE SO SORRY! WE'LL BE OUT IN JUST A FEW MINUTES.
NO, NO. IT'S OKAY. OUR MEETING ISN'T SUPPOSED TO START UNTIL THREE.
WE'LL JUST WAIT OUTSIDE...
...?
HUH?

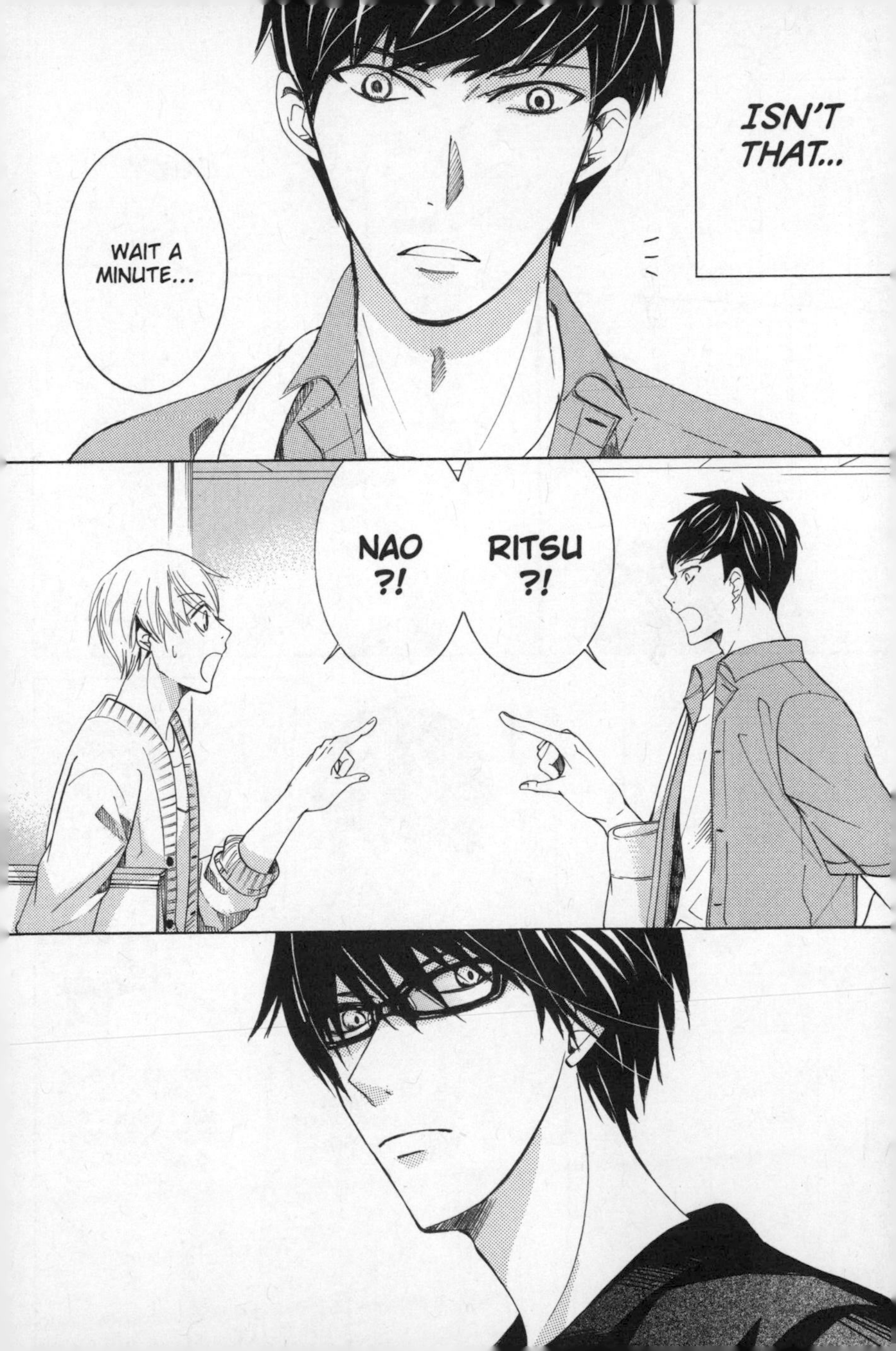
ISN'T THAT...
WAIT A MINUTE...
RITSU ?!
NAO ?!

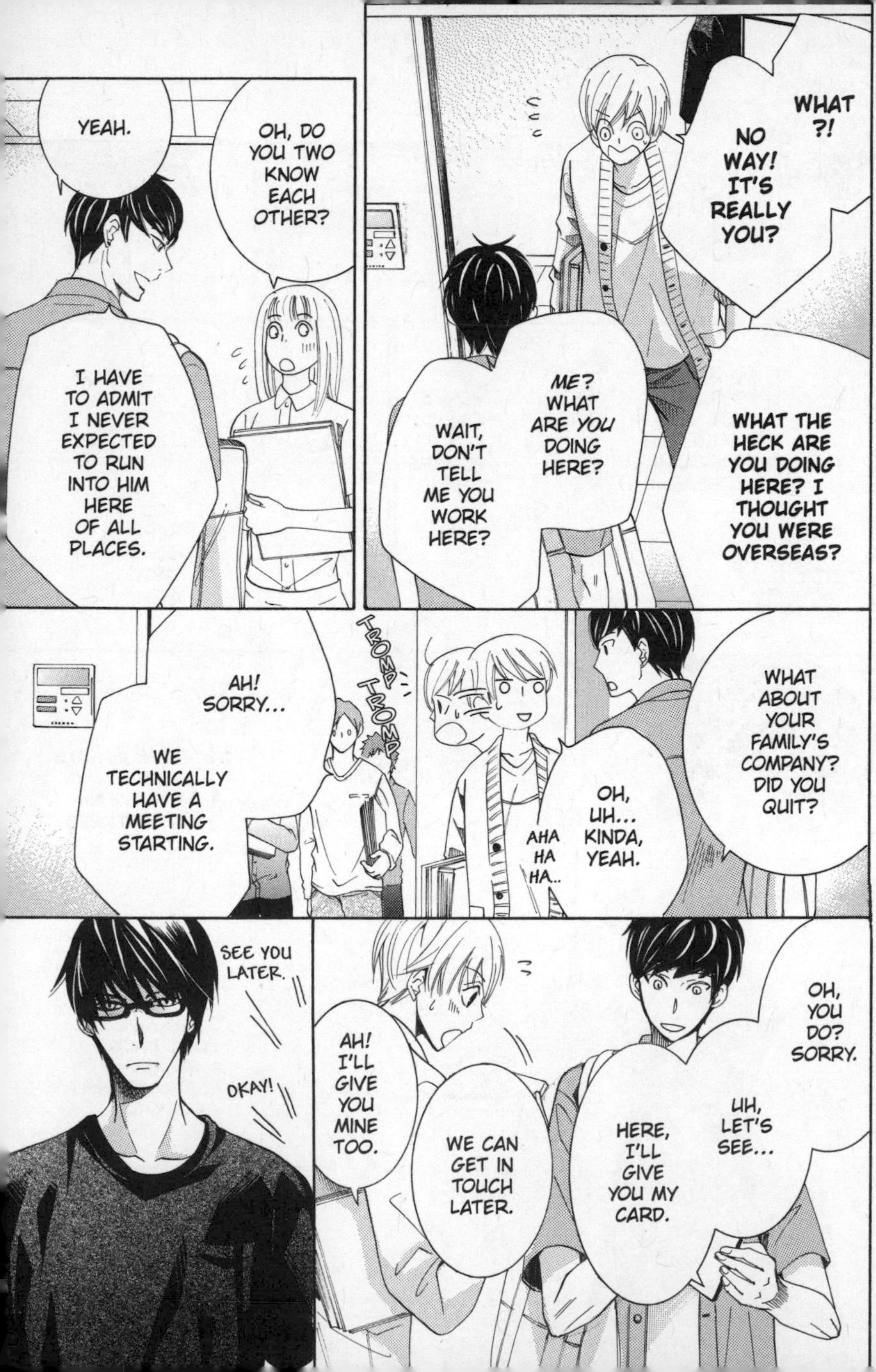
WHAT ?!
NO WAY! IT'S REALLY YOU?
WHAT THE HECK ARE YOU DOING HERE? I THOUGHT YOU WERE OVERSEAS?
ME? WHAT ARE YOU DOING HERE?
WAIT, DON'T TELL ME YOU WORK HERE?
OH, DO YOU TWO KNOW EACH OTHER?
YEAH.
I HAVE TO ADMIT I NEVER EXPECTED TO RUN INTO HIM HERE OF ALL PLACES.
WHAT ABOUT YOUR FAMILY'S COMPANY? DID YOU QUIT?
OH, UH... KINDA, YEAH.
AHA HA HA...
TROMP TROMP TROMP
AH! SORRY...
WE TECHNICALLY HAVE A MEETING STARTING.
OH, YOU DO? SORRY.
UH, LET'S SEE...
HERE, I'LL GIVE YOU MY CARD.
WE CAN GET IN TOUCH LATER.
AH! I'LL GIVE YOU MINE TOO.
SEE YOU LATER.
OKAY!

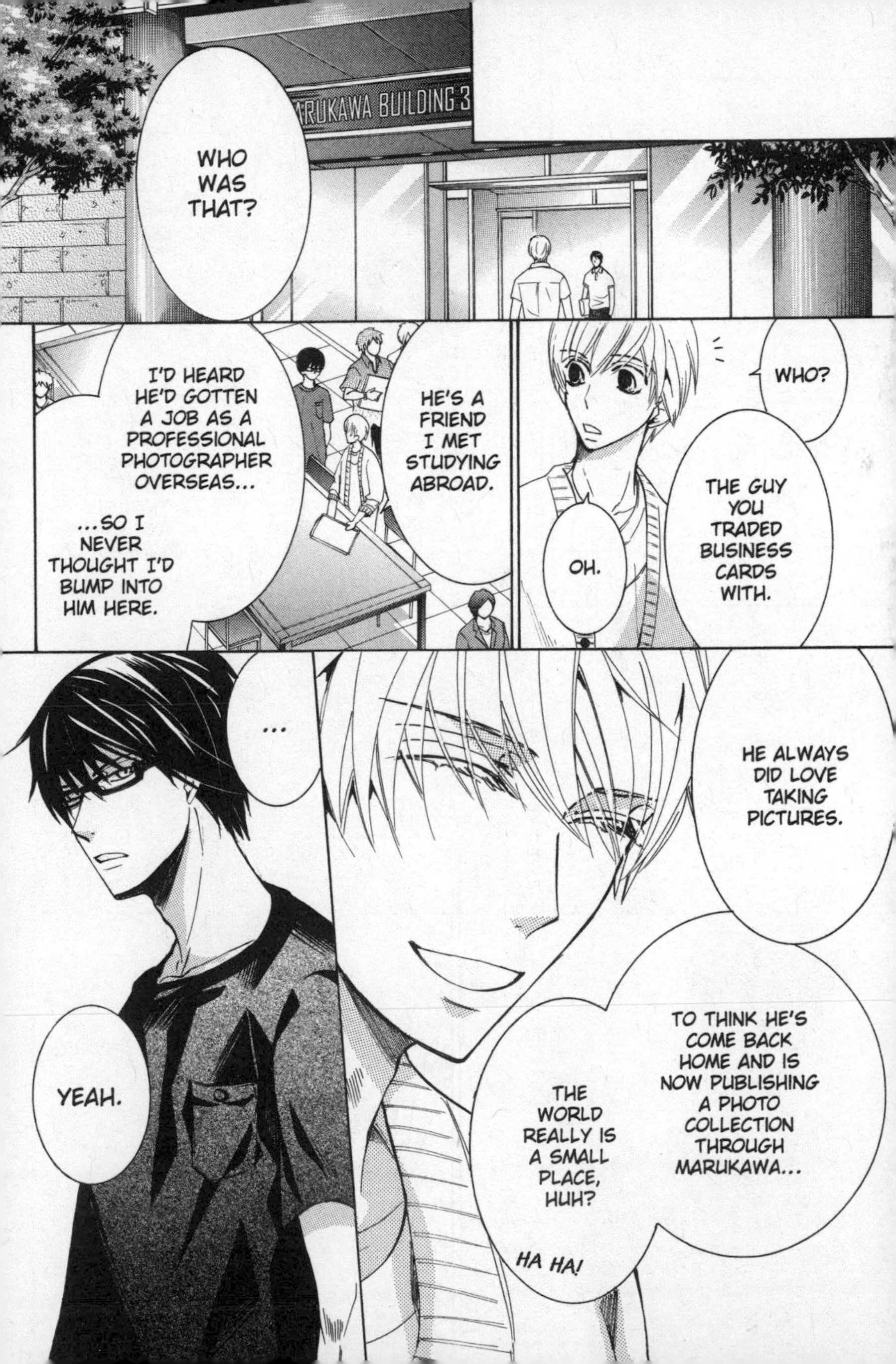
ARUKAWA BUILDING 3
WHO WAS THAT?
WHO?
THE GUY YOU TRADED BUSINESS CARDS WITH.
OH.
HE'S A FRIEND I MET STUDYING ABROAD.
I'D HEARD HE'D GOTTEN A JOB AS A PROFESSIONAL PHOTOGRAPHER OVERSEAS...
...SO I NEVER THOUGHT I'D BUMP INTO HIM HERE.
HE ALWAYS DID LOVE TAKING PICTURES.
TO THINK HE'S COME BACK HOME AND IS NOW PUBLISHING A PHOTO COLLECTION THROUGH MARUKAWA...
THE WORLD REALLY IS A SMALL PLACE, HUH?
HA HA!
...
YEAH.

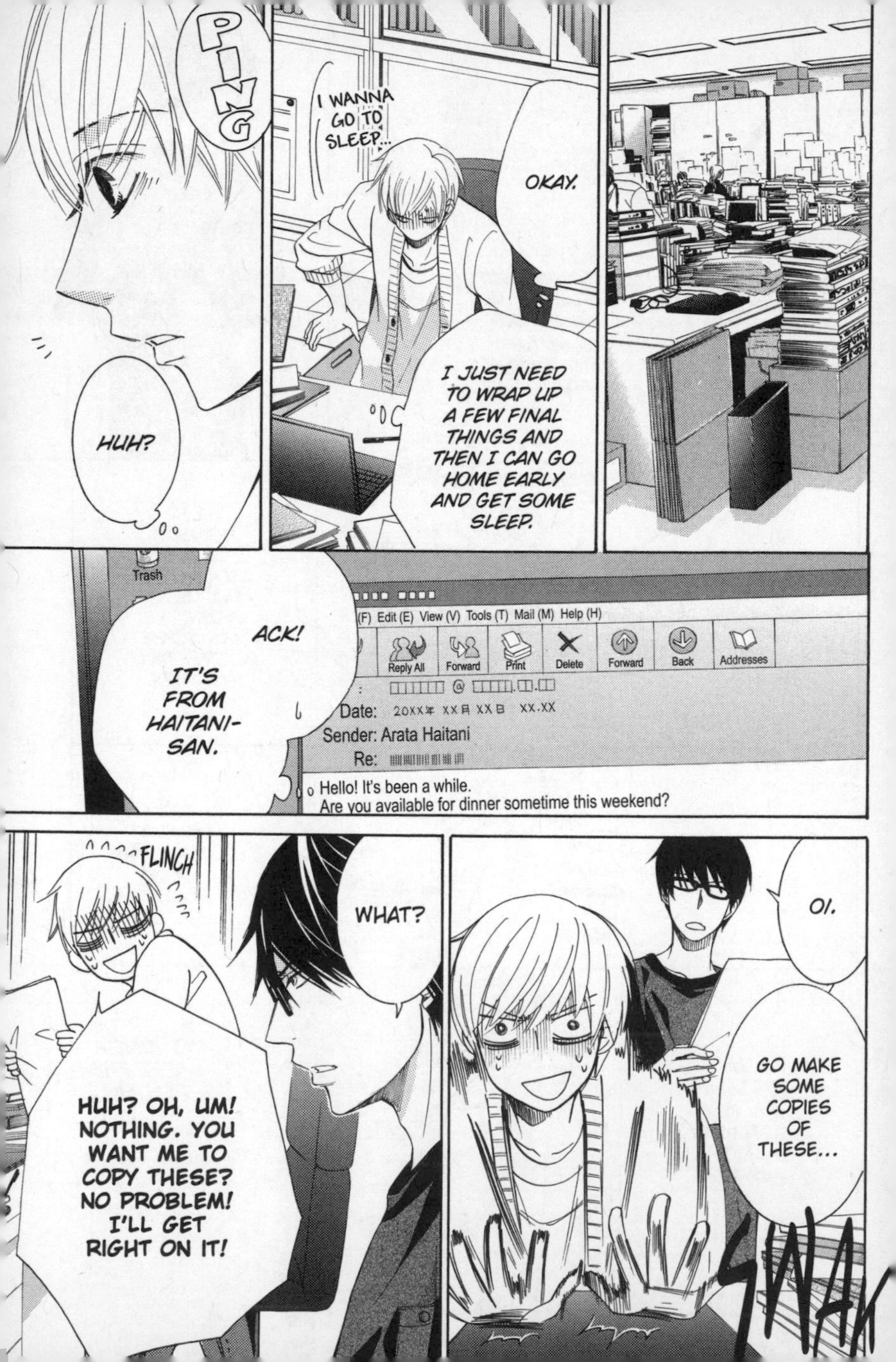
I WANNA GO TO SLEEP...
OKAY.
I JUST NEED TO WRAP UP A FEW FINAL THINGS AND THEN I CAN GO HOME EARLY AND GET SOME SLEEP.
PING
HUH?
Trash
(F) Edit (E) View (V) Tools (T) Mail (M) Help (H)
Reply All
Forward
Print
Delete
Forward
Back
Addresses
Date: 20XX年 XX月 XX日 XX.XX
Sender: Arata Haitani
Re:
Hello! It's been a while.
Are you available for dinner sometime this weekend?
ACK!
IT'S FROM HAITANI-SAN.
OI.
GO MAKE SOME COPIES OF THESE...
SWAK
WHAT?
FLINCH
HUH? OH, UM! NOTHING. YOU WANT ME TO COPY THESE? NO PROBLEM! I'LL GET RIGHT ON IT!

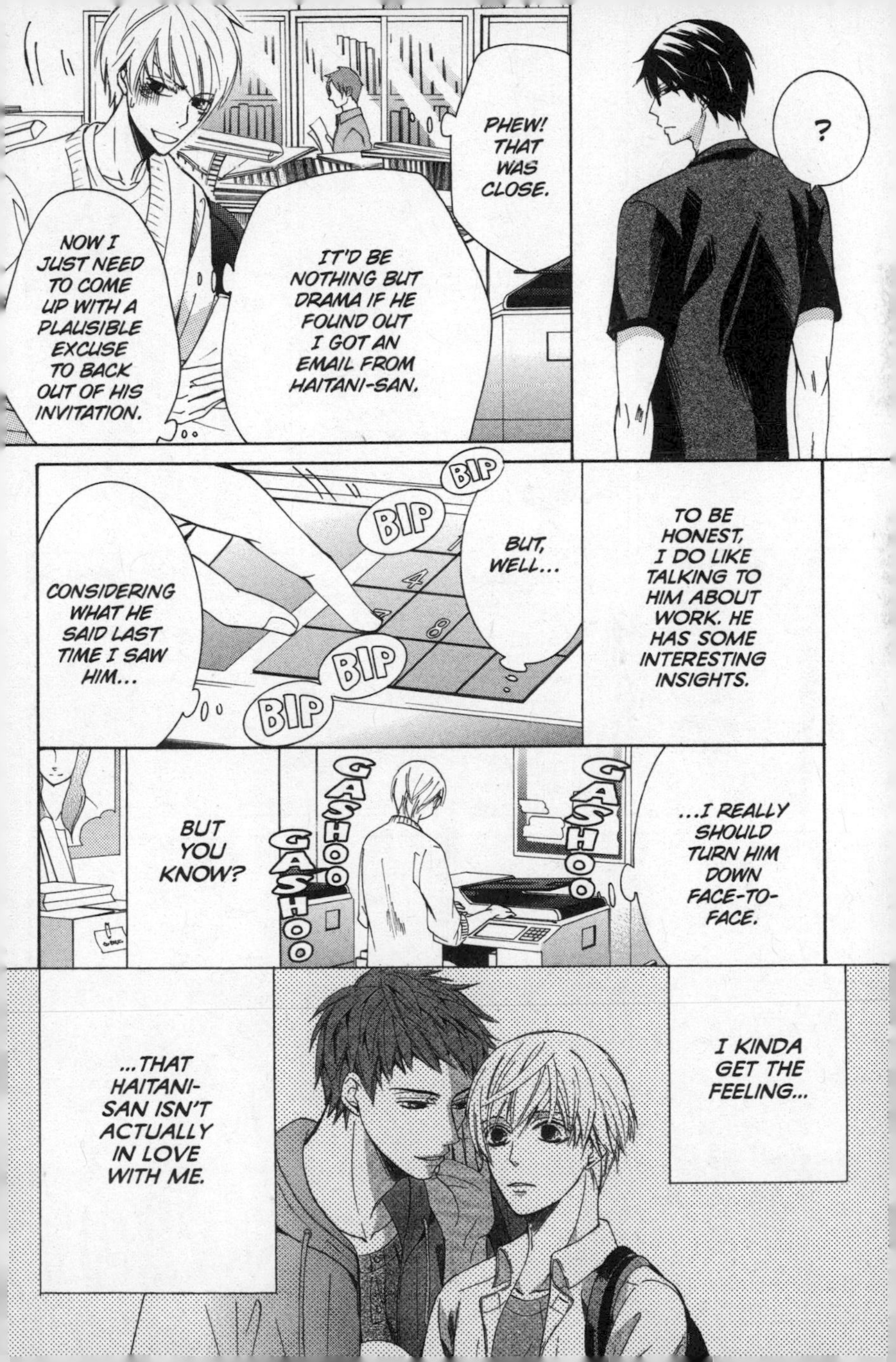
?
PHEW! THAT WAS CLOSE.
IT'D BE NOTHING BUT DRAMA IF HE FOUND OUT I GOT AN EMAIL FROM HAITANI-SAN.
NOW I JUST NEED TO COME UP WITH A PLAUSIBLE EXCUSE TO BACK OUT OF HIS INVITATION.
TO BE HONEST, I DO LIKE TALKING TO HIM ABOUT WORK. HE HAS SOME INTERESTING INSIGHTS.
BIP
BUT, WELL...
BIP
BIP
BIP
CONSIDERING WHAT HE SAID LAST TIME I SAW HIM...
...I REALLY SHOULD TURN HIM DOWN FACE-TO-FACE.
GASHOO
GASHOO
GASHOO
BUT YOU KNOW?
I KINDA GET THE FEELING...
...THAT HAITANI-SAN ISN'T ACTUALLY IN LOVE WITH ME.

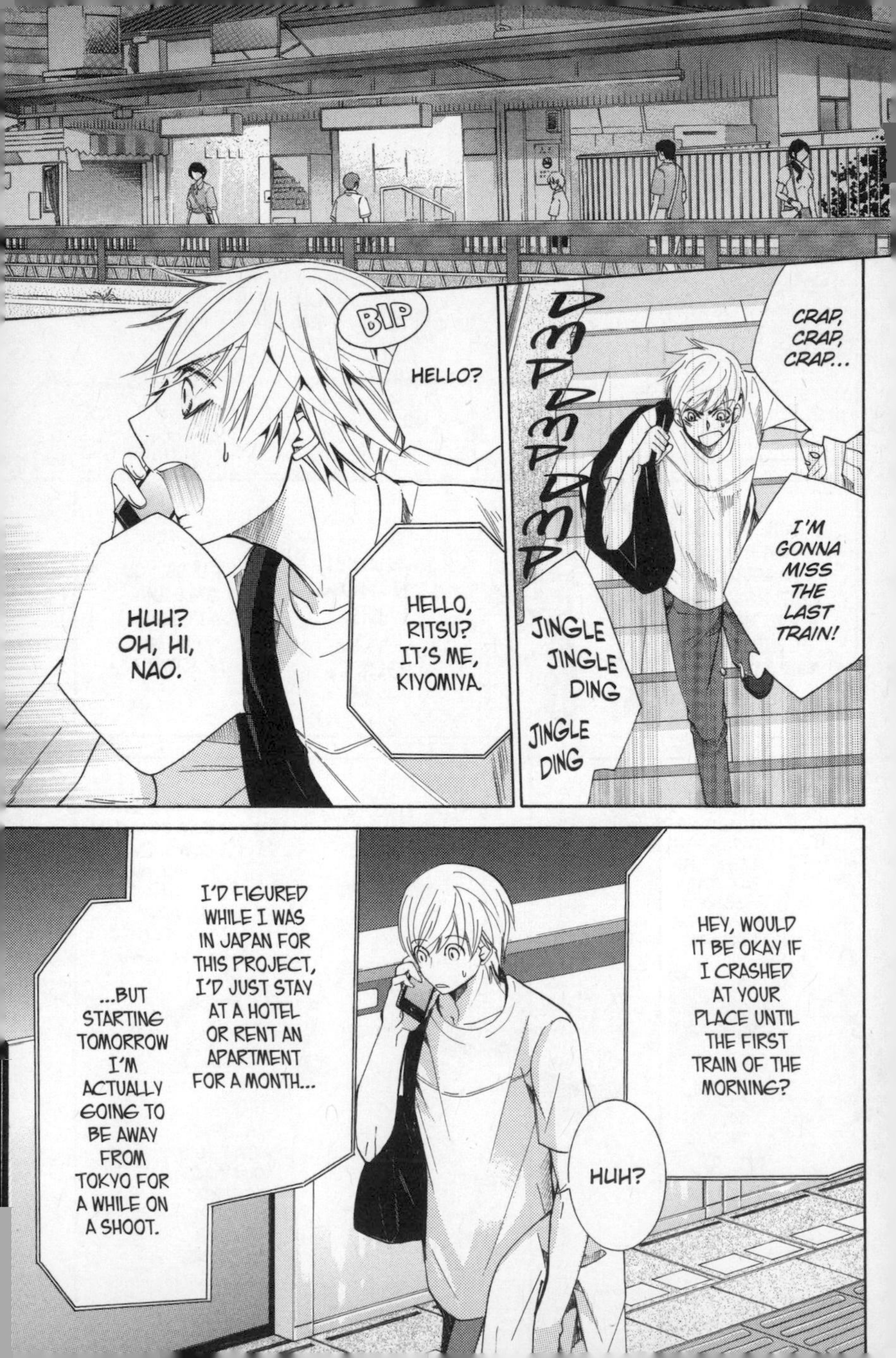
CRAP, CRAP, CRAP...
I'M GONNA MISS THE LAST TRAIN!
JINGLE JINGLE DING
JINGLE DING
BIP
HELLO?
HELLO, RITSU? IT'S ME, KIYOMIYA.
HUH? OH, HI, NAO.
HEY, WOULD IT BE OKAY IF I CRASHED AT YOUR PLACE UNTIL THE FIRST TRAIN OF THE MORNING?
HUH?
I'D FIGURED WHILE I WAS IN JAPAN FOR THIS PROJECT, I'D JUST STAY AT A HOTEL OR RENT AN APARTMENT FOR A MONTH...
...BUT STARTING TOMORROW I'M ACTUALLY GOING TO BE AWAY FROM TOKYO FOR A WHILE ON A SHOOT.

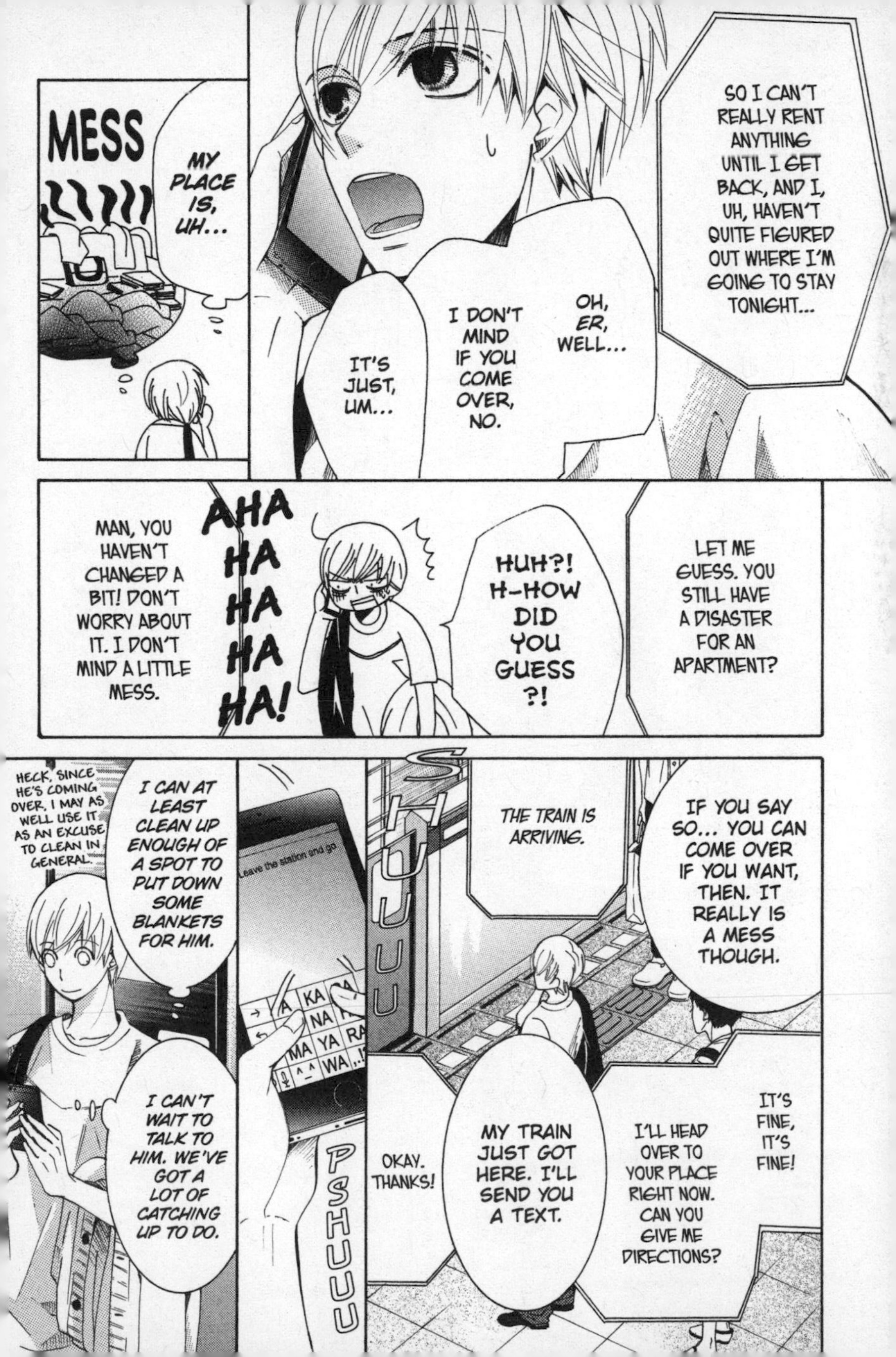
SO I CAN'T REALLY RENT ANYTHING UNTIL I GET BACK, AND I, UH, HAVEN'T QUITE FIGURED OUT WHERE I'M GOING TO STAY TONIGHT...
OH, ER, WELL...
I DON'T MIND IF YOU COME OVER, NO.
IT'S JUST, UM...
MY PLACE IS, UH...
MESS
LET ME GUESS. YOU STILL HAVE A DISASTER FOR AN APARTMENT?
HUH?! H-HOW DID YOU GUESS?!
AHA HA HA HA HA!
MAN, YOU HAVEN'T CHANGED A BIT! DON'T WORRY ABOUT IT. I DON'T MIND A LITTLE MESS.
IF YOU SAY SO... YOU CAN COME OVER IF YOU WANT, THEN. IT REALLY IS A MESS THOUGH.
THE TRAIN IS ARRIVING.
SHUUUUU
IT'S FINE, IT'S FINE!
I'LL HEAD OVER TO YOUR PLACE RIGHT NOW. CAN YOU GIVE ME DIRECTIONS?
MY TRAIN JUST GOT HERE. I'LL SEND YOU A TEXT.
OKAY. THANKS!
PSHUUU
Leave the station and go
HECK, SINCE HE'S COMING OVER, I MAY AS WELL USE IT AS AN EXCUSE TO CLEAN IN GENERAL.
I CAN AT LEAST CLEAN UP ENOUGH OF A SPOT TO PUT DOWN SOME BLANKETS FOR HIM.
I CAN'T WAIT TO TALK TO HIM. WE'VE GOT A LOT OF CATCHING UP TO DO.

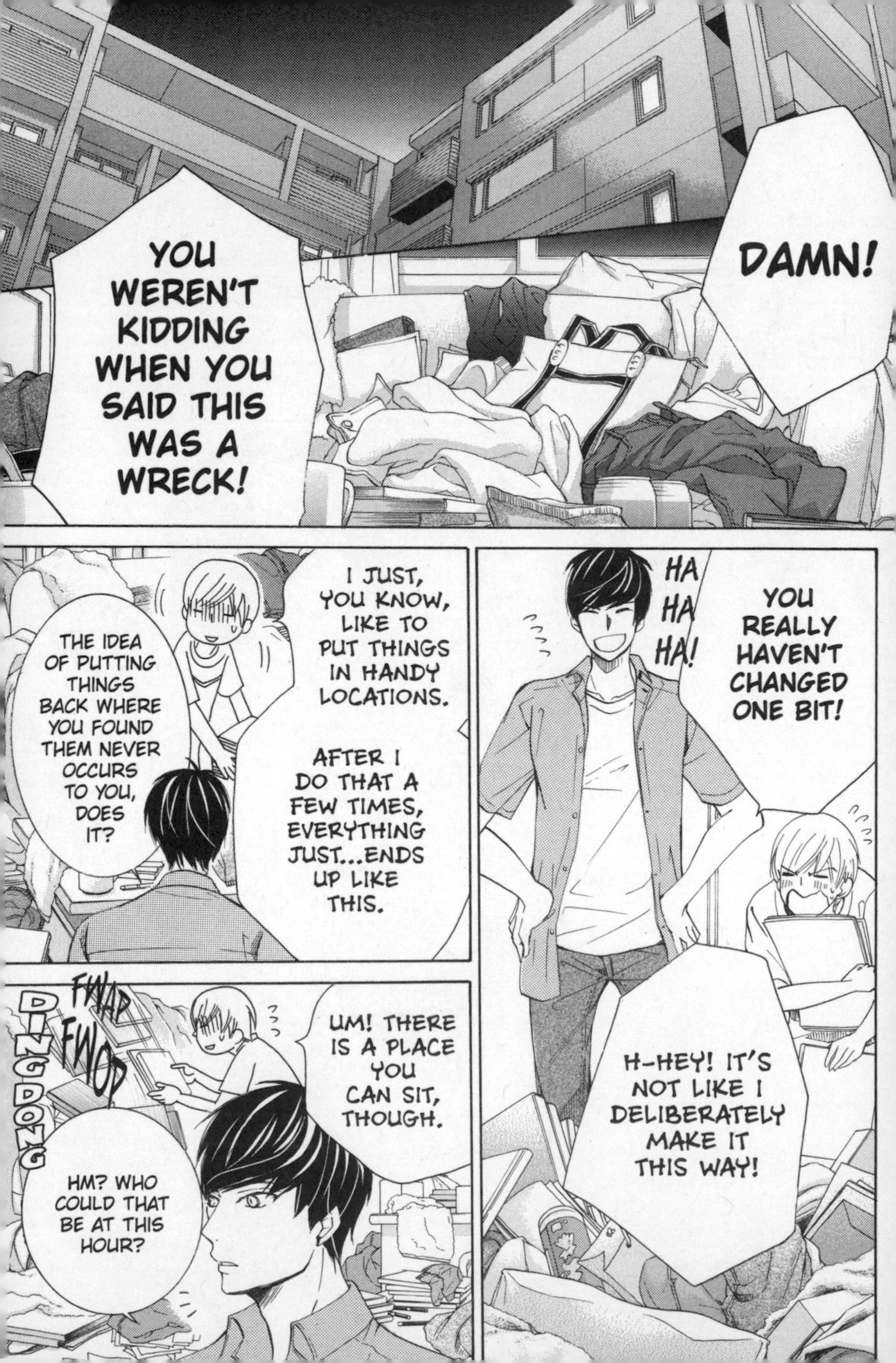
DAMN!
YOU WEREN'T KIDDING WHEN YOU SAID THIS WAS A WRECK!
HA HA HA!
YOU REALLY HAVEN'T CHANGED ONE BIT!
H-HEY! IT'S NOT LIKE I DELIBERATELY MAKE IT THIS WAY!
I JUST, YOU KNOW, LIKE TO PUT THINGS IN HANDY LOCATIONS.
AFTER I DO THAT A FEW TIMES, EVERYTHING JUST...ENDS UP LIKE THIS.
THE IDEA OF PUTTING THINGS BACK WHERE YOU FOUND THEM NEVER OCCURS TO YOU, DOES IT?
FWAP FWOP
UM! THERE IS A PLACE YOU CAN SIT, THOUGH.
DING DONG
HM? WHO COULD THAT BE AT THIS HOUR?

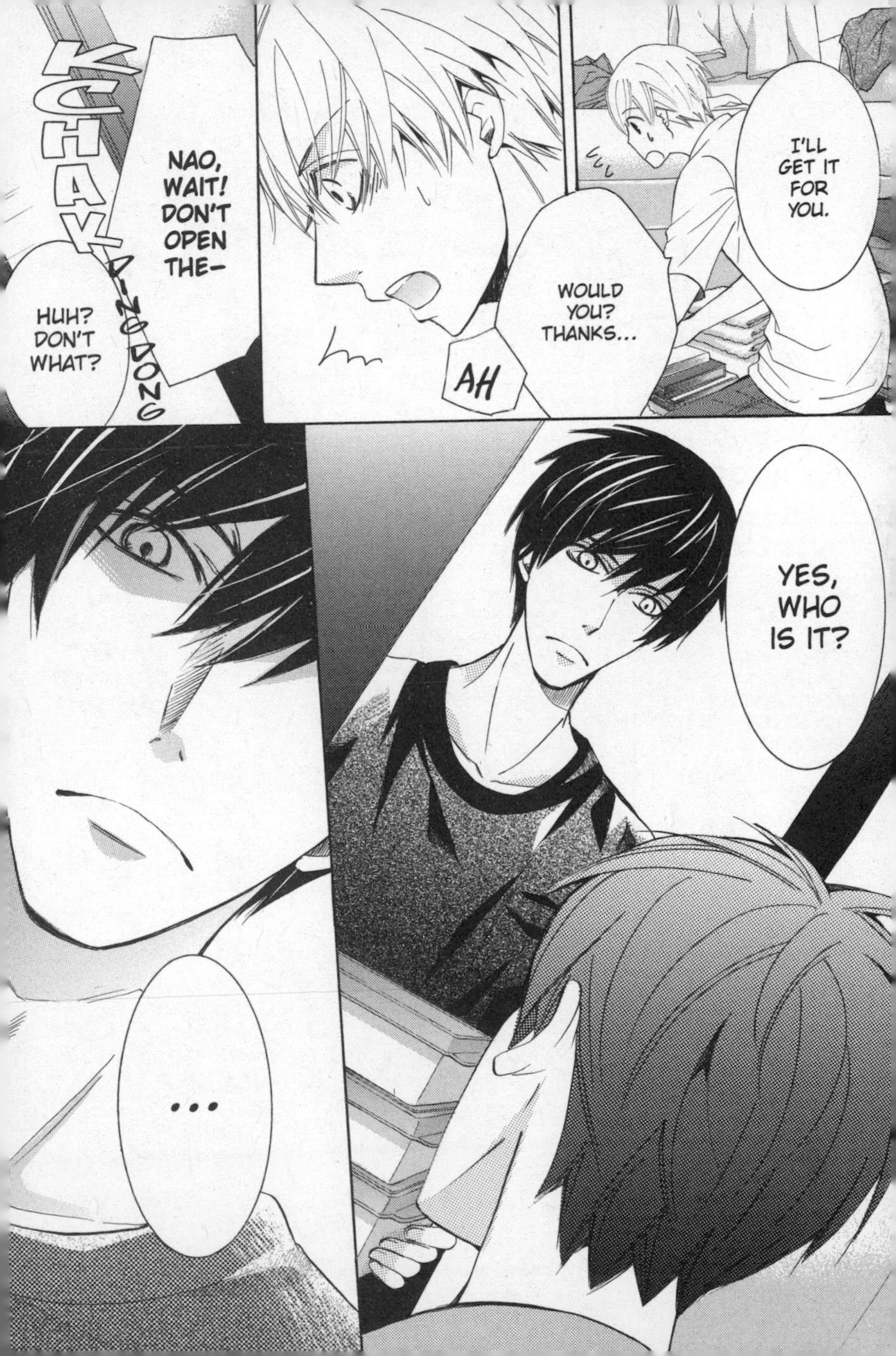

I'LL GET IT FOR YOU.
WOULD YOU? THANKS...
AH
NAO, WAIT! DON'T OPEN THE-
KCHAK
DING DONG
HUH? DON'T WHAT?
YES, WHO IS IT?
...

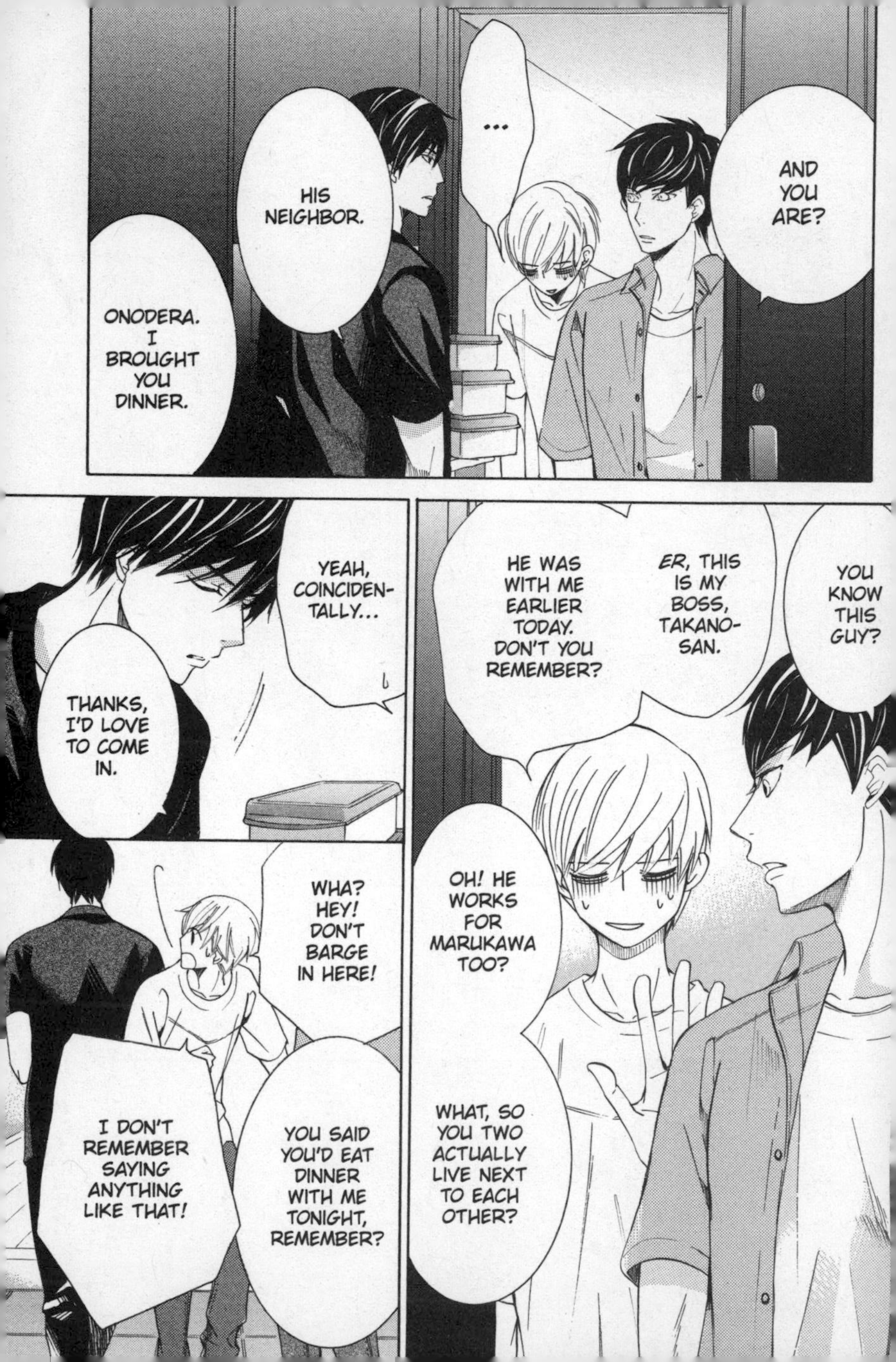
AND YOU ARE?
...
HIS NEIGHBOR.
ONODERA. I BROUGHT YOU DINNER.
YOU KNOW THIS GUY?
ER, THIS IS MY BOSS, TAKANO-SAN.
HE WAS WITH ME EARLIER TODAY. DON'T YOU REMEMBER?
OH! HE WORKS FOR MARUKAWA TOO?
WHAT, SO YOU TWO ACTUALLY LIVE NEXT TO EACH OTHER?
YEAH, COINCIDEN-TALLY...
THANKS, I'D LOVE TO COME IN.
WHA? HEY! DON'T BARGE IN HERE!
YOU SAID YOU'D EAT DINNER WITH ME TONIGHT, REMEMBER?
I DON'T REMEMBER SAYING ANYTHING LIKE THAT!

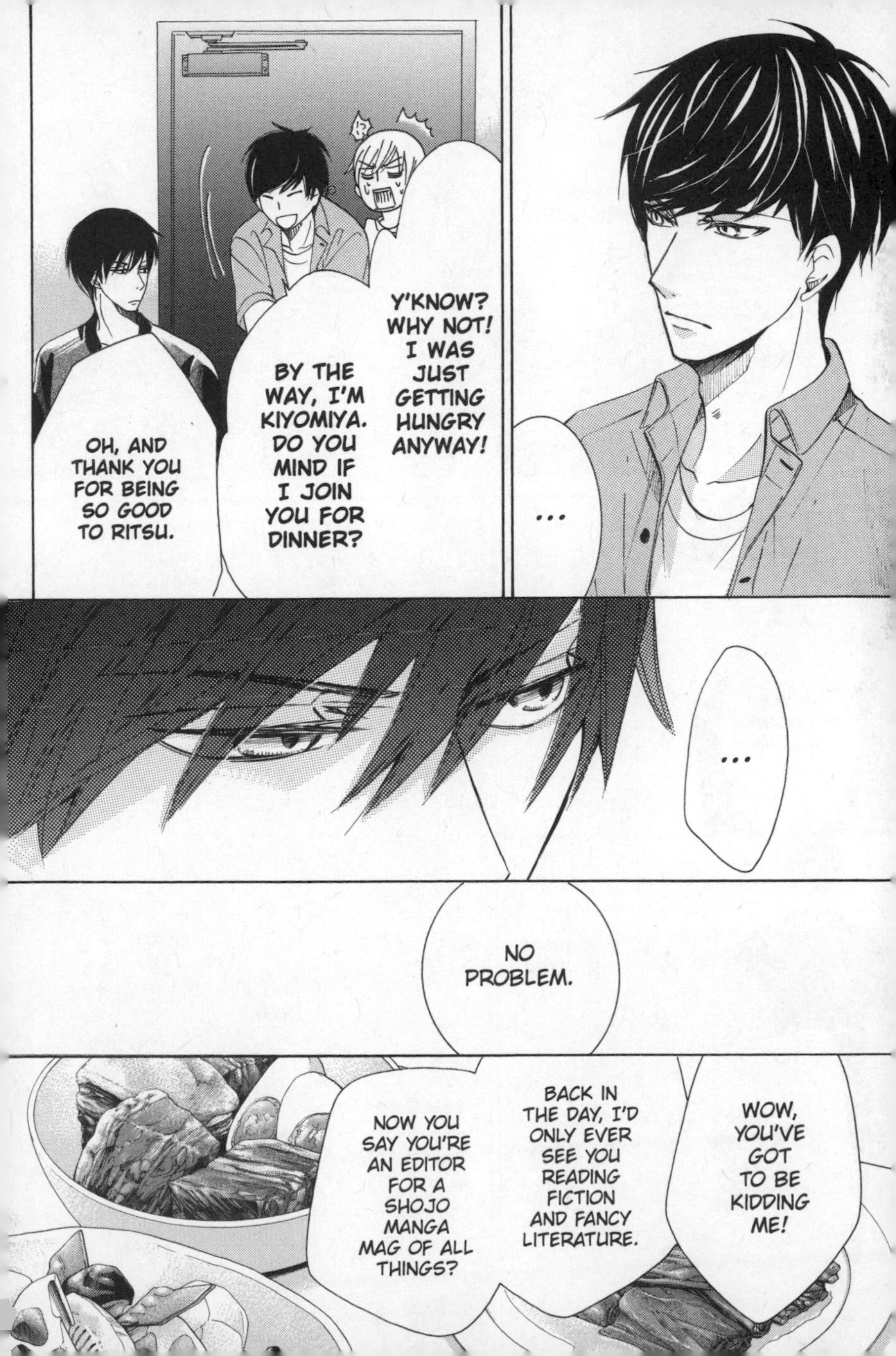
...
!?
Y'KNOW? WHY NOT! I WAS JUST GETTING HUNGRY ANYWAY!
BY THE WAY, I'M KIYOMIYA. DO YOU MIND IF I JOIN YOU FOR DINNER?
OH, AND THANK YOU FOR BEING SO GOOD TO RITSU.
...
NO PROBLEM.
WOW, YOU'VE GOT TO BE KIDDING ME!
BACK IN THE DAY, I'D ONLY EVER SEE YOU READING FICTION AND FANCY LITERATURE.
NOW YOU SAY YOU'RE AN EDITOR FOR A SHOJO MANGA MAG OF ALL THINGS?

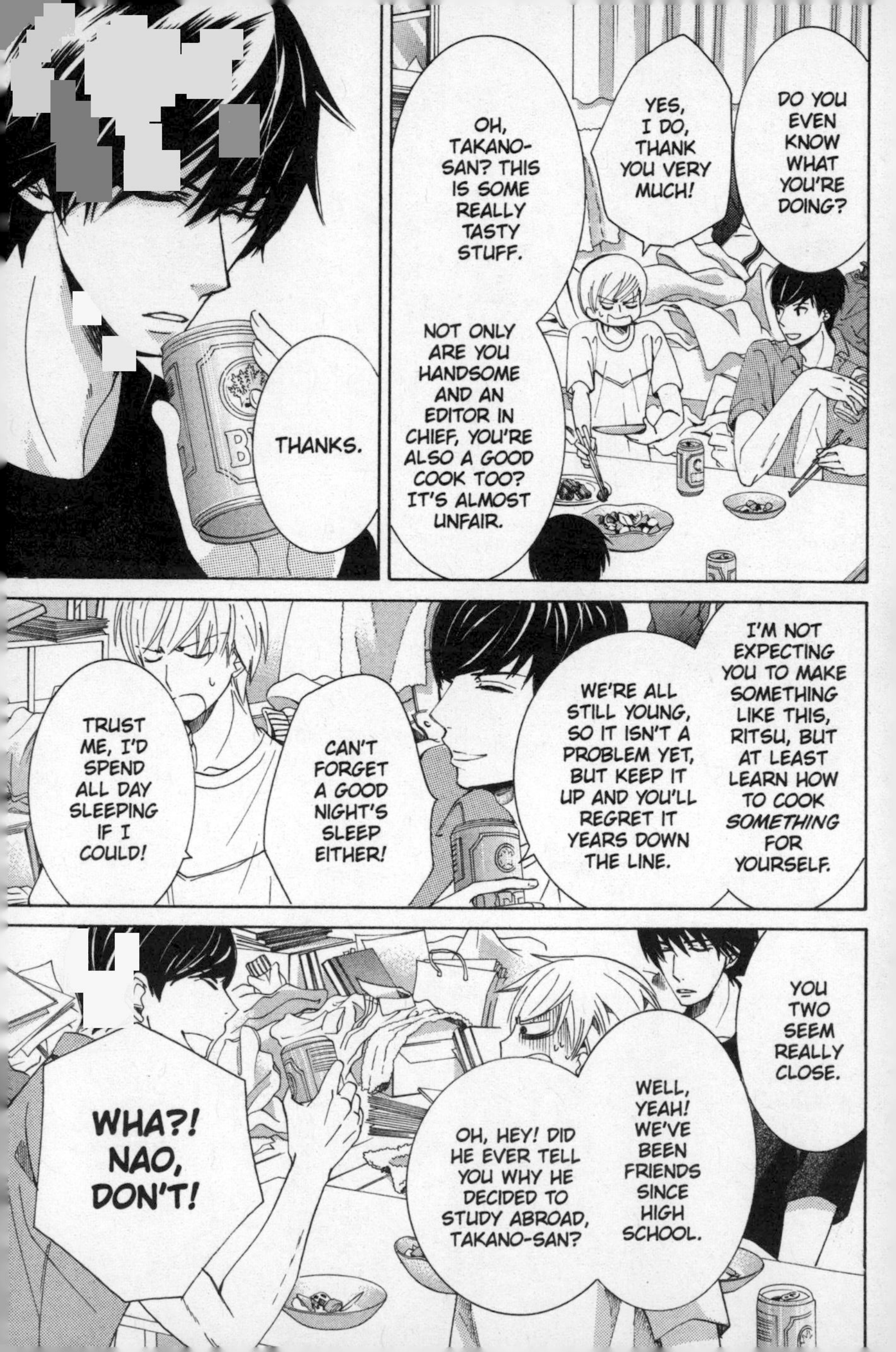
DO YOU EVEN KNOW WHAT YOU'RE DOING?
YES, I DO, THANK YOU VERY MUCH!
OH, TAKANO-SAN? THIS IS SOME REALLY TASTY STUFF.
NOT ONLY ARE YOU HANDSOME AND AN EDITOR IN CHIEF, YOU'RE ALSO A GOOD COOK TOO? IT'S ALMOST UNFAIR.
THANKS.
I'M NOT EXPECTING YOU TO MAKE SOMETHING LIKE THIS, RITSU, BUT AT LEAST LEARN HOW TO COOK *SOMETHING* FOR YOURSELF.
WE'RE ALL STILL YOUNG, SO IT ISN'T A PROBLEM YET, BUT KEEP IT UP AND YOU'LL REGRET IT YEARS DOWN THE LINE.
CAN'T FORGET A GOOD NIGHT'S SLEEP EITHER!
TRUST ME, I'D SPEND ALL DAY SLEEPING IF I COULD!
YOU TWO SEEM REALLY CLOSE.
WELL, YEAH! WE'VE BEEN FRIENDS SINCE HIGH SCHOOL.
OH, HEY! DID HE EVER TELL YOU WHY HE DECIDED TO STUDY ABROAD, TAKANO-SAN?
WHA?! NAO, DON'T!

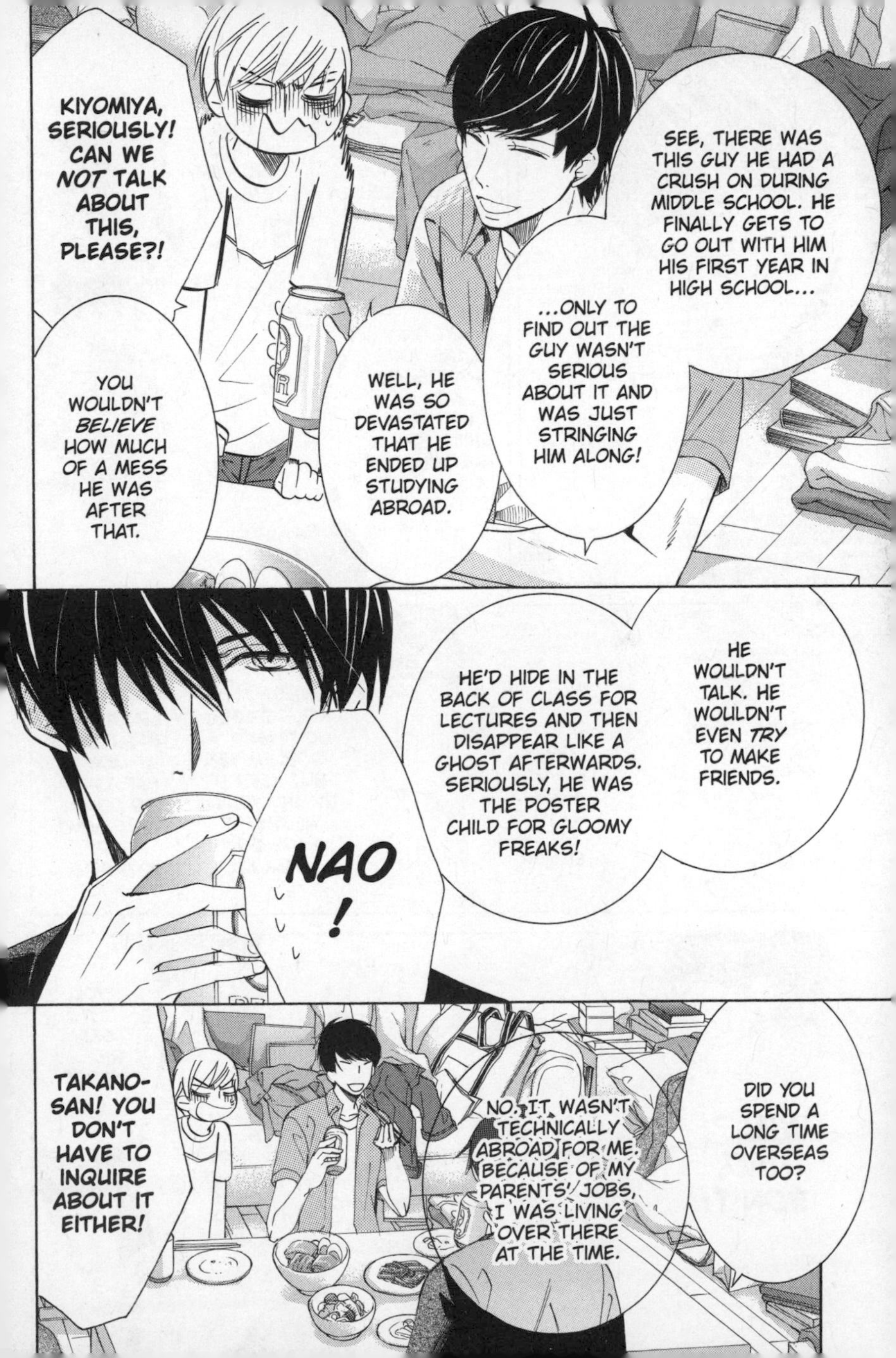
SEE, THERE WAS THIS GUY HE HAD A CRUSH ON DURING MIDDLE SCHOOL. HE FINALLY GETS TO GO OUT WITH HIM HIS FIRST YEAR IN HIGH SCHOOL...
...ONLY TO FIND OUT THE GUY WASN'T SERIOUS ABOUT IT AND WAS JUST STRINGING HIM ALONG!
WELL, HE WAS SO DEVASTATED THAT HE ENDED UP STUDYING ABROAD.
KIYOMIYA, SERIOUSLY! CAN WE *NOT* TALK ABOUT THIS, PLEASE?!
YOU WOULDN'T *BELIEVE* HOW MUCH OF A MESS HE WAS AFTER THAT.
HE WOULDN'T TALK. HE WOULDN'T EVEN *TRY* TO MAKE FRIENDS.
HE'D HIDE IN THE BACK OF CLASS FOR LECTURES AND THEN DISAPPEAR LIKE A GHOST AFTERWARDS. SERIOUSLY, HE WAS THE POSTER CHILD FOR GLOOMY FREAKS!
NAO!
DID YOU SPEND A LONG TIME OVERSEAS TOO?
NO. IT WASN'T TECHNICALLY ABROAD FOR ME. BECAUSE OF MY PARENTS' JOBS, I WAS LIVING OVER THERE AT THE TIME.
TAKANO-SAN! YOU DON'T HAVE TO INQUIRE ABOUT IT EITHER!

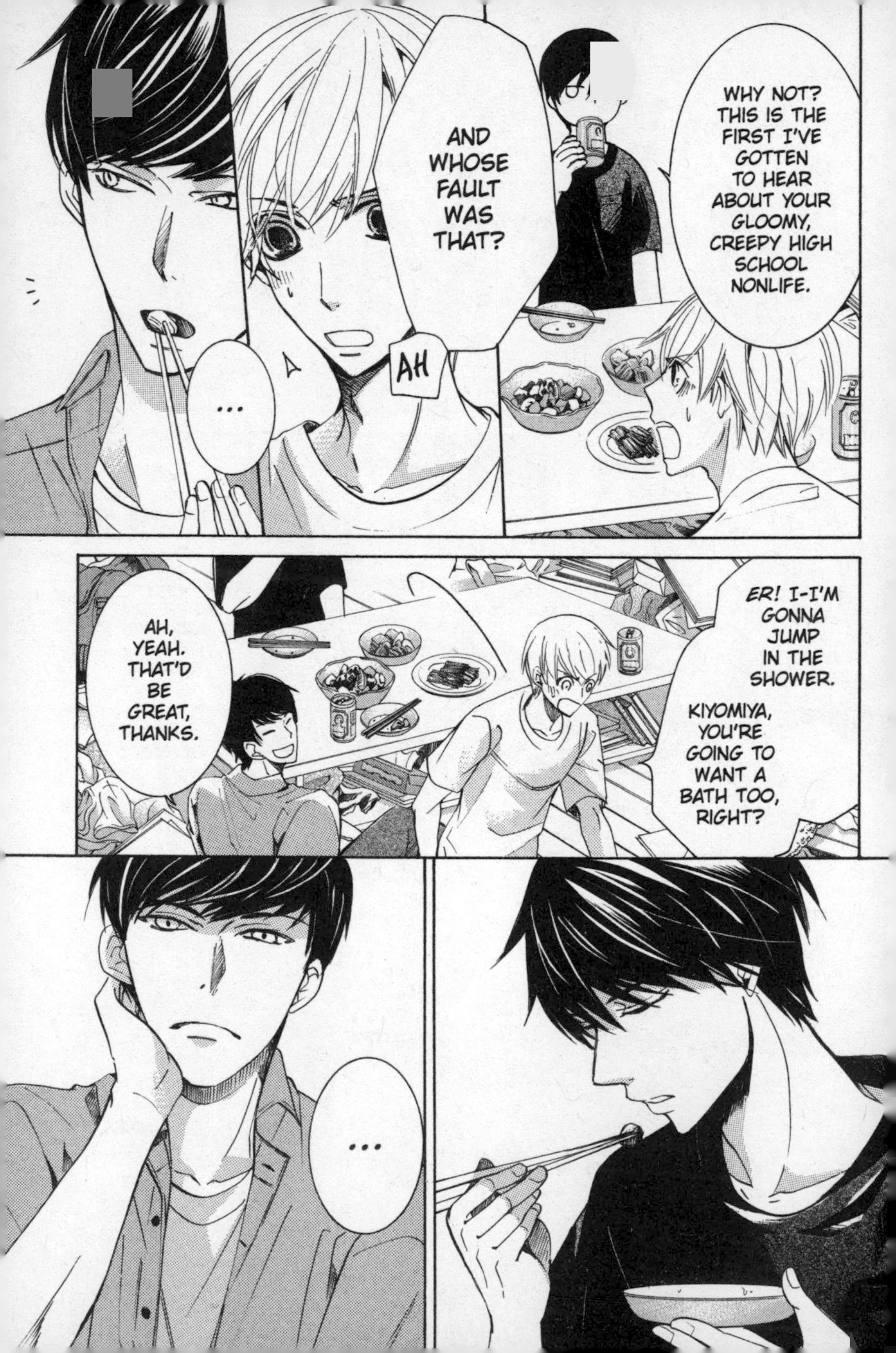
WHY NOT? THIS IS THE FIRST I'VE GOTTEN TO HEAR ABOUT YOUR GLOOMY, CREEPY HIGH SCHOOL NONLIFE.
AND WHOSE FAULT WAS THAT?
AH
...
ER! I-I'M GONNA JUMP IN THE SHOWER.
KIYOMIYA, YOU'RE GOING TO WANT A BATH TOO, RIGHT?
AH, YEAH. THAT'D BE GREAT, THANKS.
...

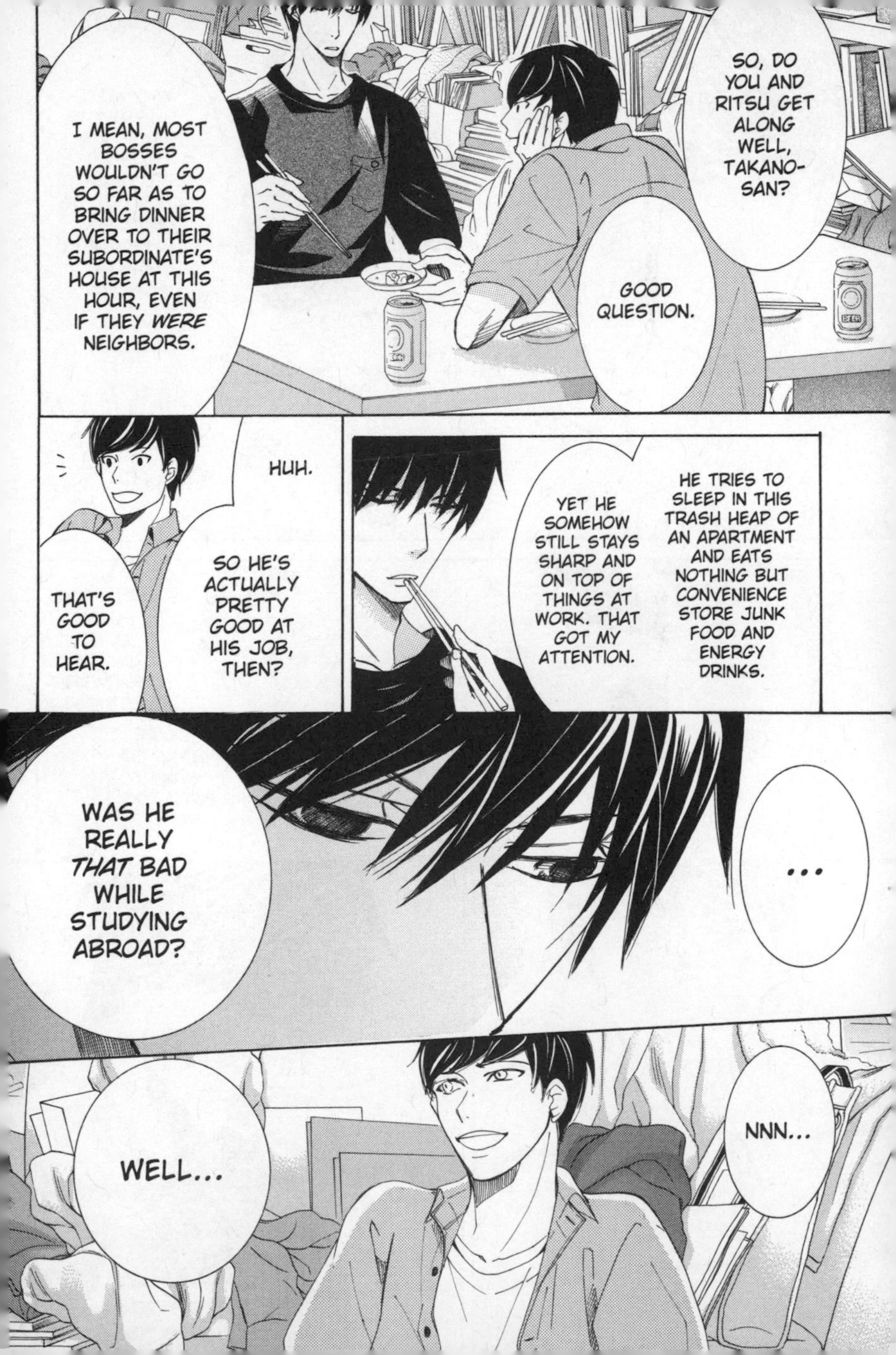
SO, DO YOU AND RITSU GET ALONG WELL, TAKANO-SAN?
GOOD QUESTION.
I MEAN, MOST BOSSES WOULDN'T GO SO FAR AS TO BRING DINNER OVER TO THEIR SUBORDINATE'S HOUSE AT THIS HOUR, EVEN IF THEY *WERE* NEIGHBORS.
HE TRIES TO SLEEP IN THIS TRASH HEAP OF AN APARTMENT AND EATS NOTHING BUT CONVENIENCE STORE JUNK FOOD AND ENERGY DRINKS.
YET HE SOMEHOW STILL STAYS SHARP AND ON TOP OF THINGS AT WORK. THAT GOT MY ATTENTION.
HUH.
SO HE'S ACTUALLY PRETTY GOOD AT HIS JOB, THEN?
THAT'S GOOD TO HEAR.
...
WAS HE REALLY *THAT* BAD WHILE STUDYING ABROAD?
NNN...
WELL...

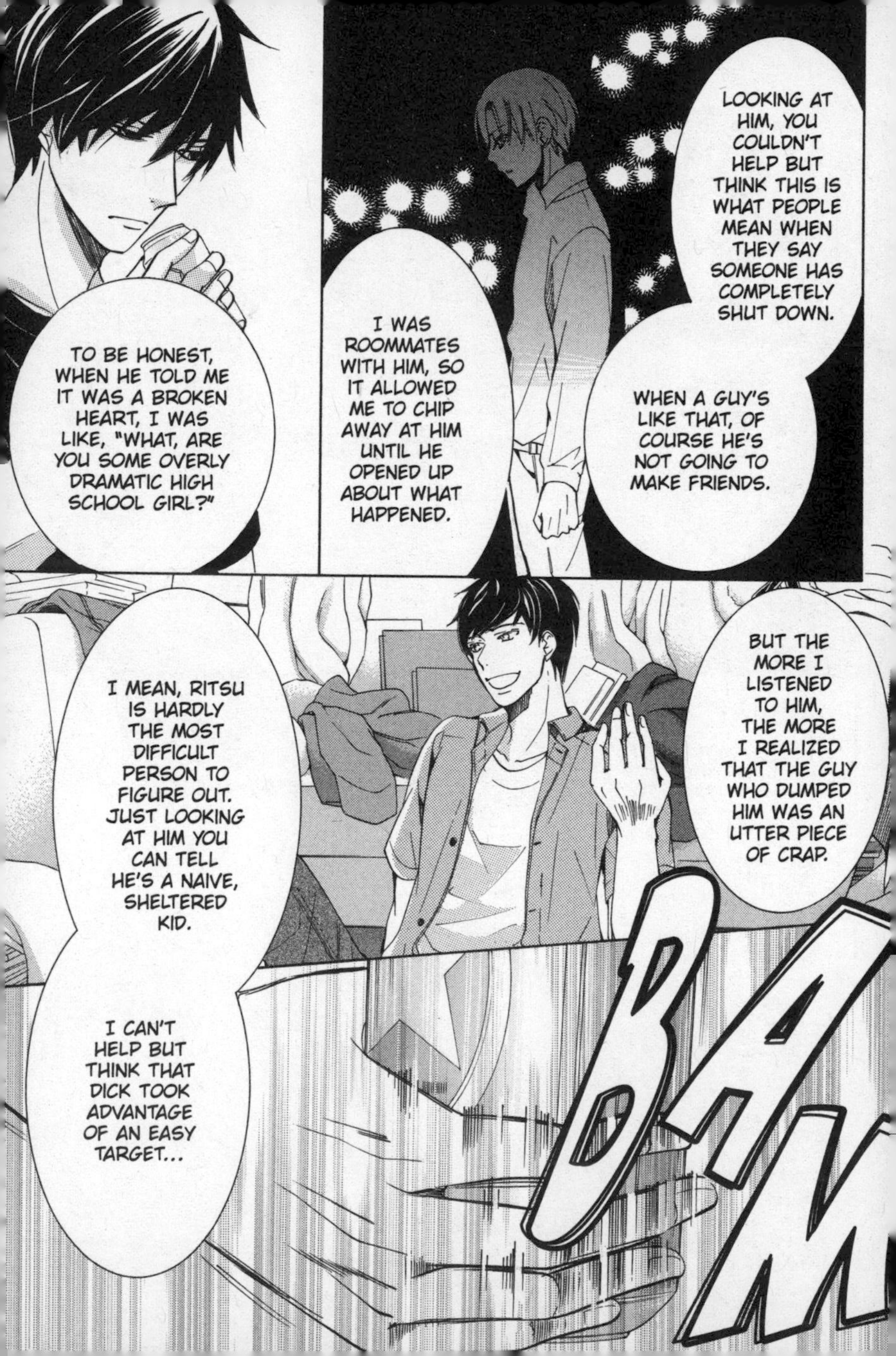

LOOKING AT HIM, YOU COULDN'T HELP BUT THINK THIS IS WHAT PEOPLE MEAN WHEN THEY SAY SOMEONE HAS COMPLETELY SHUT DOWN.
WHEN A GUY'S LIKE THAT, OF COURSE HE'S NOT GOING TO MAKE FRIENDS.
I WAS ROOMMATES WITH HIM, SO IT ALLOWED ME TO CHIP AWAY AT HIM UNTIL HE OPENED UP ABOUT WHAT HAPPENED.
TO BE HONEST, WHEN HE TOLD ME IT WAS A BROKEN HEART, I WAS LIKE, "WHAT, ARE YOU SOME OVERLY DRAMATIC HIGH SCHOOL GIRL?"
BUT THE MORE I LISTENED TO HIM, THE MORE I REALIZED THAT THE GUY WHO DUMPED HIM WAS AN UTTER PIECE OF CRAP.
I MEAN, RITSU IS HARDLY THE MOST DIFFICULT PERSON TO FIGURE OUT. JUST LOOKING AT HIM YOU CAN TELL HE'S A NAIVE, SHELTERED KID.
I CAN'T HELP BUT THINK THAT DICK TOOK ADVANTAGE OF AN EASY TARGET...
BAM

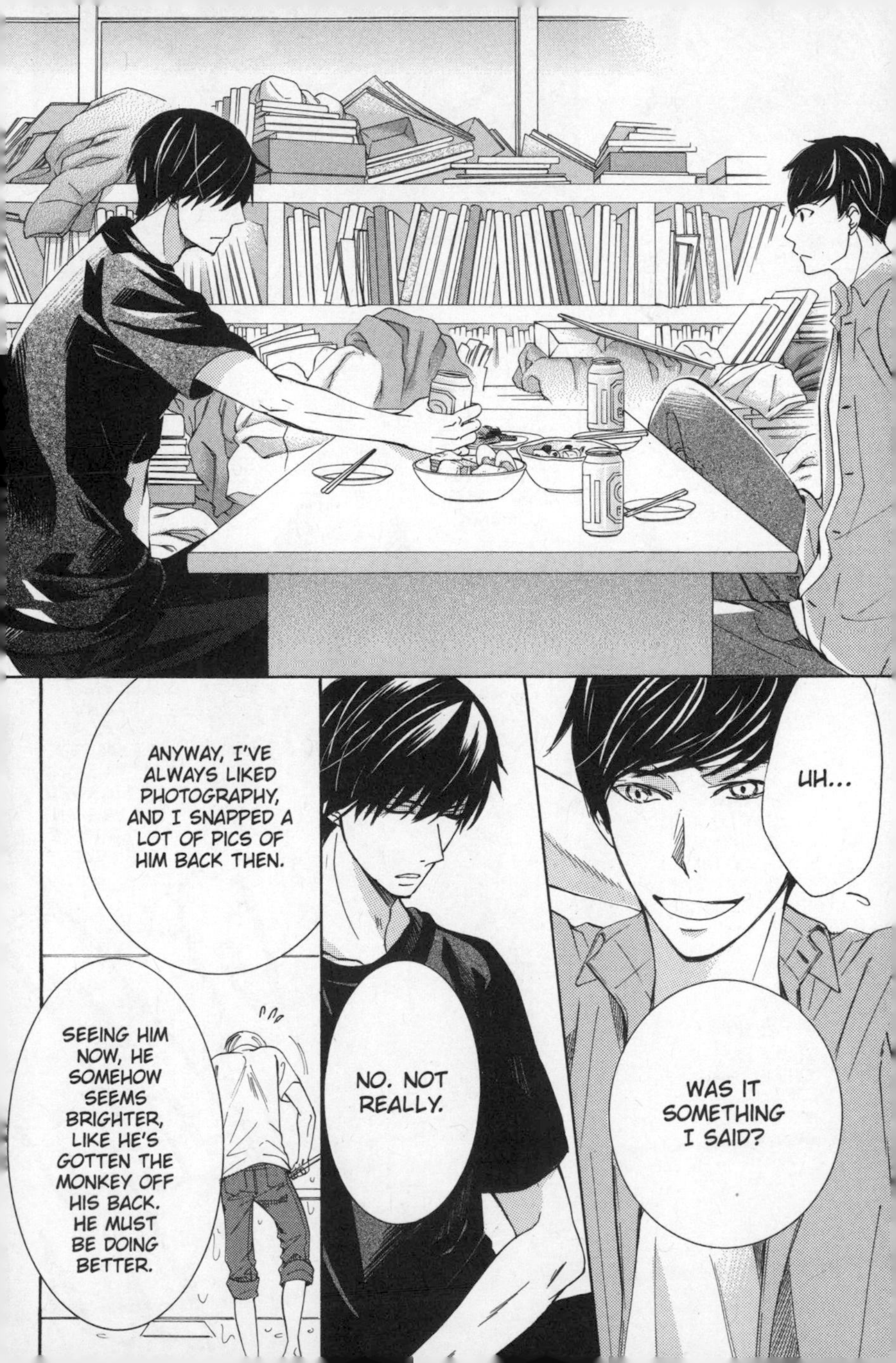
UH...
WAS IT SOMETHING I SAID?
NO. NOT REALLY.
ANYWAY, I'VE ALWAYS LIKED PHOTOGRAPHY, AND I SNAPPED A LOT OF PICS OF HIM BACK THEN.
SEEING HIM NOW, HE SOMEHOW SEEMS BRIGHTER, LIKE HE'S GOTTEN THE MONKEY OFF HIS BACK. HE MUST BE DOING BETTER.

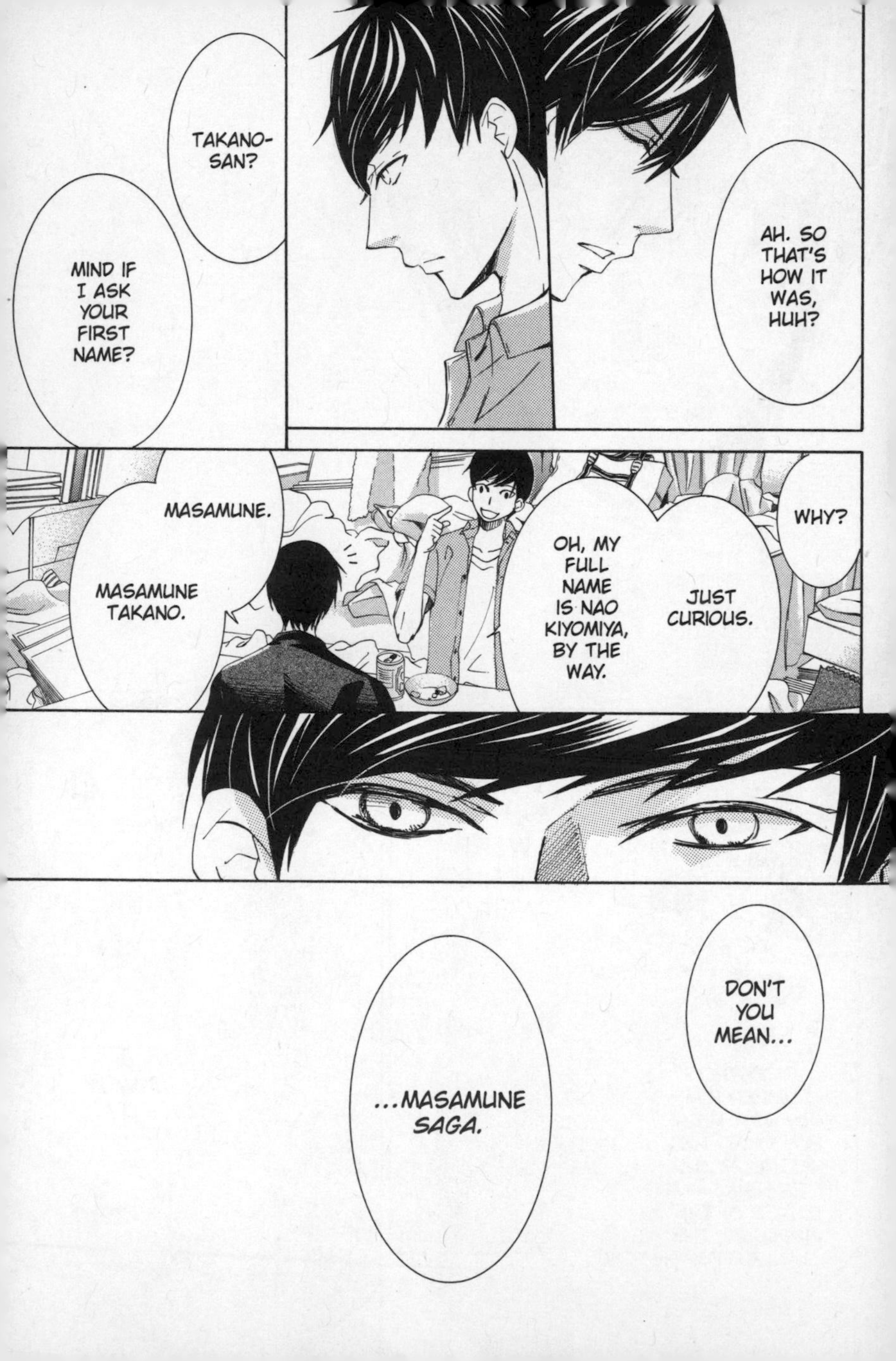
AH. SO THAT'S HOW IT WAS, HUH?
TAKANO-SAN?
MIND IF I ASK YOUR FIRST NAME?
WHY?
JUST CURIOUS.
OH, MY FULL NAME IS NAO KIYOMIYA, BY THE WAY.
MASAMUNE.
MASAMUNE TAKANO.
DON'T YOU MEAN...
...MASAMUNE SAGA.

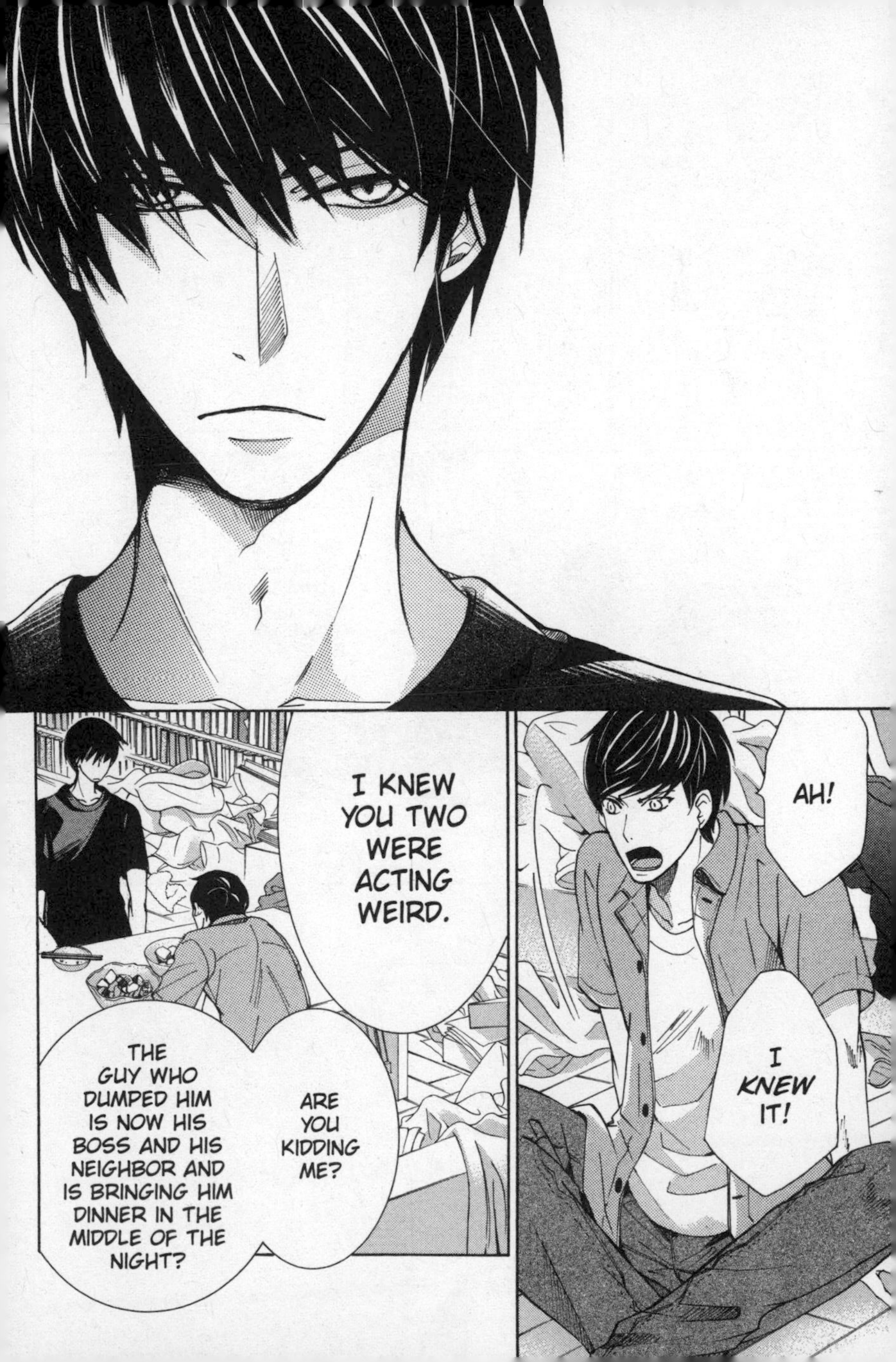
AH!
I KNEW IT!
I KNEW YOU TWO WERE ACTING WEIRD.
ARE YOU KIDDING ME?
THE GUY WHO DUMPED HIM IS NOW HIS BOSS AND HIS NEIGHBOR AND IS BRINGING HIM DINNER IN THE MIDDLE OF THE NIGHT?

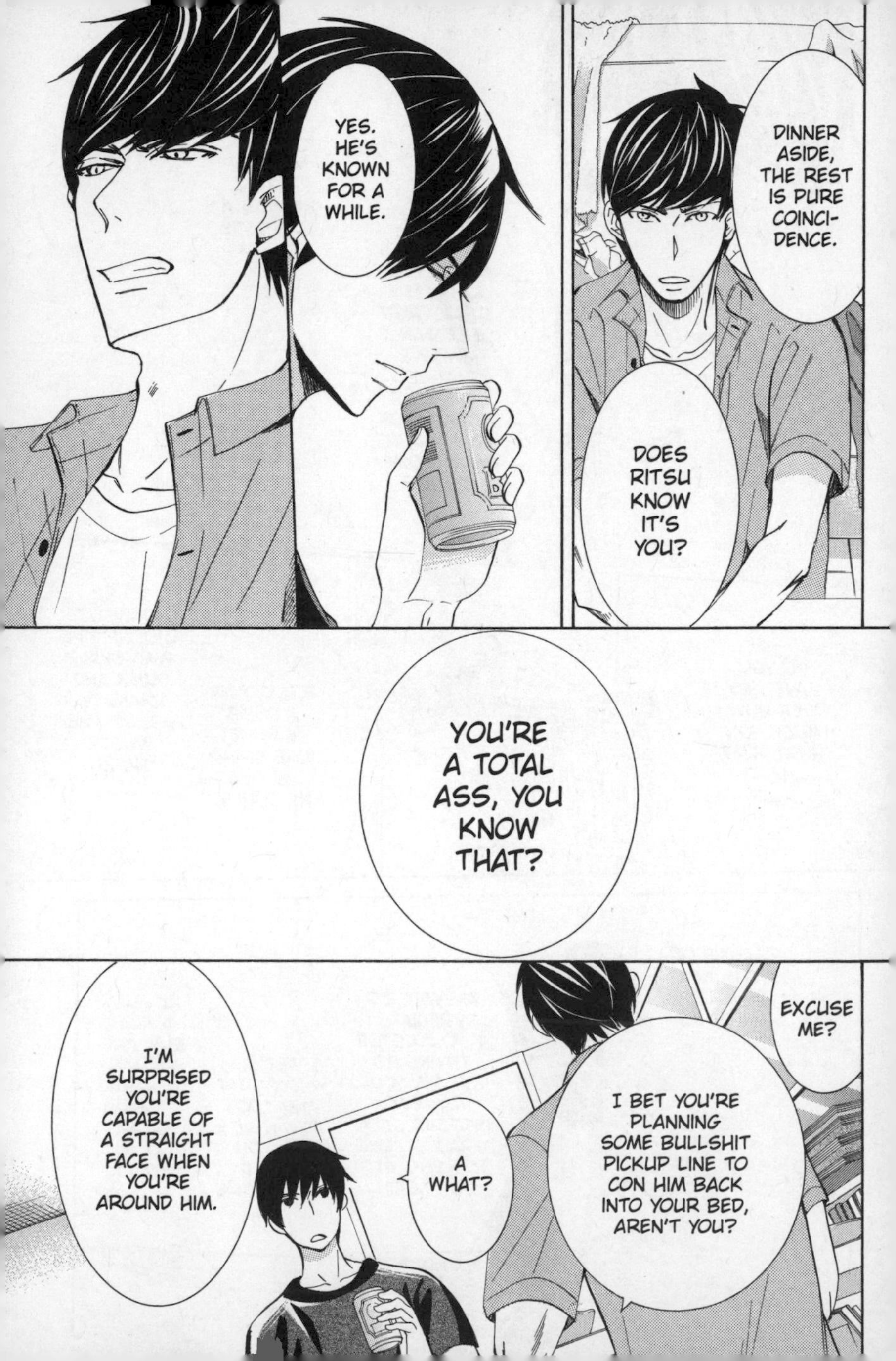
DINNER ASIDE, THE REST IS PURE COINCIDENCE.
DOES RITSU KNOW IT'S YOU?
YES. HE'S KNOWN FOR A WHILE.
YOU'RE A TOTAL ASS, YOU KNOW THAT?
EXCUSE ME?
I BET YOU'RE PLANNING SOME BULLSHIT PICKUP LINE TO CON HIM BACK INTO YOUR BED, AREN'T YOU?
A WHAT?
I'M SURPRISED YOU'RE CAPABLE OF A STRAIGHT FACE WHEN YOU'RE AROUND HIM.

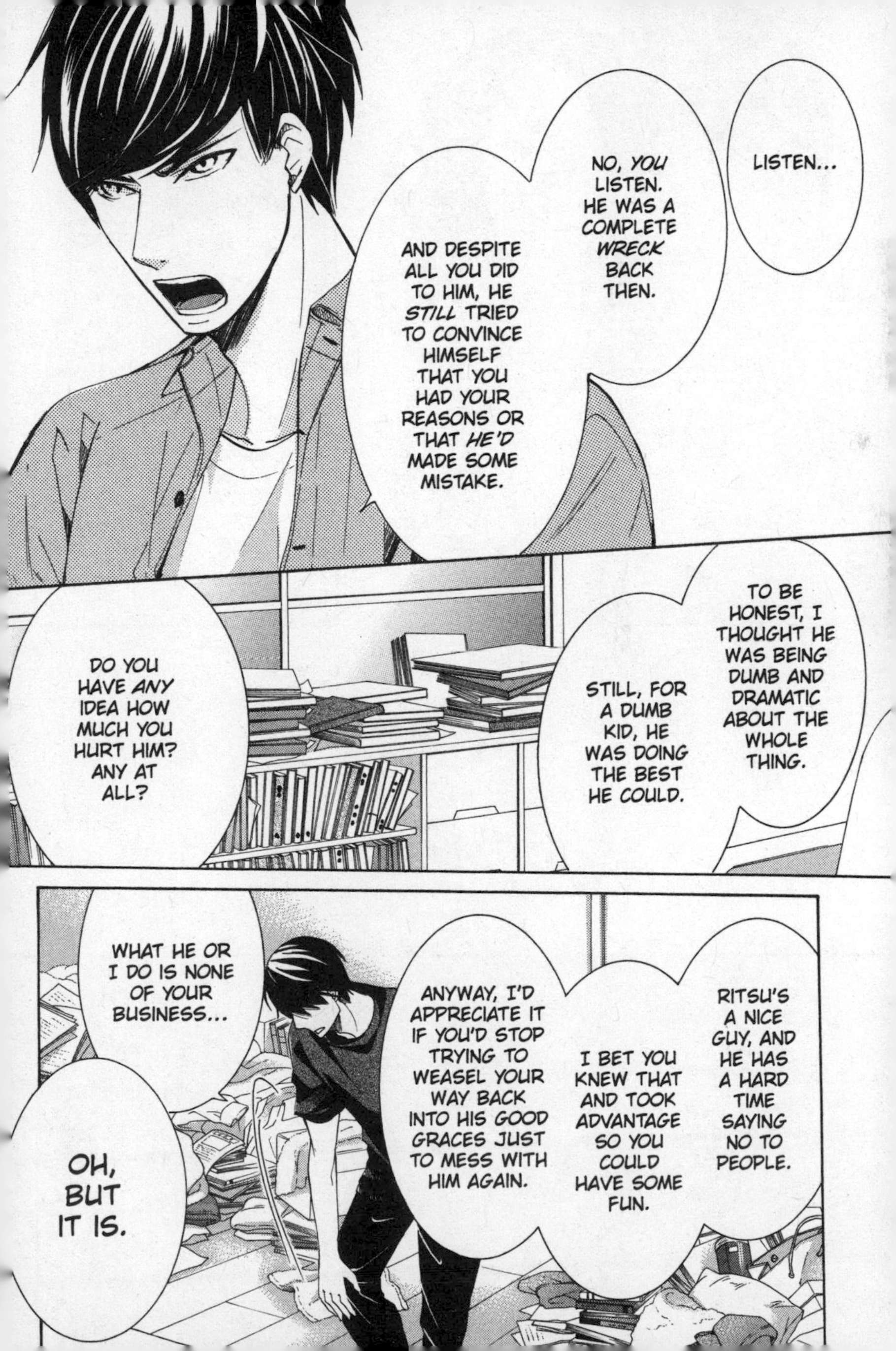
LISTEN...
NO, *YOU* LISTEN. HE WAS A COMPLETE *WRECK* BACK THEN.
AND DESPITE ALL YOU DID TO HIM, HE *STILL* TRIED TO CONVINCE HIMSELF THAT YOU HAD YOUR REASONS OR THAT *HE'D* MADE SOME MISTAKE.
TO BE HONEST, I THOUGHT HE WAS BEING DUMB AND DRAMATIC ABOUT THE WHOLE THING.
STILL, FOR A DUMB KID, HE WAS DOING THE BEST HE COULD.
DO YOU HAVE *ANY* IDEA HOW MUCH YOU HURT HIM? ANY AT ALL?
RITSU'S A NICE GUY, AND HE HAS A HARD TIME SAYING NO TO PEOPLE.
I BET YOU KNEW THAT AND TOOK ADVANTAGE SO YOU COULD HAVE SOME FUN.
ANYWAY, I'D APPRECIATE IT IF YOU'D STOP TRYING TO WEASEL YOUR WAY BACK INTO HIS GOOD GRACES JUST TO MESS WITH HIM AGAIN.
WHAT HE OR I DO IS NONE OF YOUR BUSINESS...
OH, BUT IT IS.

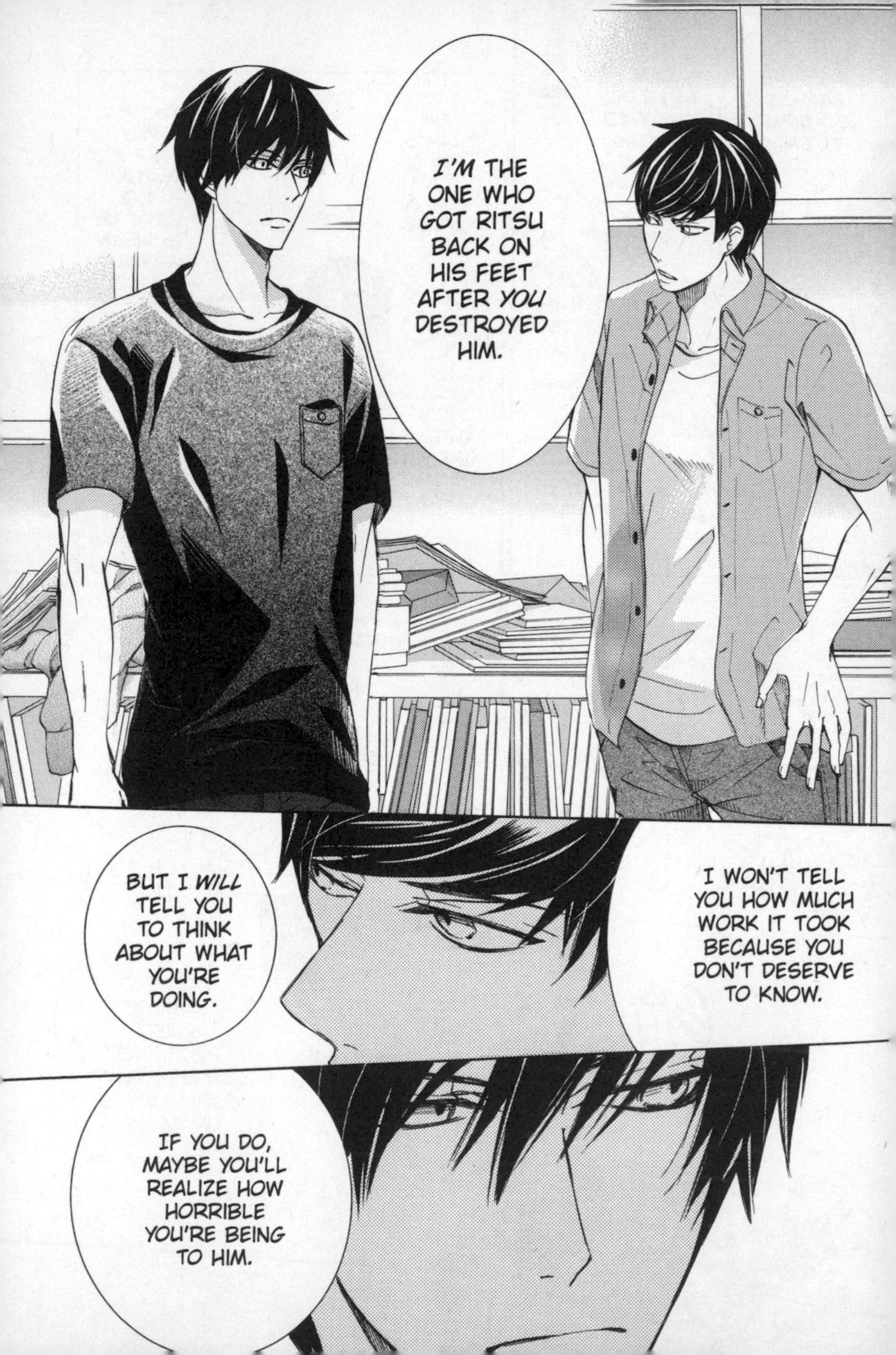
I'M THE ONE WHO GOT RITSU BACK ON HIS FEET AFTER *YOU* DESTROYED HIM.
I WON'T TELL YOU HOW MUCH WORK IT TOOK BECAUSE YOU DON'T DESERVE TO KNOW.
BUT I *WILL* TELL YOU TO THINK ABOUT WHAT YOU'RE DOING.
IF YOU DO, MAYBE YOU'LL REALIZE HOW HORRIBLE YOU'RE BEING TO HIM.

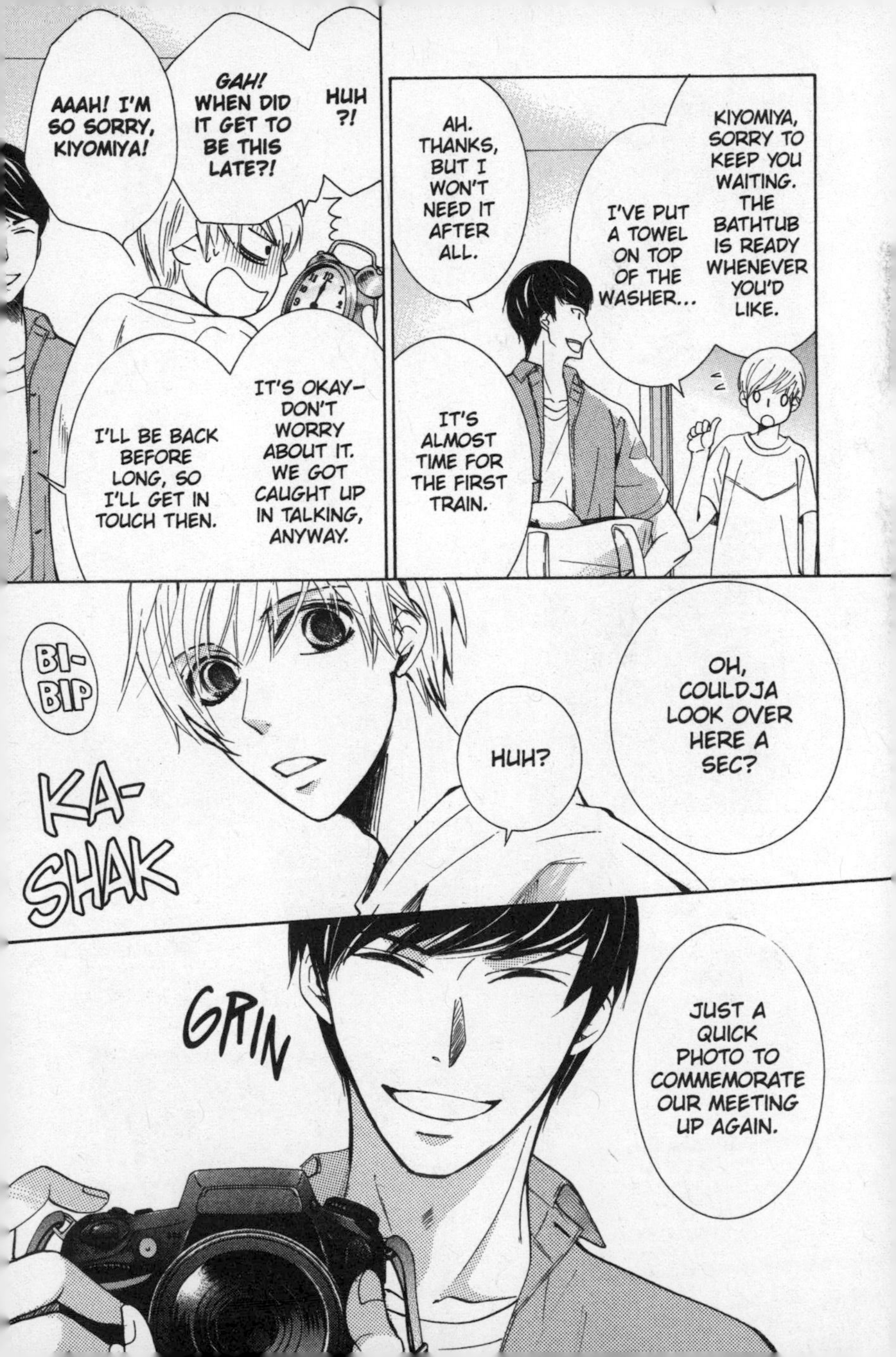
KIYOMIYA, SORRY TO KEEP YOU WAITING. THE BATHTUB IS READY WHENEVER YOU'D LIKE.
I'VE PUT A TOWEL ON TOP OF THE WASHER...
AH. THANKS, BUT I WON'T NEED IT AFTER ALL.
IT'S ALMOST TIME FOR THE FIRST TRAIN.
HUH ?!
GAH! WHEN DID IT GET TO BE THIS LATE?!
AAAH! I'M SO SORRY, KIYOMIYA!
IT'S OKAY—DON'T WORRY ABOUT IT. WE GOT CAUGHT UP IN TALKING, ANYWAY.
I'LL BE BACK BEFORE LONG, SO I'LL GET IN TOUCH THEN.
OH, COULDJA LOOK OVER HERE A SEC?
HUH?
BI-BIP
KA-SHAK
JUST A QUICK PHOTO TO COMMEMORATE OUR MEETING UP AGAIN.
GRIN

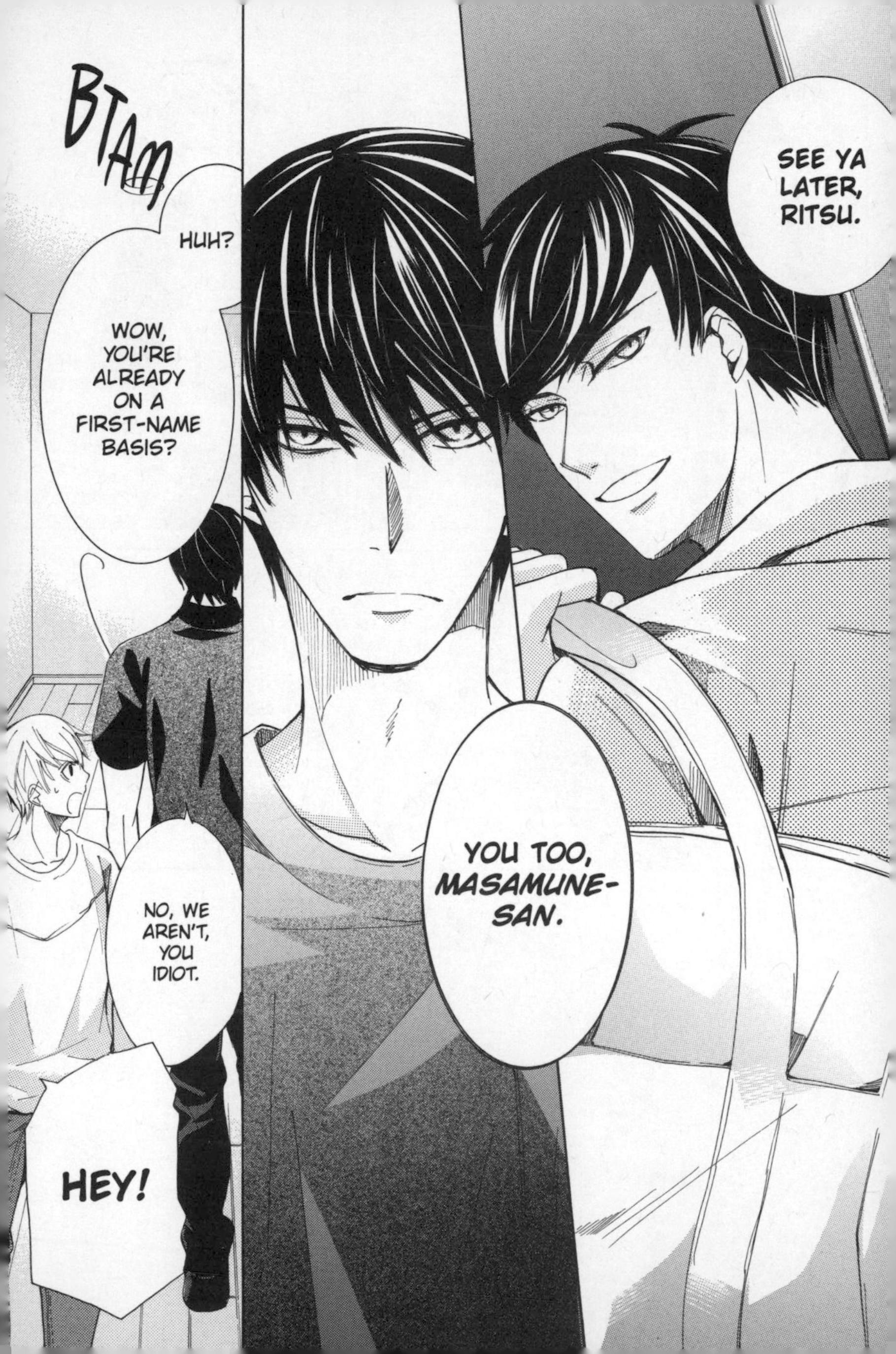
SEE YA LATER, RITSU.
YOU TOO, MASAMUNE-SAN.
BTAM
HUH?
WOW, YOU'RE ALREADY ON A FIRST-NAME BASIS?
NO, WE AREN'T, YOU IDIOT.
HEY!

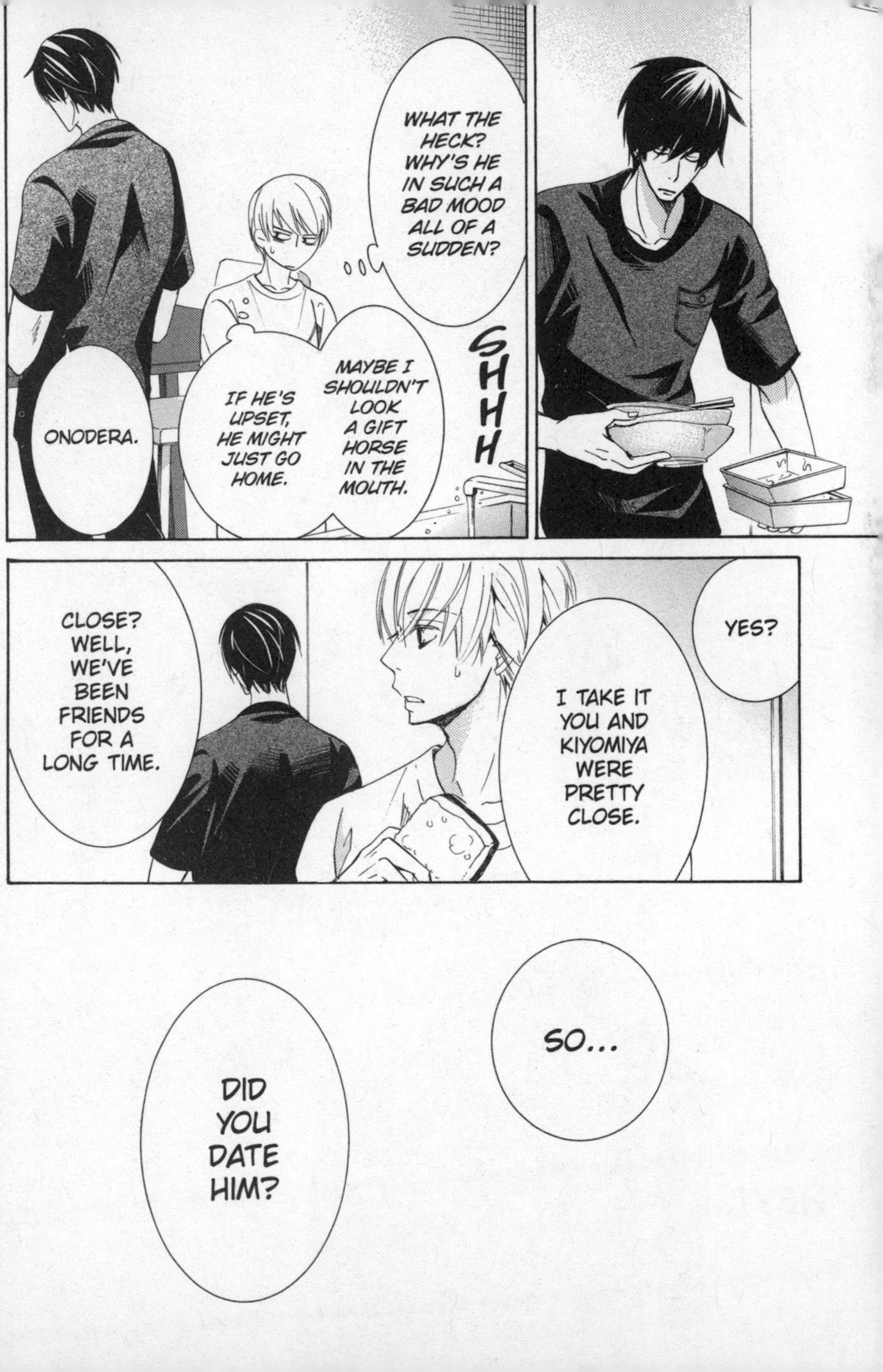
WHAT THE HECK? WHY'S HE IN SUCH A BAD MOOD ALL OF A SUDDEN?
SHHH
MAYBE I SHOULDN'T LOOK A GIFT HORSE IN THE MOUTH.
IF HE'S UPSET, HE MIGHT JUST GO HOME.
ONODERA.
YES?
I TAKE IT YOU AND KIYOMIYA WERE PRETTY CLOSE.
CLOSE? WELL, WE'VE BEEN FRIENDS FOR A LONG TIME.
SO...
DID YOU DATE HIM?

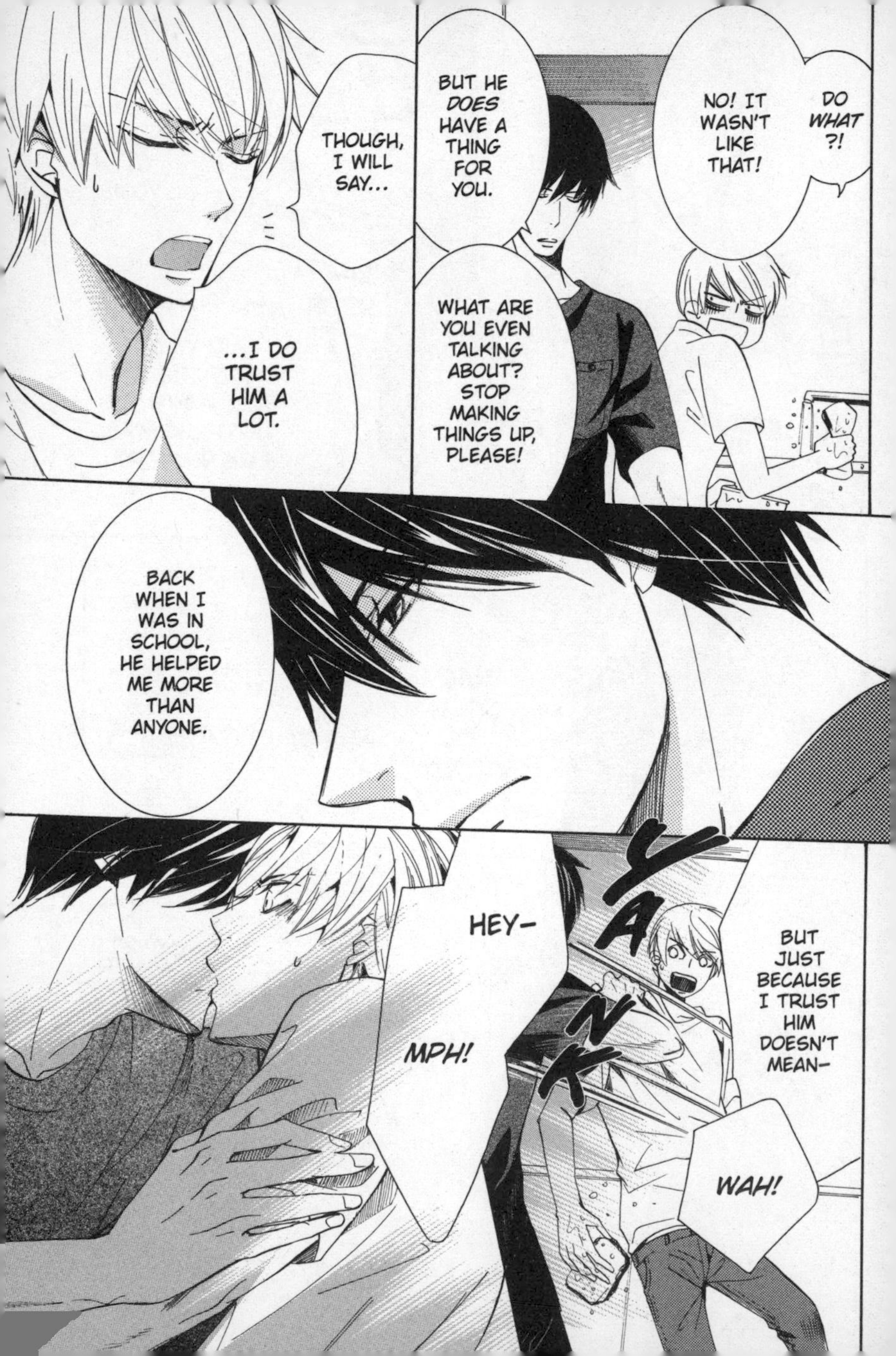
DO WHAT?!
NO! IT WASN'T LIKE THAT!
BUT HE DOES HAVE A THING FOR YOU.
WHAT ARE YOU EVEN TALKING ABOUT? STOP MAKING THINGS UP, PLEASE!
THOUGH, I WILL SAY...
...I DO TRUST HIM A LOT.
BACK WHEN I WAS IN SCHOOL, HE HELPED ME MORE THAN ANYONE.
BUT JUST BECAUSE I TRUST HIM DOESN'T MEAN-
YANK
WAH!
HEY-
MPH!

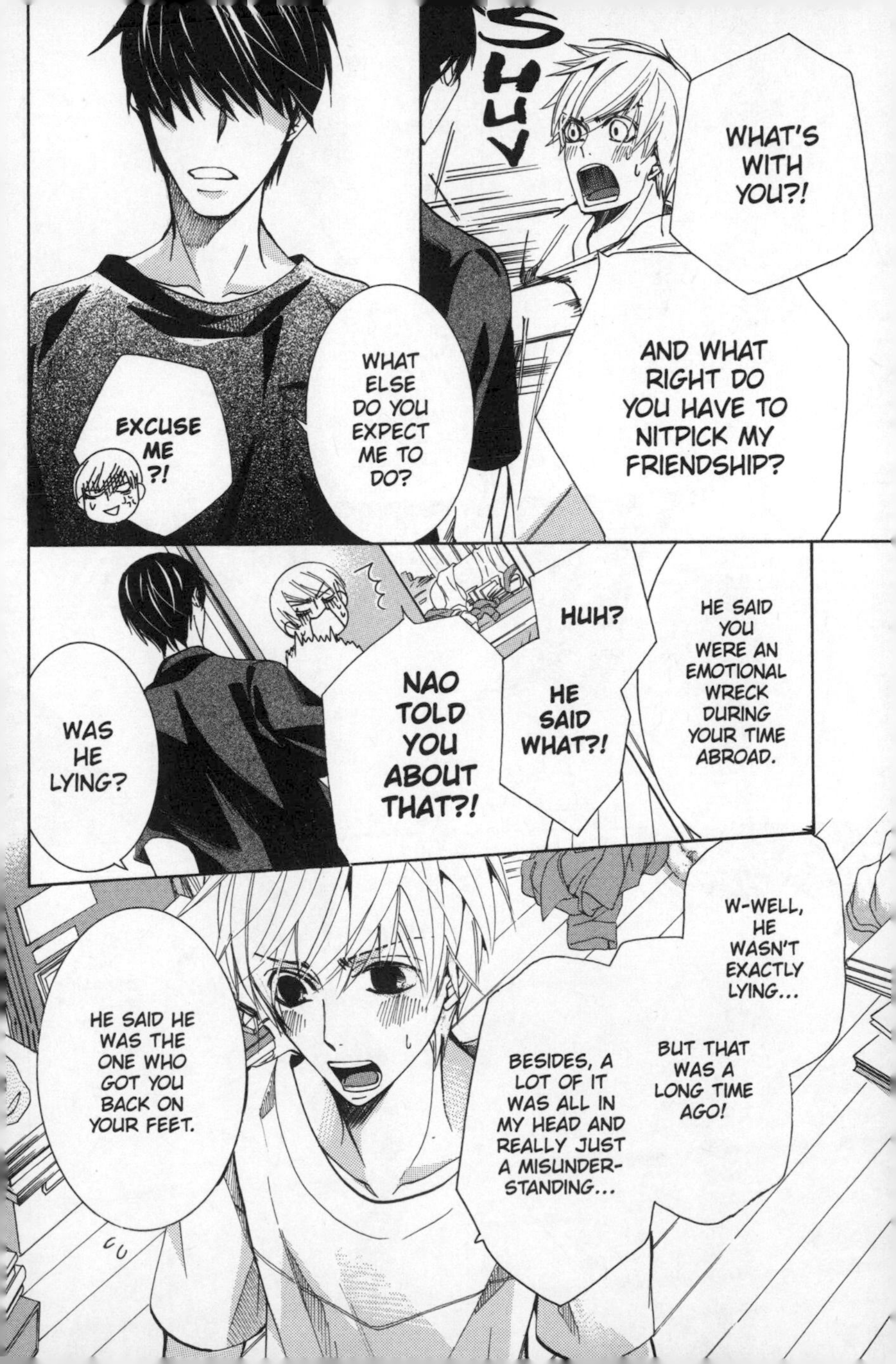
SHUV
WHAT'S WITH YOU?!
AND WHAT RIGHT DO YOU HAVE TO NITPICK MY FRIENDSHIP?
WHAT ELSE DO YOU EXPECT ME TO DO?
EXCUSE ME ?!
HE SAID YOU WERE AN EMOTIONAL WRECK DURING YOUR TIME ABROAD.
HUH?
HE SAID WHAT?!
NAO TOLD YOU ABOUT THAT?!
WAS HE LYING?
W-WELL, HE WASN'T EXACTLY LYING...
BUT THAT WAS A LONG TIME AGO!
BESIDES, A LOT OF IT WAS ALL IN MY HEAD AND REALLY JUST A MISUNDER-STANDING...
HE SAID HE WAS THE ONE WHO GOT YOU BACK ON YOUR FEET.

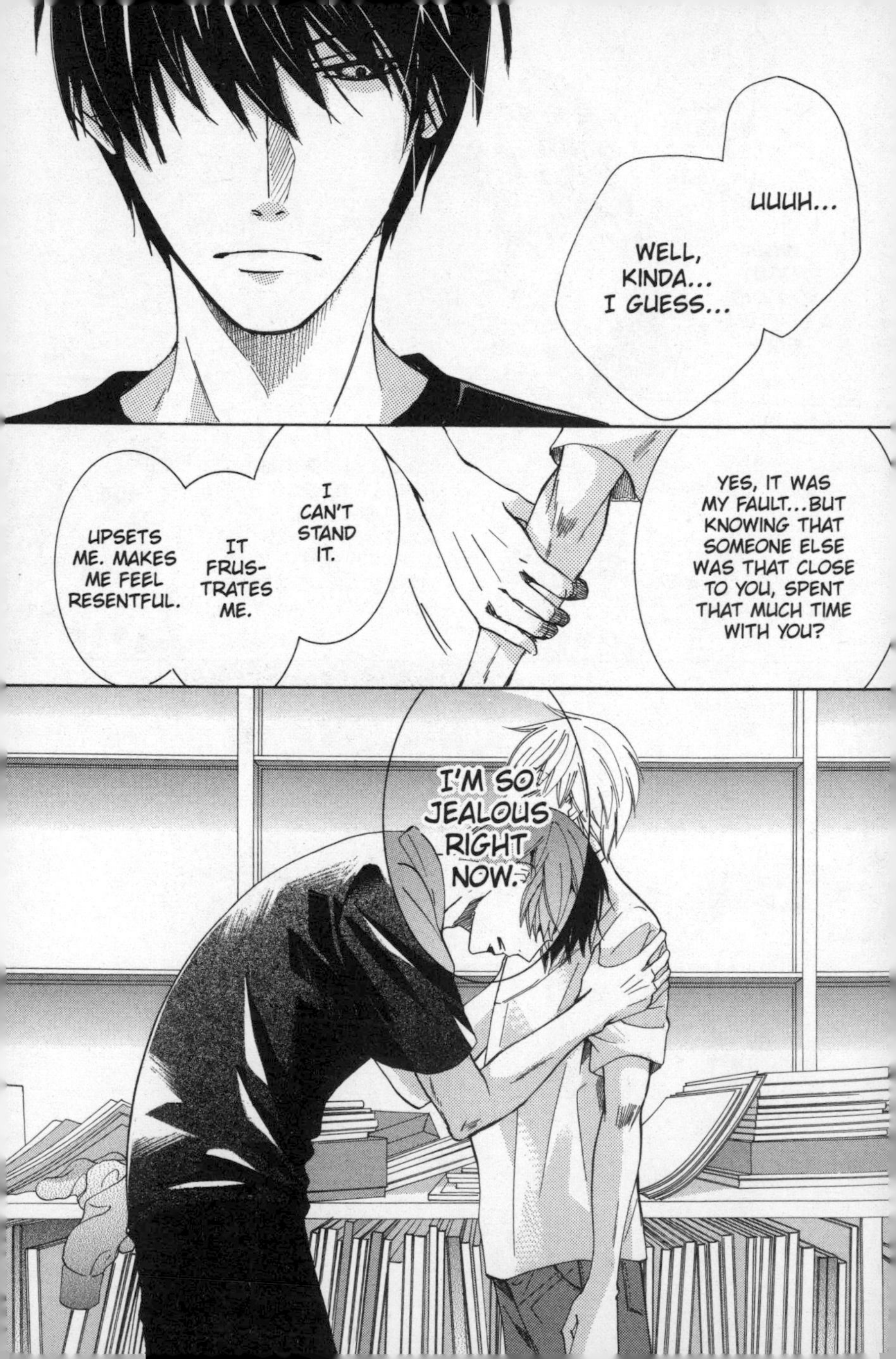
UUUH...
WELL, KINDA... I GUESS...
YES, IT WAS MY FAULT...BUT KNOWING THAT SOMEONE ELSE WAS THAT CLOSE TO YOU, SPENT THAT MUCH TIME WITH YOU?
I CAN'T STAND IT.
IT FRUS-TRATES ME.
UPSETS ME. MAKES ME FEEL RESENTFUL.
I'M SO JEALOUS RIGHT NOW.

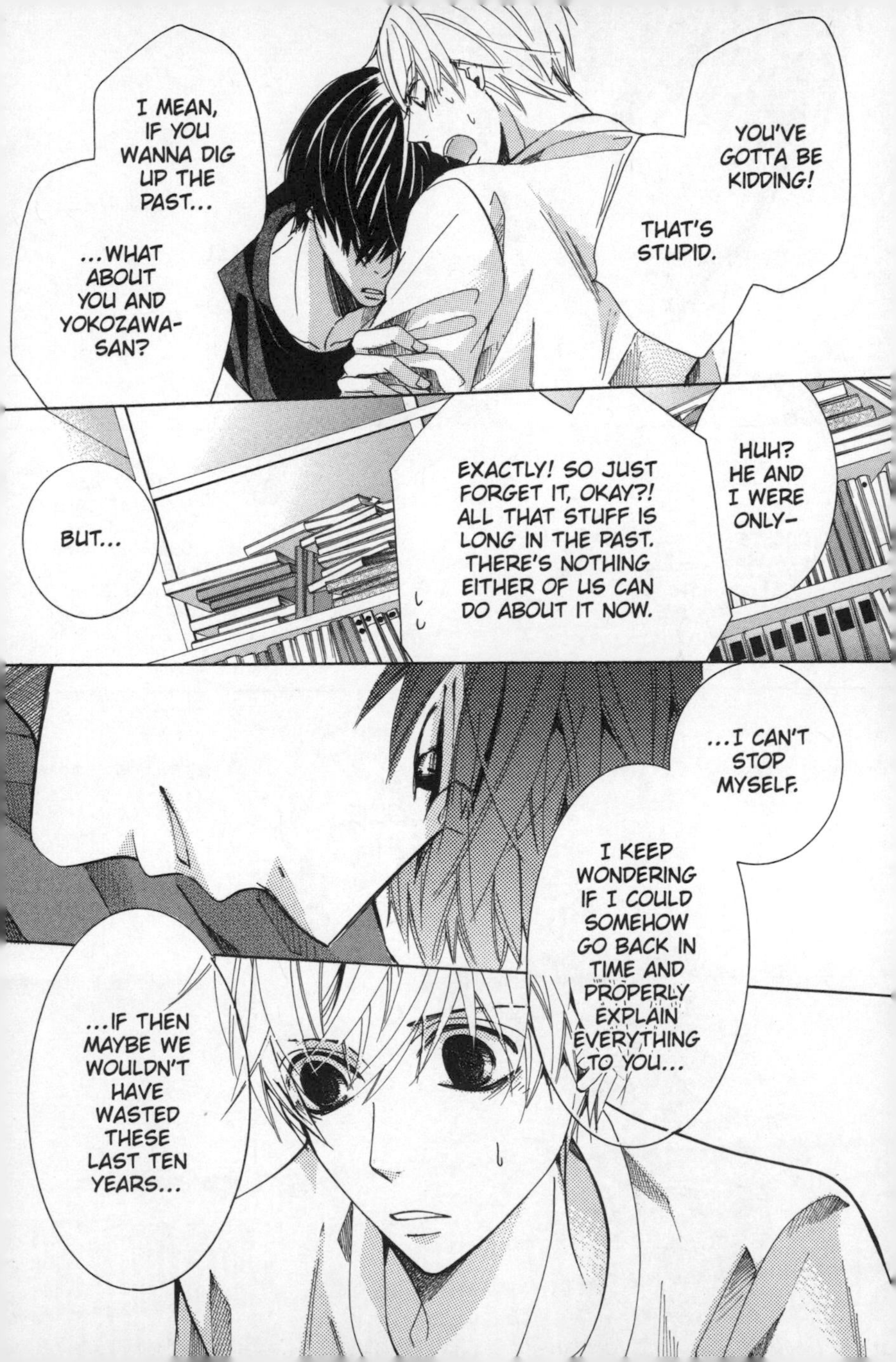
YOU'VE GOTTA BE KIDDING!
THAT'S STUPID.
I MEAN, IF YOU WANNA DIG UP THE PAST...
...WHAT ABOUT YOU AND YOKOZAWA-SAN?
HUH? HE AND I WERE ONLY-
EXACTLY! SO JUST FORGET IT, OKAY?! ALL THAT STUFF IS LONG IN THE PAST. THERE'S NOTHING EITHER OF US CAN DO ABOUT IT NOW.
BUT...
...I CAN'T STOP MYSELF.
I KEEP WONDERING IF I COULD SOMEHOW GO BACK IN TIME AND PROPERLY EXPLAIN EVERYTHING TO YOU...
...IF THEN MAYBE WE WOULDN'T HAVE WASTED THESE LAST TEN YEARS...

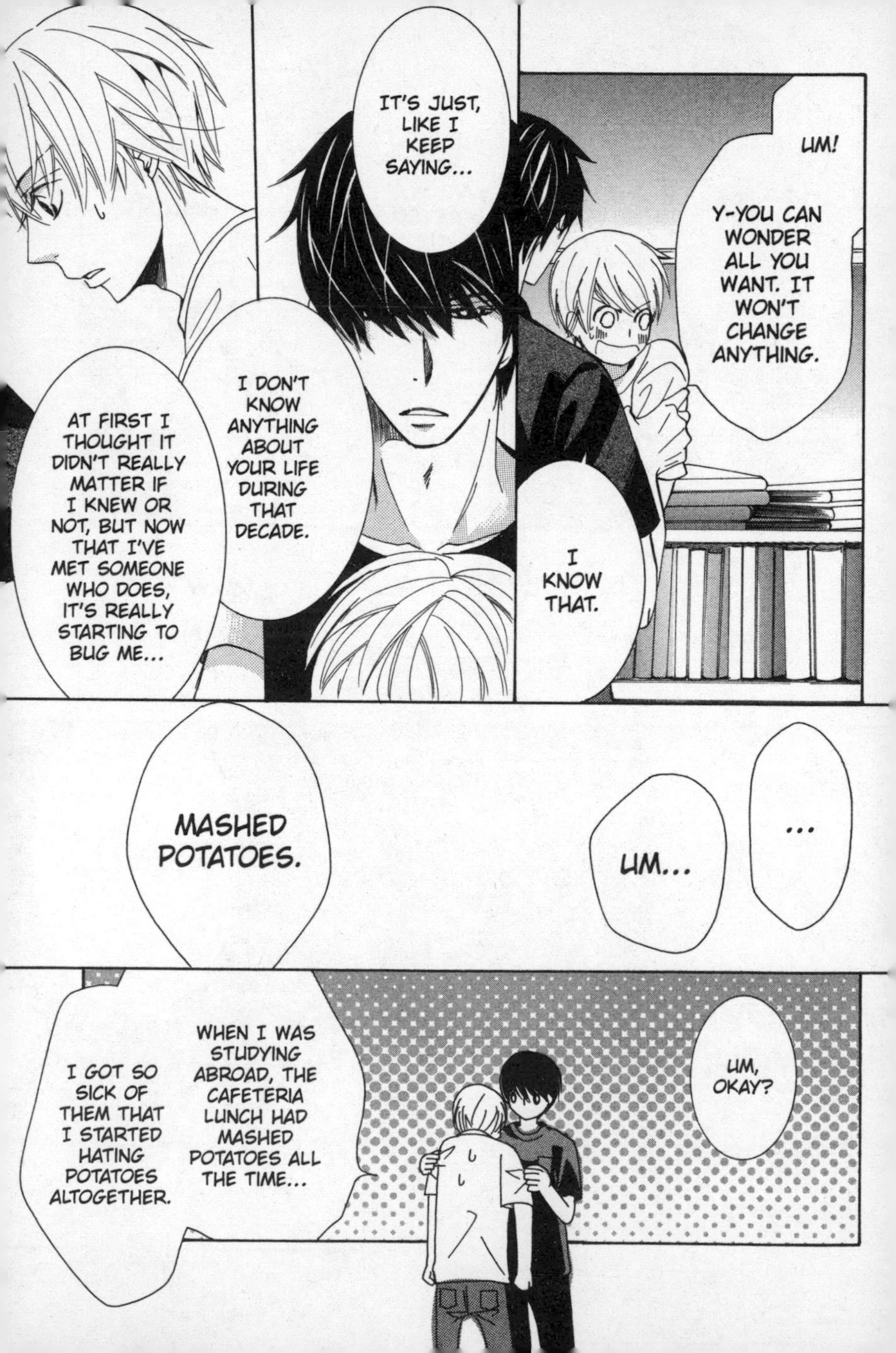
UM!
Y-YOU CAN WONDER ALL YOU WANT. IT WON'T CHANGE ANYTHING.
I KNOW THAT.
IT'S JUST, LIKE I KEEP SAYING...
I DON'T KNOW ANYTHING ABOUT YOUR LIFE DURING THAT DECADE.
AT FIRST I THOUGHT IT DIDN'T REALLY MATTER IF I KNEW OR NOT, BUT NOW THAT I'VE MET SOMEONE WHO DOES, IT'S REALLY STARTING TO BUG ME...
...
UM...
MASHED POTATOES.
UM, OKAY?
WHEN I WAS STUDYING ABROAD, THE CAFETERIA LUNCH HAD MASHED POTATOES ALL THE TIME...
I GOT SO SICK OF THEM THAT I STARTED HATING POTATOES ALTOGETHER.

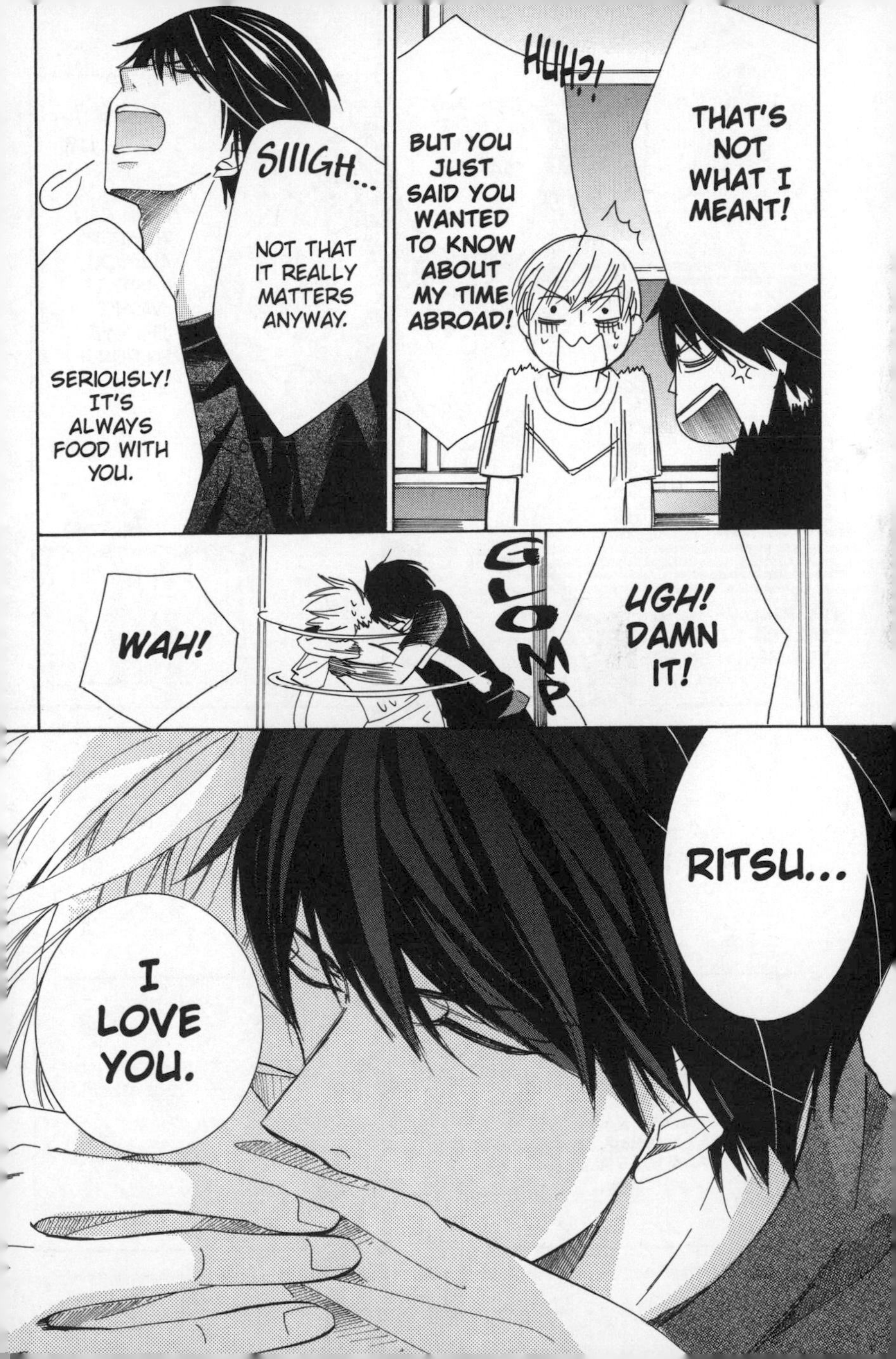
THAT'S NOT WHAT I MEANT!
HUH?!
BUT YOU JUST SAID YOU WANTED TO KNOW ABOUT MY TIME ABROAD!
SIIIGH...
NOT THAT IT REALLY MATTERS ANYWAY.
SERIOUSLY! IT'S ALWAYS FOOD WITH YOU.
UGH! DAMN IT!
GLOMP
WAH!
RITSU...
I LOVE YOU.

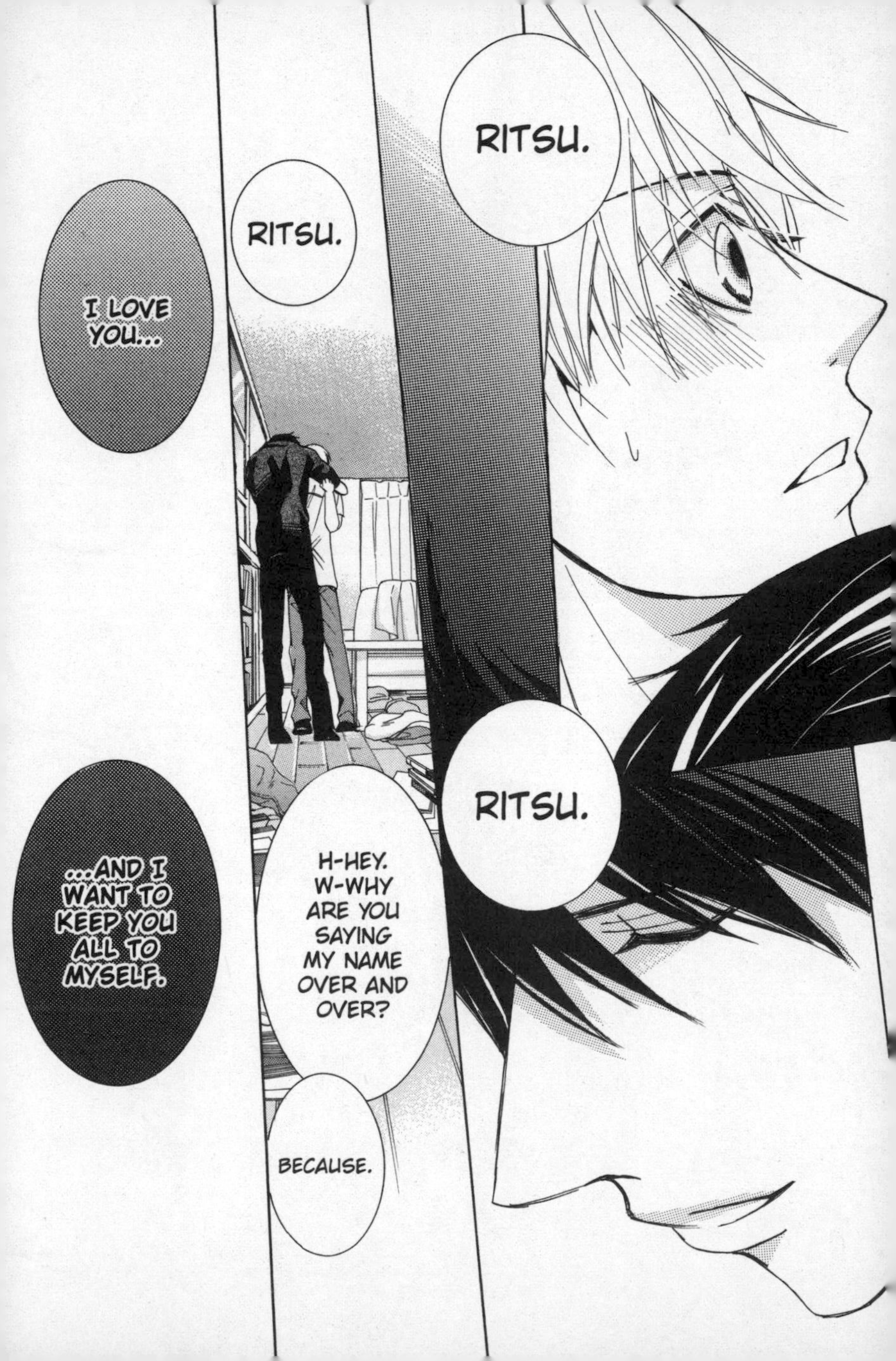
RITSU.
RITSU.
RITSU.
H-HEY. W-WHY ARE YOU SAYING MY NAME OVER AND OVER?
BECAUSE.
I LOVE YOU...
...AND I WANT TO KEEP YOU ALL TO MYSELF.

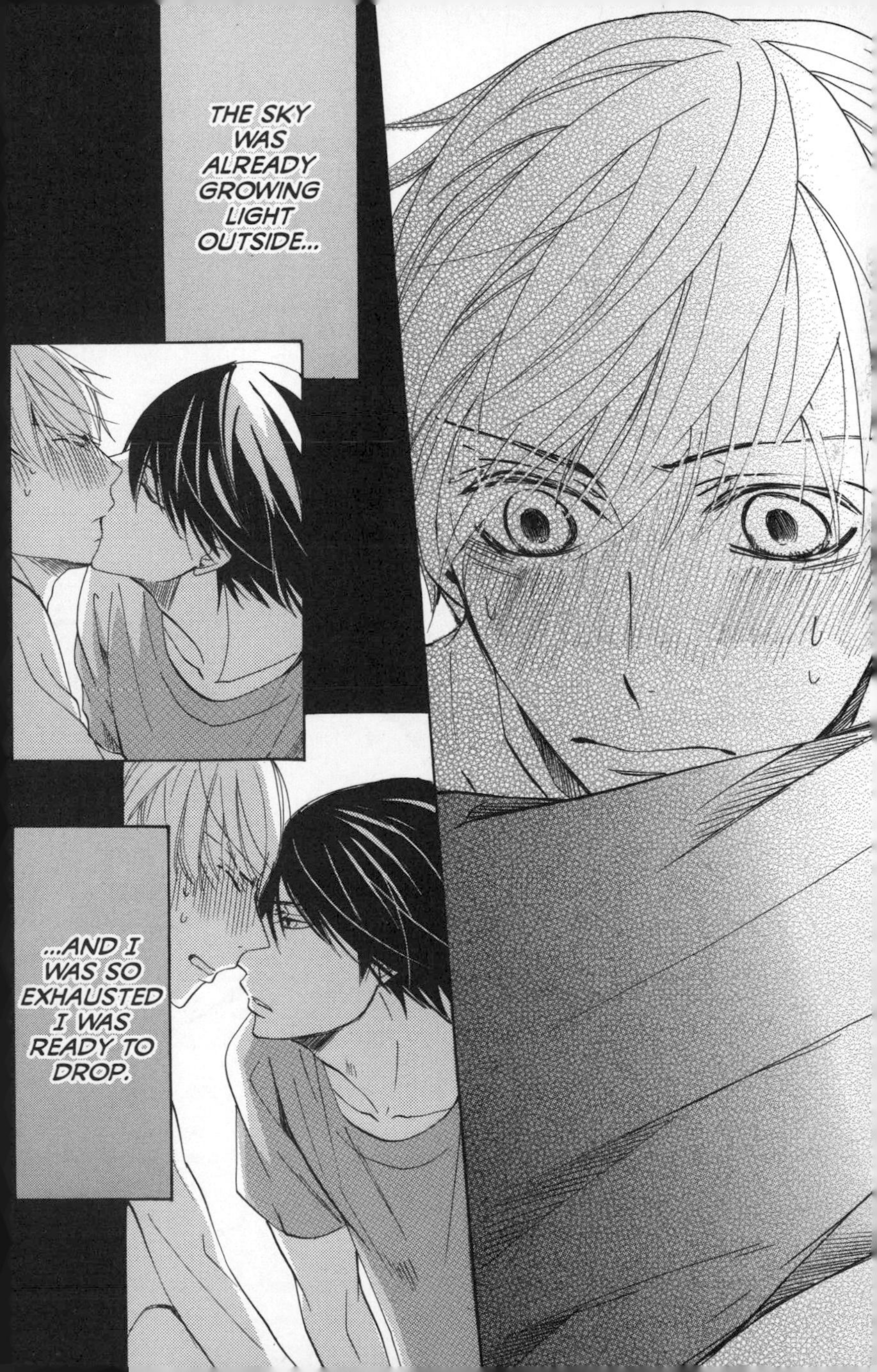
THE SKY WAS ALREADY GROWING LIGHT OUTSIDE...
...AND I WAS SO EXHAUSTED I WAS READY TO DROP.

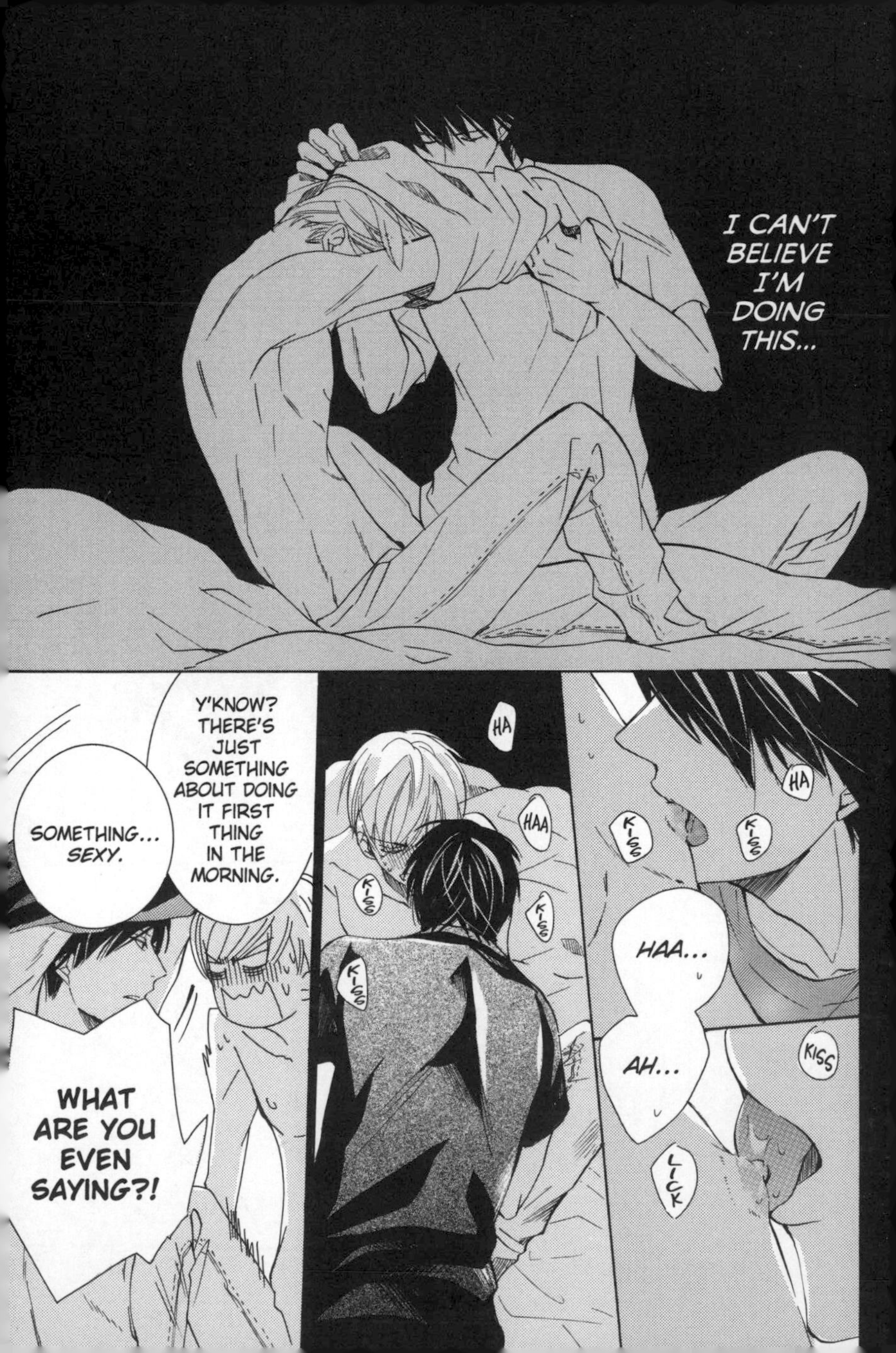
I CAN'T BELIEVE I'M DOING THIS...
HA
KISS
KISS
HAA...
AH...
KISS
LICK
HA
HAA
KISS
KISS
KISS
Y'KNOW? THERE'S JUST SOMETHING ABOUT DOING IT FIRST THING IN THE MORNING.
SOMETHING... SEXY.
WHAT ARE YOU EVEN SAYING?!

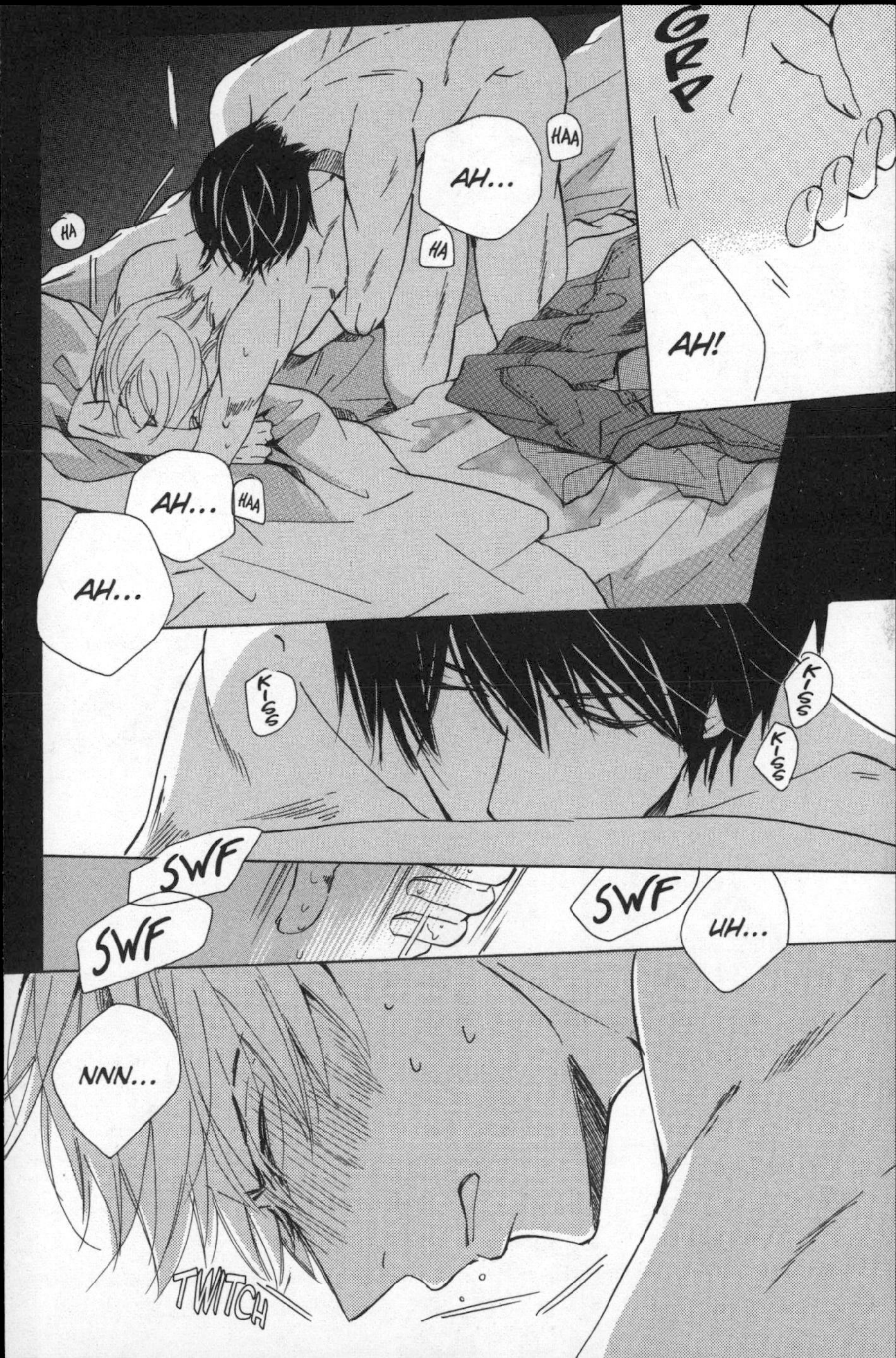
GRP
AH!
HAA
AH...
HA
HA
HAA
AH...
AH...
KISS
KISS
KISS
UH...
SWF
SWF
SWF
NNN...
TWITCH

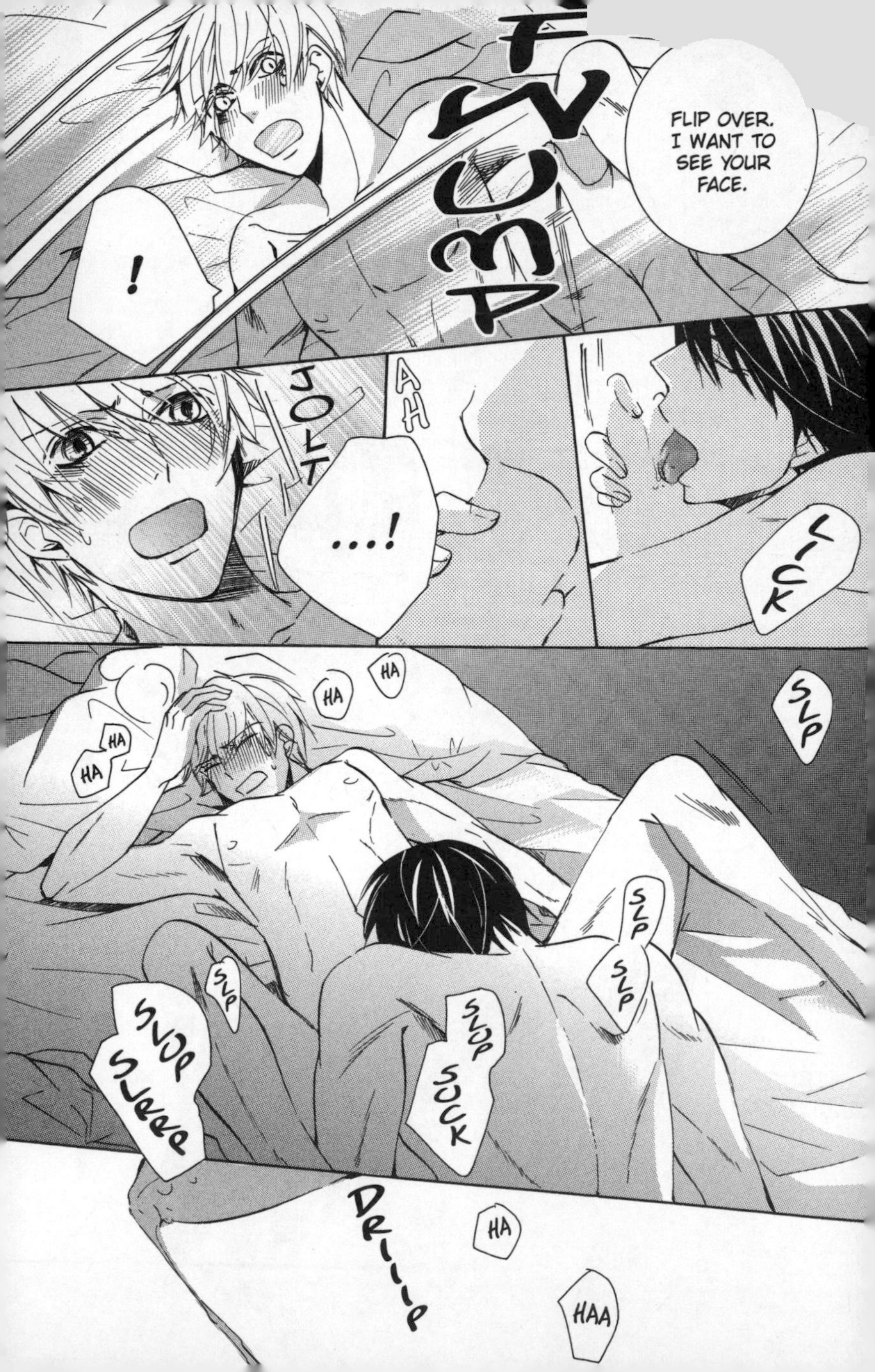
FLIP OVER. I WANT TO SEE YOUR FACE.
FUMP
!
LICK
AH
JOLT
...!
SLP
HA
HA
HA
HA
SLP
SLP
SLURP
SUCK
SLP
SLURP
SLURRP
DRIIIP
HA
HAA

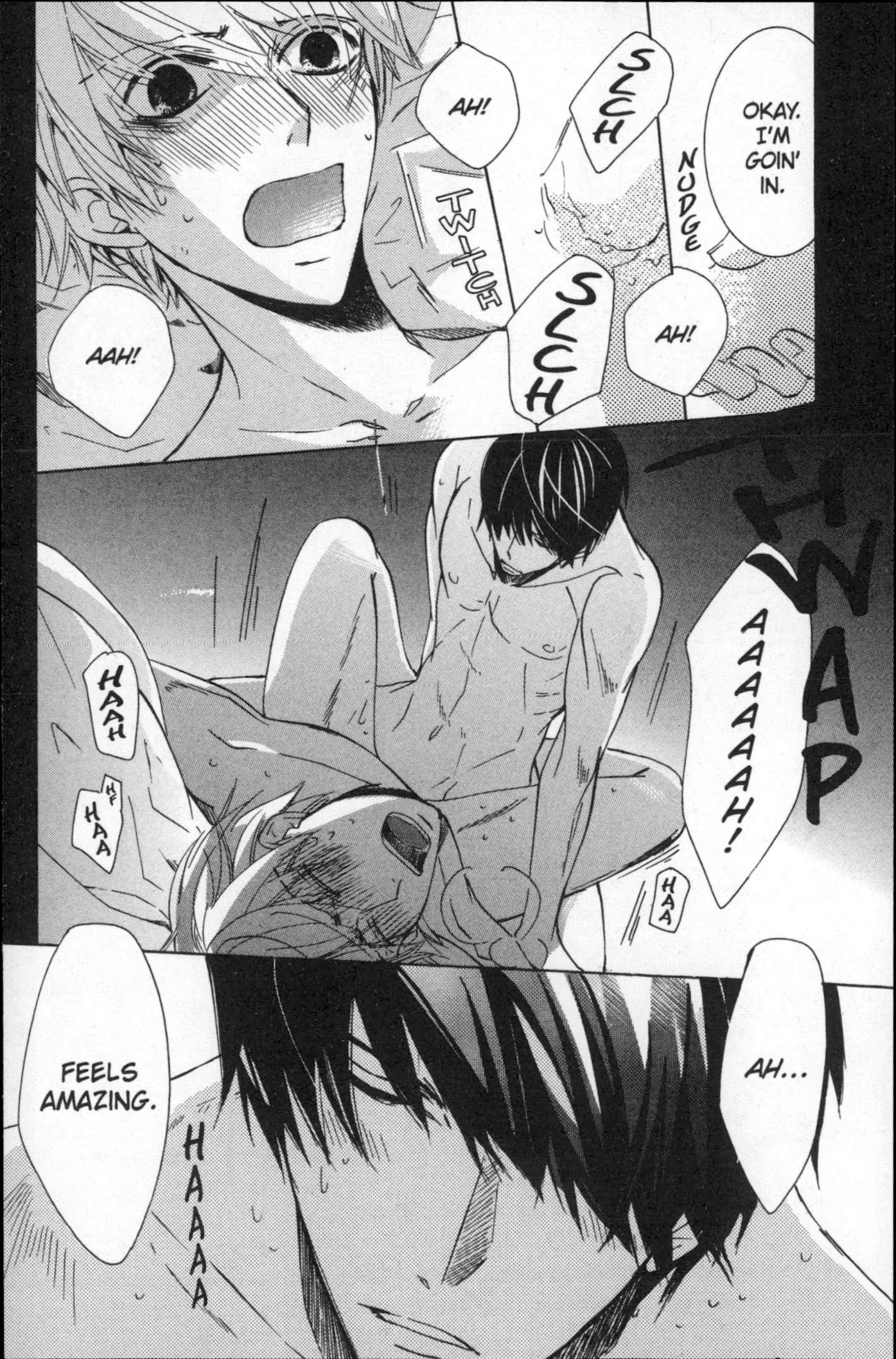
OKAY. I'M GOIN' IN.
NUDGE
SLCH
AH!
AH!
SLCH
TWITCH
AAH!
THWAP
AAAAAAAH!
HAA
HAAAH
HF
HAA
AH...
HAAAA
FEELS AMAZING.

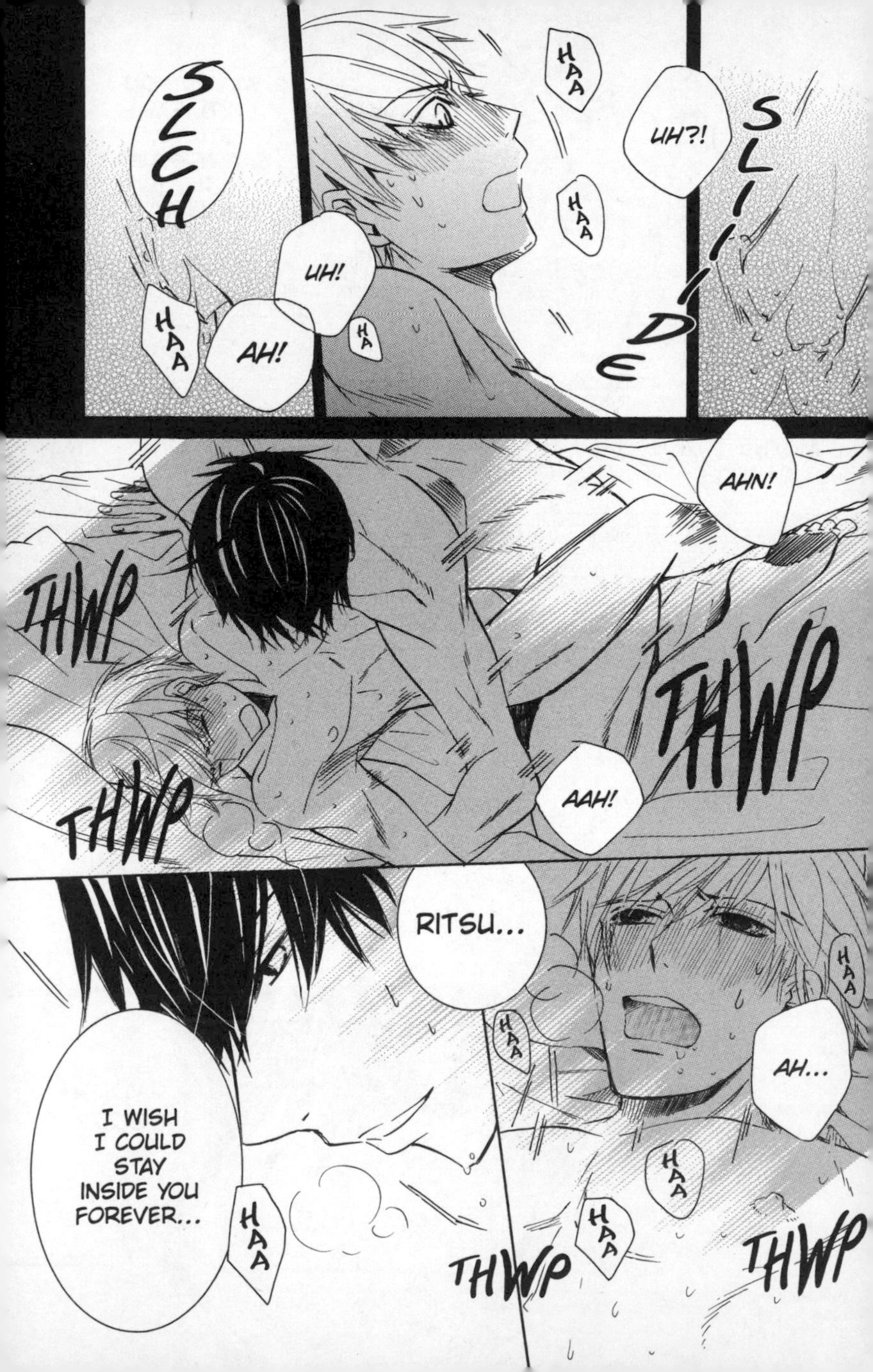
SLIIIIDE
UH?!
HAA
HAA
UH!
HA
SLCH
AH!
HAA
AHN!
THWP
AAH!
THWP
THWP
RITSU...
HAA
AH...
HAA
HAA
HAA
THWP
THWP
I WISH I COULD STAY INSIDE YOU FOREVER...
HAA

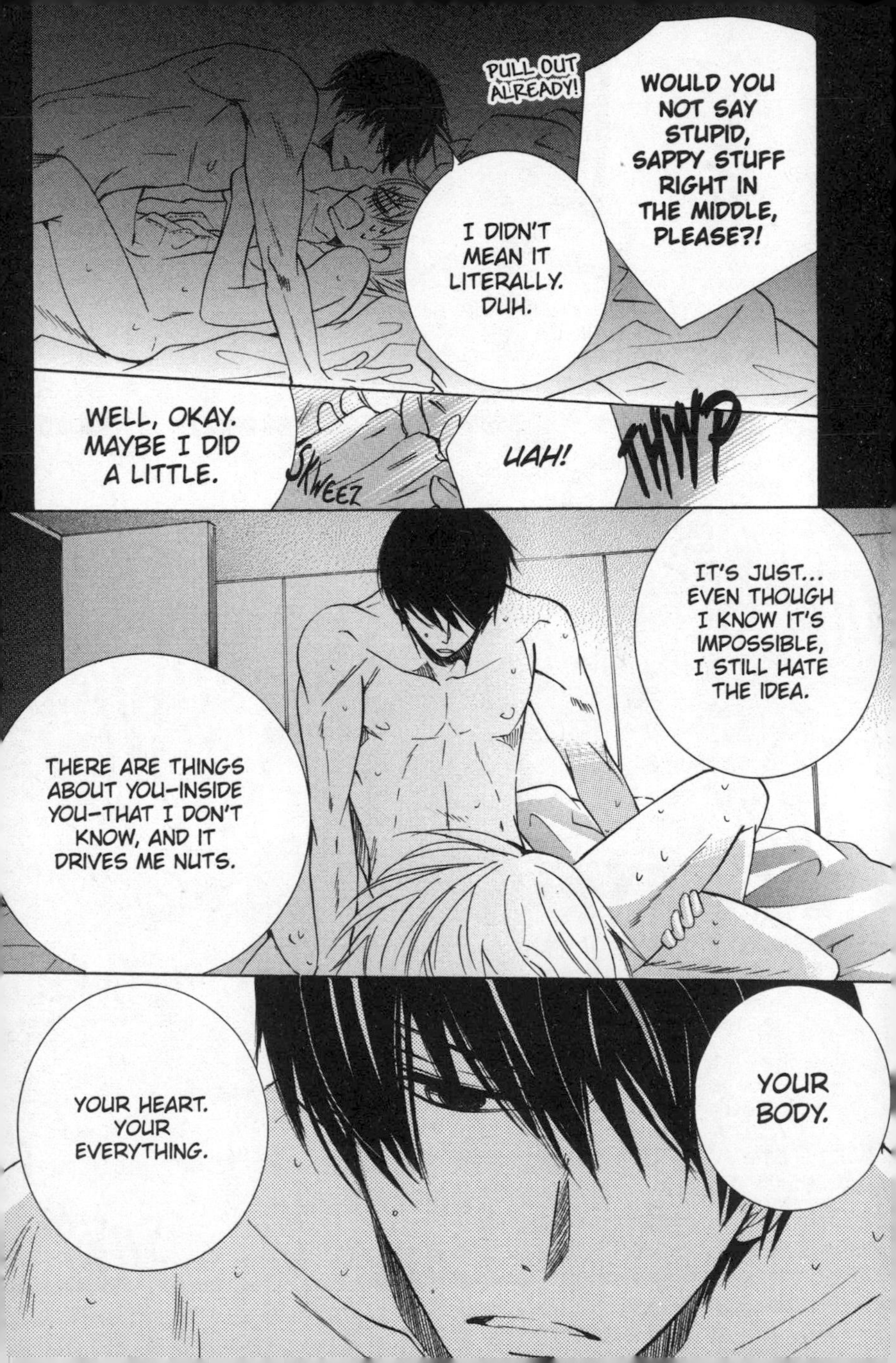
WOULD YOU NOT SAY STUPID, SAPPY STUFF RIGHT IN THE MIDDLE, PLEASE?!
PULL OUT ALREADY!
I DIDN'T MEAN IT LITERALLY. DUH.
THWP
UAH!
SKWEEZ
WELL, OKAY. MAYBE I DID A LITTLE.
IT'S JUST... EVEN THOUGH I KNOW IT'S IMPOSSIBLE, I STILL HATE THE IDEA.
THERE ARE THINGS ABOUT YOU–INSIDE YOU–THAT I DON'T KNOW, AND IT DRIVES ME NUTS.
YOUR BODY.
YOUR HEART. YOUR EVERYTHING.

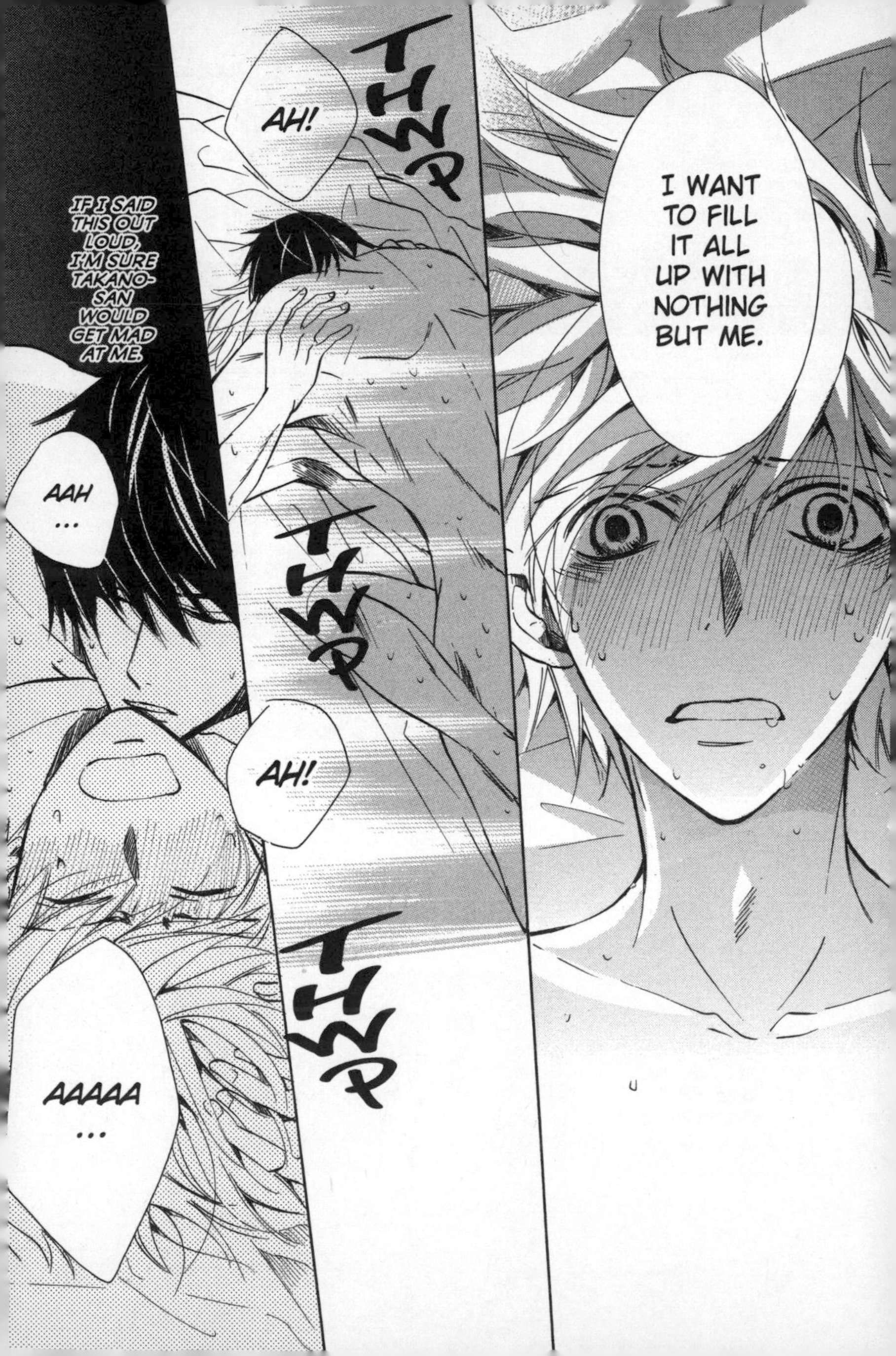
I WANT TO FILL IT ALL UP WITH NOTHING BUT ME.
THWP
AH!
THWP
AH!
THWP
IF I SAID THIS OUT LOUD, I'M SURE TAKANO-SAN WOULD GET MAD AT ME.
AAH ...
AAAAA ...

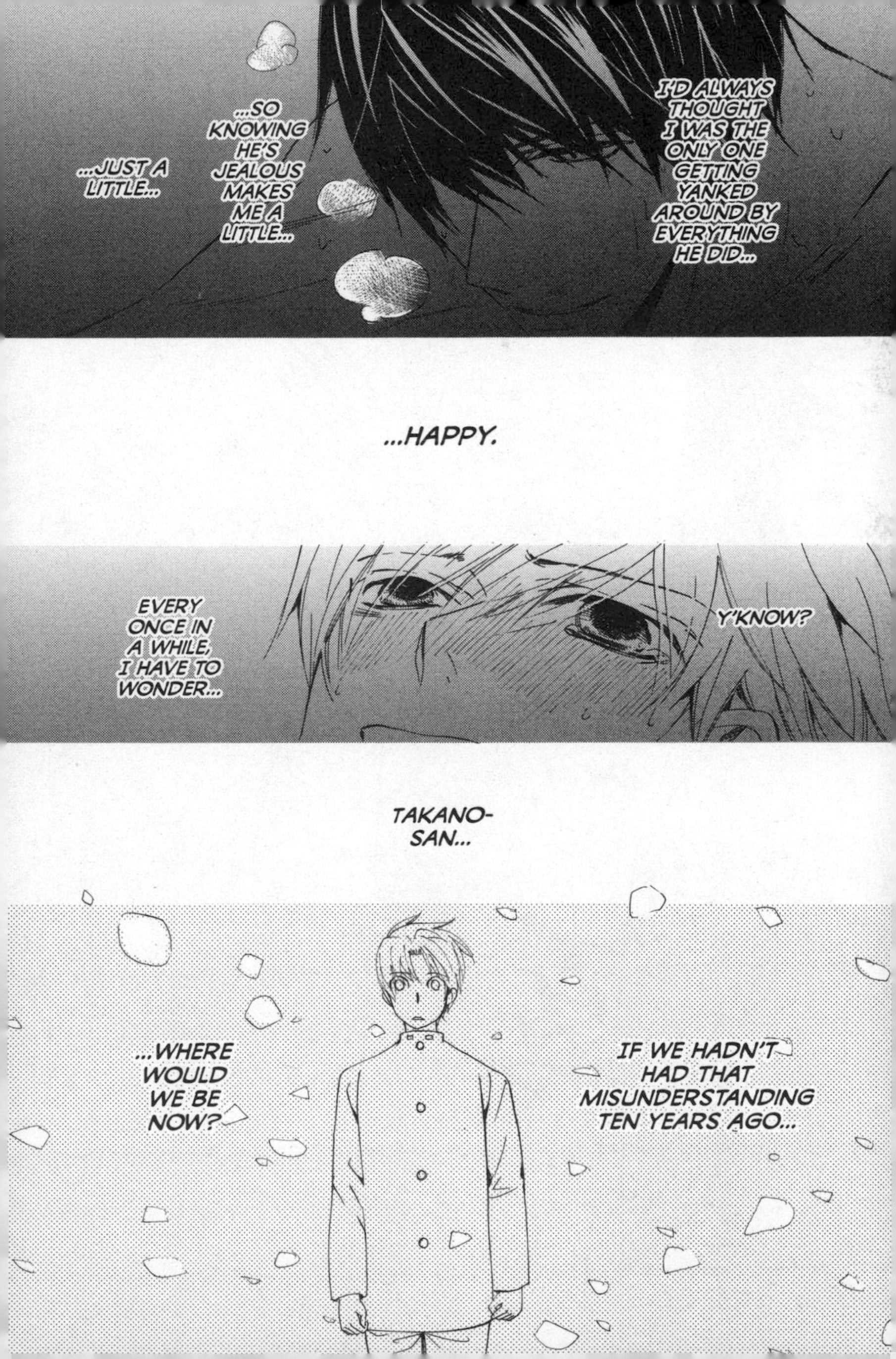
I'D ALWAYS THOUGHT I WAS THE ONLY ONE GETTING YANKED AROUND BY EVERYTHING HE DID...
...SO KNOWING HE'S JEALOUS MAKES ME A LITTLE...
...JUST A LITTLE...
...HAPPY.
Y'KNOW?
EVERY ONCE IN A WHILE, I HAVE TO WONDER...
TAKANO-SAN...
IF WE HADN'T HAD THAT MISUNDERSTANDING TEN YEARS AGO...
...WHERE WOULD WE BE NOW?

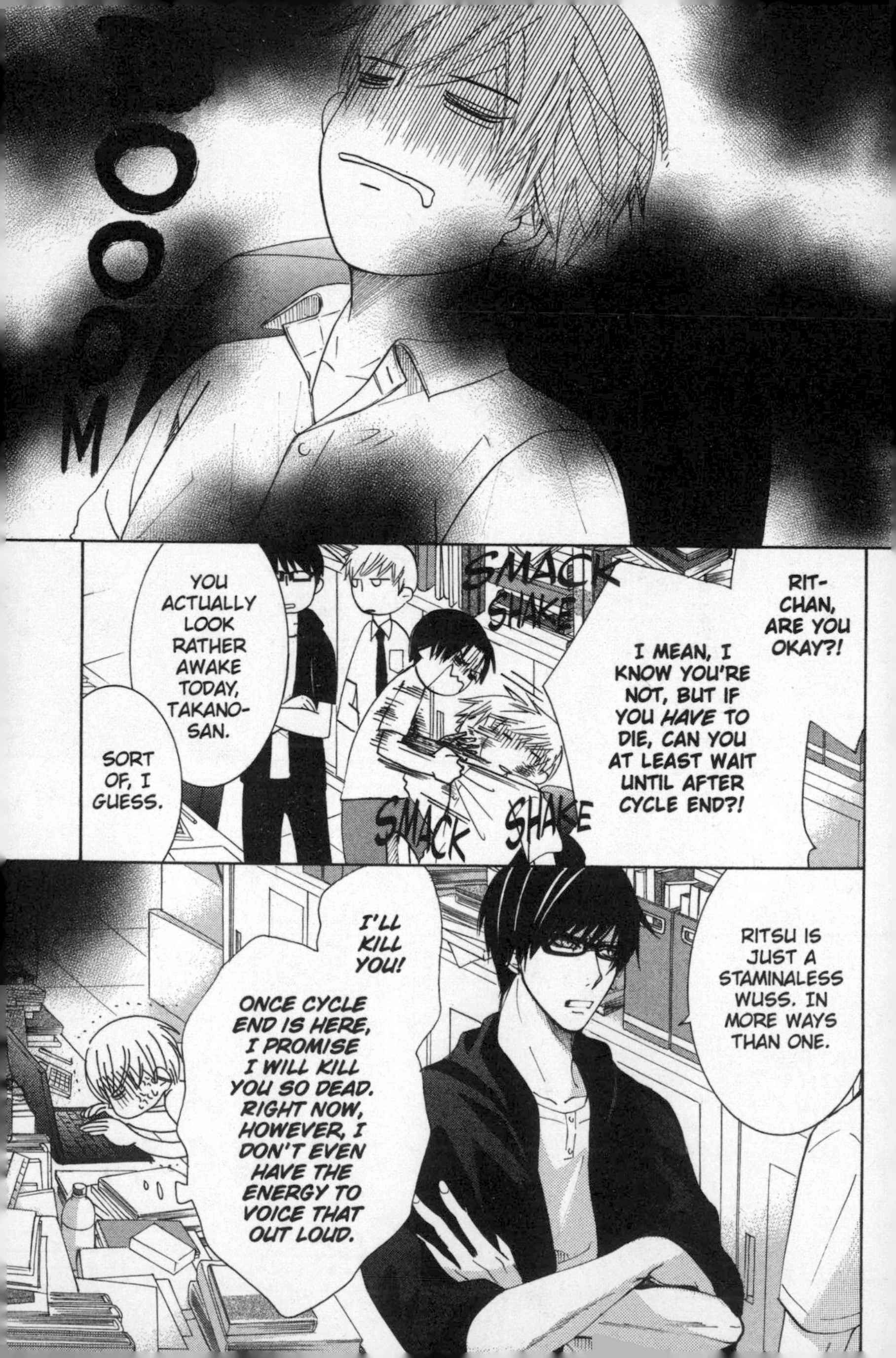
DOOOM
RIT-CHAN, ARE YOU OKAY?!
I MEAN, I KNOW YOU'RE NOT, BUT IF YOU *HAVE* TO DIE, CAN YOU AT LEAST WAIT UNTIL AFTER CYCLE END?!
SMACK
SHAKE
SMACK
SHAKE
YOU ACTUALLY LOOK RATHER AWAKE TODAY, TAKANO-SAN.
SORT OF, I GUESS.
RITSU IS JUST A STAMINALESS WUSS. IN MORE WAYS THAN ONE.
I'LL KILL YOU!
ONCE CYCLE END IS HERE, I PROMISE I WILL KILL YOU SO DEAD. RIGHT NOW, HOWEVER, I DON'T EVEN HAVE THE ENERGY TO VOICE THAT OUT LOUD.

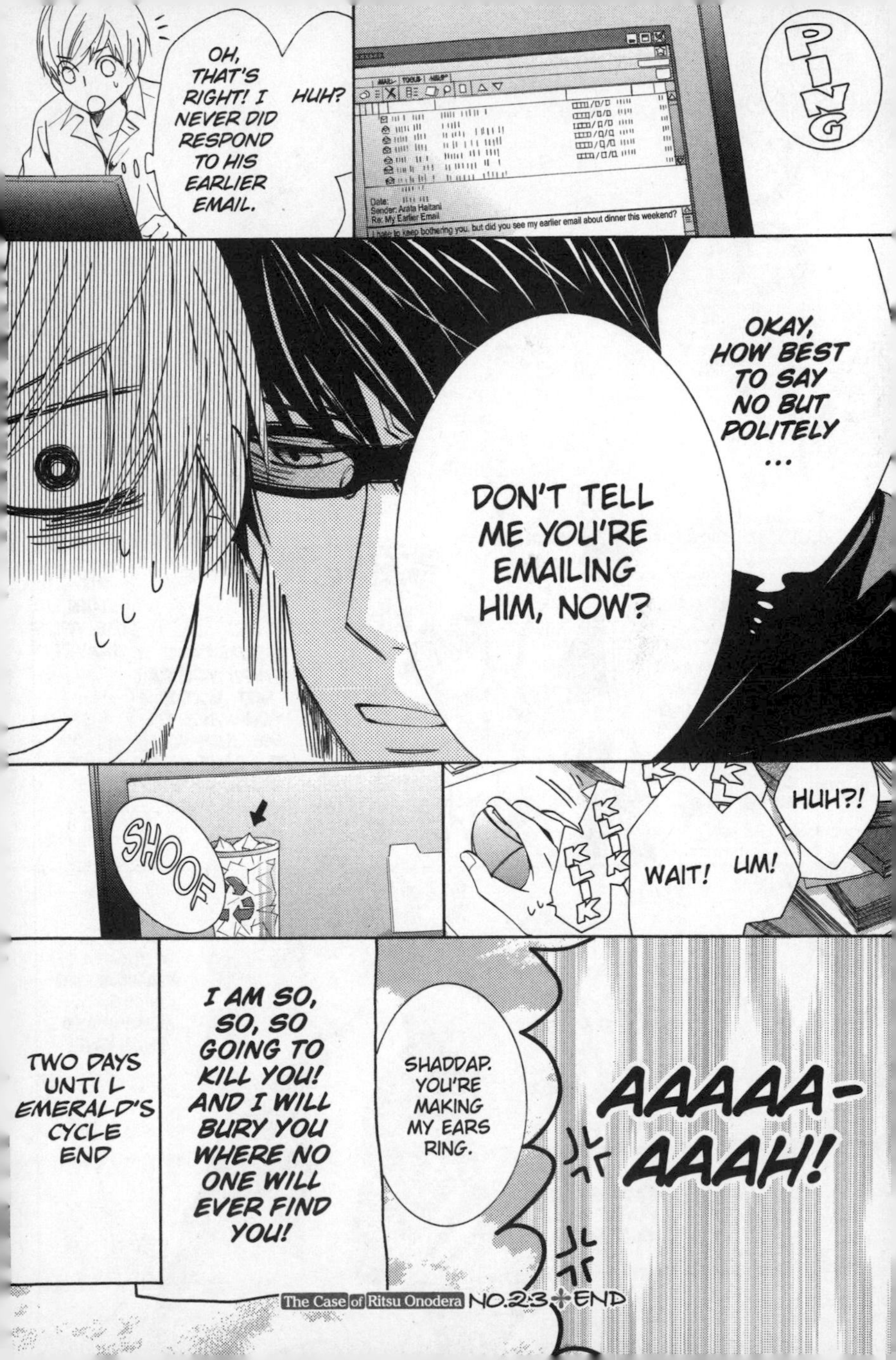
PING
Date:
Sender: Arata Haitani
Re: My Earlier Email
I hate to keep bothering you, but did you see my earlier email about dinner this weekend?
HUH?
OH, THAT'S RIGHT! I NEVER DID RESPOND TO HIS EARLIER EMAIL.
OKAY, HOW BEST TO SAY NO BUT POLITELY ...
DON'T TELL ME YOU'RE EMAILING HIM, NOW?
HUH?!
UM!
WAIT!
KLIK
KLIK
KLIK
SHOOF
AAAAA-AAAH!
SHADDAP. YOU'RE MAKING MY EARS RING.
I AM SO, SO, SO GOING TO KILL YOU! AND I WILL BURY YOU WHERE NO ONE WILL EVER FIND YOU!
TWO DAYS UNTI L EMERALD'S CYCLE END
The Case of Ritsu Onodera NO.23 END

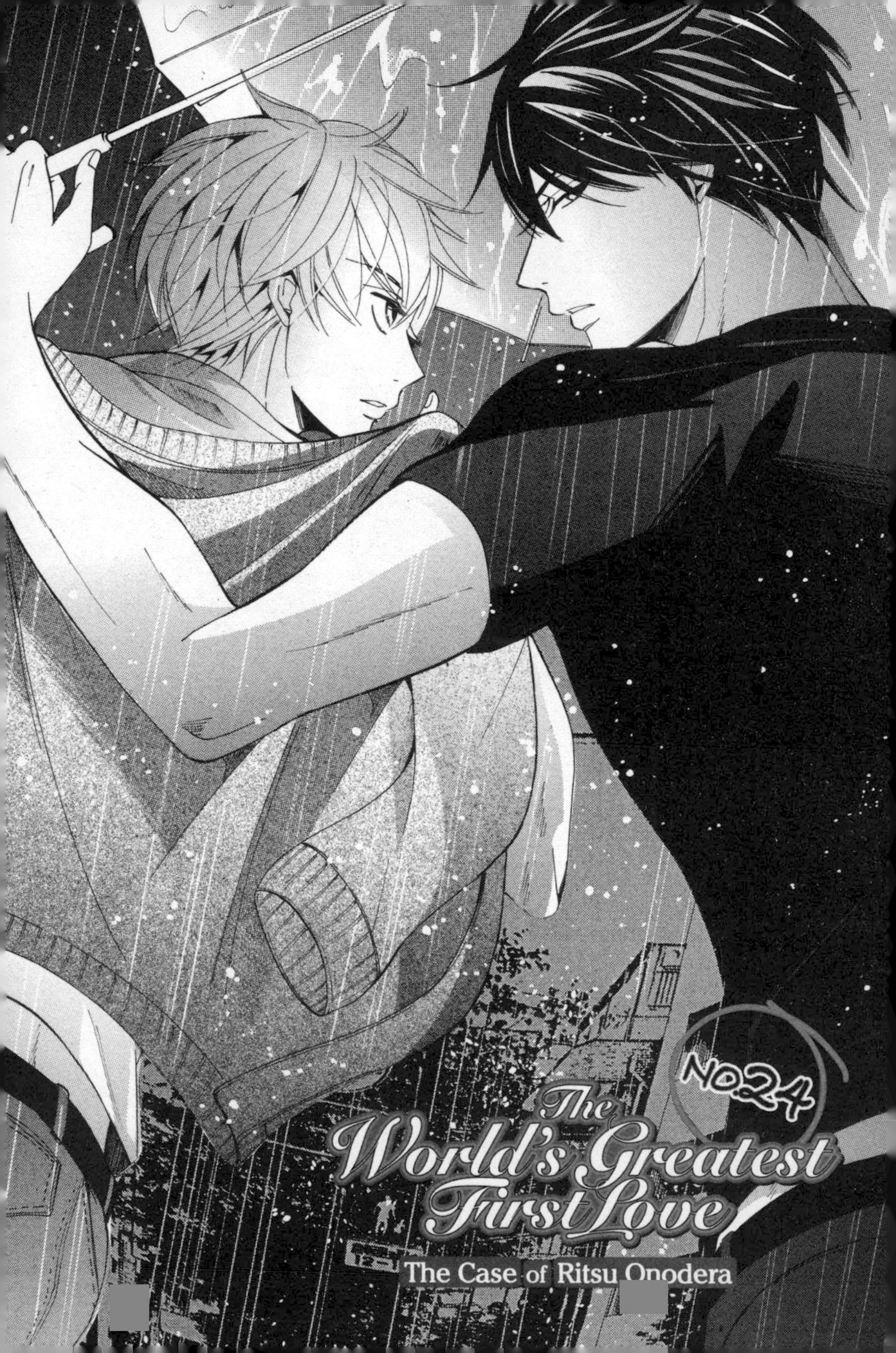
No.24
The World's Greatest First Love
The Case of Ritsu Onodera

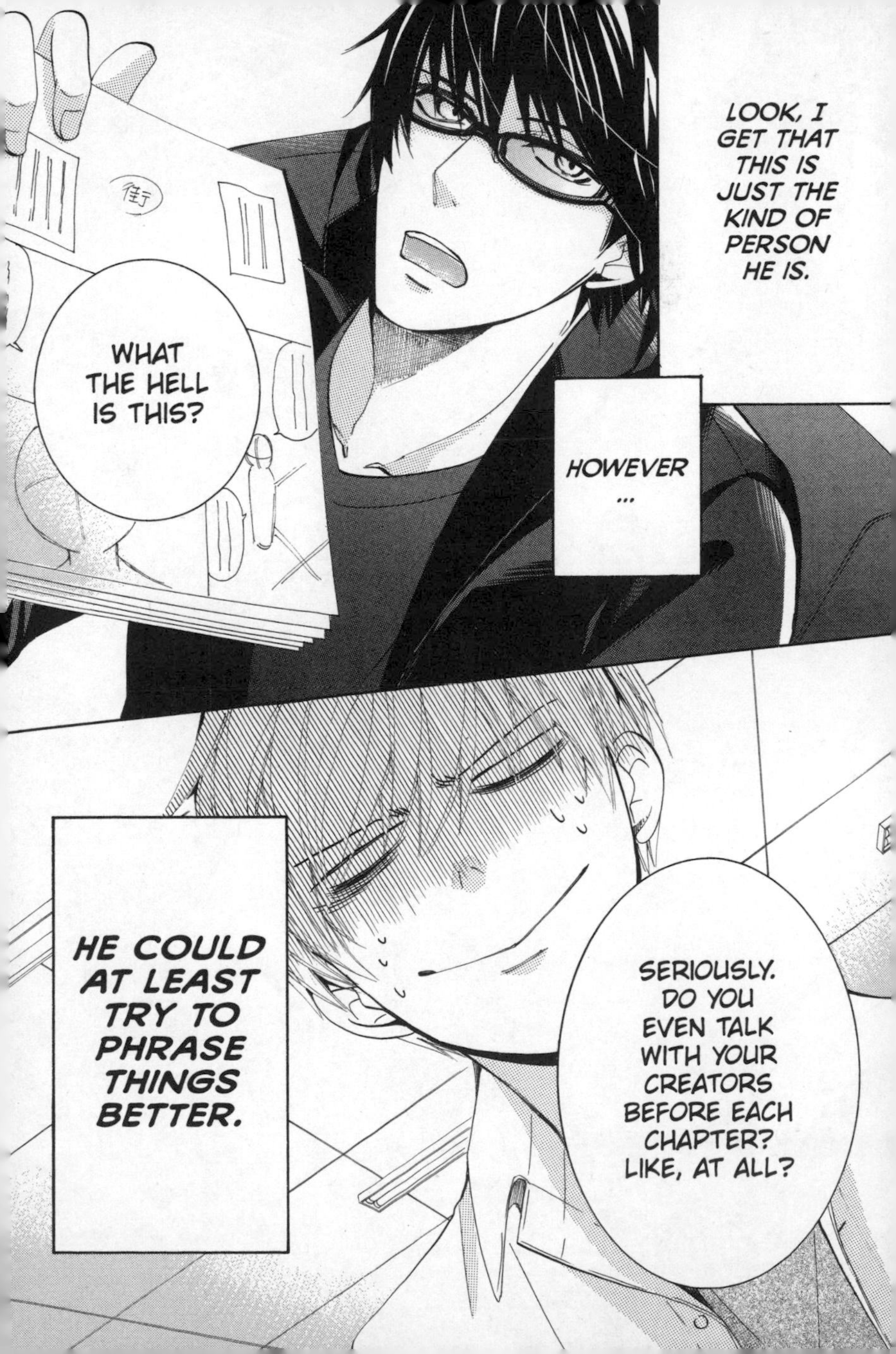
LOOK, I GET THAT THIS IS JUST THE KIND OF PERSON HE IS.
WHAT THE HELL IS THIS?
HOWEVER ...
SERIOUSLY. DO YOU EVEN TALK WITH YOUR CREATORS BEFORE EACH CHAPTER? LIKE, AT ALL?
HE COULD AT LEAST TRY TO PHRASE THINGS BETTER.

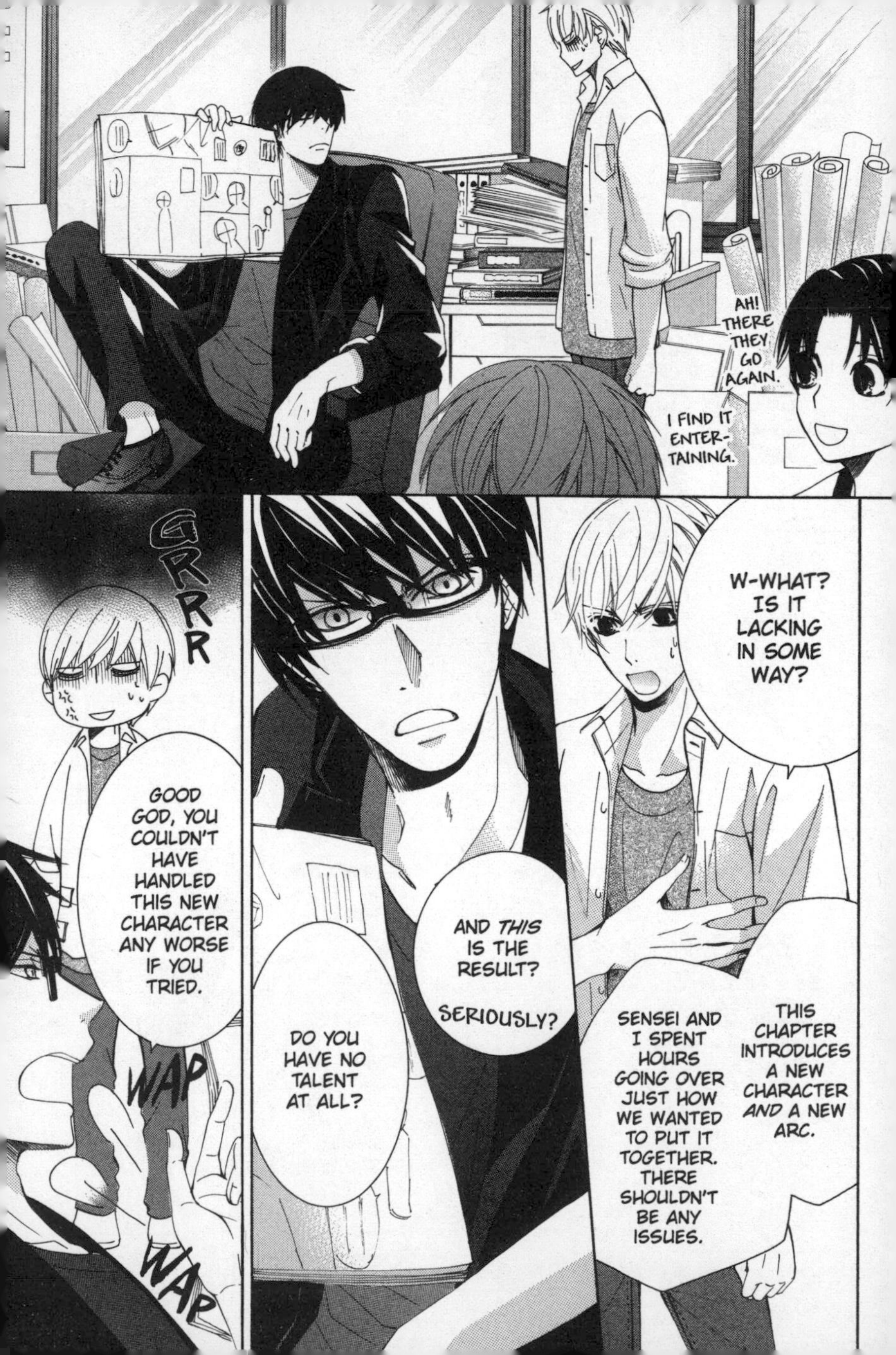
AH! THERE THEY GO AGAIN.
I FIND IT ENTER-TAINING.
W-WHAT? IS IT LACKING IN SOME WAY?
THIS CHAPTER INTRODUCES A NEW CHARACTER *AND* A NEW ARC.
SENSEI AND I SPENT HOURS GOING OVER JUST HOW WE WANTED TO PUT IT TOGETHER. THERE SHOULDN'T BE ANY ISSUES.
AND *THIS* IS THE RESULT?
SERIOUSLY?
DO YOU HAVE NO TALENT AT ALL?
GRRR
GOOD GOD, YOU COULDN'T HAVE HANDLED THIS NEW CHARACTER ANY WORSE IF YOU TRIED.
WAP
WAP

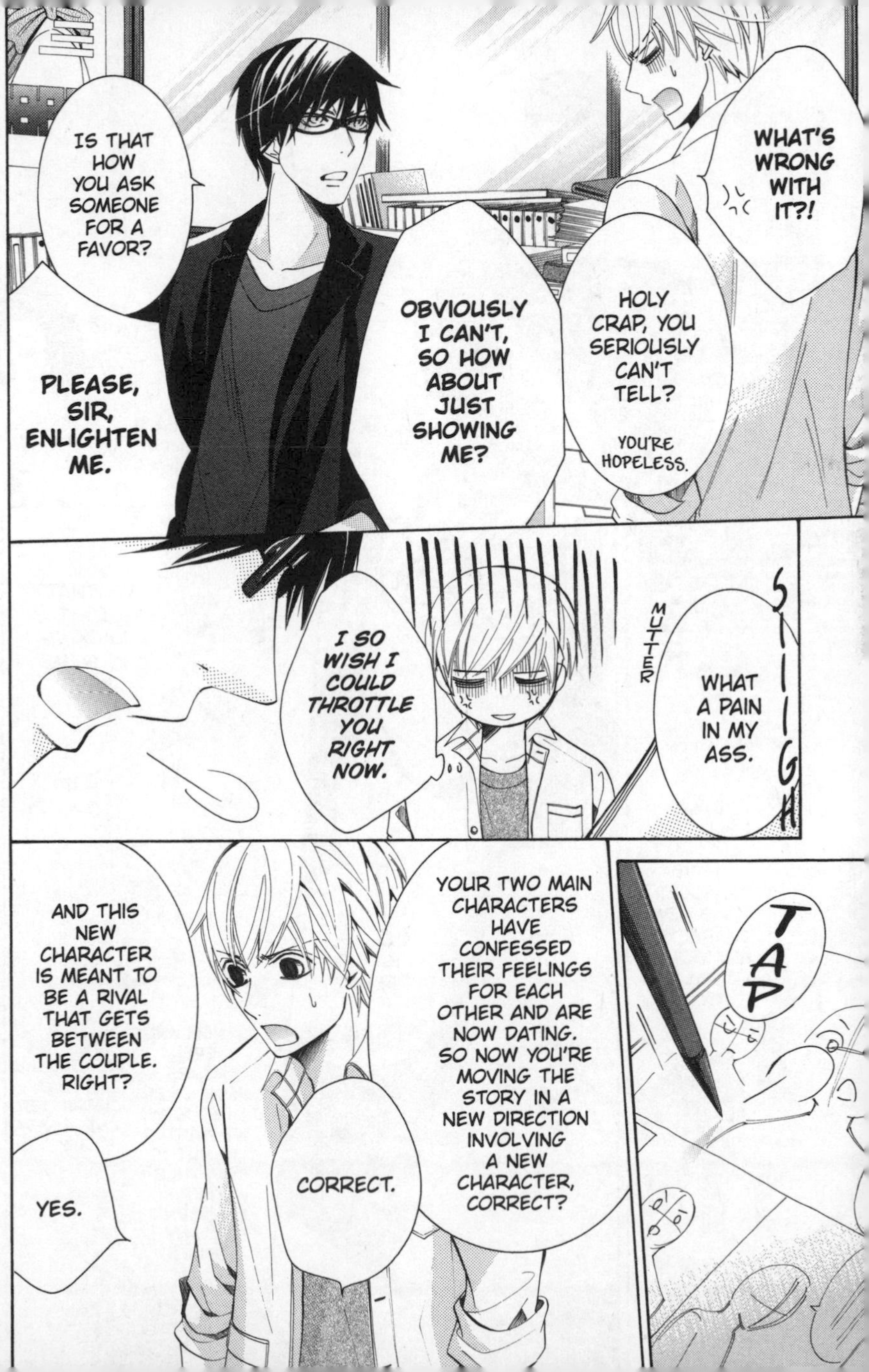

WHAT'S WRONG WITH IT?!
IS THAT HOW YOU ASK SOMEONE FOR A FAVOR?
HOLY CRAP, YOU SERIOUSLY CAN'T TELL?
YOU'RE HOPELESS.
OBVIOUSLY I CAN'T, SO HOW ABOUT JUST SHOWING ME?
PLEASE, SIR, ENLIGHTEN ME.
SIIIGH
MUTTER
WHAT A PAIN IN MY ASS.
I SO WISH I COULD THROTTLE YOU RIGHT NOW.
TAP
YOUR TWO MAIN CHARACTERS HAVE CONFESSED THEIR FEELINGS FOR EACH OTHER AND ARE NOW DATING. SO NOW YOU'RE MOVING THE STORY IN A NEW DIRECTION INVOLVING A NEW CHARACTER, CORRECT?
CORRECT.
AND THIS NEW CHARACTER IS MEANT TO BE A RIVAL THAT GETS BETWEEN THE COUPLE. RIGHT?
YES.

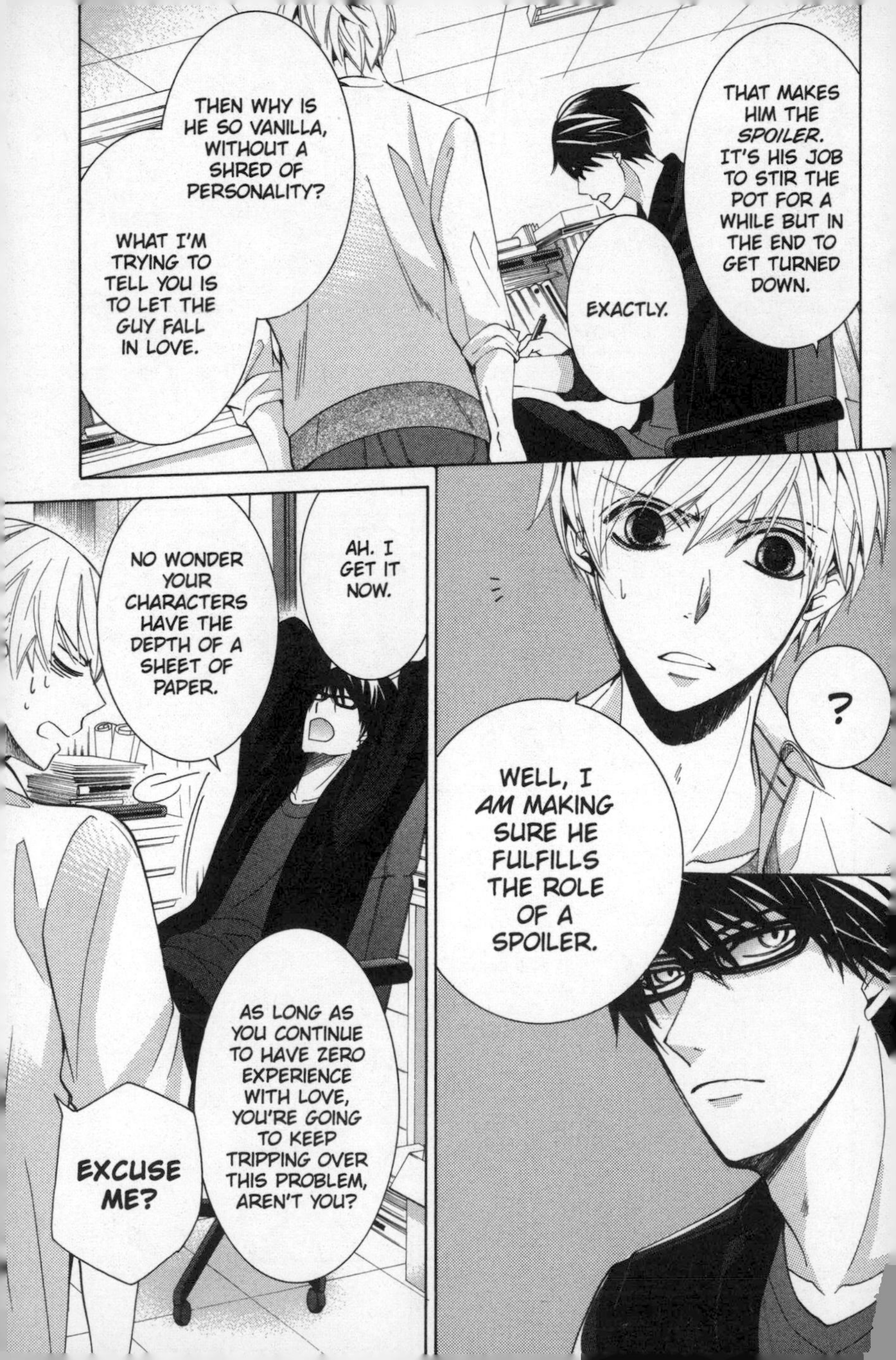
THAT MAKES HIM THE *SPOILER*. IT'S HIS JOB TO STIR THE POT FOR A WHILE BUT IN THE END TO GET TURNED DOWN.
THEN WHY IS HE SO VANILLA, WITHOUT A SHRED OF PERSONALITY?
EXACTLY.
WHAT I'M TRYING TO TELL YOU IS TO LET THE GUY FALL IN LOVE.
?
WELL, I *AM* MAKING SURE HE FULFILLS THE ROLE OF A SPOILER.
AH. I GET IT NOW.
NO WONDER YOUR CHARACTERS HAVE THE DEPTH OF A SHEET OF PAPER.
AS LONG AS YOU CONTINUE TO HAVE ZERO EXPERIENCE WITH LOVE, YOU'RE GOING TO KEEP TRIPPING OVER THIS PROBLEM, AREN'T YOU?
EXCUSE ME?

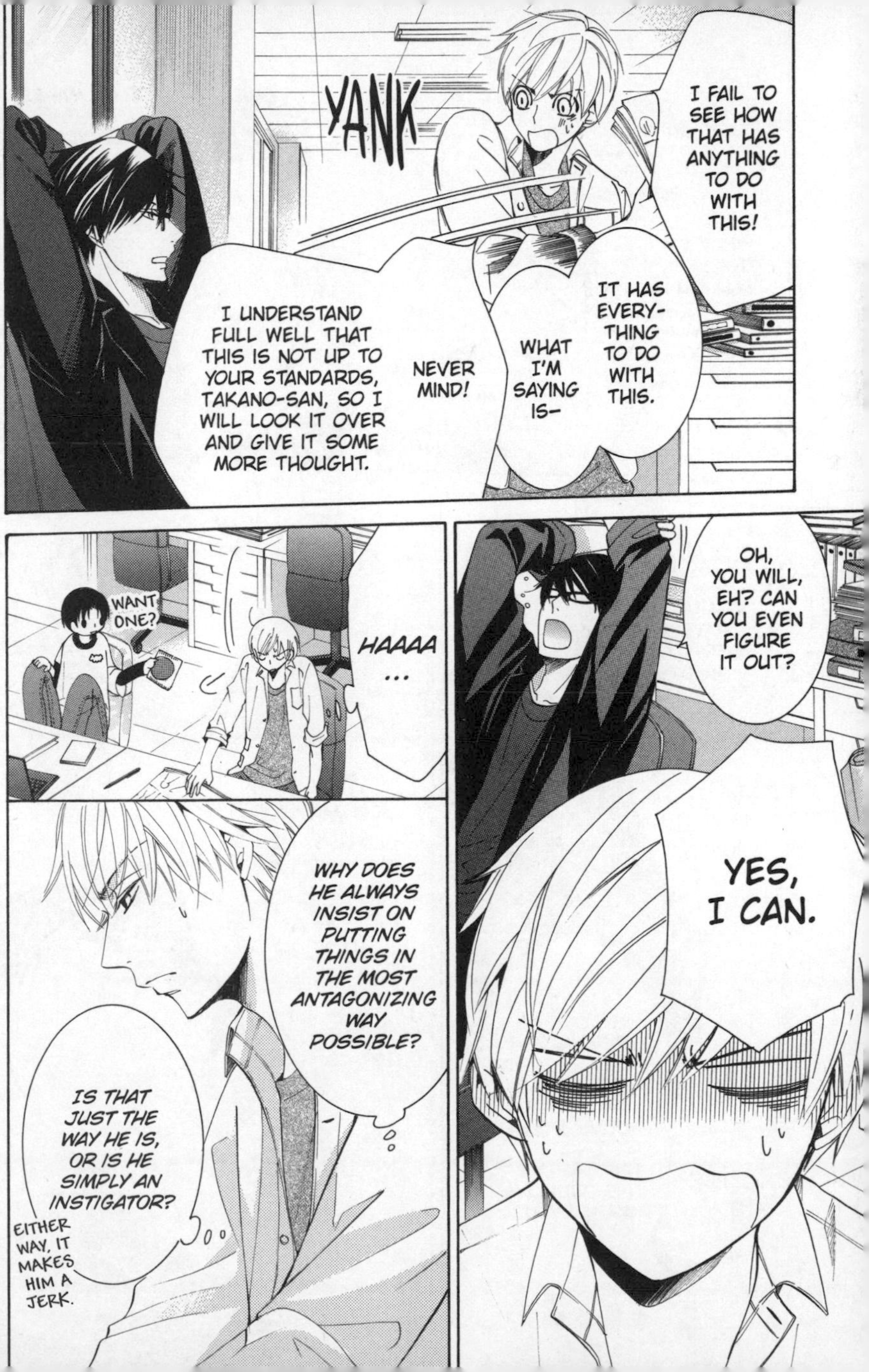
I FAIL TO SEE HOW THAT HAS ANYTHING TO DO WITH THIS!
YANK
IT HAS EVERYTHING TO DO WITH THIS.
WHAT I'M SAYING IS—
NEVER MIND!
I UNDERSTAND FULL WELL THAT THIS IS NOT UP TO YOUR STANDARDS, TAKANO-SAN, SO I WILL LOOK IT OVER AND GIVE IT SOME MORE THOUGHT.
OH, YOU WILL, EH? CAN YOU EVEN FIGURE IT OUT?
YES, I CAN.
HAAAA...
WANT ONE?
WHY DOES HE ALWAYS INSIST ON PUTTING THINGS IN THE MOST ANTAGONIZING WAY POSSIBLE?
IS THAT JUST THE WAY HE IS, OR IS HE SIMPLY AN INSTIGATOR?
EITHER WAY, IT MAKES HIM A JERK.

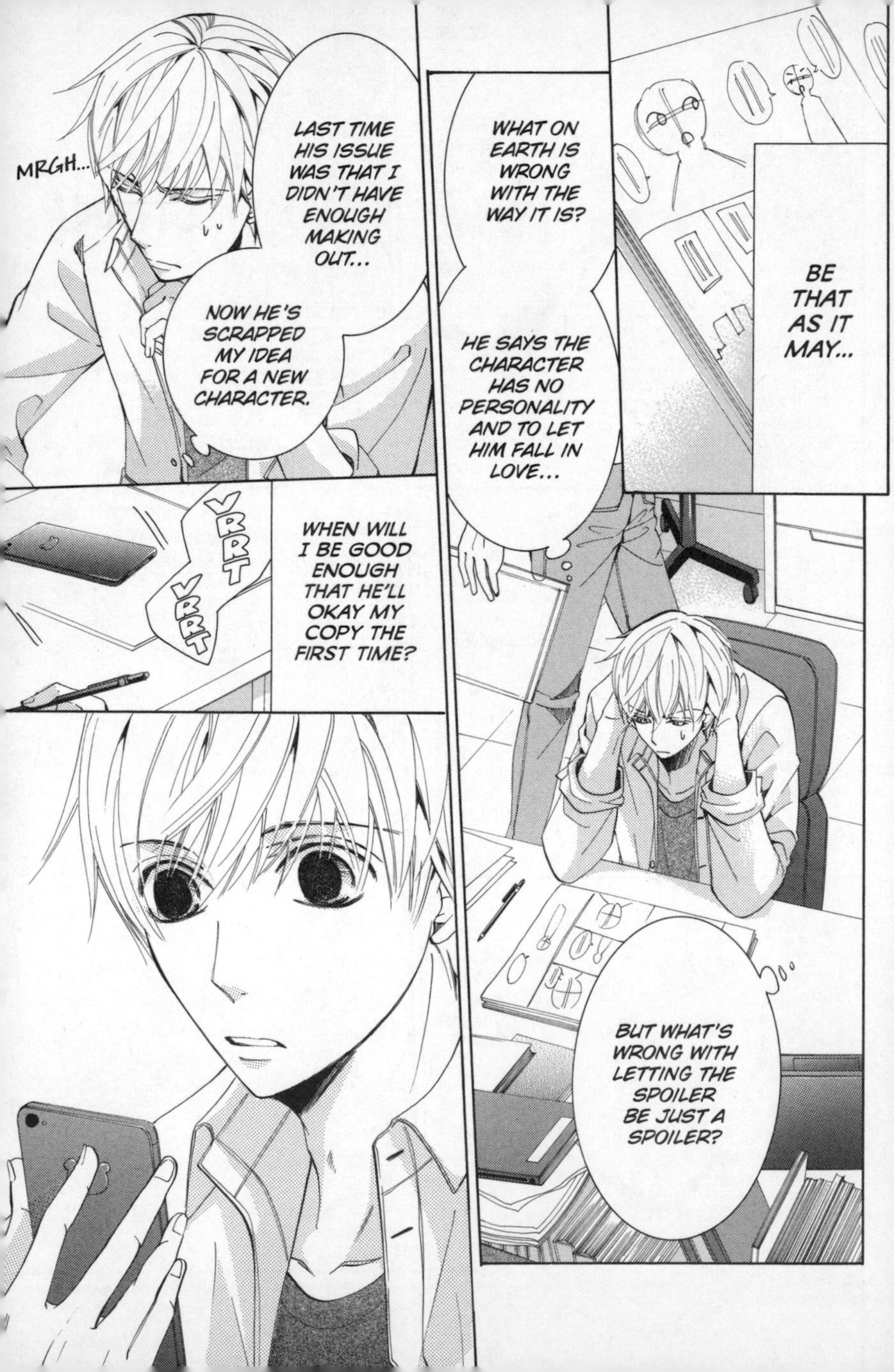
BE THAT AS IT MAY...
WHAT ON EARTH IS WRONG WITH THE WAY IT IS?
HE SAYS THE CHARACTER HAS NO PERSONALITY AND TO LET HIM FALL IN LOVE...
BUT WHAT'S WRONG WITH LETTING THE SPOILER BE JUST A SPOILER?
LAST TIME HIS ISSUE WAS THAT I DIDN'T HAVE ENOUGH MAKING OUT...
NOW HE'S SCRAPPED MY IDEA FOR A NEW CHARACTER.
MRGH...
WHEN WILL I BE GOOD ENOUGH THAT HE'LL OKAY MY COPY THE FIRST TIME?
VRRT
VRRT

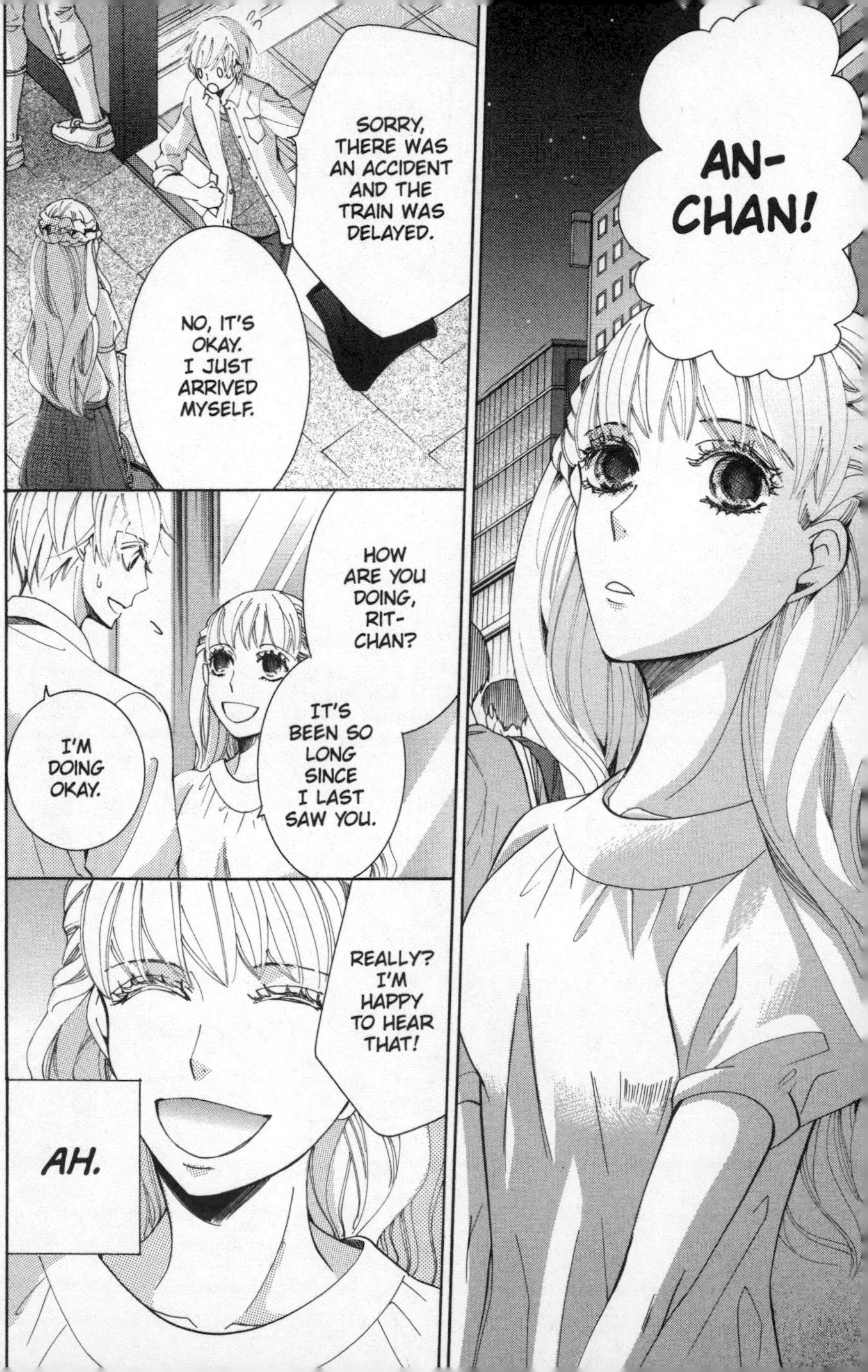

AN-CHAN!
SORRY, THERE WAS AN ACCIDENT AND THE TRAIN WAS DELAYED.
NO, IT'S OKAY. I JUST ARRIVED MYSELF.
HOW ARE YOU DOING, RIT-CHAN?
IT'S BEEN SO LONG SINCE I LAST SAW YOU.
I'M DOING OKAY.
REALLY? I'M HAPPY TO HEAR THAT!
AH.

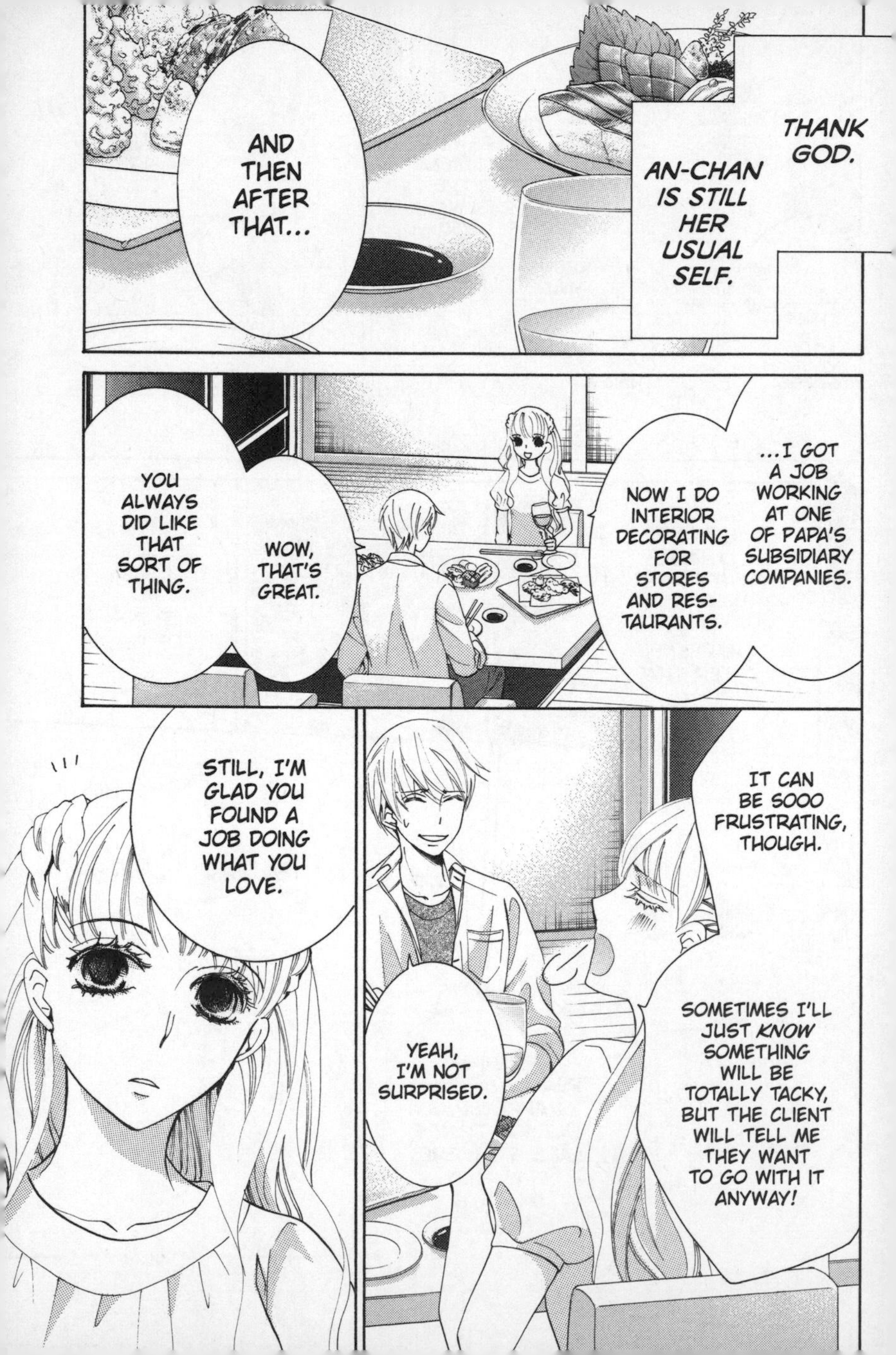
THANK GOD.
AN-CHAN IS STILL HER USUAL SELF.
AND THEN AFTER THAT...
...I GOT A JOB WORKING AT ONE OF PAPA'S SUBSIDIARY COMPANIES.
NOW I DO INTERIOR DECORATING FOR STORES AND RES-TAURANTS.
WOW, THAT'S GREAT.
YOU ALWAYS DID LIKE THAT SORT OF THING.
IT CAN BE SOOO FRUSTRATING, THOUGH.
SOMETIMES I'LL JUST KNOW SOMETHING WILL BE TOTALLY TACKY, BUT THE CLIENT WILL TELL ME THEY WANT TO GO WITH IT ANYWAY!
YEAH, I'M NOT SURPRISED.
STILL, I'M GLAD YOU FOUND A JOB DOING WHAT YOU LOVE.

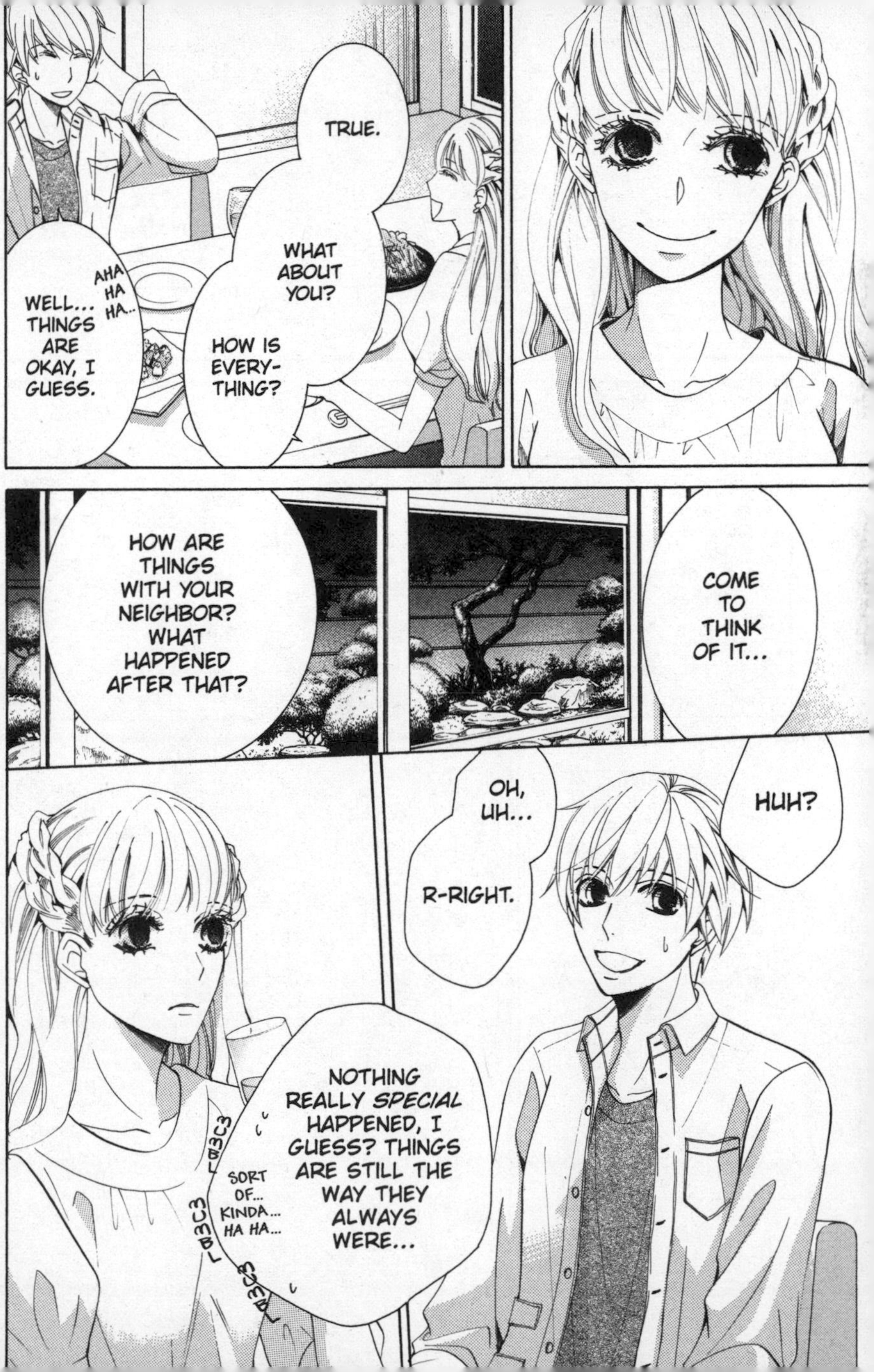
TRUE.
WHAT ABOUT YOU?
HOW IS EVERYTHING?
AHA HA HA...
WELL... THINGS ARE OKAY, I GUESS.
COME TO THINK OF IT...
HOW ARE THINGS WITH YOUR NEIGHBOR? WHAT HAPPENED AFTER THAT?
HUH?
OH, UH...
R-RIGHT.
NOTHING REALLY *SPECIAL* HAPPENED, I GUESS? THINGS ARE STILL THE WAY THEY ALWAYS WERE...
SORT OF... KINDA... HA HA...

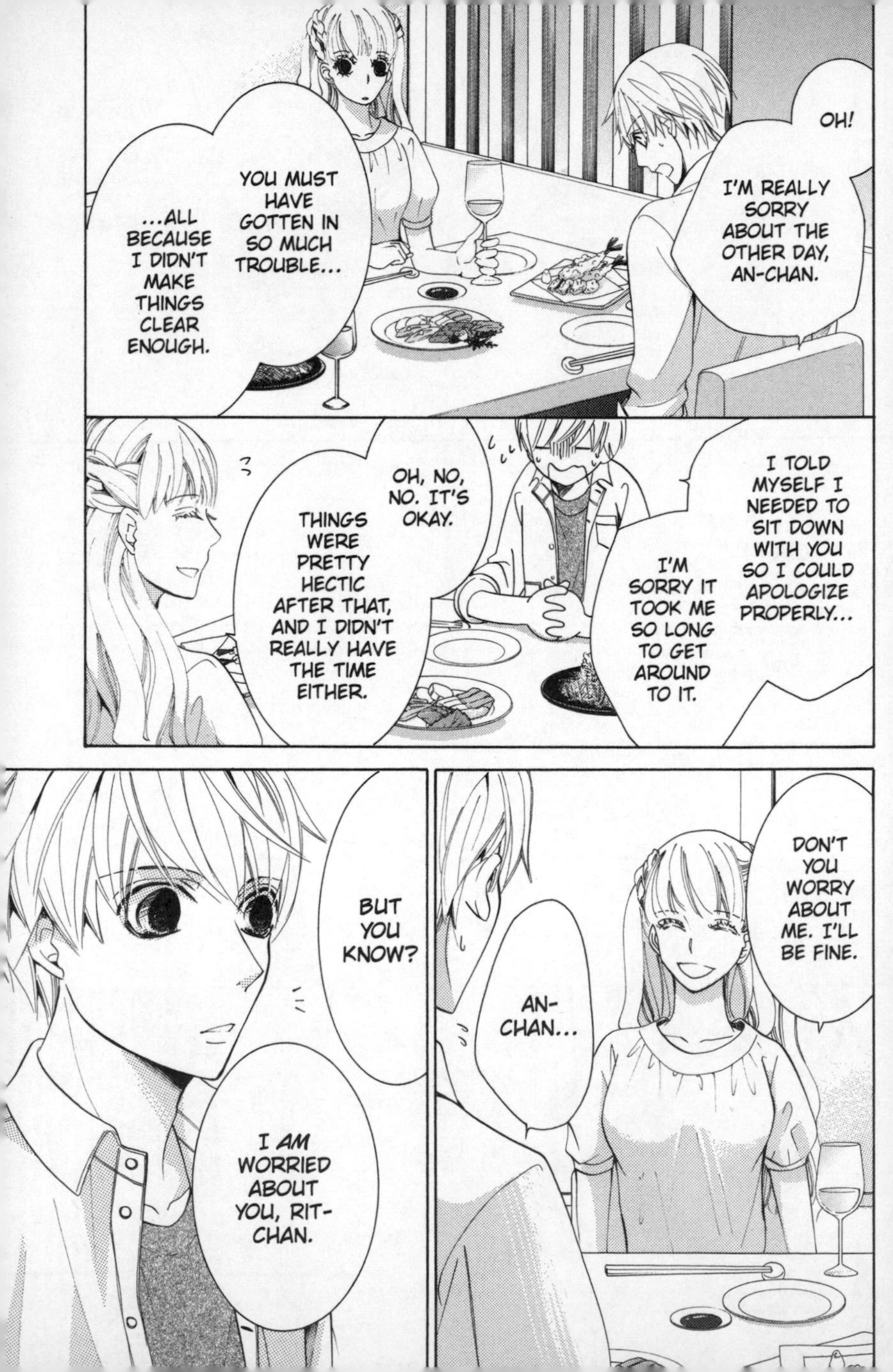
OH!
I'M REALLY SORRY ABOUT THE OTHER DAY, AN-CHAN.
YOU MUST HAVE GOTTEN IN SO MUCH TROUBLE...
...ALL BECAUSE I DIDN'T MAKE THINGS CLEAR ENOUGH.
I TOLD MYSELF I NEEDED TO SIT DOWN WITH YOU SO I COULD APOLOGIZE PROPERLY...
I'M SORRY IT TOOK ME SO LONG TO GET AROUND TO IT.
OH, NO, NO. IT'S OKAY.
THINGS WERE PRETTY HECTIC AFTER THAT, AND I DIDN'T REALLY HAVE THE TIME EITHER.
DON'T YOU WORRY ABOUT ME. I'LL BE FINE.
AN-CHAN...
BUT YOU KNOW?
I *AM* WORRIED ABOUT YOU, RIT-CHAN.

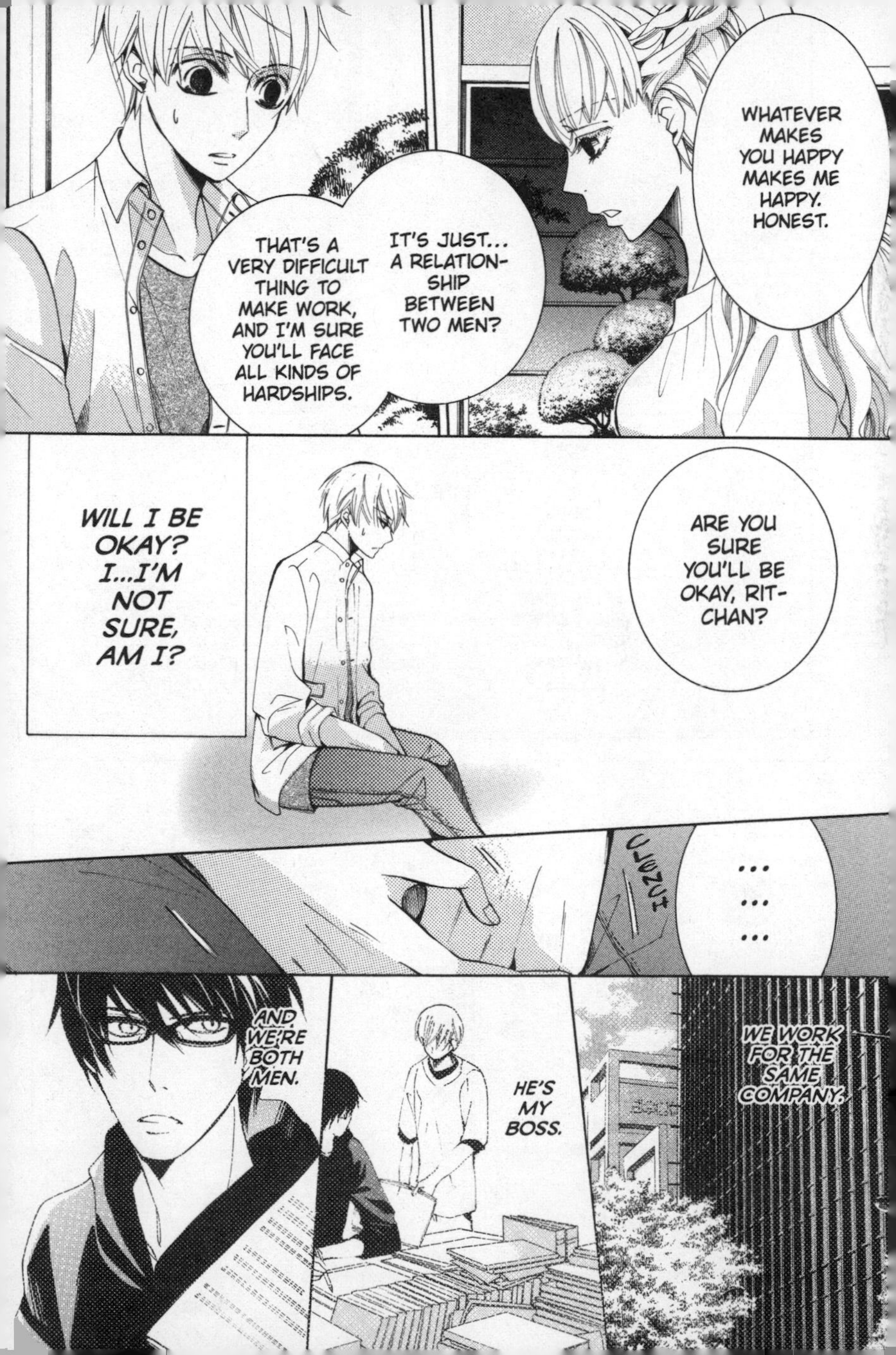
WHATEVER MAKES YOU HAPPY MAKES ME HAPPY. HONEST.
IT'S JUST... A RELATIONSHIP BETWEEN TWO MEN?
THAT'S A VERY DIFFICULT THING TO MAKE WORK, AND I'M SURE YOU'LL FACE ALL KINDS OF HARDSHIPS.
ARE YOU SURE YOU'LL BE OKAY, RIT-CHAN?
WILL I BE OKAY? I...I'M NOT SURE, AM I?
... ...
CLENCH
WE WORK FOR THE SAME COMPANY.
HE'S MY BOSS.
AND WE'RE BOTH MEN.

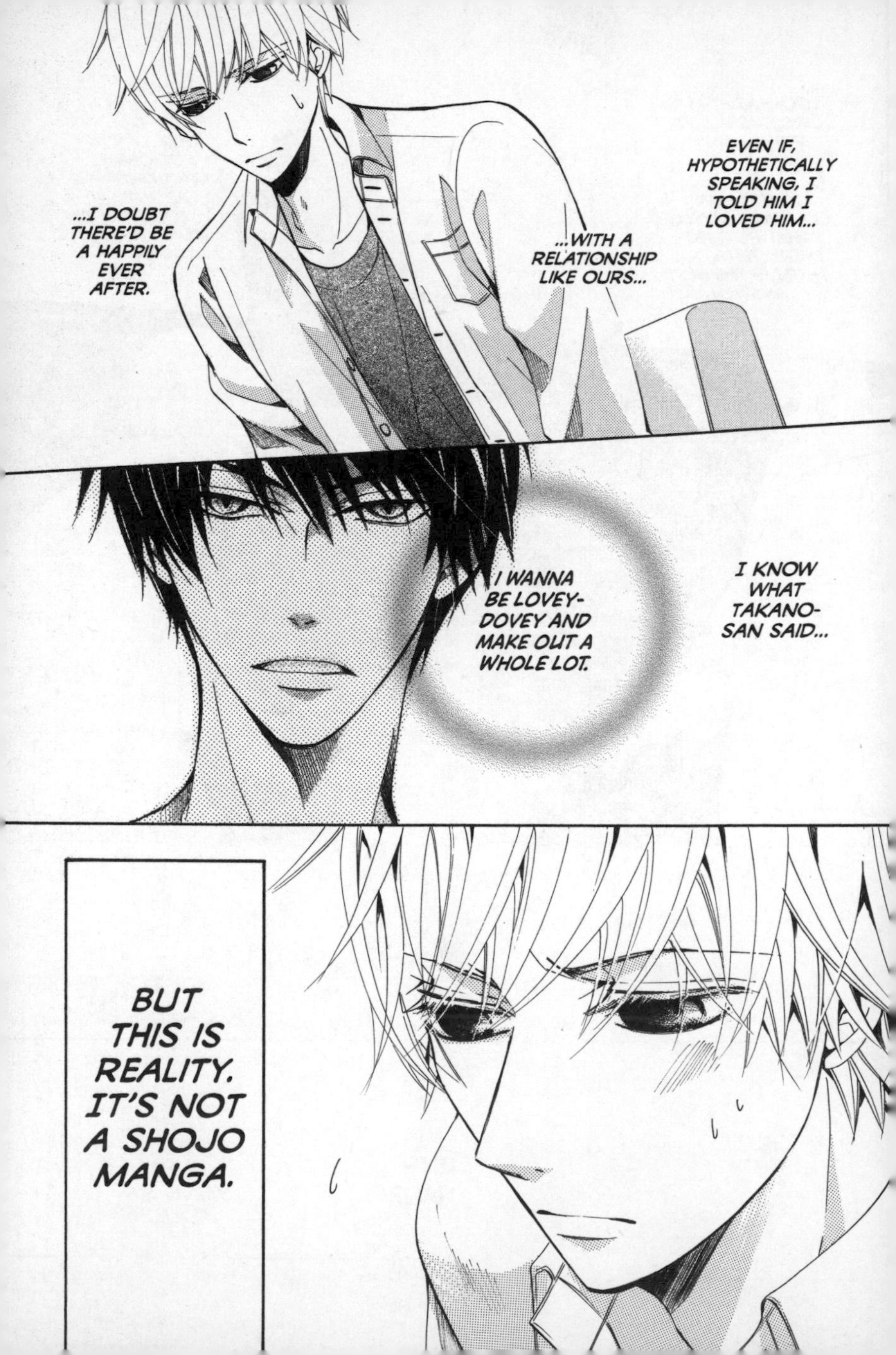
EVEN IF, HYPOTHETICALLY SPEAKING, I TOLD HIM I LOVED HIM...
...WITH A RELATIONSHIP LIKE OURS...
...I DOUBT THERE'D BE A HAPPILY EVER AFTER.
I KNOW WHAT TAKANO-SAN SAID...
I WANNA BE LOVEY-DOVEY AND MAKE OUT A WHOLE LOT.
BUT THIS IS REALITY. IT'S NOT A SHOJO MANGA.

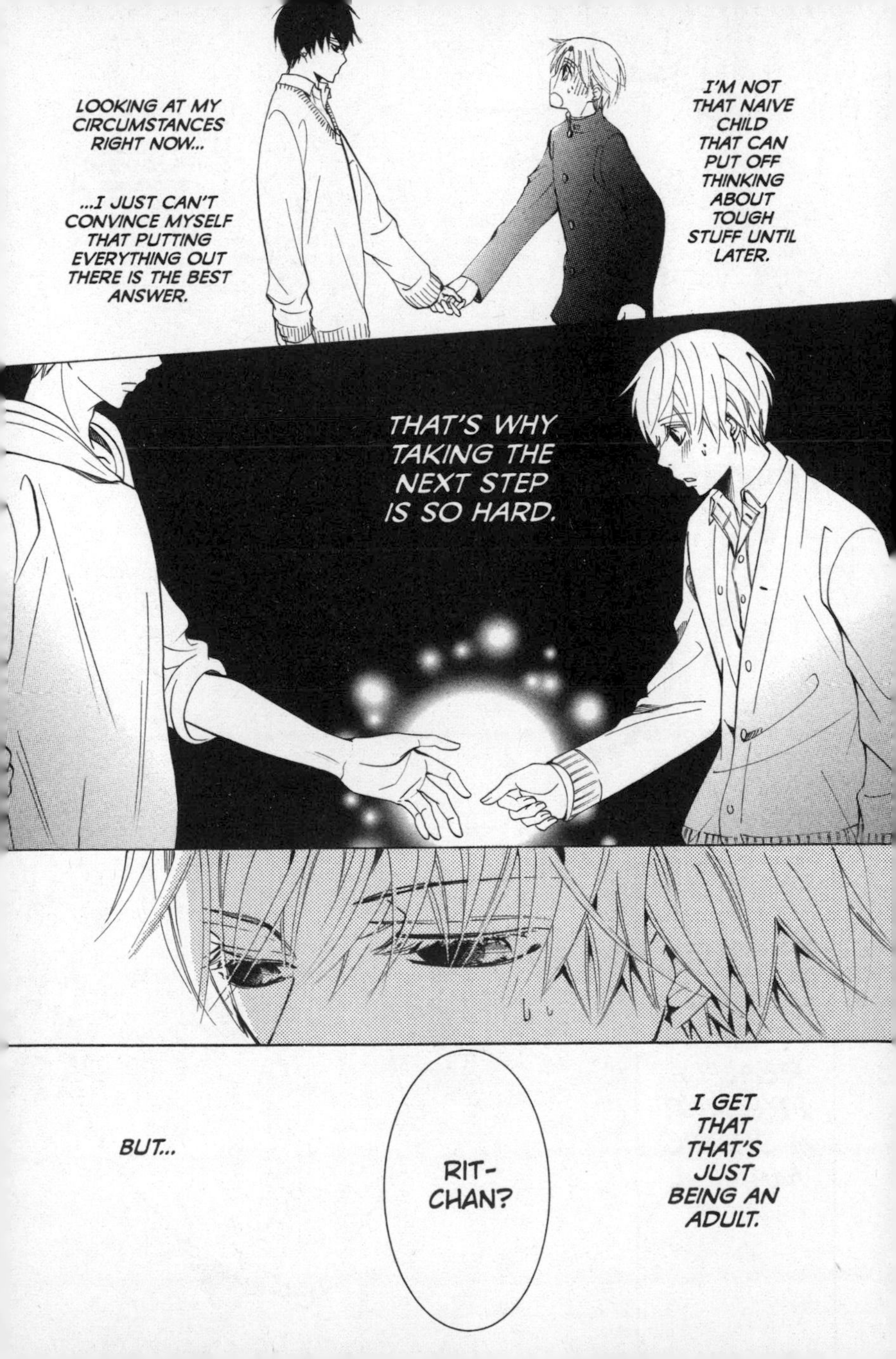
I'M NOT THAT NAIVE CHILD THAT CAN PUT OFF THINKING ABOUT TOUGH STUFF UNTIL LATER.
LOOKING AT MY CIRCUMSTANCES RIGHT NOW...
...I JUST CAN'T CONVINCE MYSELF THAT PUTTING EVERYTHING OUT THERE IS THE BEST ANSWER.
THAT'S WHY TAKING THE NEXT STEP IS SO HARD.
I GET THAT THAT'S JUST BEING AN ADULT.
RIT-CHAN?
BUT...

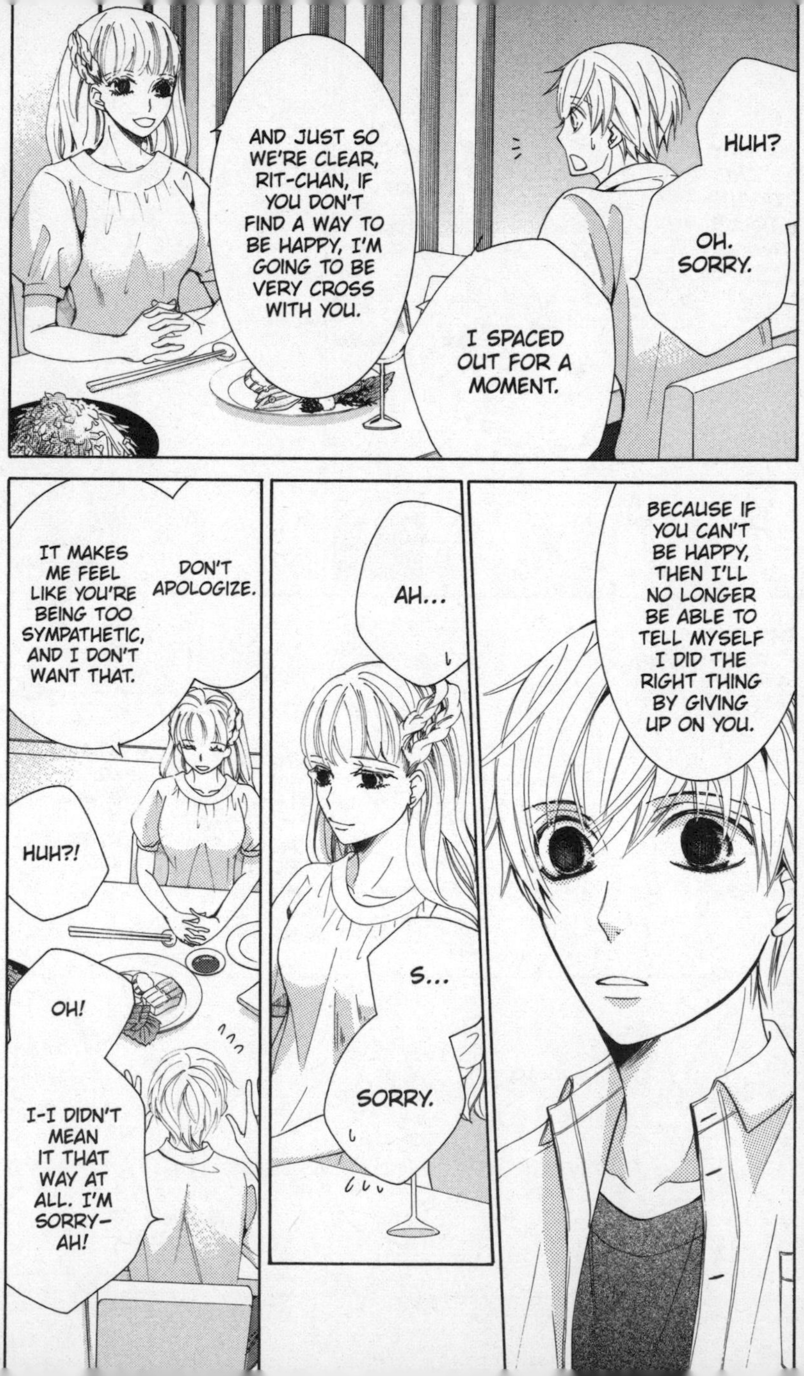

HUH?
OH. SORRY.
I SPACED OUT FOR A MOMENT.
AND JUST SO WE'RE CLEAR, RIT-CHAN, IF YOU DON'T FIND A WAY TO BE HAPPY, I'M GOING TO BE VERY CROSS WITH YOU.
BECAUSE IF YOU CAN'T BE HAPPY, THEN I'LL NO LONGER BE ABLE TO TELL MYSELF I DID THE RIGHT THING BY GIVING UP ON YOU.
AH...
S...
SORRY.
DON'T APOLOGIZE.
IT MAKES ME FEEL LIKE YOU'RE BEING TOO SYMPATHETIC, AND I DON'T WANT THAT.
HUH?!
OH!
I-I DIDN'T MEAN IT THAT WAY AT ALL. I'M SORRY—AH!

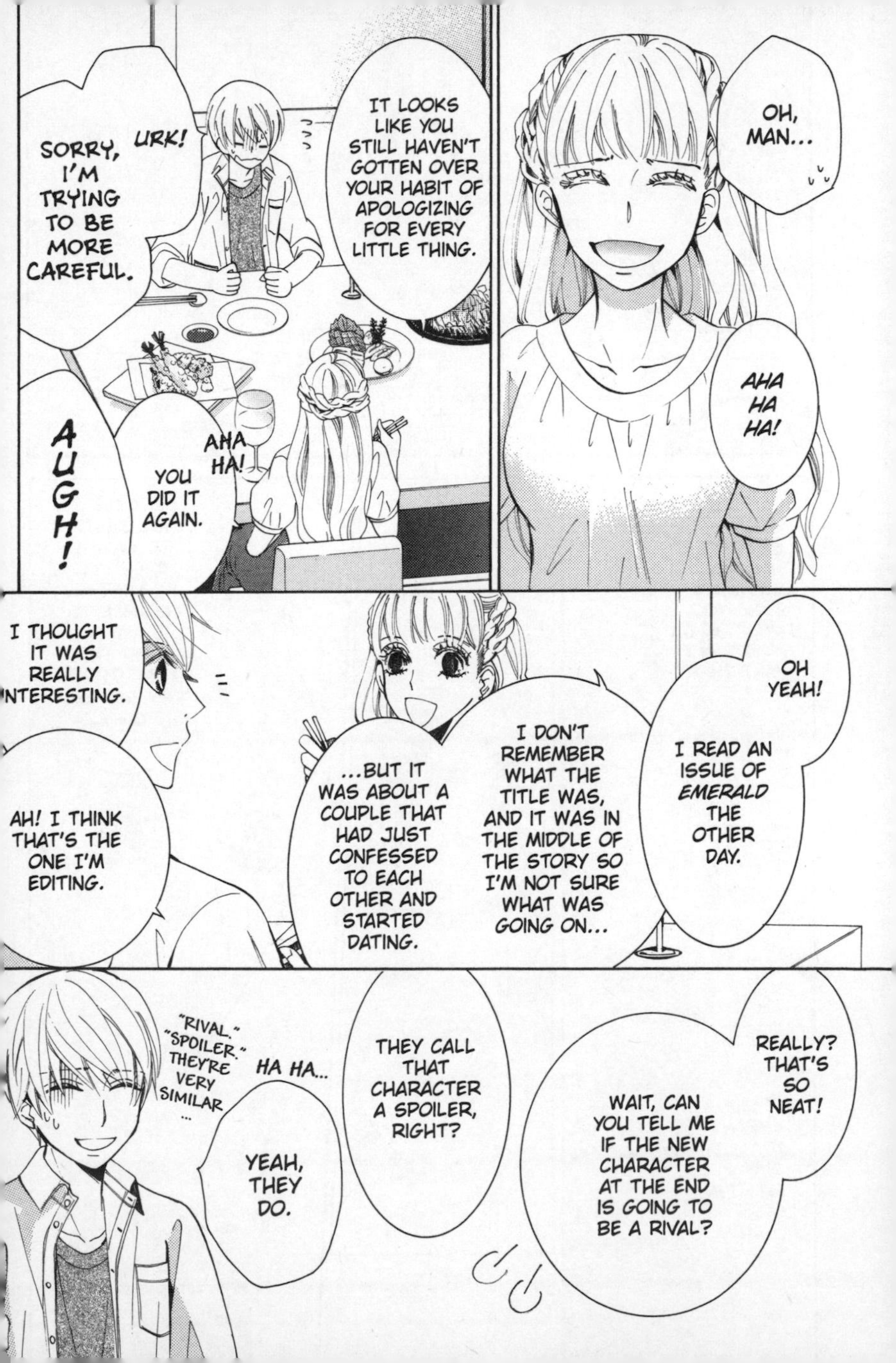
OH, MAN...
AHA HA HA!
IT LOOKS LIKE YOU STILL HAVEN'T GOTTEN OVER YOUR HABIT OF APOLOGIZING FOR EVERY LITTLE THING.
URK!
SORRY, I'M TRYING TO BE MORE CAREFUL.
AHA HA!
YOU DID IT AGAIN.
AUGH!
OH YEAH!
I READ AN ISSUE OF *EMERALD* THE OTHER DAY.
I DON'T REMEMBER WHAT THE TITLE WAS, AND IT WAS IN THE MIDDLE OF THE STORY SO I'M NOT SURE WHAT WAS GOING ON...
...BUT IT WAS ABOUT A COUPLE THAT HAD JUST CONFESSED TO EACH OTHER AND STARTED DATING.
I THOUGHT IT WAS REALLY INTERESTING.
AH! I THINK THAT'S THE ONE I'M EDITING.
REALLY? THAT'S SO NEAT!
WAIT, CAN YOU TELL ME IF THE NEW CHARACTER AT THE END IS GOING TO BE A RIVAL?
THEY CALL THAT CHARACTER A SPOILER, RIGHT?
HA HA...
YEAH, THEY DO.
"RIVAL." "SPOILER." THEY'RE VERY SIMILAR...

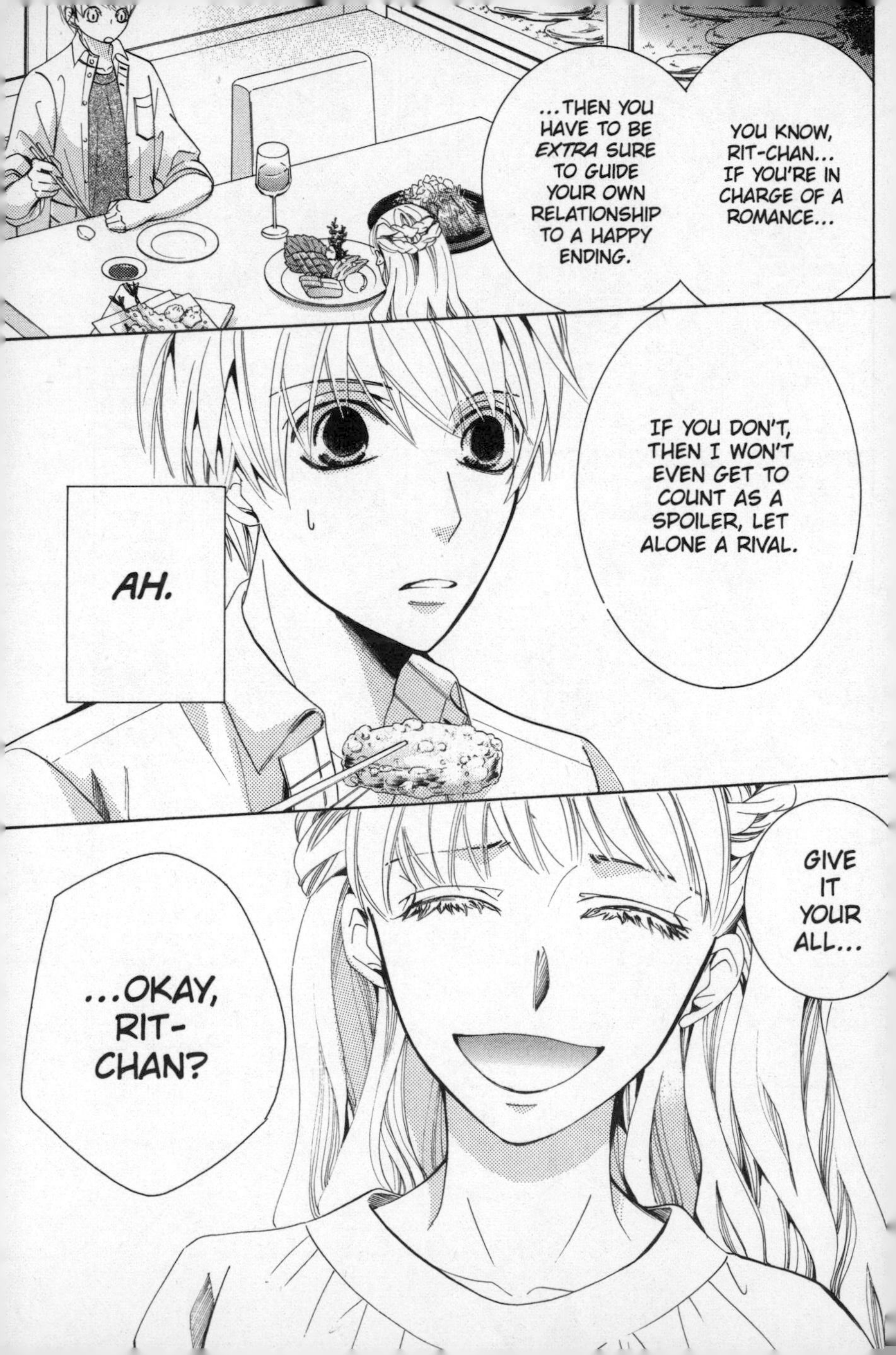
YOU KNOW, RIT-CHAN... IF YOU'RE IN CHARGE OF A ROMANCE...
...THEN YOU HAVE TO BE *EXTRA* SURE TO GUIDE YOUR OWN RELATIONSHIP TO A HAPPY ENDING.
IF YOU DON'T, THEN I WON'T EVEN GET TO COUNT AS A SPOILER, LET ALONE A RIVAL.
AH.
GIVE IT YOUR ALL...
...OKAY, RIT-CHAN?

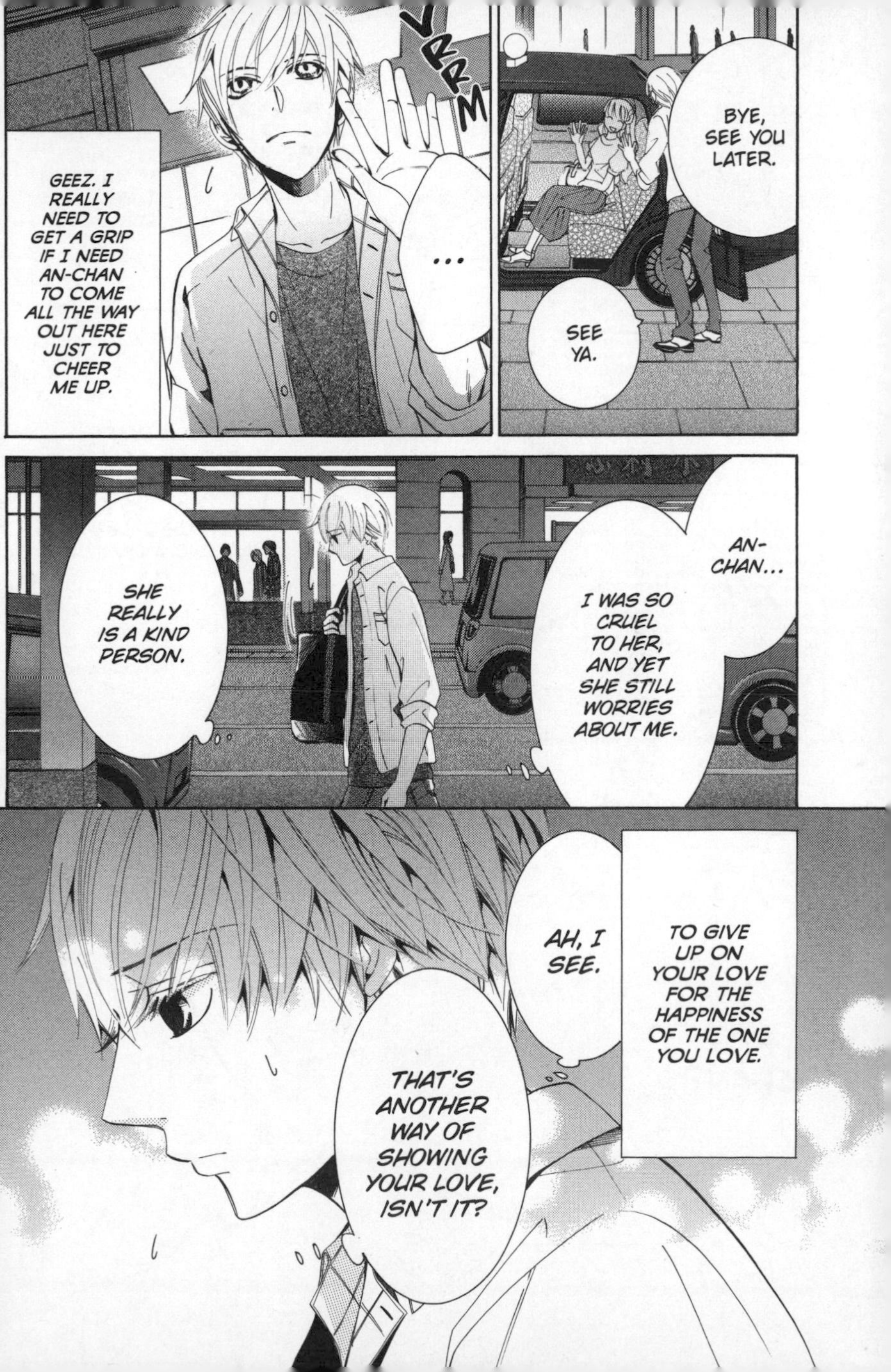
BYE, SEE YOU LATER.
SEE YA.
VRRM
...
GEEZ. I REALLY NEED TO GET A GRIP IF I NEED AN-CHAN TO COME ALL THE WAY OUT HERE JUST TO CHEER ME UP.
AN-CHAN...
I WAS SO CRUEL TO HER, AND YET SHE STILL WORRIES ABOUT ME.
SHE REALLY IS A KIND PERSON.
TO GIVE UP ON YOUR LOVE FOR THE HAPPINESS OF THE ONE YOU LOVE.
AH, I SEE.
THAT'S ANOTHER WAY OF SHOWING YOUR LOVE, ISN'T IT?

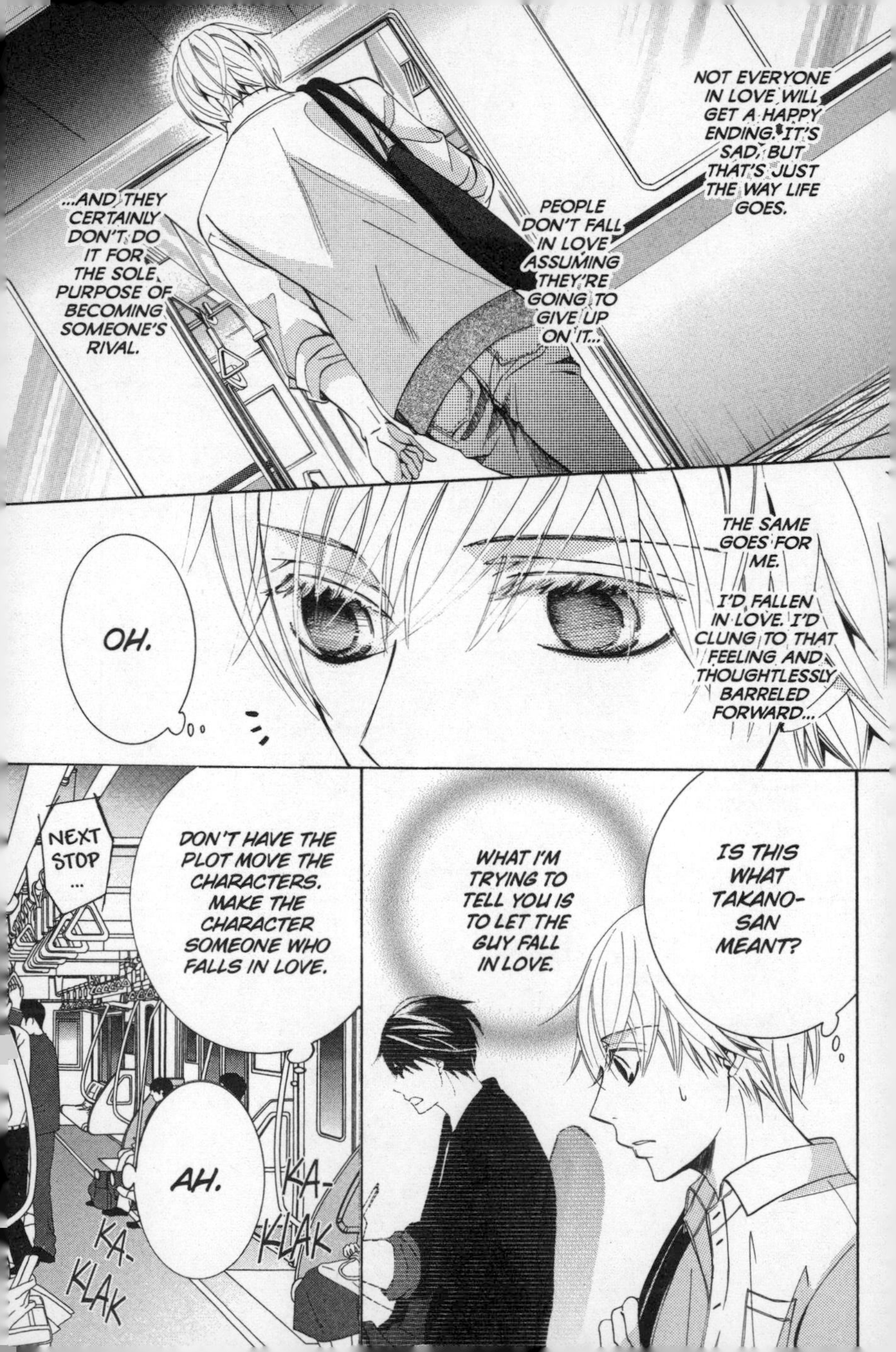
NOT EVERYONE IN LOVE WILL GET A HAPPY ENDING. IT'S SAD, BUT THAT'S JUST THE WAY LIFE GOES.
PEOPLE DON'T FALL IN LOVE ASSUMING THEY'RE GOING TO GIVE UP ON IT...
...AND THEY CERTAINLY DON'T DO IT FOR THE SOLE PURPOSE OF BECOMING SOMEONE'S RIVAL.
THE SAME GOES FOR ME.
I'D FALLEN IN LOVE. I'D CLUNG TO THAT FEELING AND THOUGHTLESSLY BARRELED FORWARD...
OH.
IS THIS WHAT TAKANO-SAN MEANT?
WHAT I'M TRYING TO TELL YOU IS TO LET THE GUY FALL IN LOVE.
DON'T HAVE THE PLOT MOVE THE CHARACTERS. MAKE THE CHARACTER SOMEONE WHO FALLS IN LOVE.
NEXT STOP ...
AH.
KA-KLAK
KA-KLAK

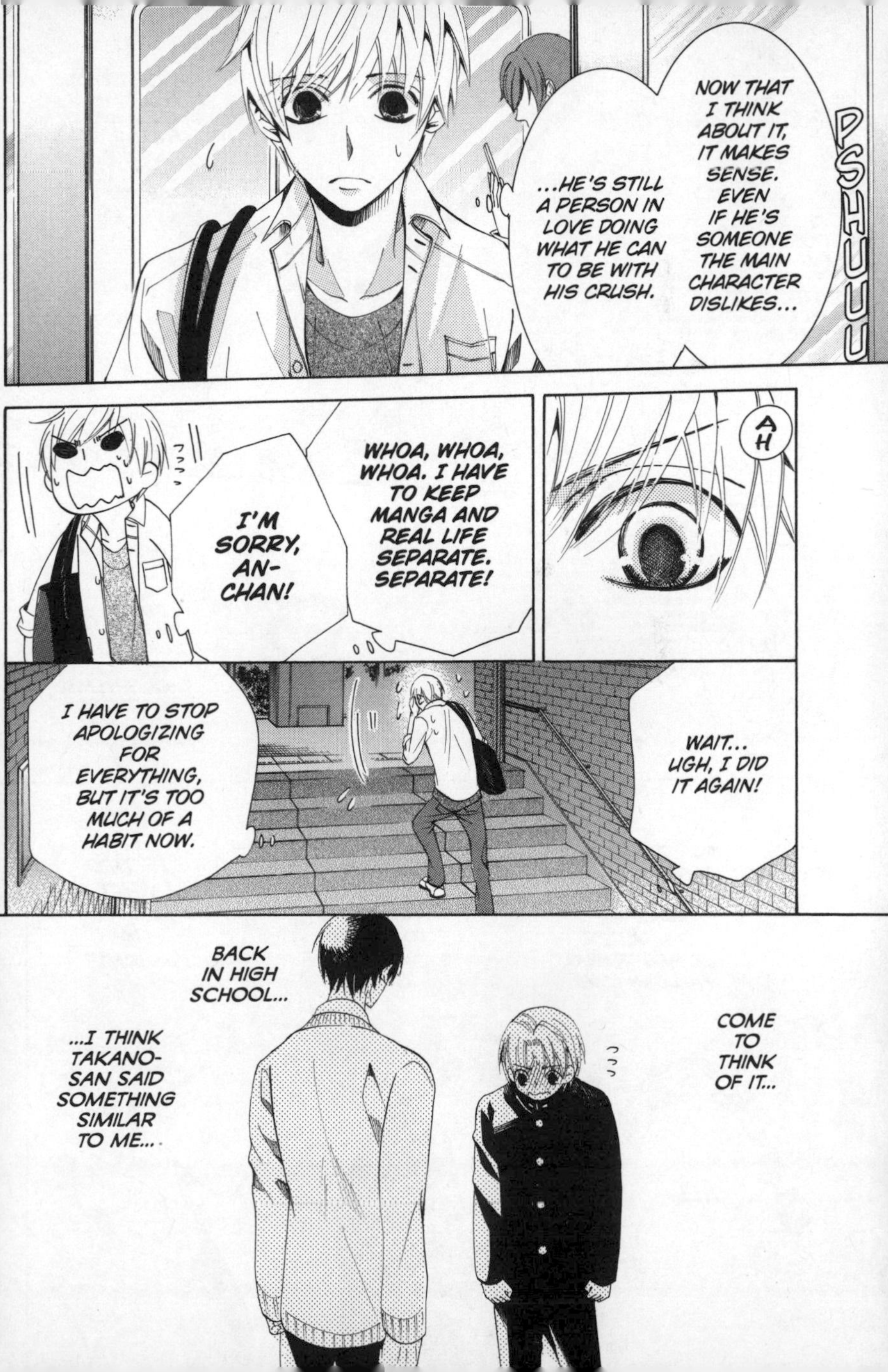
PSHUUU
NOW THAT I THINK ABOUT IT, IT MAKES SENSE. EVEN IF HE'S SOMEONE THE MAIN CHARACTER DISLIKES...
...HE'S STILL A PERSON IN LOVE DOING WHAT HE CAN TO BE WITH HIS CRUSH.
AH
WHOA, WHOA, WHOA. I HAVE TO KEEP MANGA AND REAL LIFE SEPARATE. SEPARATE!
I'M SORRY, AN-CHAN!
WAIT... UGH, I DID IT AGAIN!
I HAVE TO STOP APOLOGIZING FOR EVERYTHING, BUT IT'S TOO MUCH OF A HABIT NOW.
COME TO THINK OF IT...
BACK IN HIGH SCHOOL...
...I THINK TAKANO-SAN SAID SOMETHING SIMILAR TO ME...

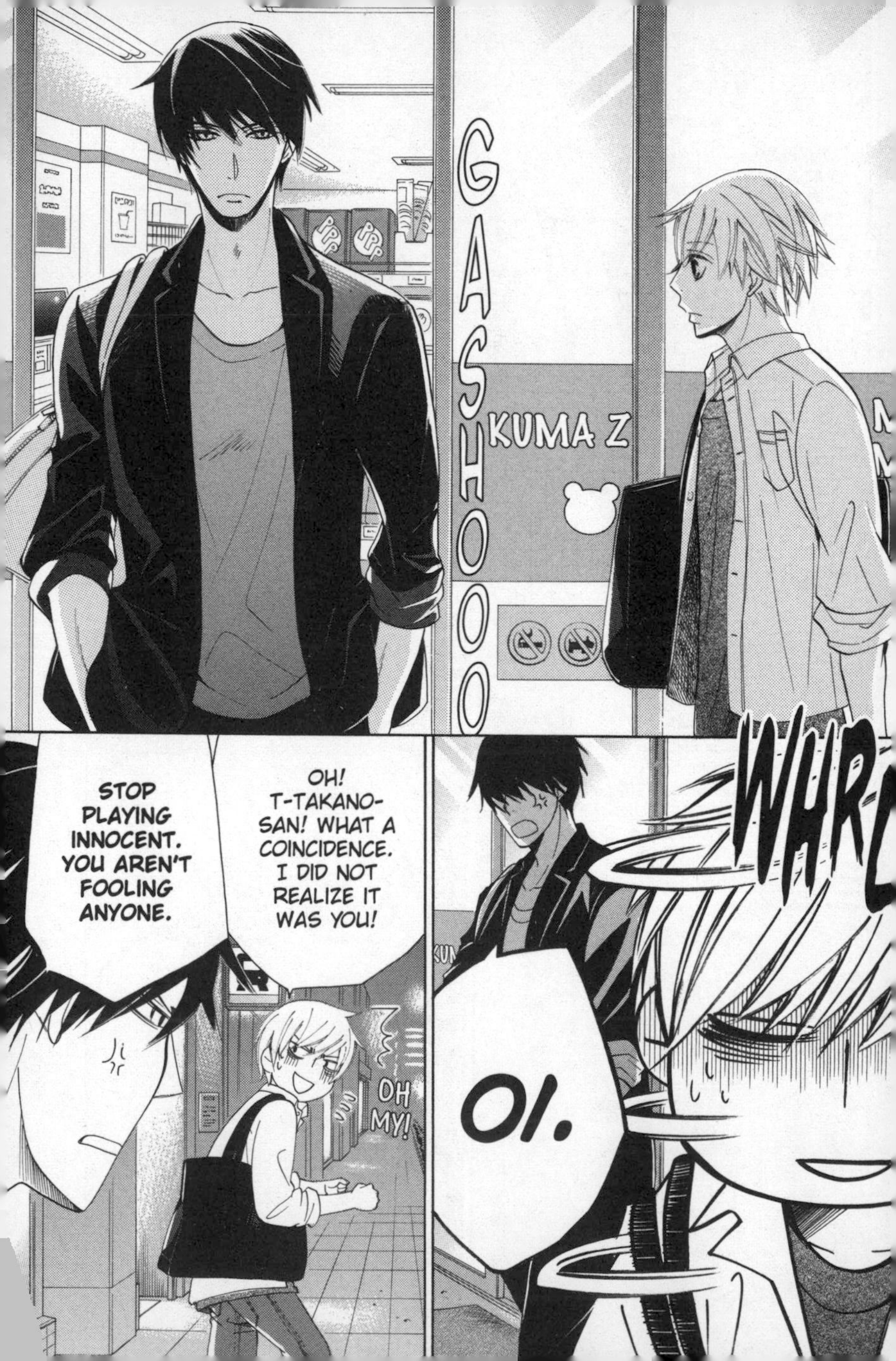
GASHOOO
KUMA Z
OI.
OH! T-TAKANO-SAN! WHAT A COINCIDENCE. I DID NOT REALIZE IT WAS YOU!
STOP PLAYING INNOCENT. YOU AREN'T FOOLING ANYONE.
OH MY!

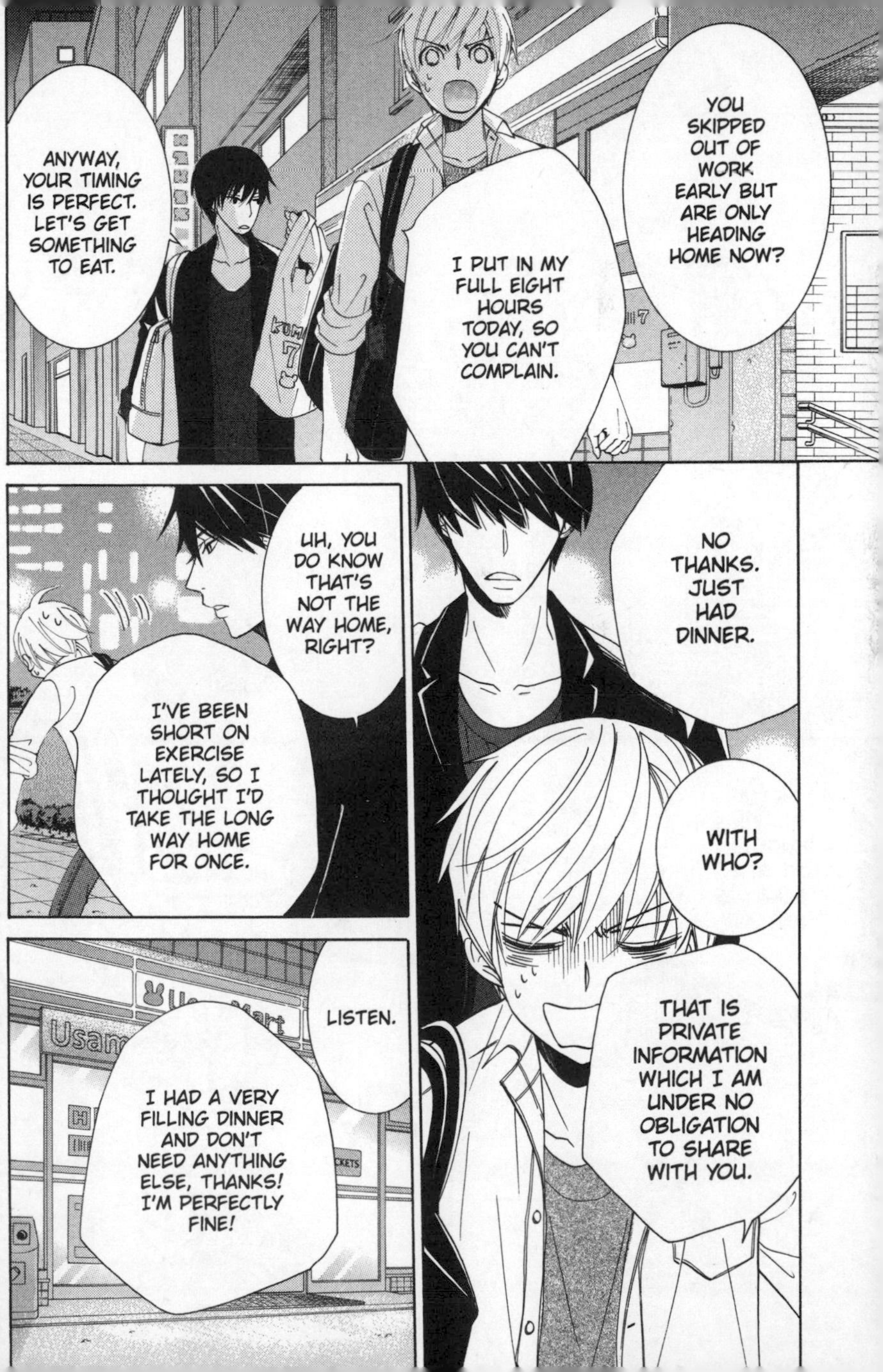
YOU SKIPPED OUT OF WORK EARLY BUT ARE ONLY HEADING HOME NOW?
I PUT IN MY FULL EIGHT HOURS TODAY, SO YOU CAN'T COMPLAIN.
ANYWAY, YOUR TIMING IS PERFECT. LET'S GET SOMETHING TO EAT.
NO THANKS. JUST HAD DINNER.
WITH WHO?
THAT IS PRIVATE INFORMATION WHICH I AM UNDER NO OBLIGATION TO SHARE WITH YOU.
UH, YOU DO KNOW THAT'S NOT THE WAY HOME, RIGHT?
I'VE BEEN SHORT ON EXERCISE LATELY, SO I THOUGHT I'D TAKE THE LONG WAY HOME FOR ONCE.
LISTEN.
I HAD A VERY FILLING DINNER AND DON'T NEED ANYTHING ELSE, THANKS! I'M PERFECTLY FINE!

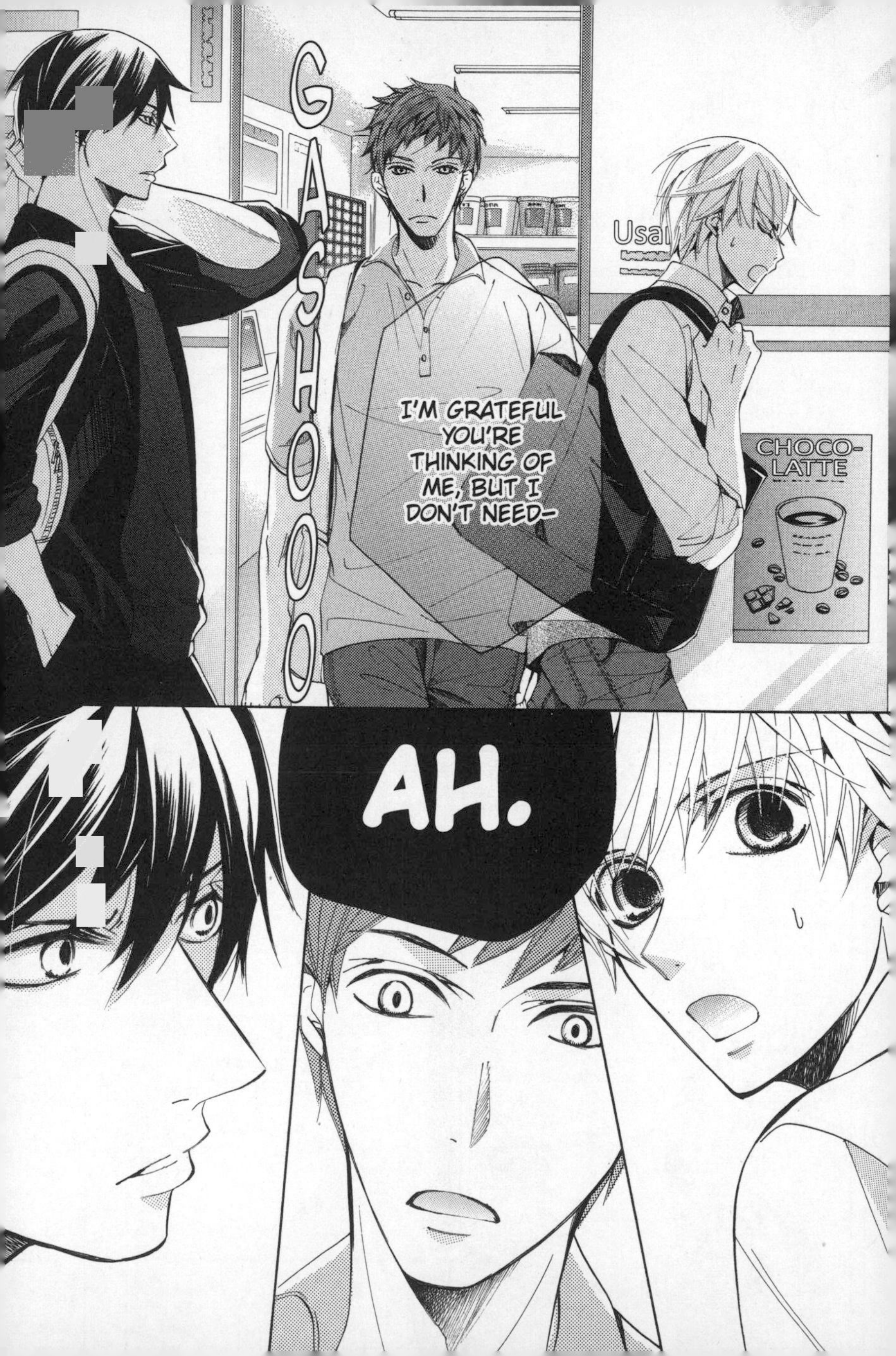
Usa
CHOCO-LATTE
I'M GRATEFUL YOU'RE THINKING OF ME, BUT I DON'T NEED-
GASHOOO
AH.

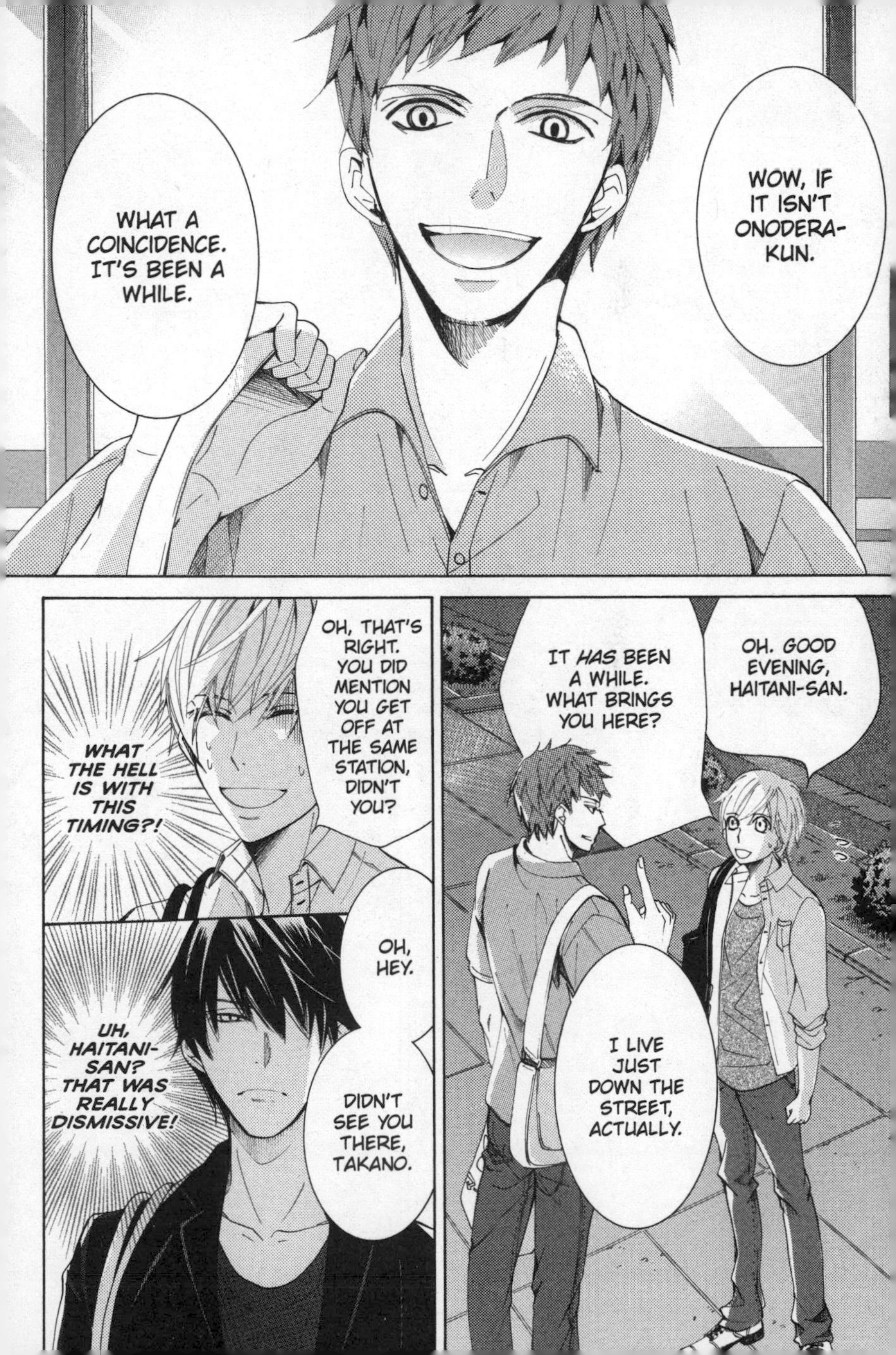
WOW, IF IT ISN'T ONODERA-KUN.
WHAT A COINCIDENCE. IT'S BEEN A WHILE.
OH. GOOD EVENING, HAITANI-SAN.
IT *HAS* BEEN A WHILE. WHAT BRINGS YOU HERE?
I LIVE JUST DOWN THE STREET, ACTUALLY.
OH, THAT'S RIGHT. YOU DID MENTION YOU GET OFF AT THE SAME STATION, DIDN'T YOU?
WHAT THE HELL IS WITH THIS TIMING?!
OH, HEY.
DIDN'T SEE YOU THERE, TAKANO.
UH, HAITANI-SAN? THAT WAS REALLY DISMISSIVE!

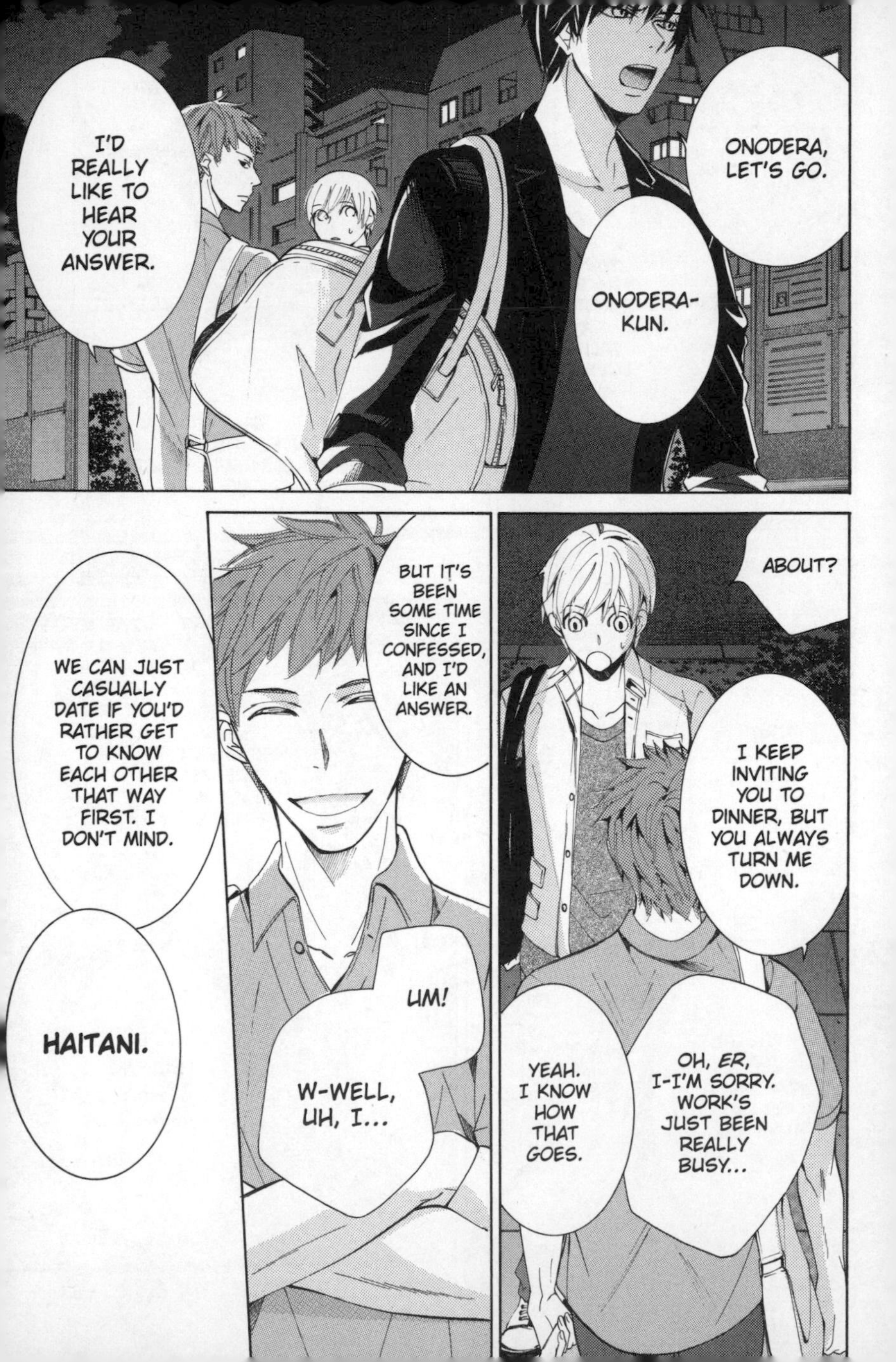
ONODERA, LET'S GO.
ONODERA-KUN.
I'D REALLY LIKE TO HEAR YOUR ANSWER.
ABOUT?
I KEEP INVITING YOU TO DINNER, BUT YOU ALWAYS TURN ME DOWN.
OH, *ER*, I-I'M SORRY. WORK'S JUST BEEN REALLY BUSY...
YEAH. I KNOW HOW THAT GOES.
BUT IT'S BEEN SOME TIME SINCE I CONFESSED, AND I'D LIKE AN ANSWER.
UM!
W-WELL, UH, I...
WE CAN JUST CASUALLY DATE IF YOU'D RATHER GET TO KNOW EACH OTHER THAT WAY FIRST. I DON'T MIND.
HAITANI.

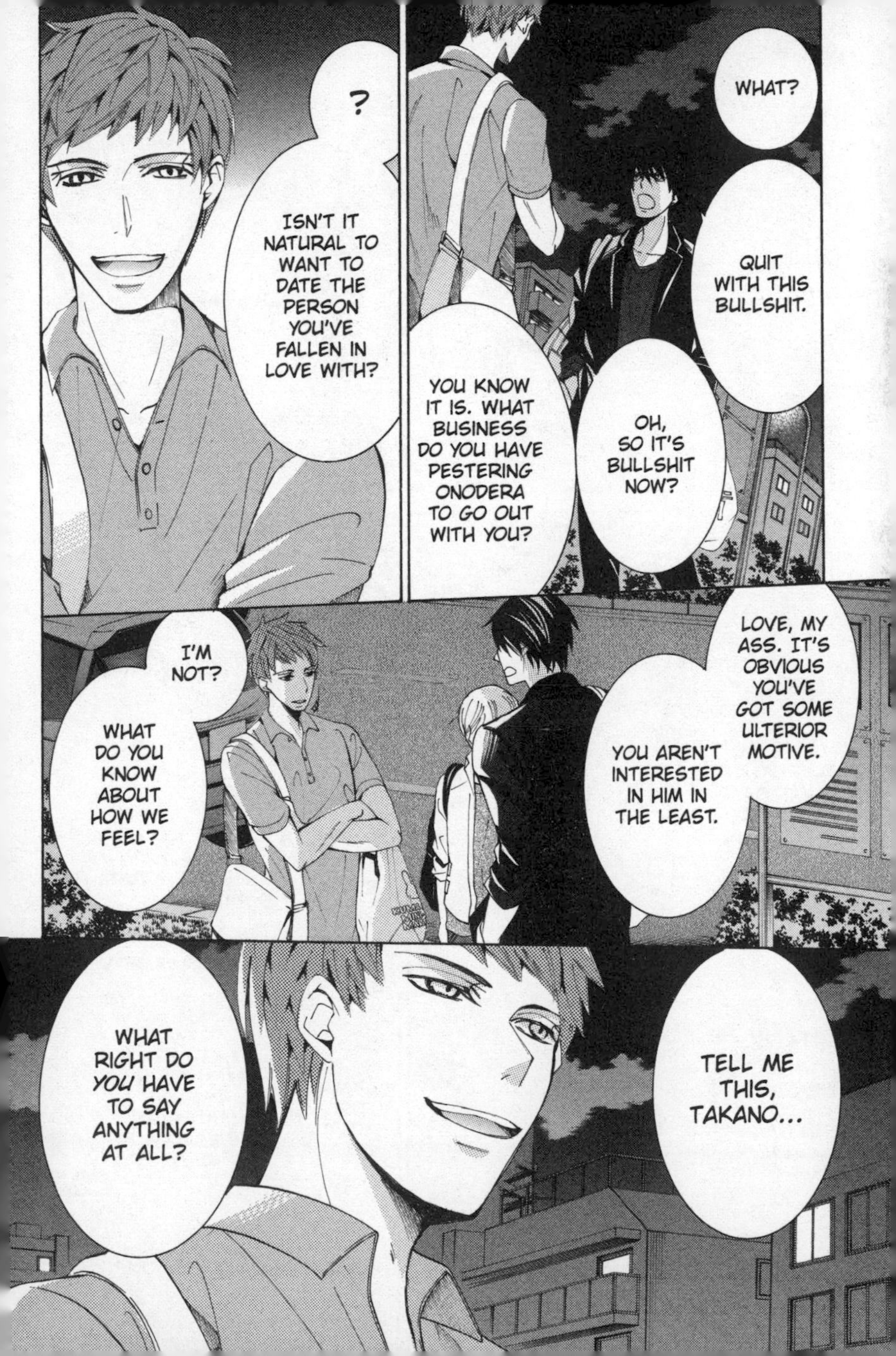
WHAT?
QUIT WITH THIS BULLSHIT.
OH, SO IT'S BULLSHIT NOW?
YOU KNOW IT IS. WHAT BUSINESS DO YOU HAVE PESTERING ONODERA TO GO OUT WITH YOU?
?
ISN'T IT NATURAL TO WANT TO DATE THE PERSON YOU'VE FALLEN IN LOVE WITH?
LOVE, MY ASS. IT'S OBVIOUS YOU'VE GOT SOME ULTERIOR MOTIVE.
YOU AREN'T INTERESTED IN HIM IN THE LEAST.
I'M NOT?
WHAT DO YOU KNOW ABOUT HOW WE FEEL?
TELL ME THIS, TAKANO...
WHAT RIGHT DO *YOU* HAVE TO SAY ANYTHING AT ALL?

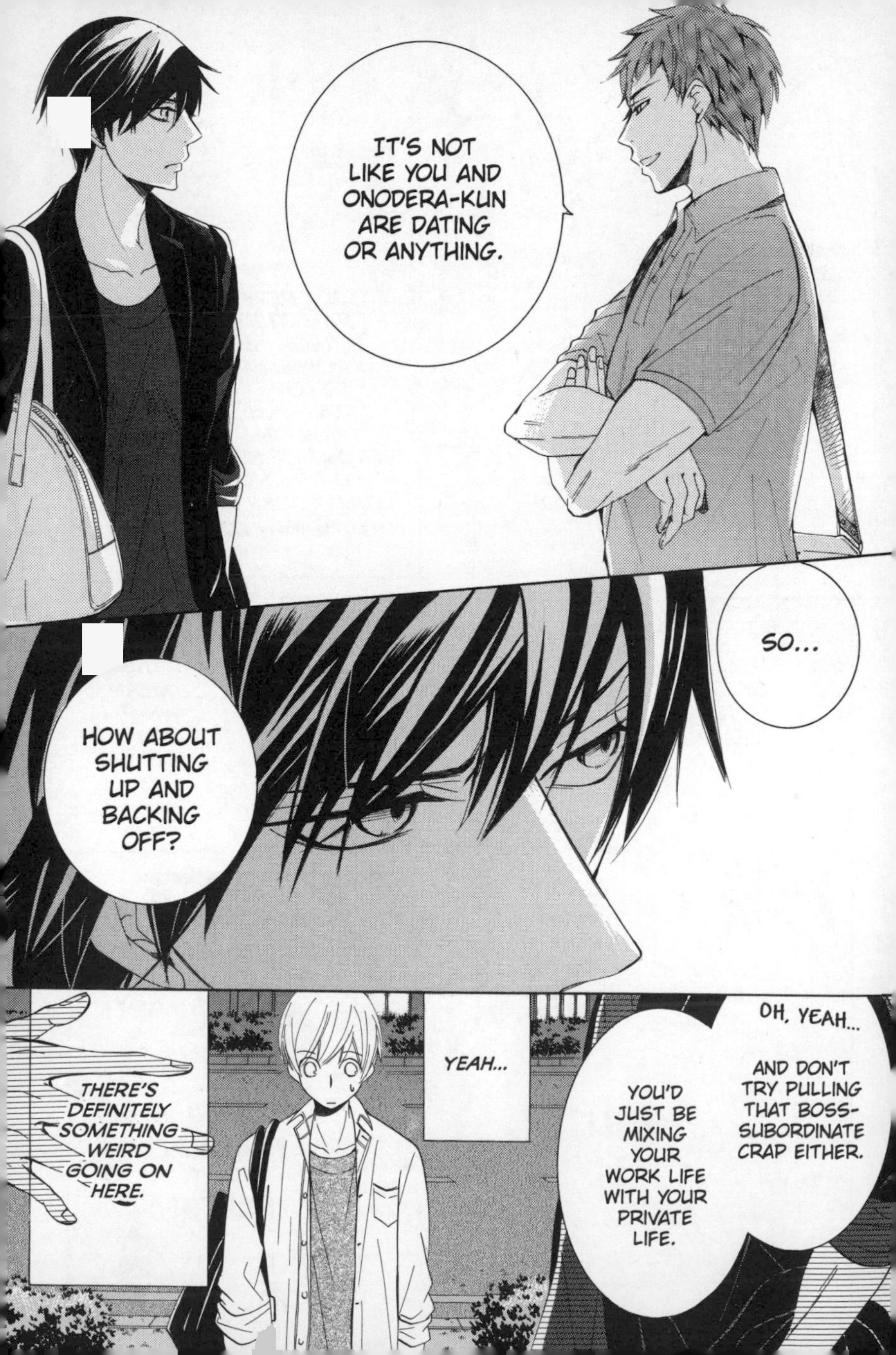
IT'S NOT LIKE YOU AND ONODERA-KUN ARE DATING OR ANYTHING.
SO...
HOW ABOUT SHUTTING UP AND BACKING OFF?
OH, YEAH...
AND DON'T TRY PULLING THAT BOSS-SUBORDINATE CRAP EITHER.
YOU'D JUST BE MIXING YOUR WORK LIFE WITH YOUR PRIVATE LIFE.
YEAH...
THERE'S DEFINITELY SOMETHING WEIRD GOING ON HERE.

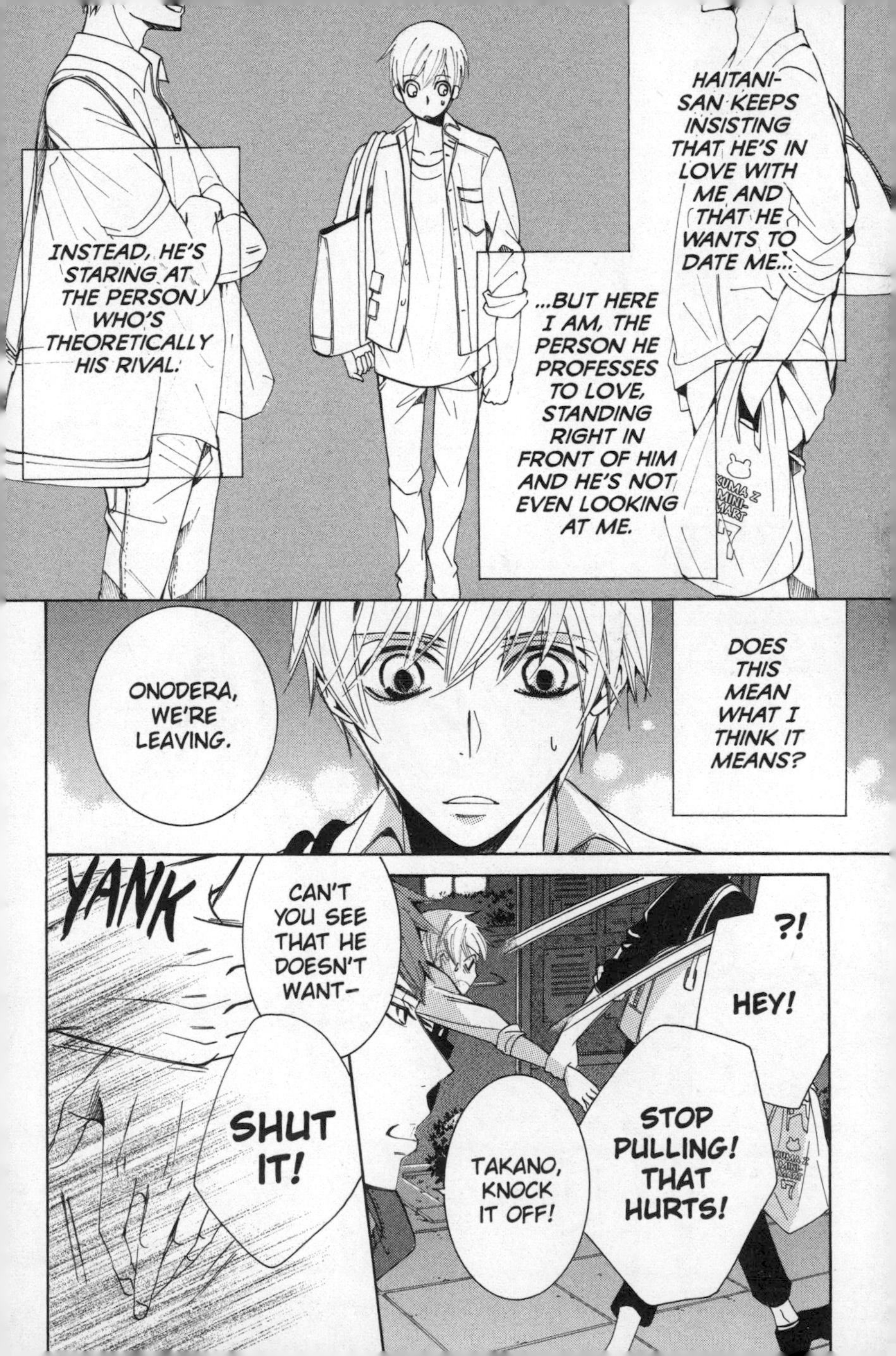
HAITANI-SAN KEEPS INSISTING THAT HE'S IN LOVE WITH ME AND THAT HE WANTS TO DATE ME...
...BUT HERE I AM, THE PERSON HE PROFESSES TO LOVE, STANDING RIGHT IN FRONT OF HIM AND HE'S NOT EVEN LOOKING AT ME.
KUMA Z MINI-MART
INSTEAD, HE'S STARING AT THE PERSON WHO'S THEORETICALLY HIS RIVAL.
DOES THIS MEAN WHAT I THINK IT MEANS?
ONODERA, WE'RE LEAVING.
?!
HEY!
CAN'T YOU SEE THAT HE DOESN'T WANT-
YANK
STOP PULLING! THAT HURTS!
TAKANO, KNOCK IT OFF!
SHUT IT!

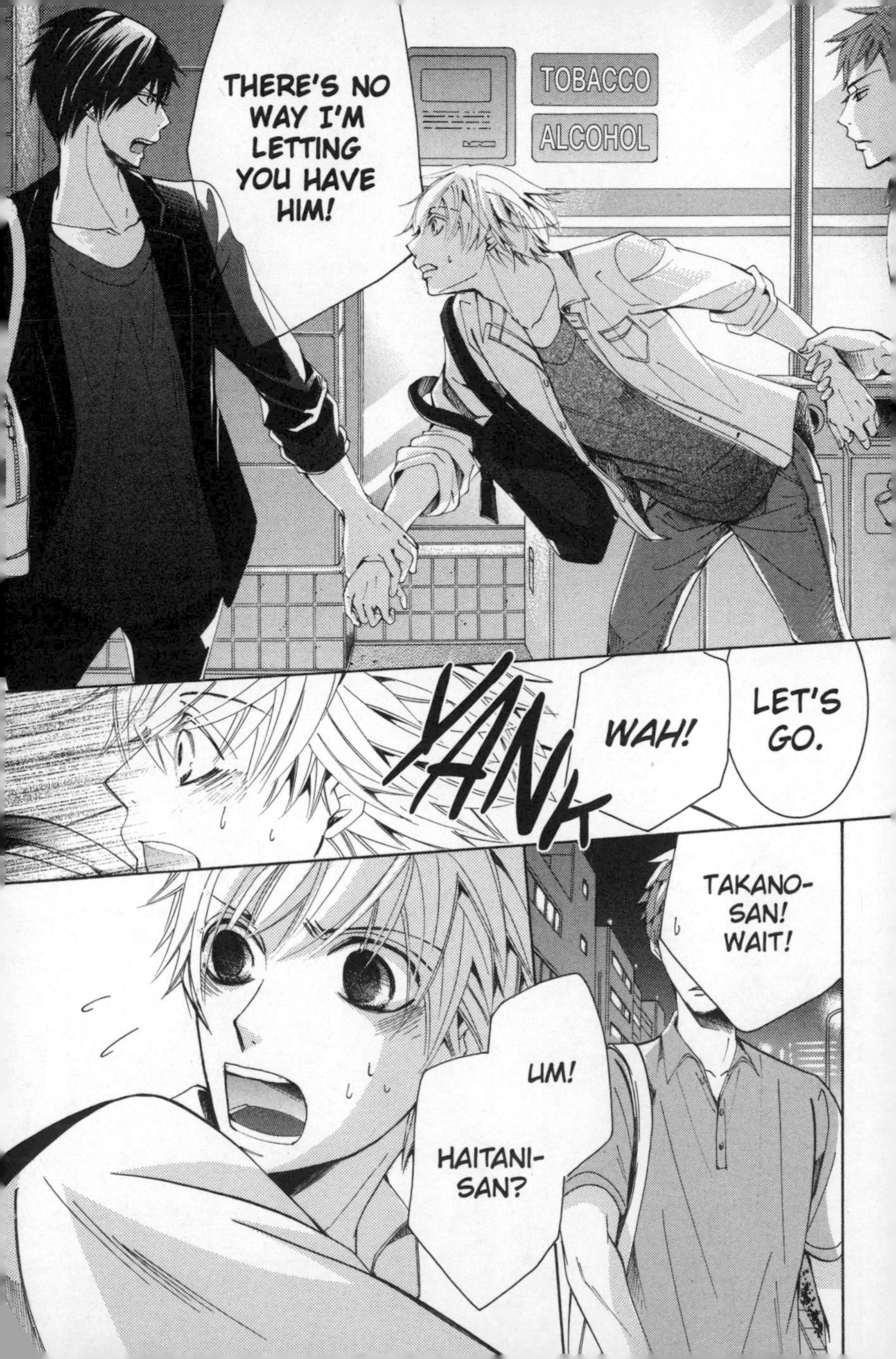
TOBACCO
ALCOHOL
THERE'S NO WAY I'M LETTING YOU HAVE HIM!
LET'S GO.
WAH!
YANK
TAKANO-SAN! WAIT!
UM!
HAITANI-SAN?

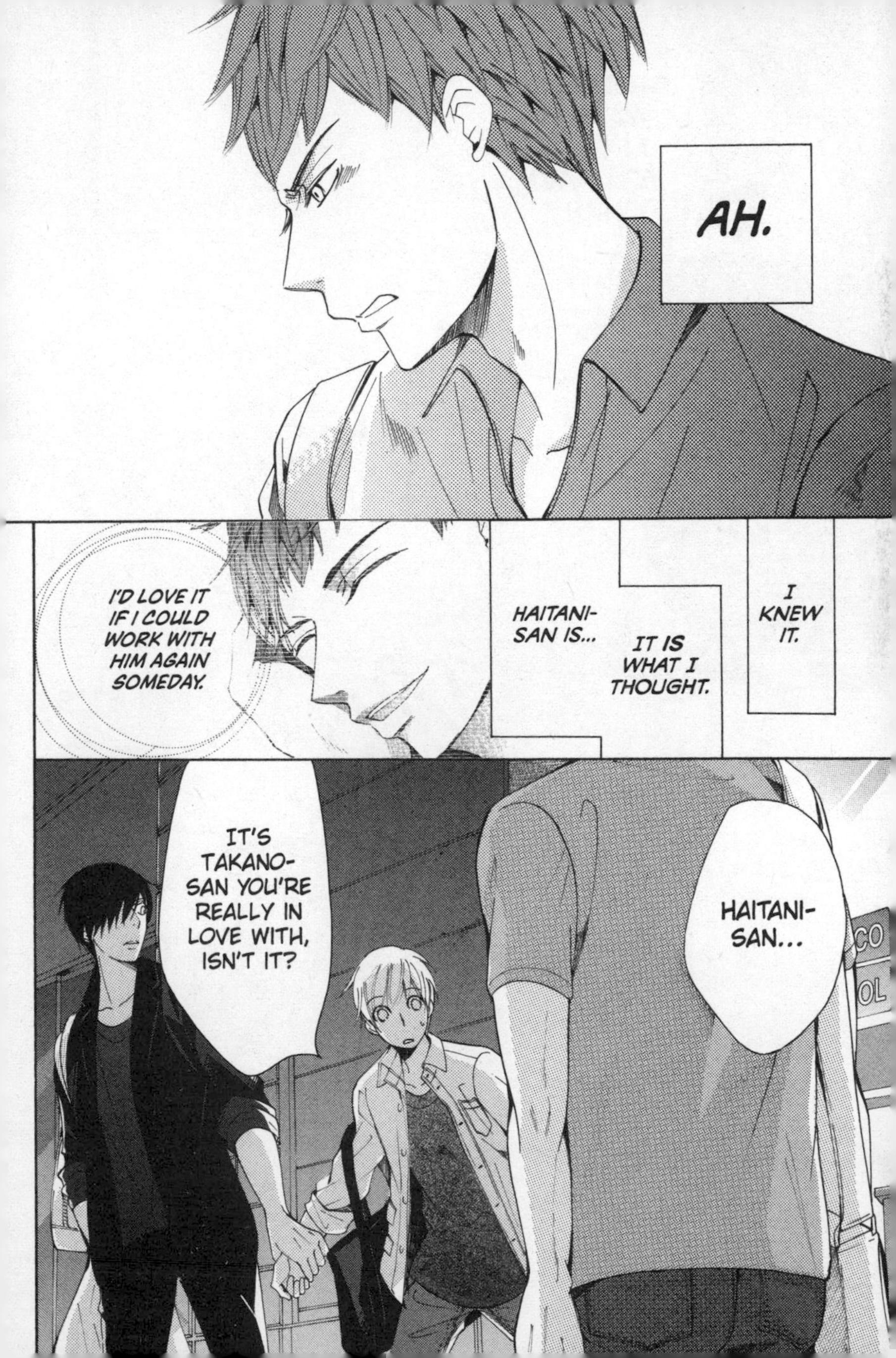
AH.
I KNEW IT.
IT IS WHAT I THOUGHT.
HAITANI-SAN IS...
I'D LOVE IT IF I COULD WORK WITH HIM AGAIN SOMEDAY.
HAITANI-SAN...
IT'S TAKANO-SAN YOU'RE REALLY IN LOVE WITH, ISN'T IT?

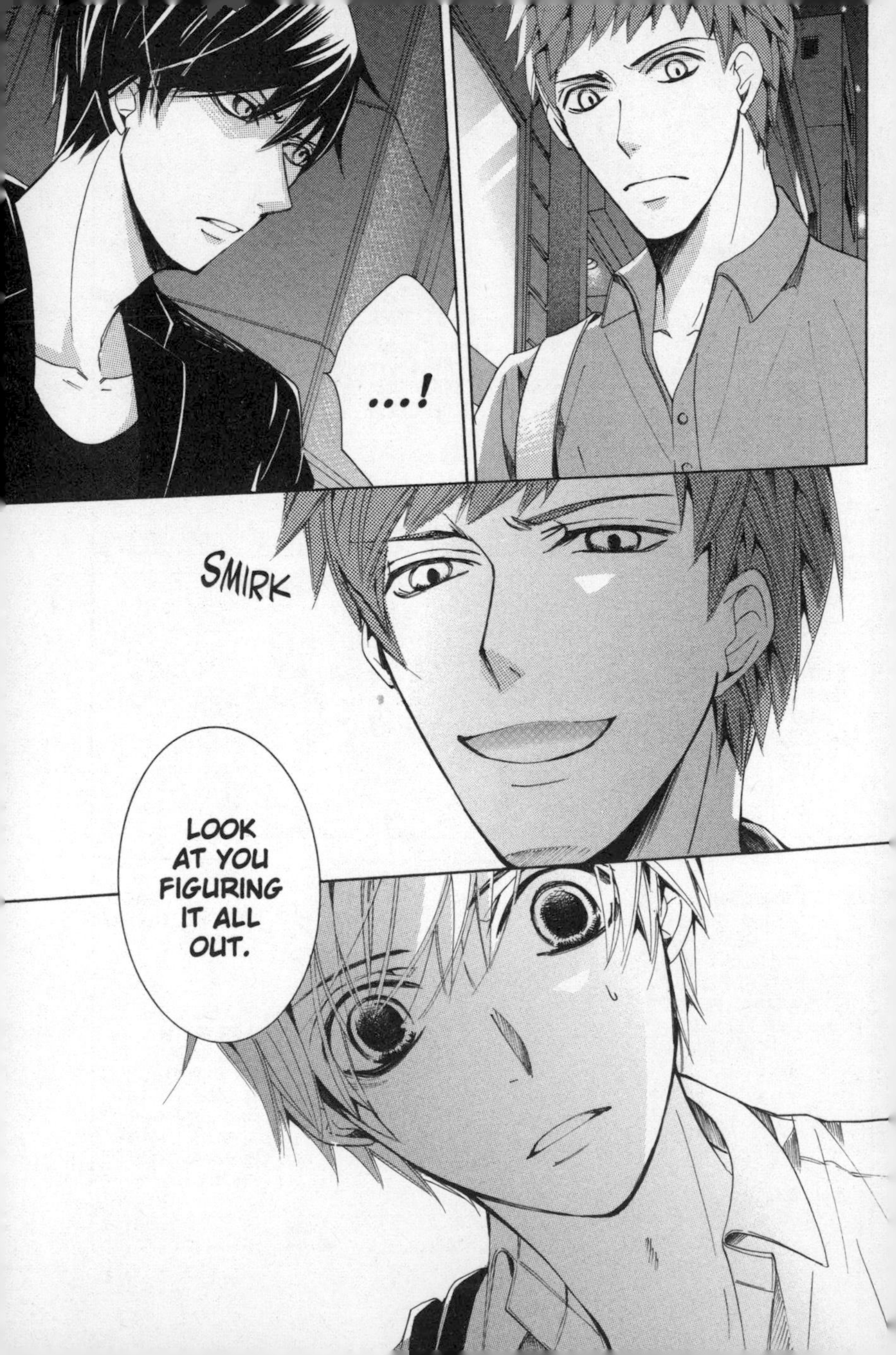
...!
SMIRK
LOOK AT YOU FIGURING IT ALL OUT.

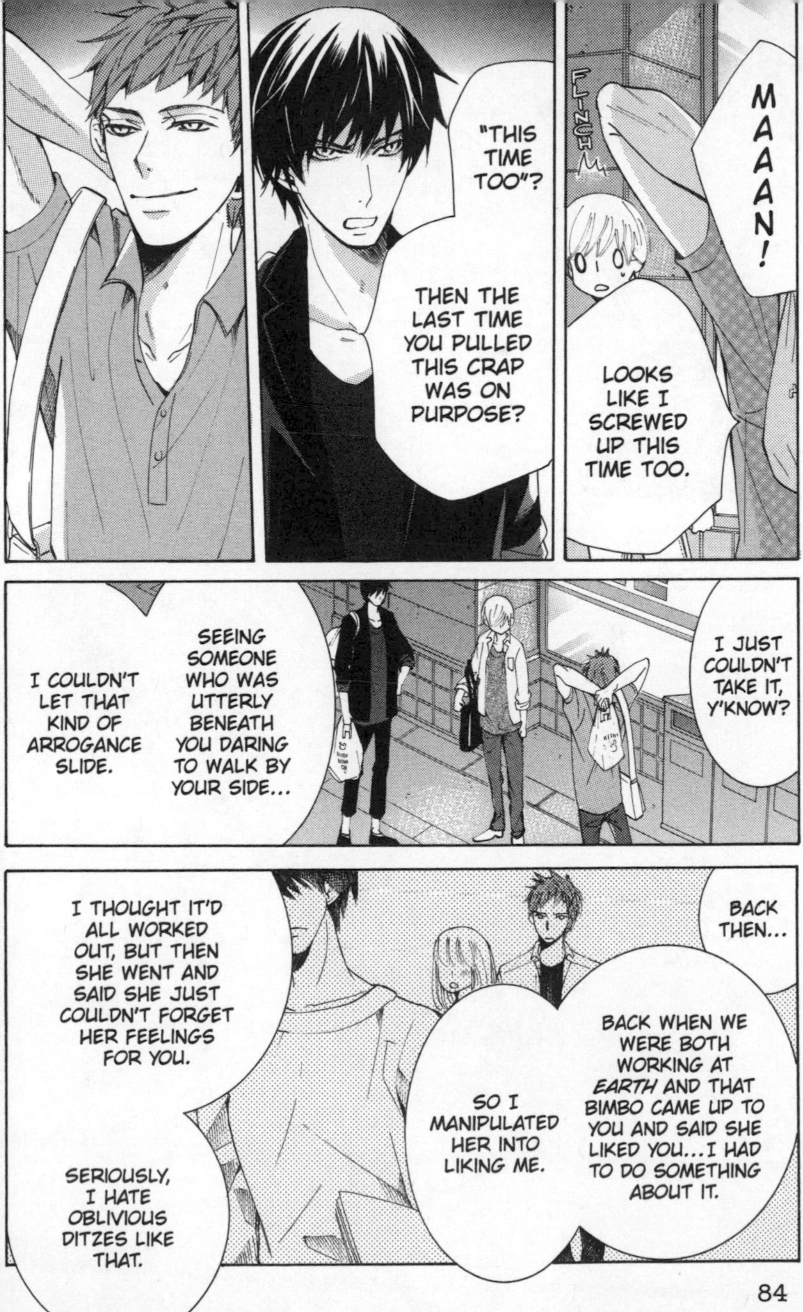
MAAAN!
FLINCH
LOOKS LIKE I SCREWED UP THIS TIME TOO.
"THIS TIME TOO"?
THEN THE LAST TIME YOU PULLED THIS CRAP WAS ON PURPOSE?
I JUST COULDN'T TAKE IT, Y'KNOW?
SEEING SOMEONE WHO WAS UTTERLY BENEATH YOU DARING TO WALK BY YOUR SIDE...
I COULDN'T LET THAT KIND OF ARROGANCE SLIDE.
BACK THEN...
BACK WHEN WE WERE BOTH WORKING AT *EARTH* AND THAT BIMBO CAME UP TO YOU AND SAID SHE LIKED YOU...I HAD TO DO SOMETHING ABOUT IT.
SO I MANIPULATED HER INTO LIKING ME.
I THOUGHT IT'D ALL WORKED OUT, BUT THEN SHE WENT AND SAID SHE JUST COULDN'T FORGET HER FEELINGS FOR YOU.
SERIOUSLY, I HATE OBLIVIOUS DITZES LIKE THAT.

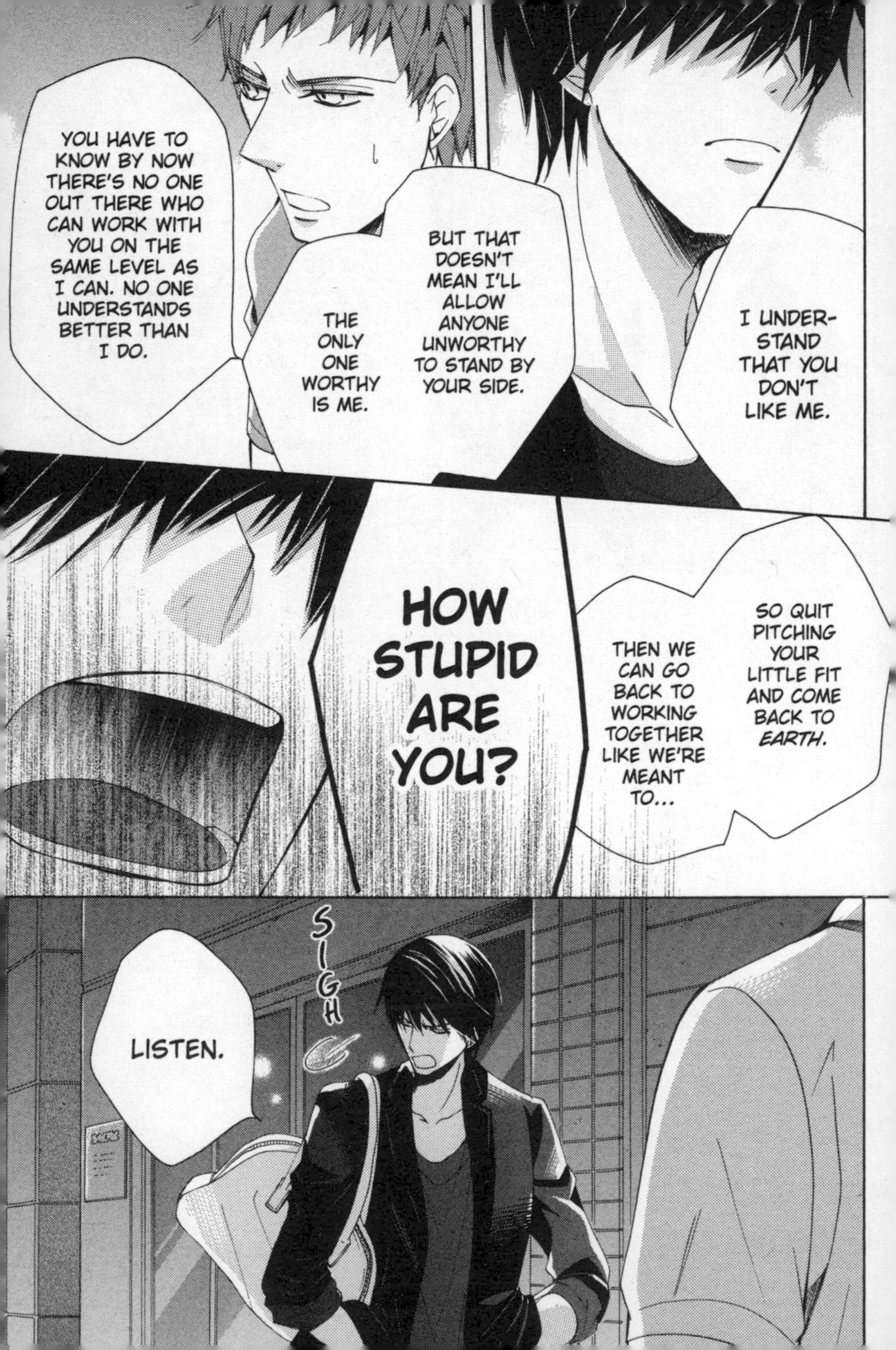
I UNDERSTAND THAT YOU DON'T LIKE ME.
BUT THAT DOESN'T MEAN I'LL ALLOW ANYONE UNWORTHY TO STAND BY YOUR SIDE.
THE ONLY ONE WORTHY IS ME.
YOU HAVE TO KNOW BY NOW THERE'S NO ONE OUT THERE WHO CAN WORK WITH YOU ON THE SAME LEVEL AS I CAN. NO ONE UNDERSTANDS BETTER THAN I DO.
SO QUIT PITCHING YOUR LITTLE FIT AND COME BACK TO *EARTH*.
THEN WE CAN GO BACK TO WORKING TOGETHER LIKE WE'RE MEANT TO...
HOW STUPID ARE YOU?
SIGH
LISTEN.

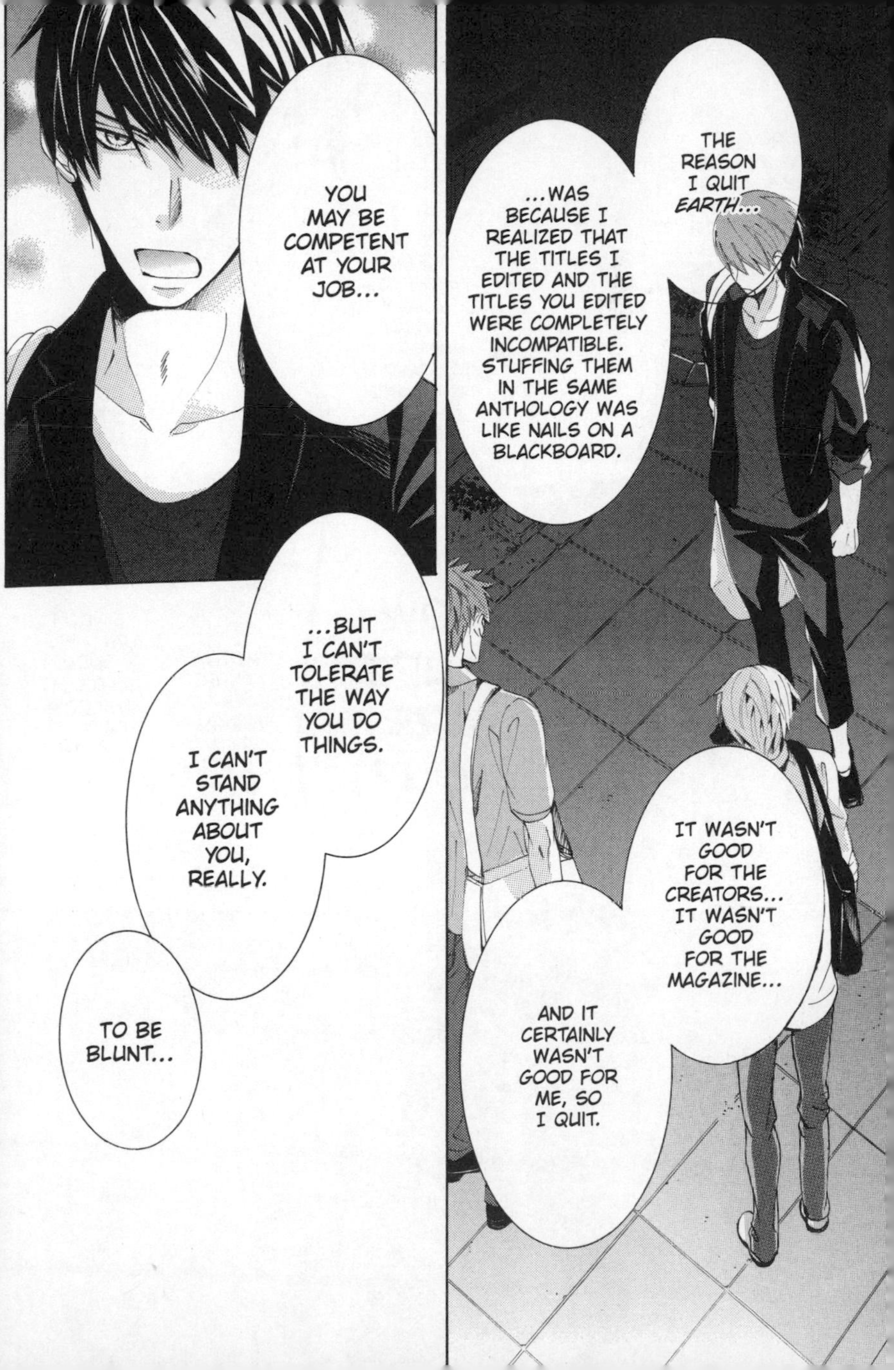
THE REASON I QUIT *EARTH*...
...WAS BECAUSE I REALIZED THAT THE TITLES I EDITED AND THE TITLES YOU EDITED WERE COMPLETELY INCOMPATIBLE. STUFFING THEM IN THE SAME ANTHOLOGY WAS LIKE NAILS ON A BLACKBOARD.
IT WASN'T GOOD FOR THE CREATORS... IT WASN'T GOOD FOR THE MAGAZINE...
AND IT CERTAINLY WASN'T GOOD FOR ME, SO I QUIT.
YOU MAY BE COMPETENT AT YOUR JOB...
...BUT I CAN'T TOLERATE THE WAY YOU DO THINGS.
I CAN'T STAND ANYTHING ABOUT YOU, REALLY.
TO BE BLUNT...

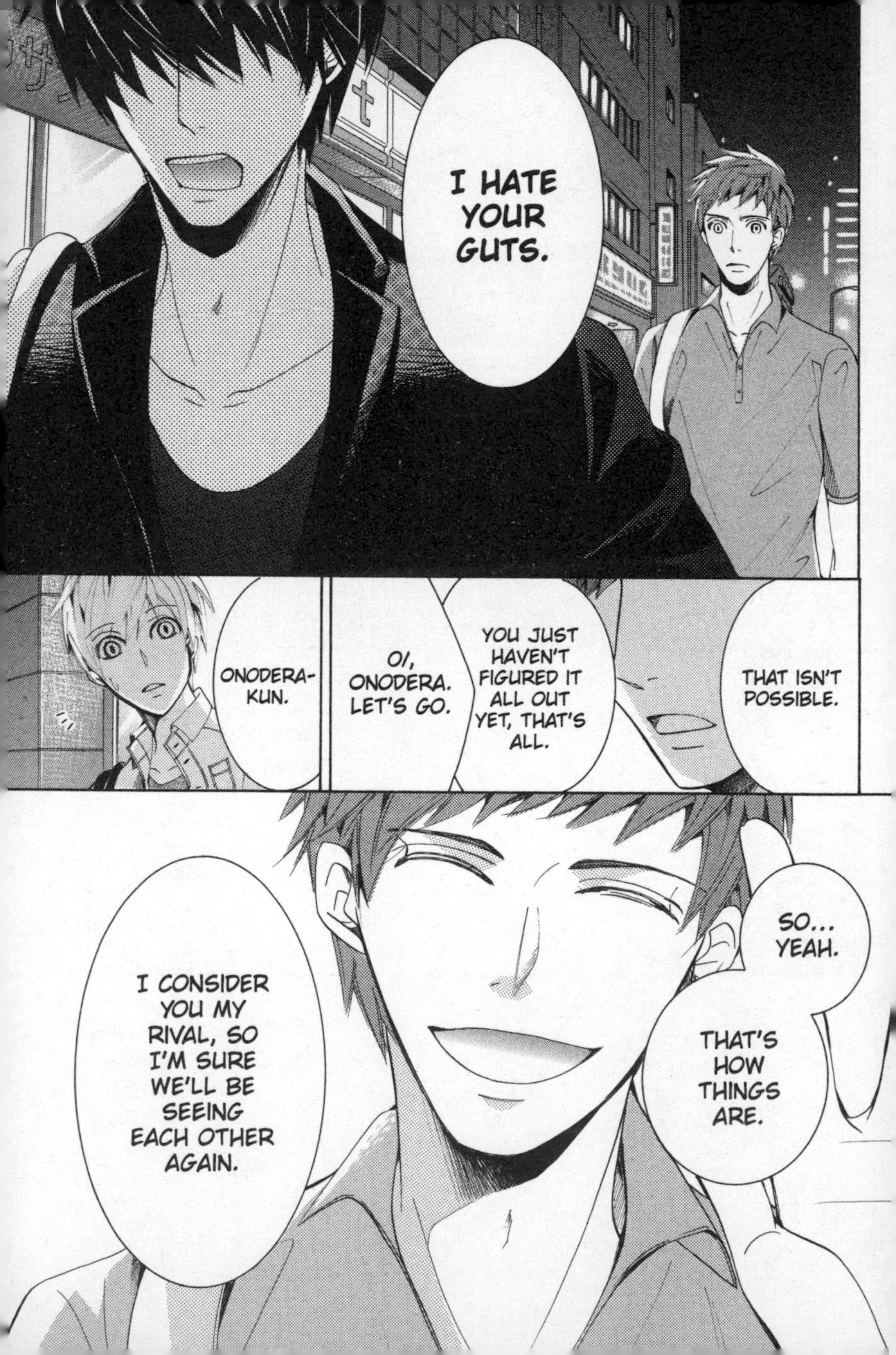
I HATE YOUR GUTS.
THAT ISN'T POSSIBLE.
YOU JUST HAVEN'T FIGURED IT ALL OUT YET, THAT'S ALL.
OI, ONODERA. LET'S GO.
ONODERA-KUN.
SO... YEAH.
THAT'S HOW THINGS ARE.
I CONSIDER YOU MY RIVAL, SO I'M SURE WE'LL BE SEEING EACH OTHER AGAIN.

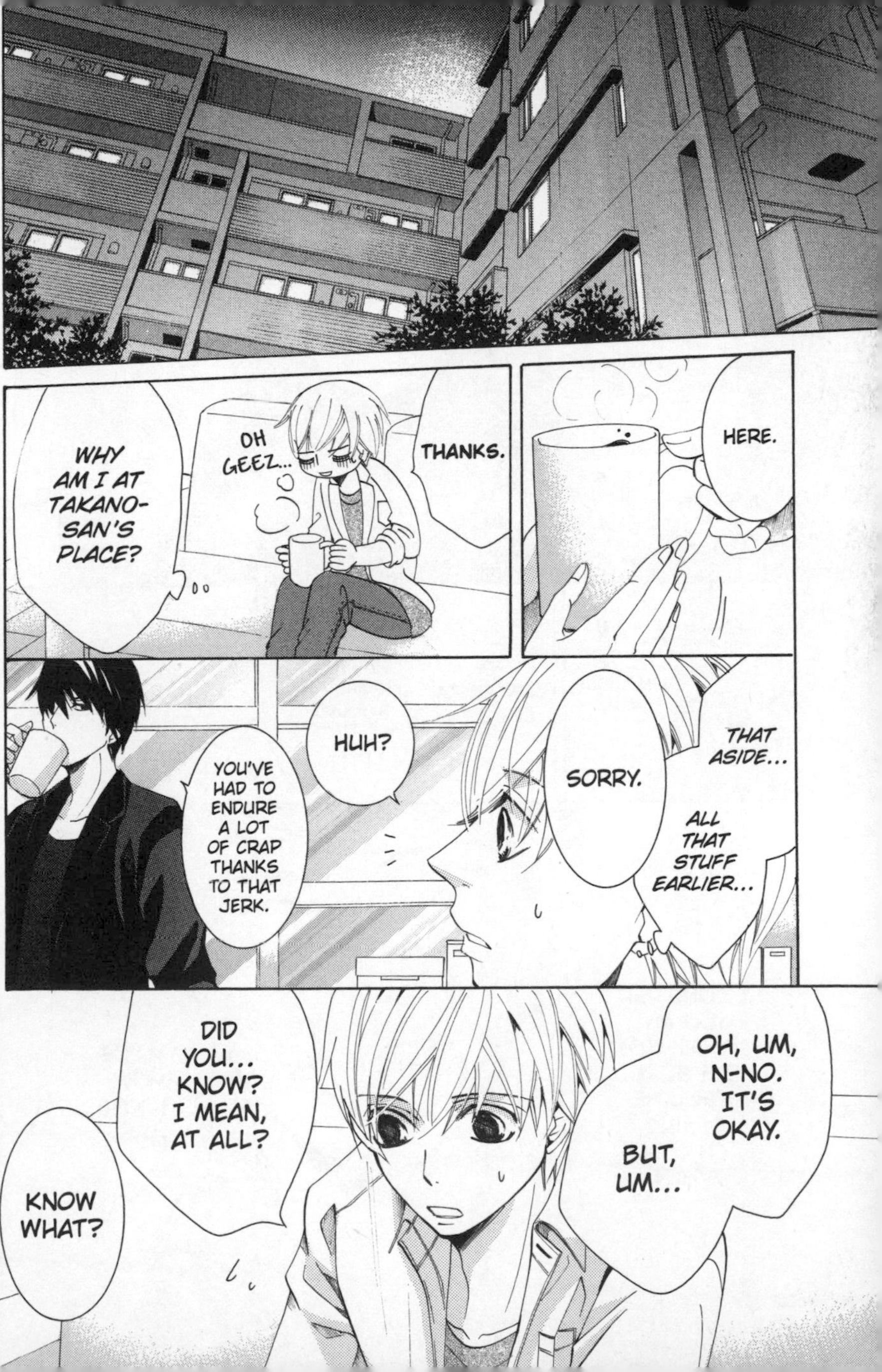
HERE.
THANKS.
OH GEEZ...
WHY AM I AT TAKANO-SAN'S PLACE?
THAT ASIDE...
ALL THAT STUFF EARLIER...
SORRY.
HUH?
YOU'VE HAD TO ENDURE A LOT OF CRAP THANKS TO THAT JERK.
OH, UM, N-NO. IT'S OKAY.
BUT, UM...
DID YOU... KNOW? I MEAN, AT ALL?
KNOW WHAT?

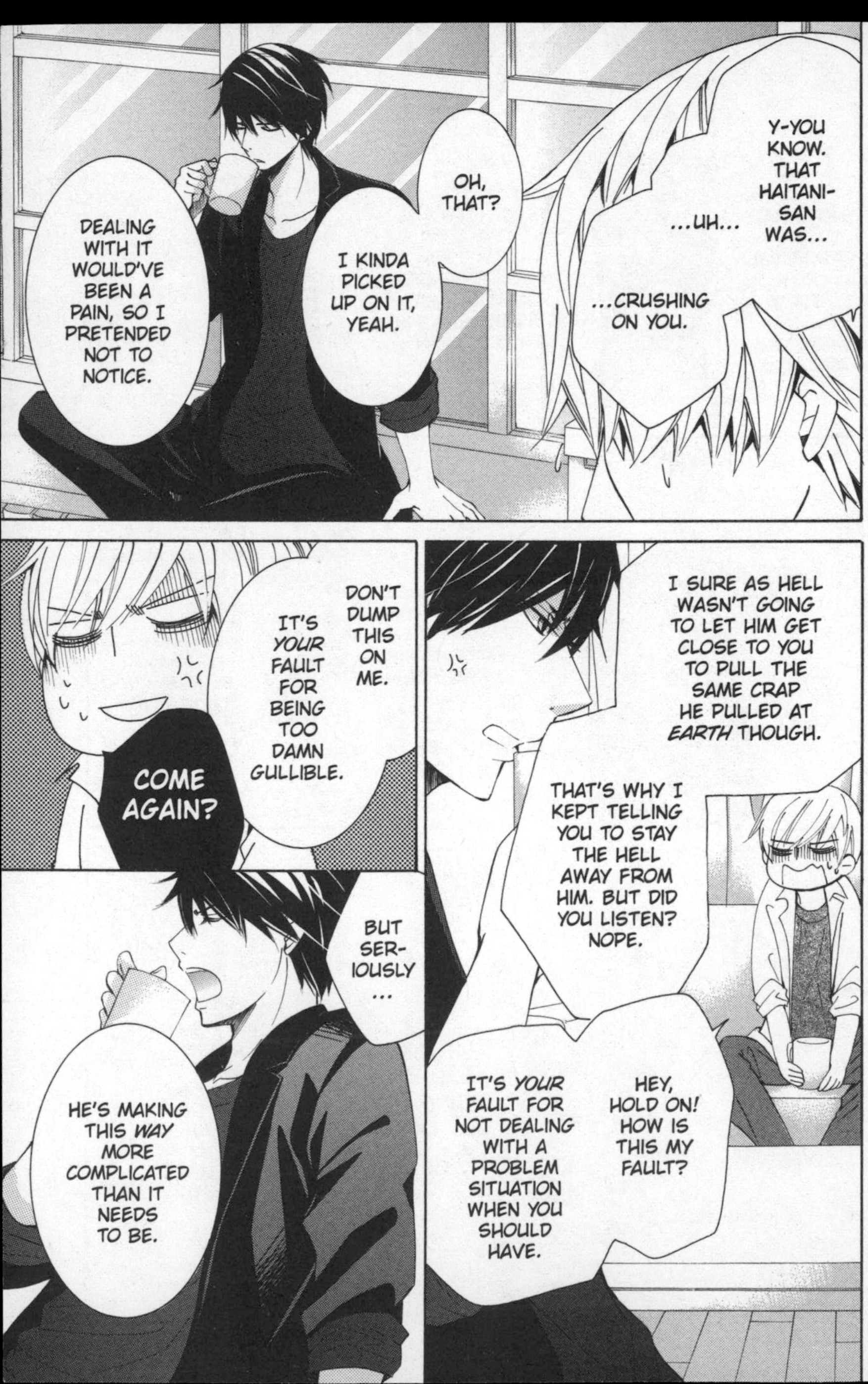
Y-YOU KNOW. THAT HAITANI-SAN WAS...
...UH...
...CRUSHING ON YOU.
OH, THAT?
I KINDA PICKED UP ON IT, YEAH.
DEALING WITH IT WOULD'VE BEEN A PAIN, SO I PRETENDED NOT TO NOTICE.
I SURE AS HELL WASN'T GOING TO LET HIM GET CLOSE TO YOU TO PULL THE SAME CRAP HE PULLED AT *EARTH* THOUGH.
THAT'S WHY I KEPT TELLING YOU TO STAY THE HELL AWAY FROM HIM. BUT DID YOU LISTEN? NOPE.
HEY, HOLD ON! HOW IS THIS MY FAULT?
IT'S *YOUR* FAULT FOR NOT DEALING WITH A PROBLEM SITUATION WHEN YOU SHOULD HAVE.
DON'T DUMP THIS ON ME.
IT'S *YOUR* FAULT FOR BEING TOO DAMN GULLIBLE.
COME AGAIN?
BUT SERIOUSLY...
HE'S MAKING THIS *WAY* MORE COMPLICATED THAN IT NEEDS TO BE.

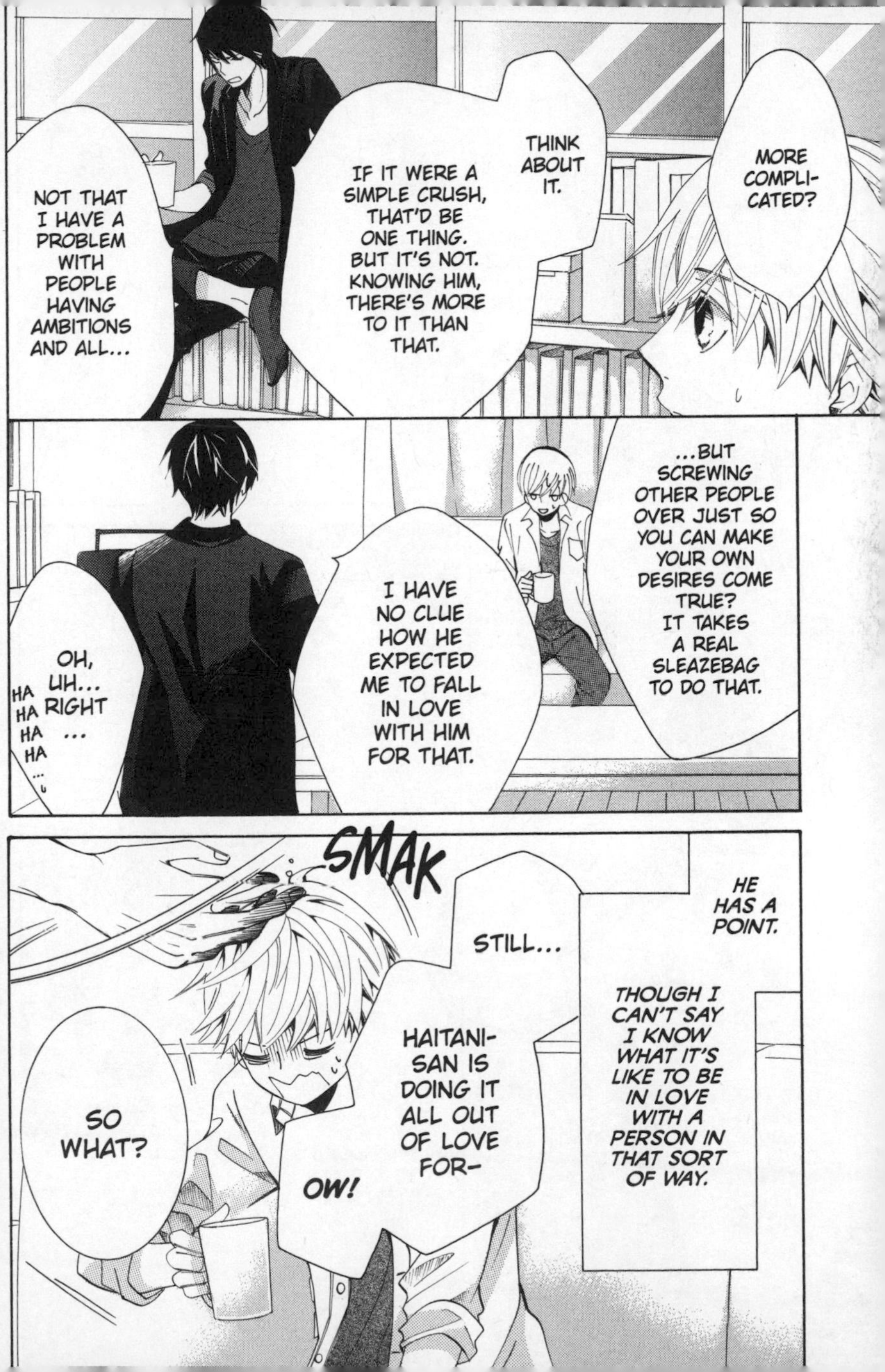
MORE COMPLI-CATED?
THINK ABOUT IT.
IF IT WERE A SIMPLE CRUSH, THAT'D BE ONE THING. BUT IT'S NOT. KNOWING HIM, THERE'S MORE TO IT THAN THAT.
NOT THAT I HAVE A PROBLEM WITH PEOPLE HAVING AMBITIONS AND ALL...
...BUT SCREWING OTHER PEOPLE OVER JUST SO YOU CAN MAKE YOUR OWN DESIRES COME TRUE? IT TAKES A REAL SLEAZEBAG TO DO THAT.
I HAVE NO CLUE HOW HE EXPECTED ME TO FALL IN LOVE WITH HIM FOR THAT.
OH, UH... RIGHT...
HA HA HA HA...
HE HAS A POINT.
THOUGH I CAN'T SAY I KNOW WHAT IT'S LIKE TO BE IN LOVE WITH A PERSON IN THAT SORT OF WAY.
STILL...
HAITANI-SAN IS DOING IT ALL OUT OF LOVE FOR-
SMAK
OW!
SO WHAT?

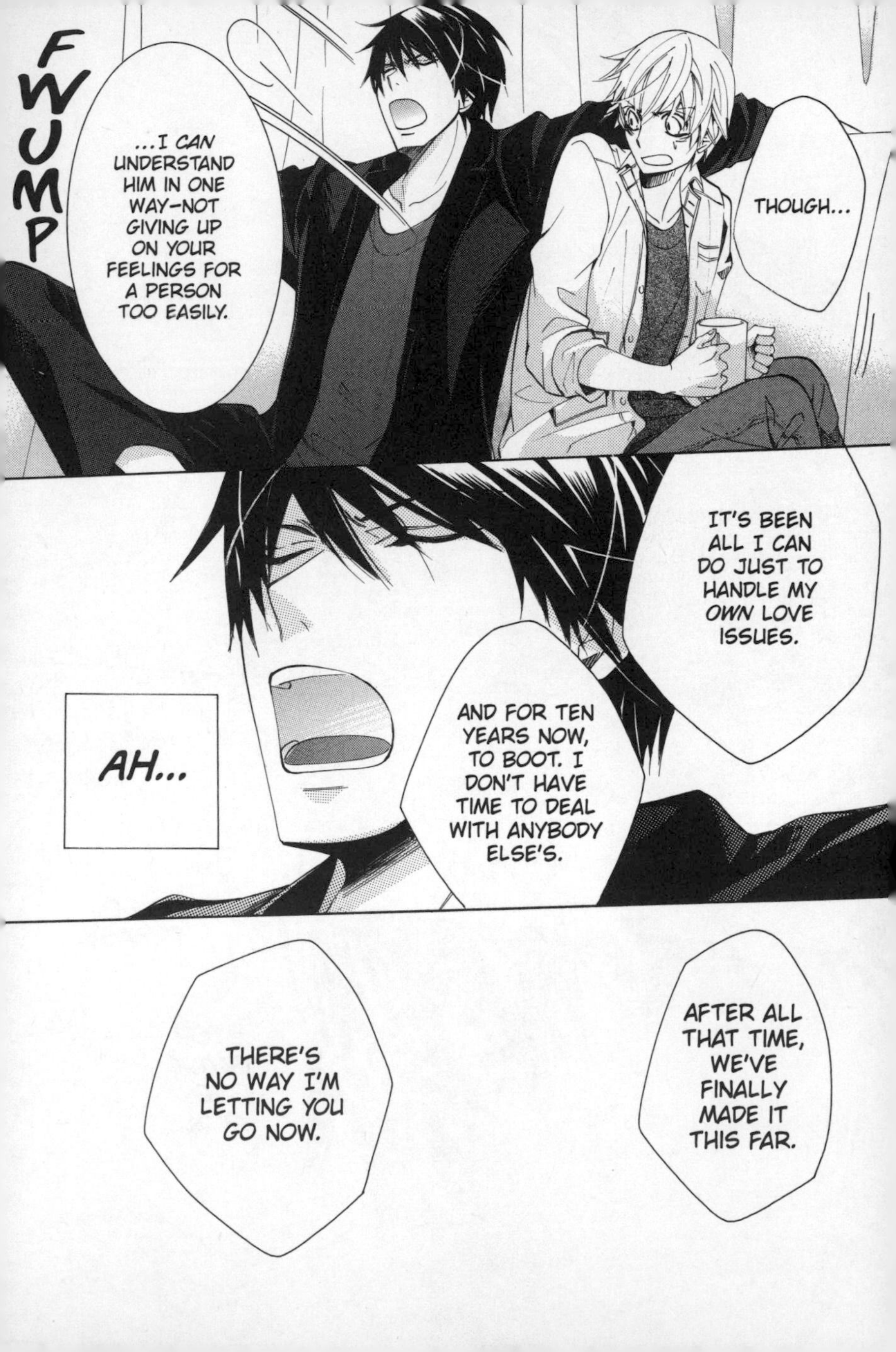
FWUMP
...I CAN UNDERSTAND HIM IN ONE WAY—NOT GIVING UP ON YOUR FEELINGS FOR A PERSON TOO EASILY.
THOUGH...
IT'S BEEN ALL I CAN DO JUST TO HANDLE MY *OWN* LOVE ISSUES.
AND FOR TEN YEARS NOW, TO BOOT. I DON'T HAVE TIME TO DEAL WITH ANYBODY ELSE'S.
AH...
AFTER ALL THAT TIME, WE'VE FINALLY MADE IT THIS FAR.
THERE'S NO WAY I'M LETTING YOU GO NOW.

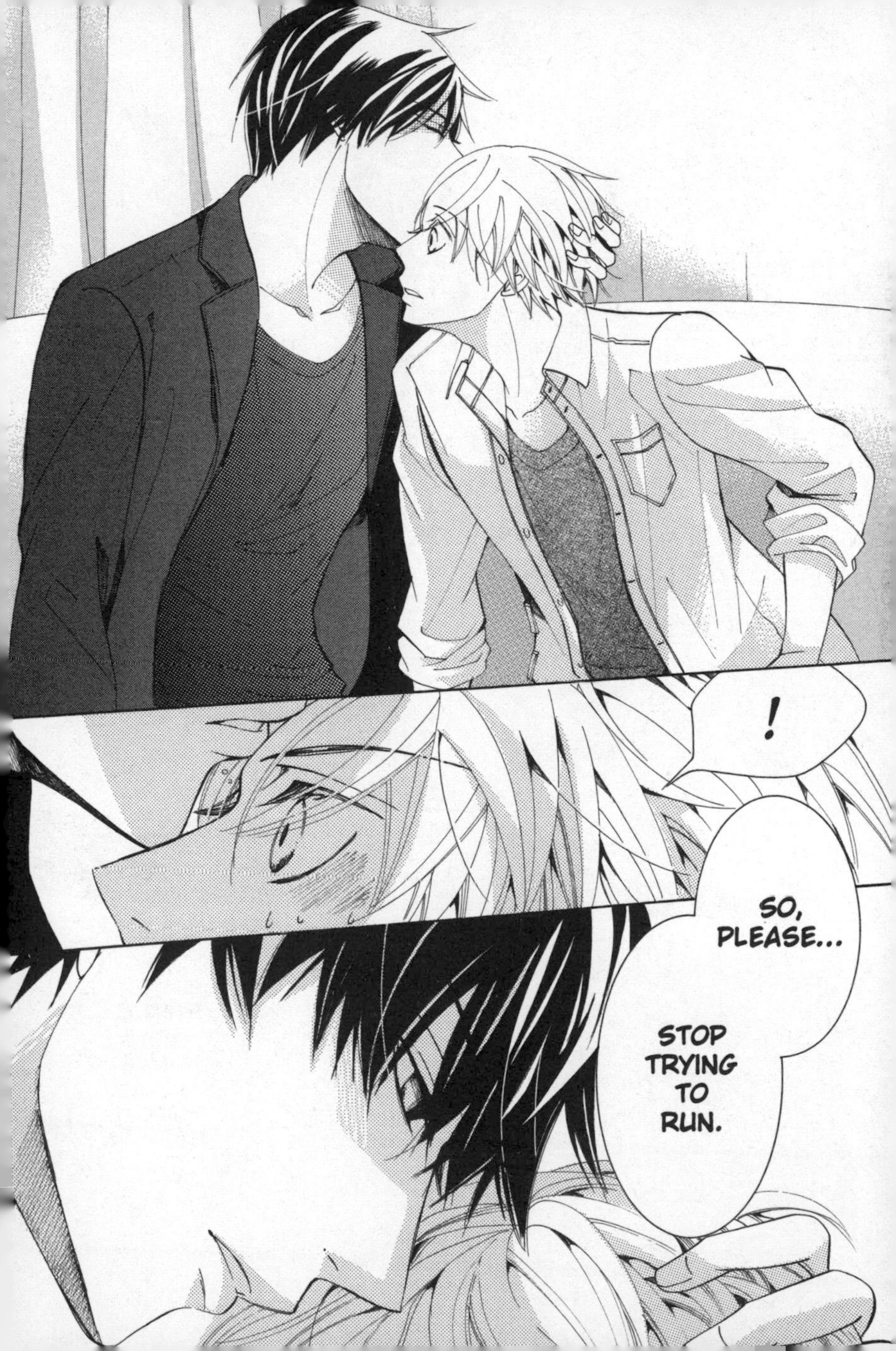
!
SO, PLEASE...
STOP TRYING TO RUN.

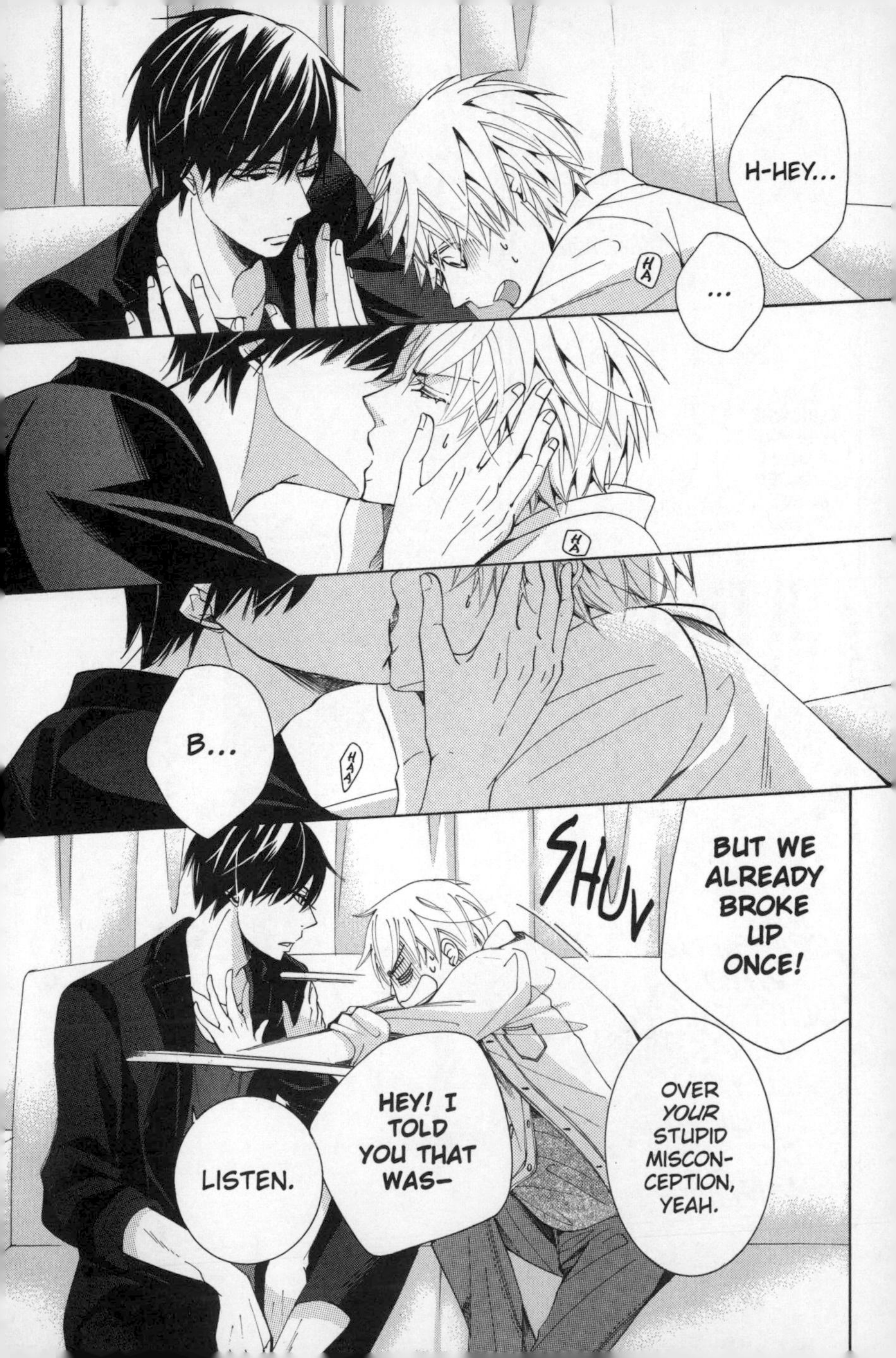
H-HEY...
...
HA
HA
B...
HA
SHUV
BUT WE ALREADY BROKE UP ONCE!
OVER YOUR STUPID MISCON-CEPTION, YEAH.
HEY! I TOLD YOU THAT WAS-
LISTEN.

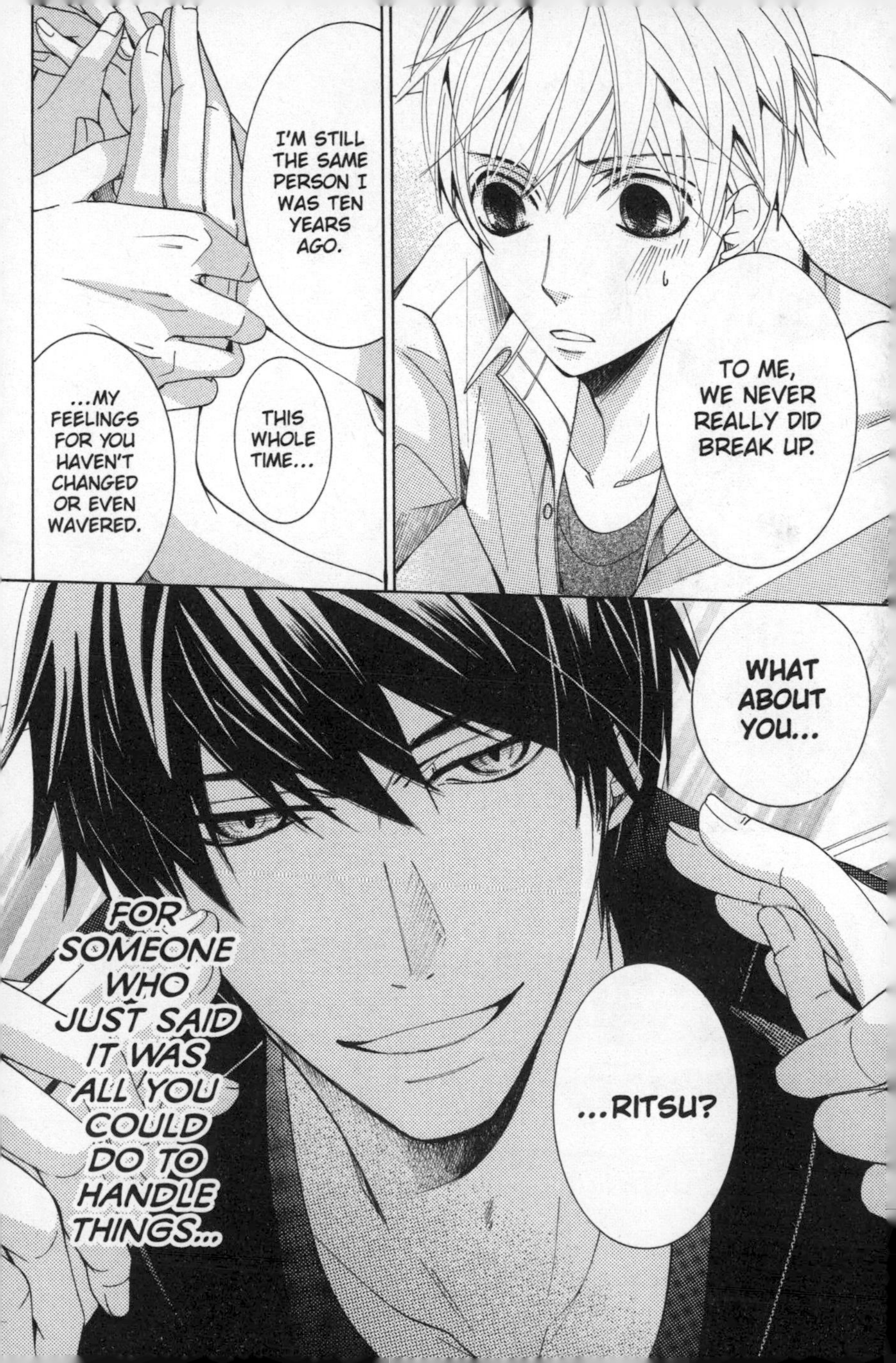
TO ME, WE NEVER REALLY DID BREAK UP.
I'M STILL THE SAME PERSON I WAS TEN YEARS AGO.
THIS WHOLE TIME...
...MY FEELINGS FOR YOU HAVEN'T CHANGED OR EVEN WAVERED.
WHAT ABOUT YOU...
...RITSU?
FOR SOMEONE WHO JUST SAID IT WAS ALL YOU COULD DO TO HANDLE THINGS...

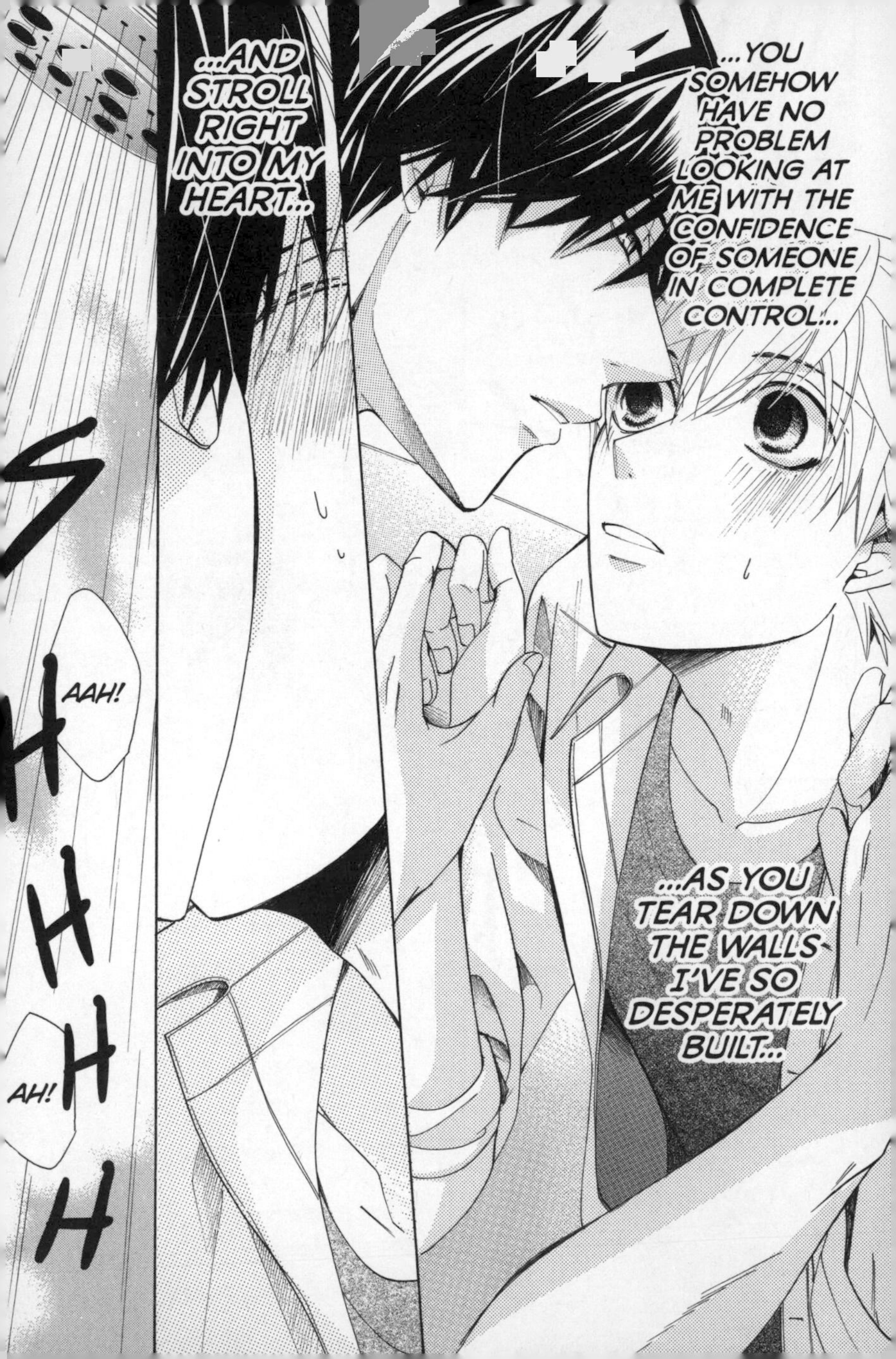
...YOU SOMEHOW HAVE NO PROBLEM LOOKING AT ME WITH THE CONFIDENCE OF SOMEONE IN COMPLETE CONTROL...
...AS YOU TEAR DOWN THE WALLS I'VE SO DESPERATELY BUILT...
...AND STROLL RIGHT INTO MY HEART...
SHHHH
AAH!
AH!

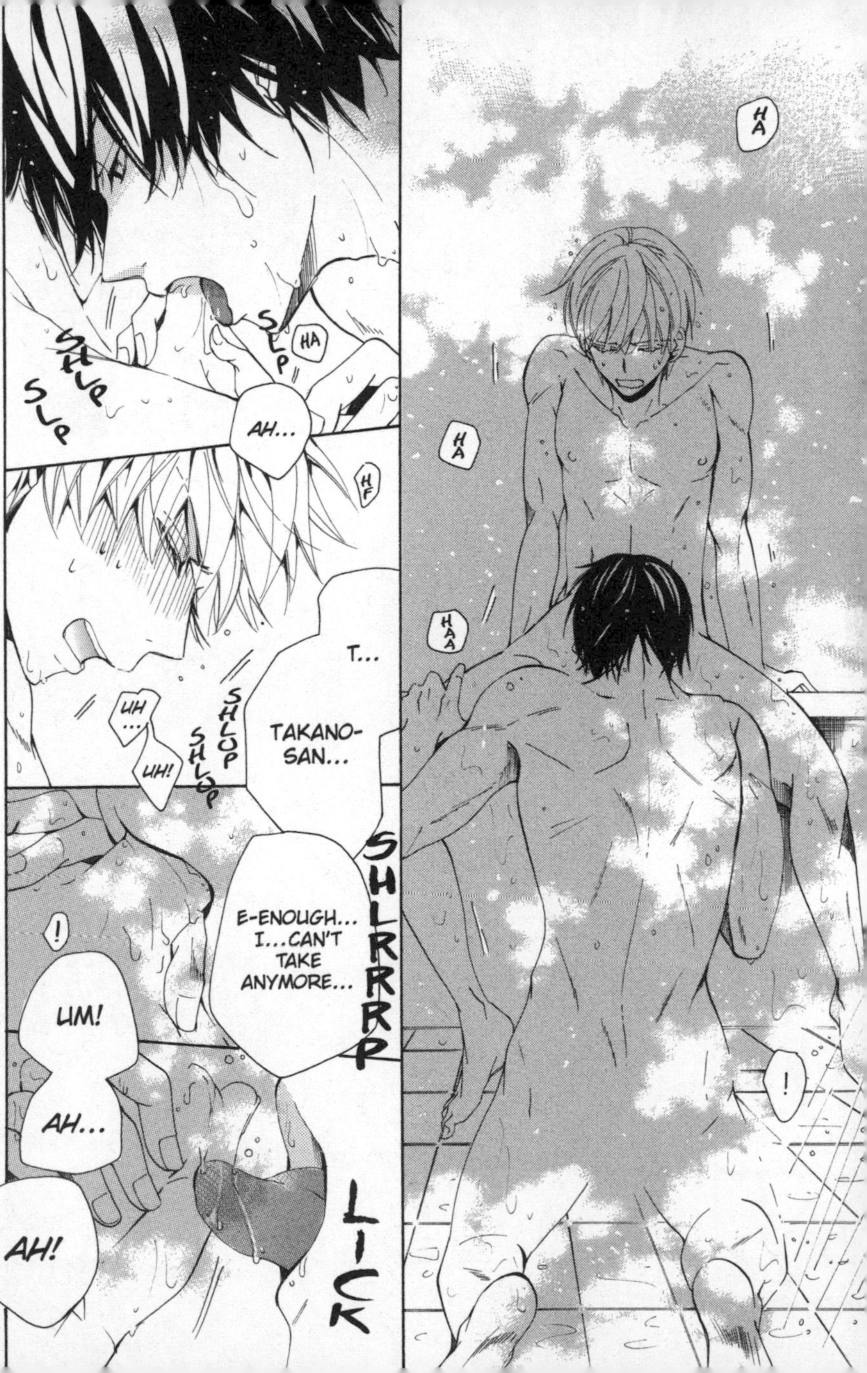
HA
HA
HAA
!
SLP
HA
SHLUP
SLP
AH...
HF
T...
TAKANO-SAN...
SHLUP
SHLUP
UH...
UH!
SHLRRRP
E-ENOUGH... I...CAN'T TAKE ANYMORE...
!
UM!
AH...
LICK
AH!

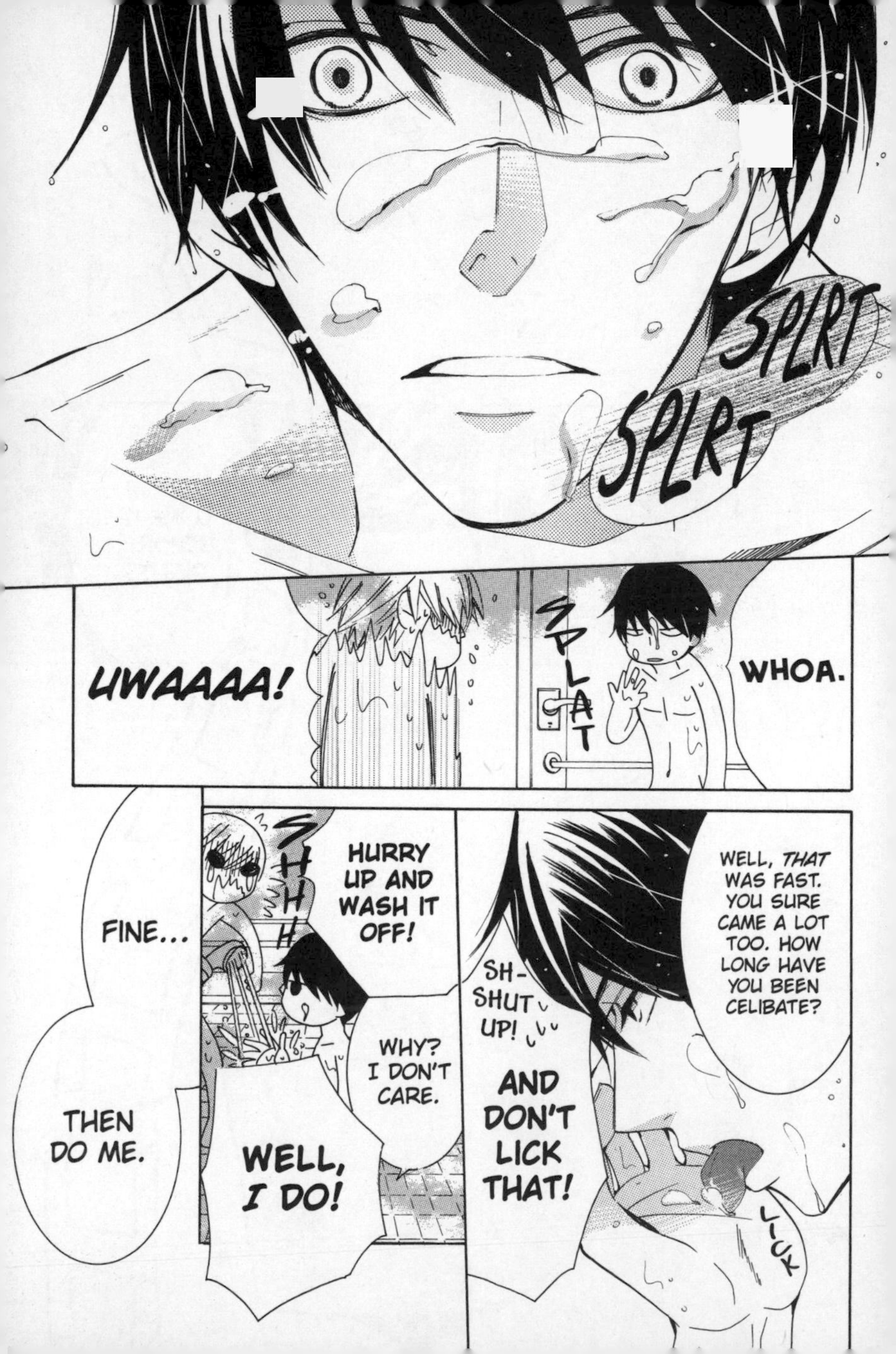
SPLRT
SPLRT
WHOA.
SPLAT
UWAAAA!
WELL, THAT WAS FAST. YOU SURE CAME A LOT TOO. HOW LONG HAVE YOU BEEN CELIBATE?
SH-SHUT UP!
AND DON'T LICK THAT!
LICK
HURRY UP AND WASH IT OFF!
SHHH
WHY? I DON'T CARE.
WELL, I DO!
FINE...
THEN DO ME.

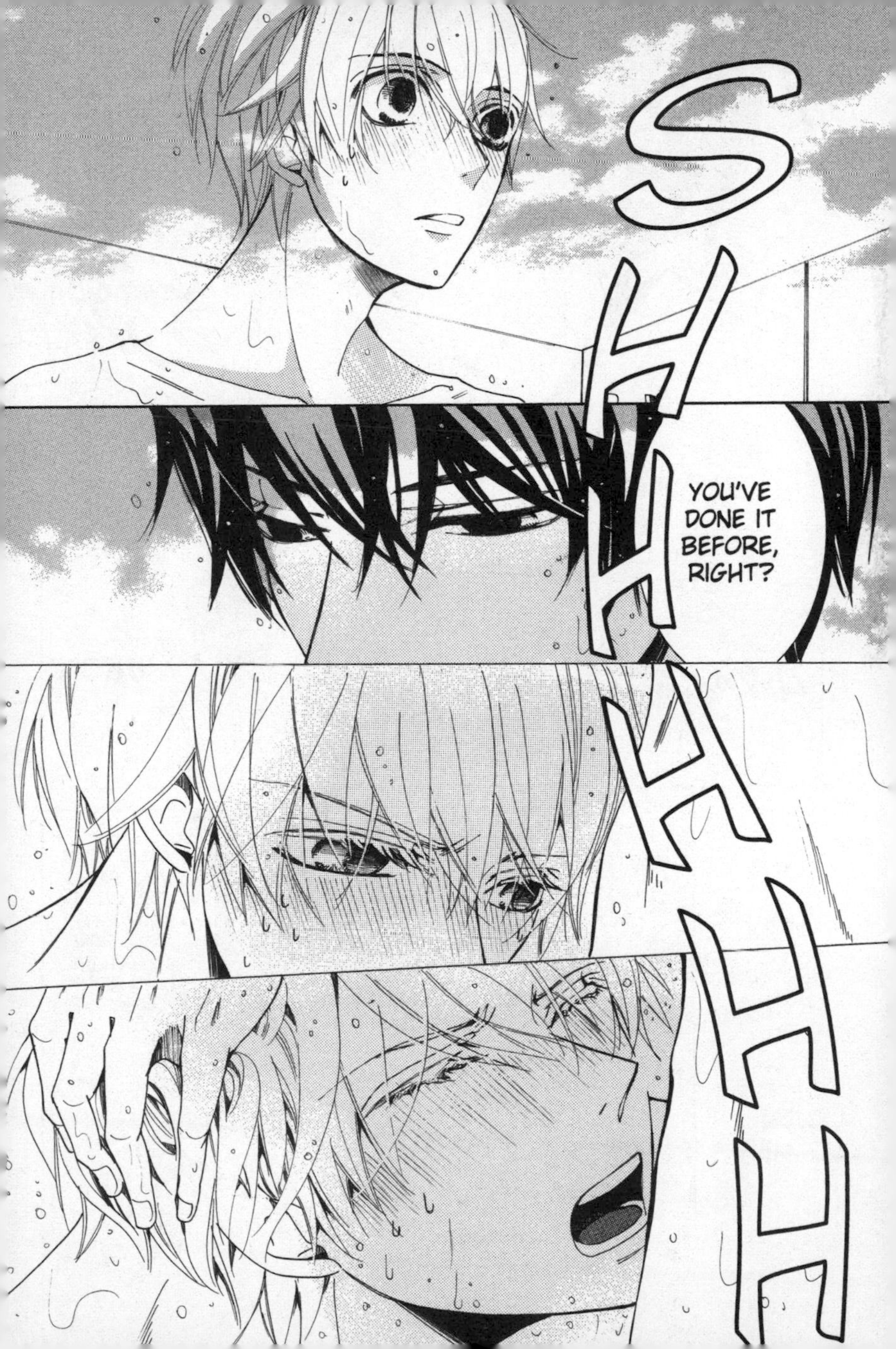
SHHHHH
YOU'VE DONE IT BEFORE, RIGHT?

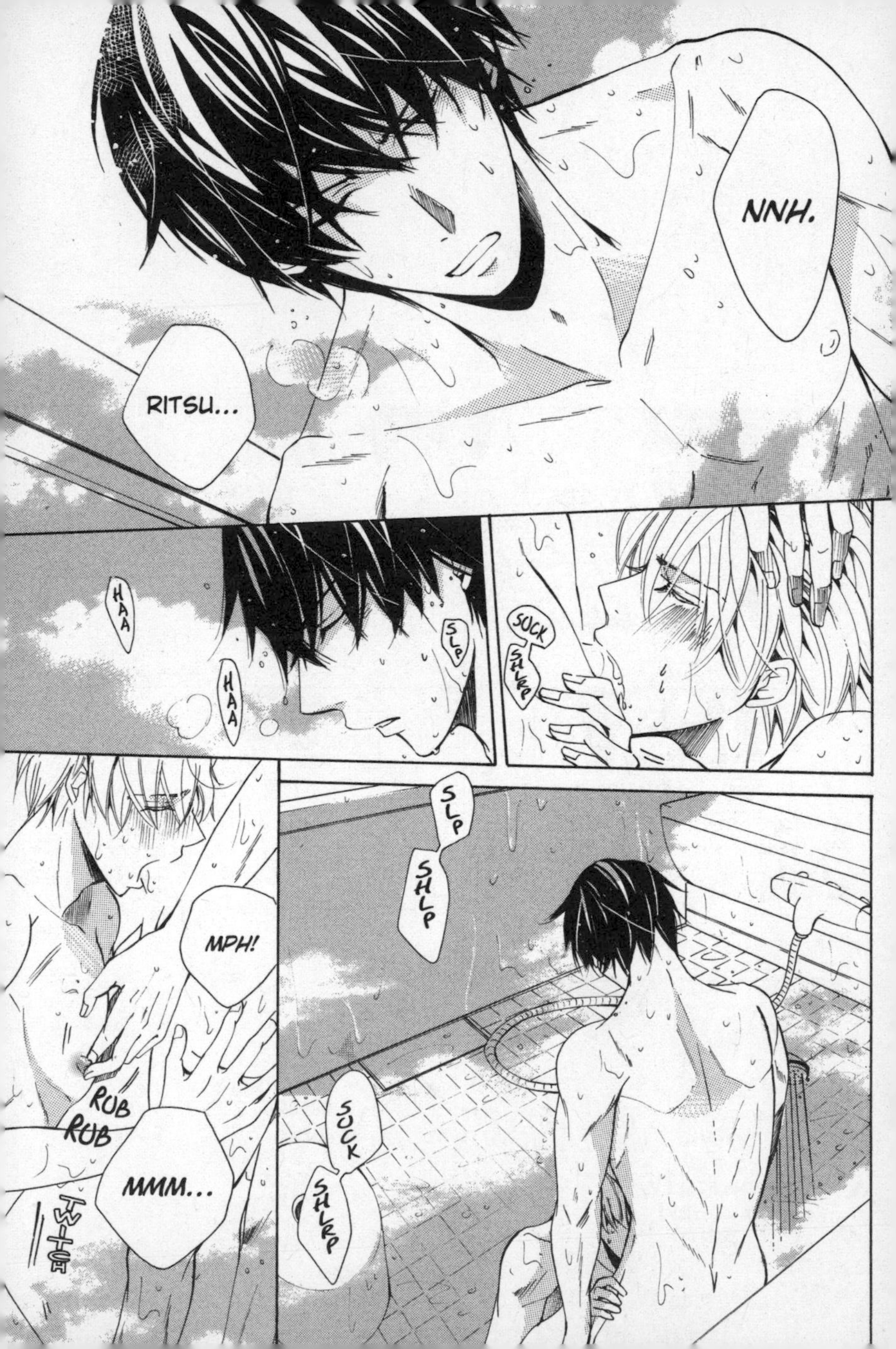
NNH.
RITSU...
SUCK
SHLRP
SLP
HAA
HAA
SLP
SHLP
SUCK
SHLRP
MPH!
RUB
RUB
MMM...
TWITCH

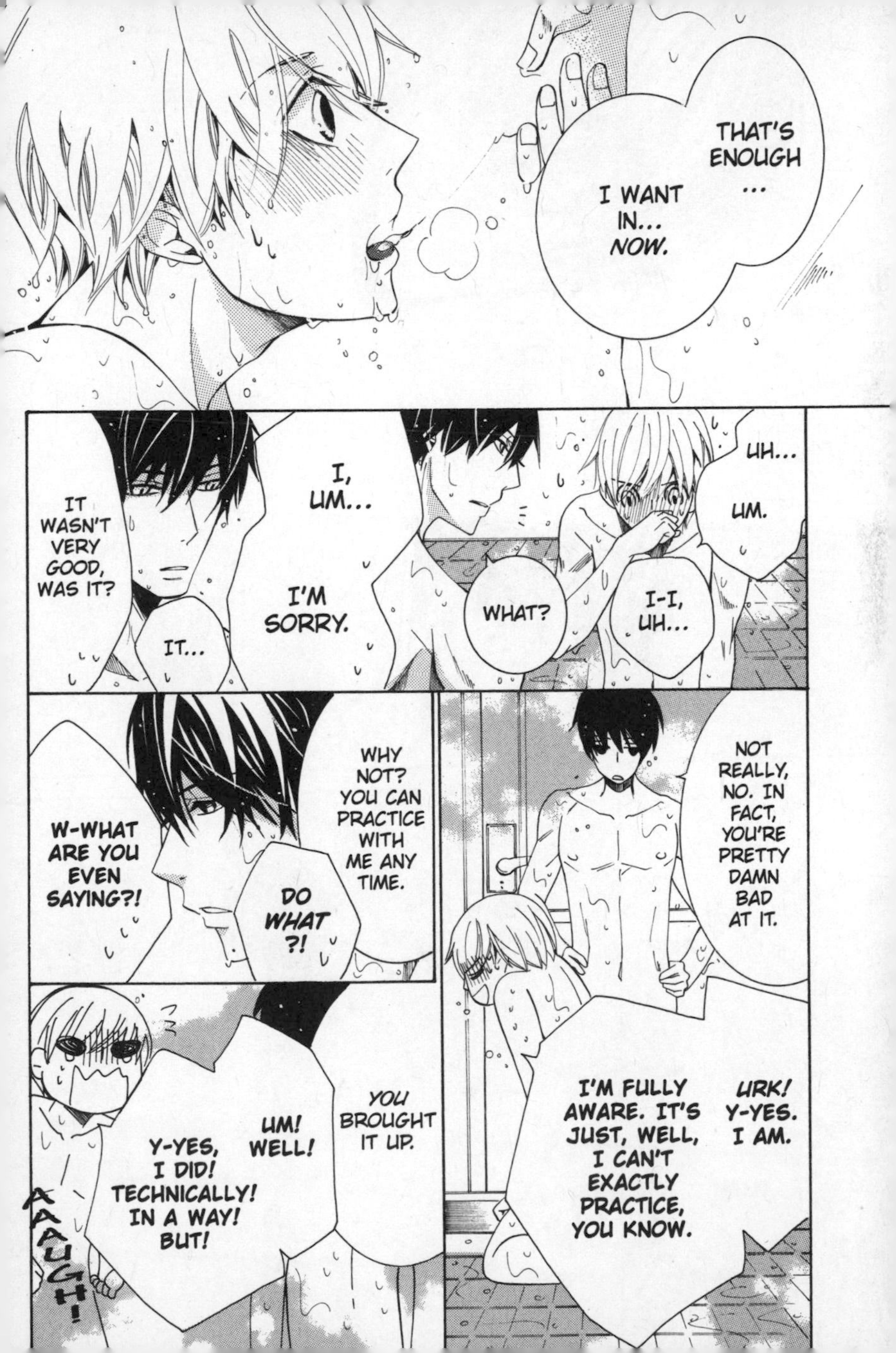
THAT'S ENOUGH...
I WANT IN... *NOW.*
UH...
UM.
I-I, UH...
WHAT?
I, UM...
I'M SORRY.
IT...
IT WASN'T VERY GOOD, WAS IT?
NOT REALLY, NO. IN FACT, YOU'RE PRETTY DAMN BAD AT IT.
URK! Y-YES. I AM.
I'M FULLY AWARE. IT'S JUST, WELL, I CAN'T EXACTLY PRACTICE, YOU KNOW.
WHY NOT? YOU CAN PRACTICE WITH ME ANY TIME.
DO *WHAT*?!
W-WHAT ARE YOU EVEN SAYING?!
YOU BROUGHT IT UP.
UM! WELL!
Y-YES, I DID! TECHNICALLY! IN A WAY! BUT!
AAAUGH!

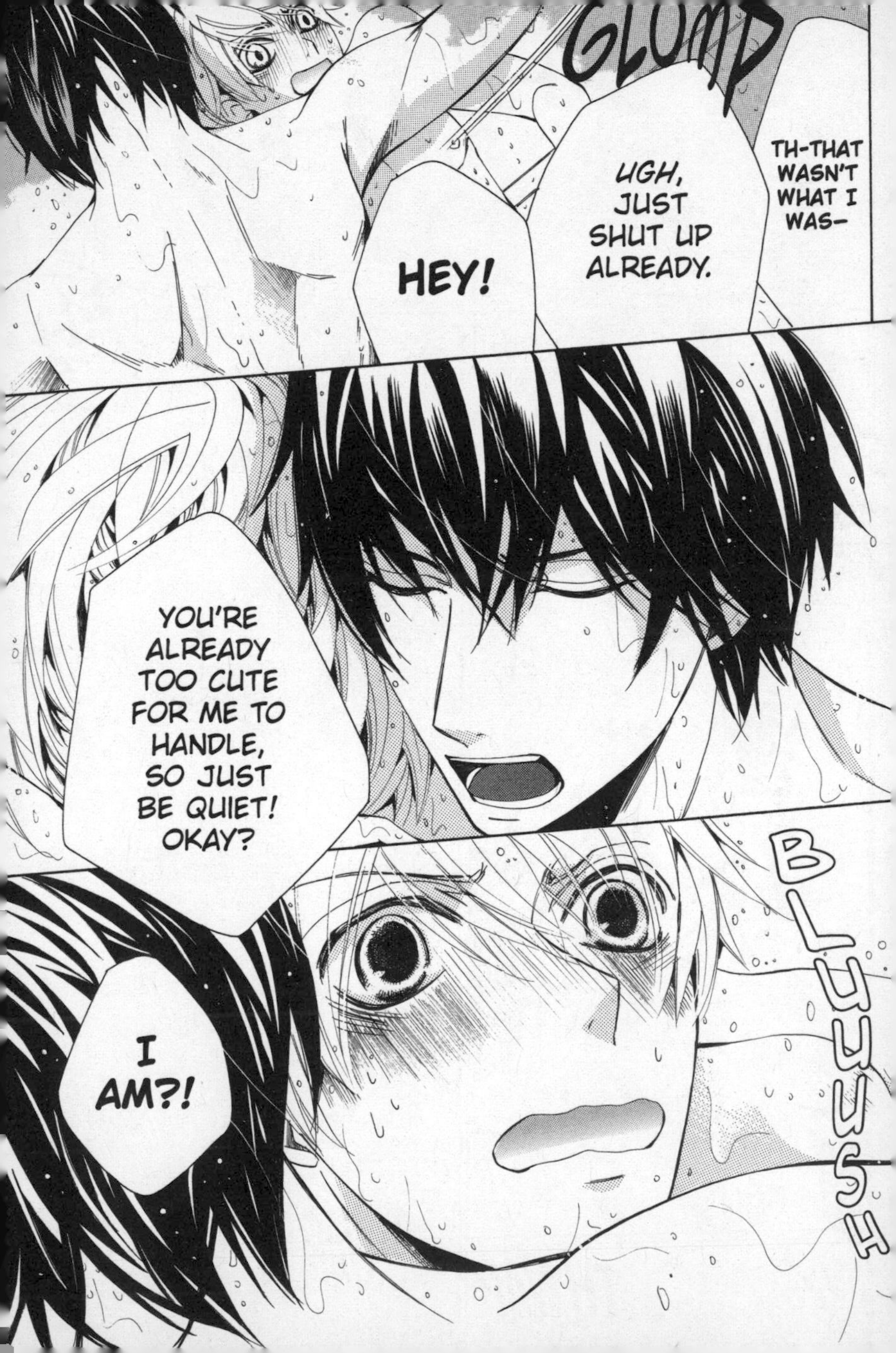
GLUMP
TH-THAT WASN'T WHAT I WAS-
UGH, JUST SHUT UP ALREADY.
HEY!
YOU'RE ALREADY TOO CUTE FOR ME TO HANDLE, SO JUST BE QUIET! OKAY?
BLUUUSH
I AM?!

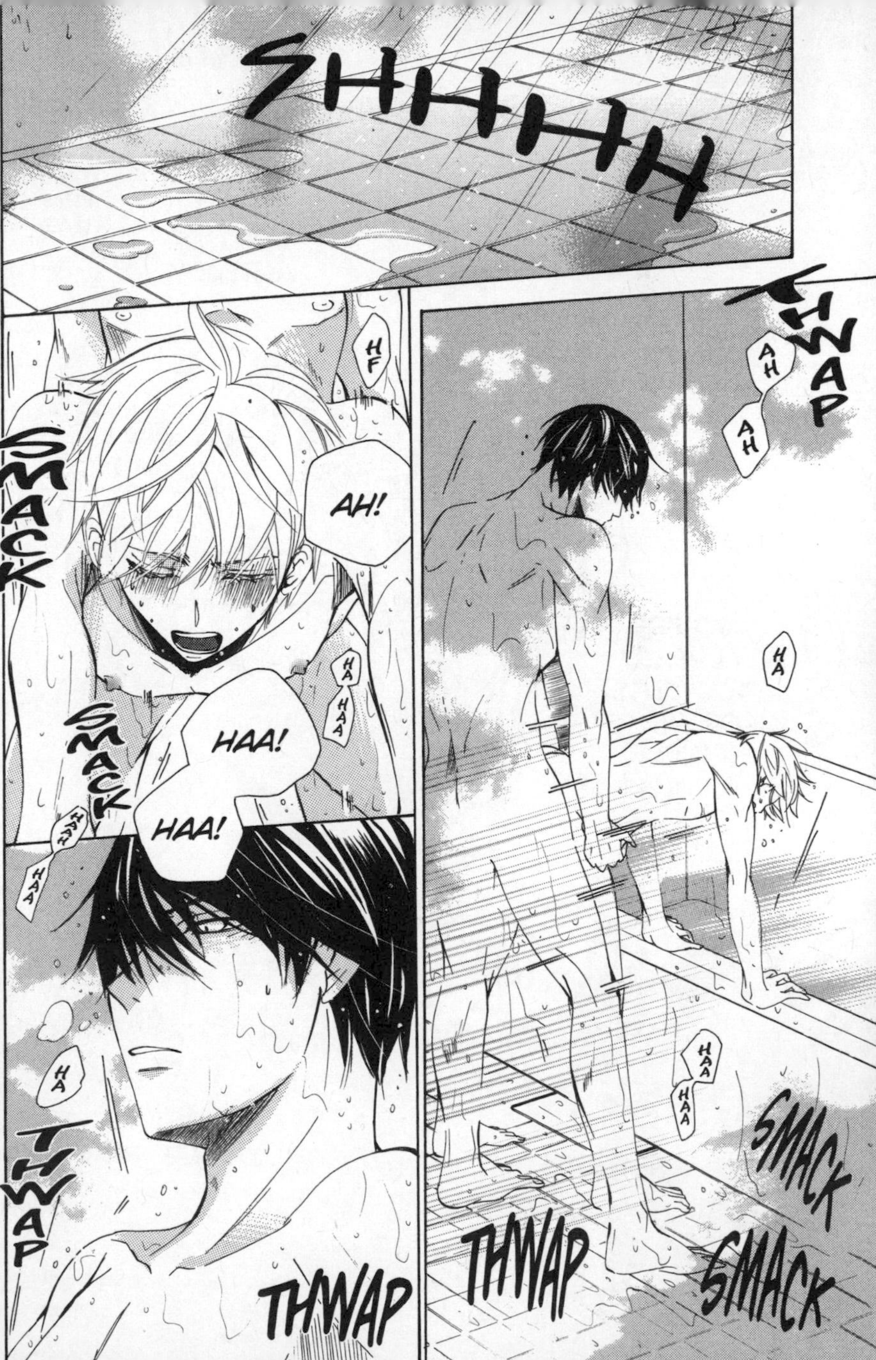
SHHHHH
THWAP
AH AH
AH
HA
HAA HAA
SMACK
SMACK
THWAP
HF
AH!
SMACK
HA HA HAA
HAA!
SMACK
HAA!
HAH HAA
HA
THWAP
THWAP

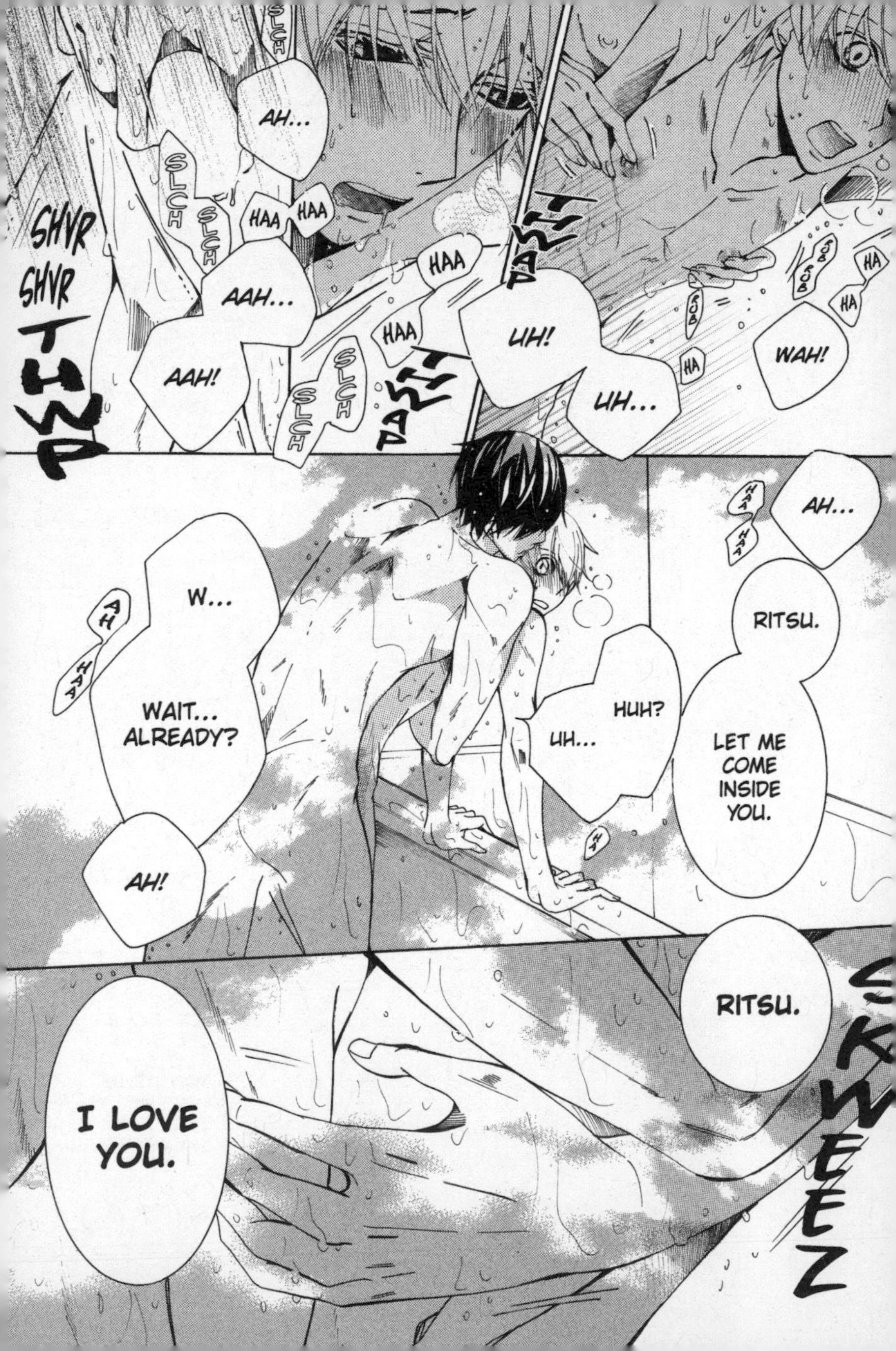
HA
HA
RUB
RUB
RUB
WAH!
HA
UH!
UH...
THWAP
SLCH
AH...
HAA
HAA
SLCH
SLCH
HAA
AAH...
AAH!
HAA
SLCH
SLCH
THWAP
SHVR
SHVR
THWP
AH...
HAA
HAA
RITSU.
LET ME COME INSIDE YOU.
HUH?
UH...
HA
W...
WAIT... ALREADY?
AH
HAA
AH!
SKWEEZ
RITSU.
I LOVE YOU.

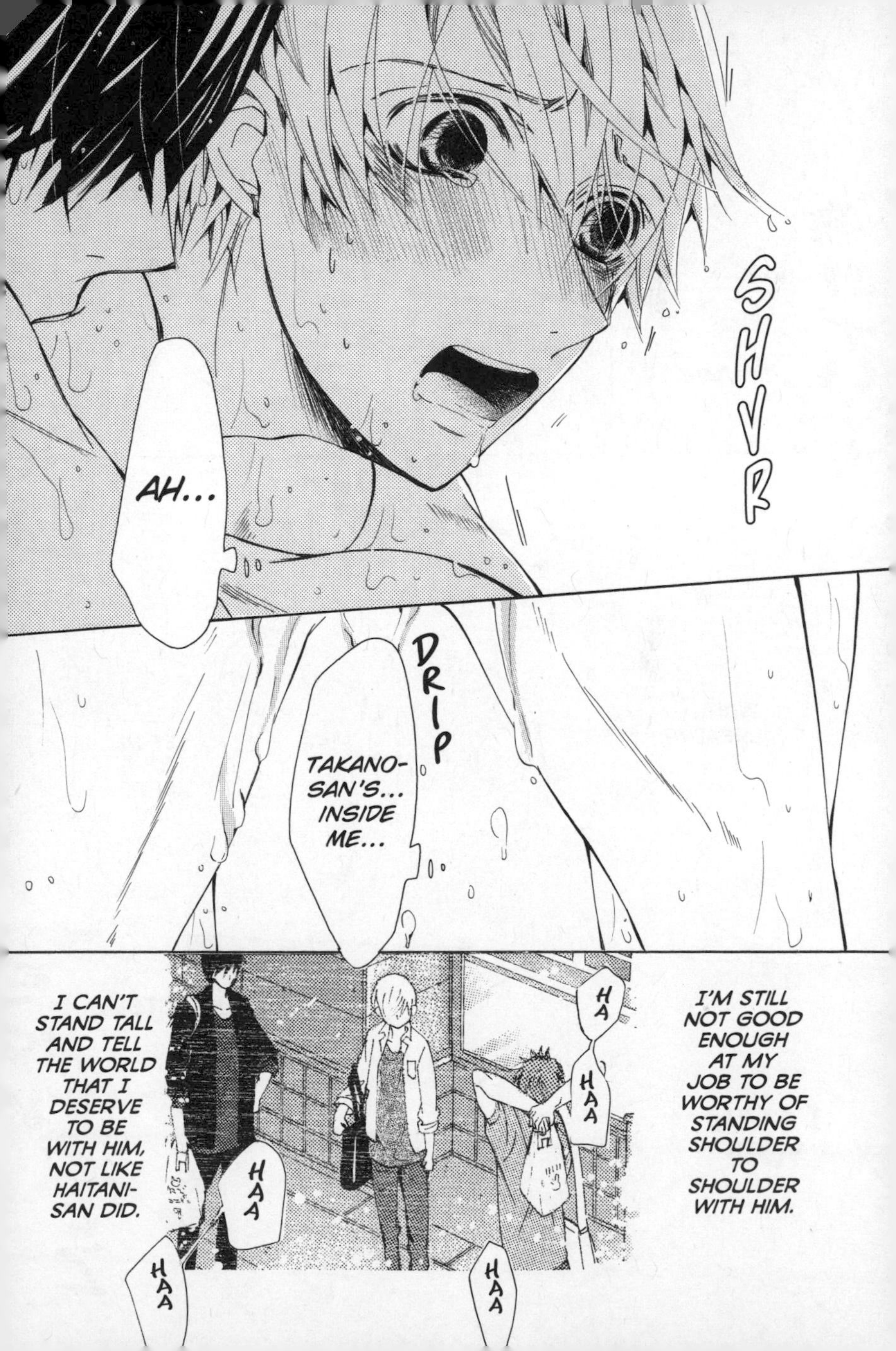
SHVR
AH...
DRIP
TAKANO-SAN'S... INSIDE ME...
I'M STILL NOT GOOD ENOUGH AT MY JOB TO BE WORTHY OF STANDING SHOULDER TO SHOULDER WITH HIM.
HA HAA
I CAN'T STAND TALL AND TELL THE WORLD THAT I DESERVE TO BE WITH HIM, NOT LIKE HAITANI-SAN DID.
HAA
HAA
HAA

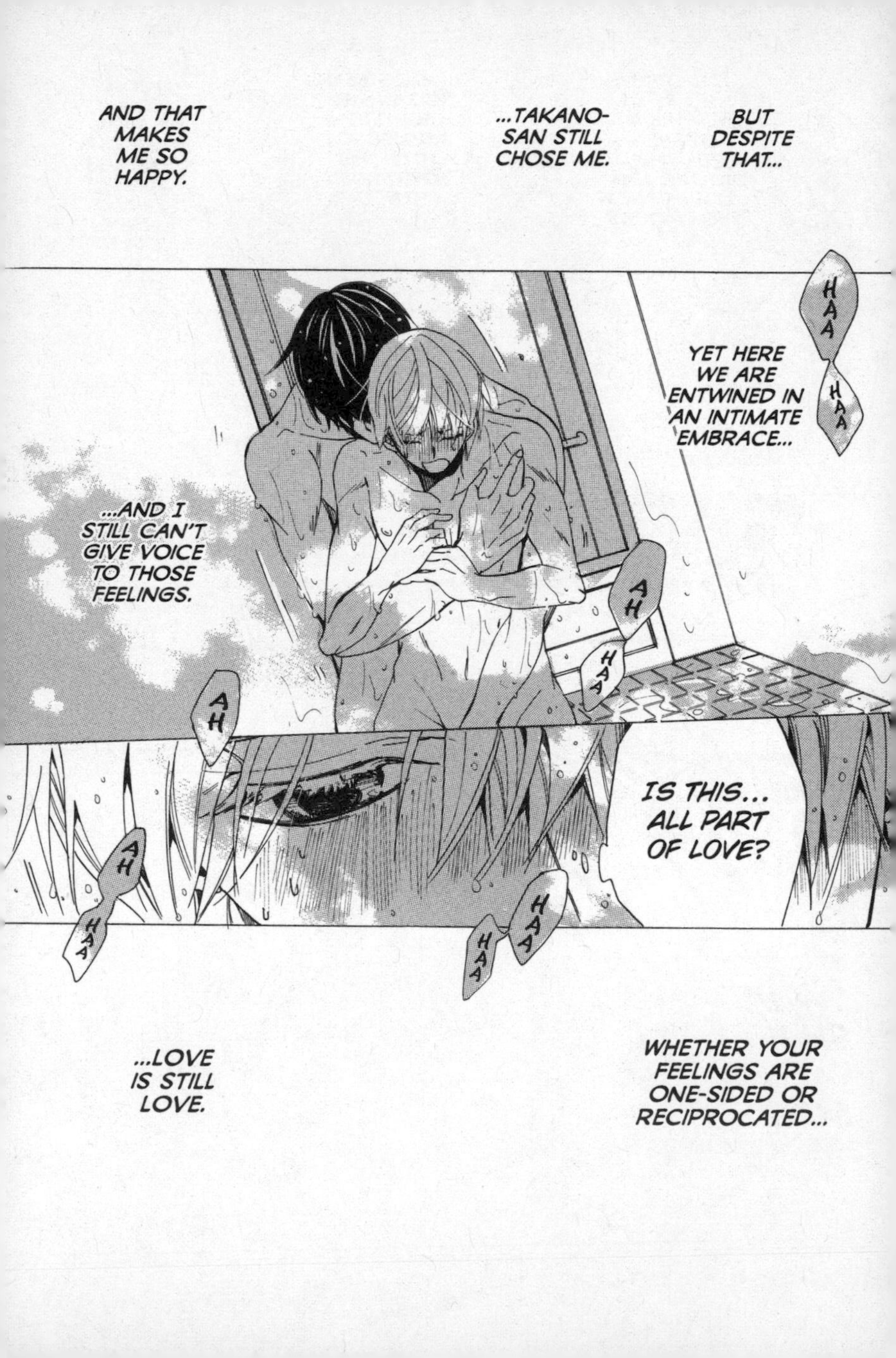
BUT DESPITE THAT...
...TAKANO-SAN STILL CHOSE ME.
AND THAT MAKES ME SO HAPPY.
HAA HAA
YET HERE WE ARE ENTWINED IN AN INTIMATE EMBRACE...
AH
HAA
...AND I STILL CAN'T GIVE VOICE TO THOSE FEELINGS.
AH
IS THIS... ALL PART OF LOVE?
HAA HAA
AH HAA
WHETHER YOUR FEELINGS ARE ONE-SIDED OR RECIPROCATED...
...LOVE IS STILL LOVE.

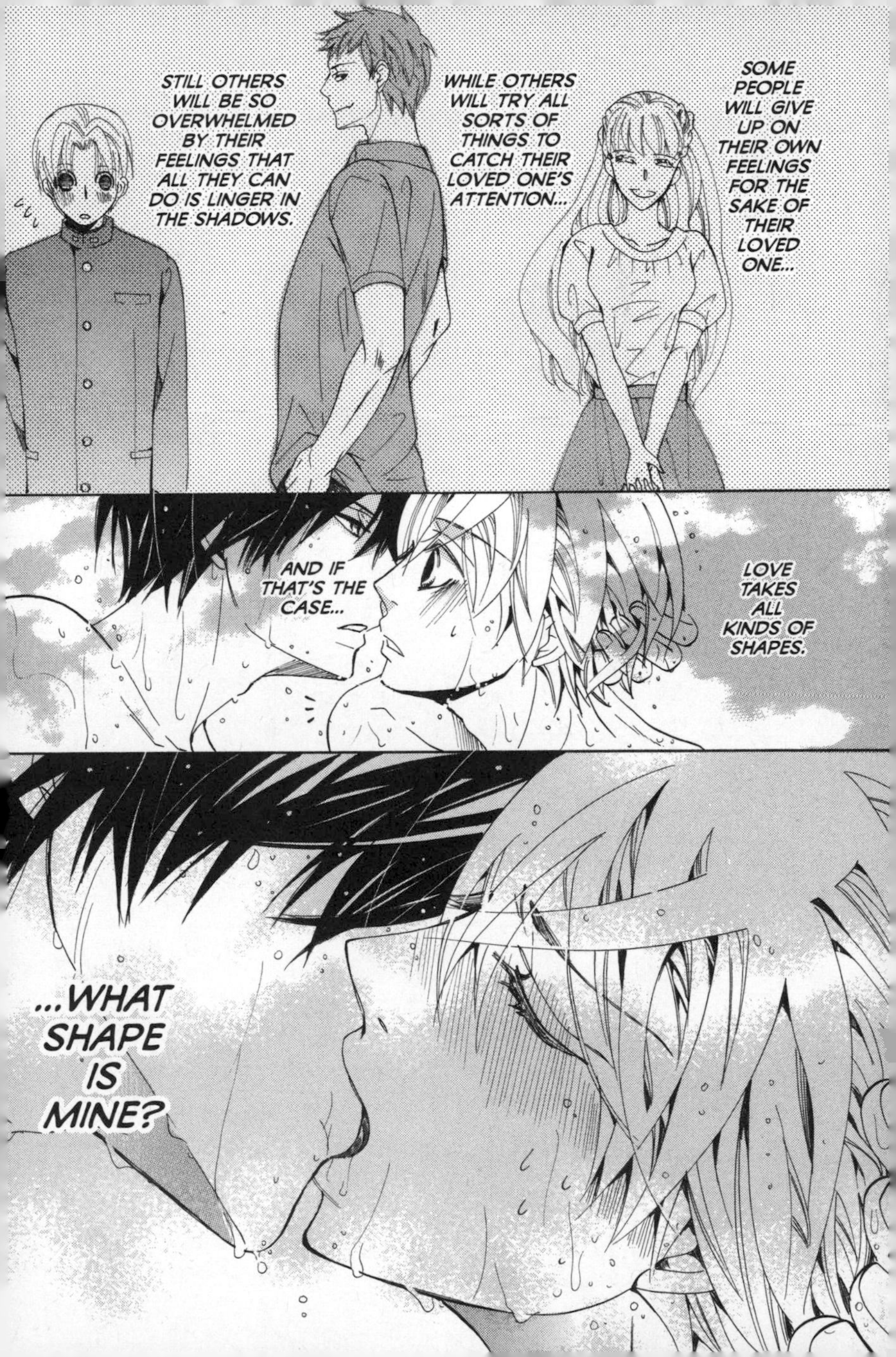
SOME PEOPLE WILL GIVE UP ON THEIR OWN FEELINGS FOR THE SAKE OF THEIR LOVED ONE...
WHILE OTHERS WILL TRY ALL SORTS OF THINGS TO CATCH THEIR LOVED ONE'S ATTENTION...
STILL OTHERS WILL BE SO OVERWHELMED BY THEIR FEELINGS THAT ALL THEY CAN DO IS LINGER IN THE SHADOWS.
LOVE TAKES ALL KINDS OF SHAPES.
AND IF THAT'S THE CASE...
...WHAT SHAPE IS MINE?

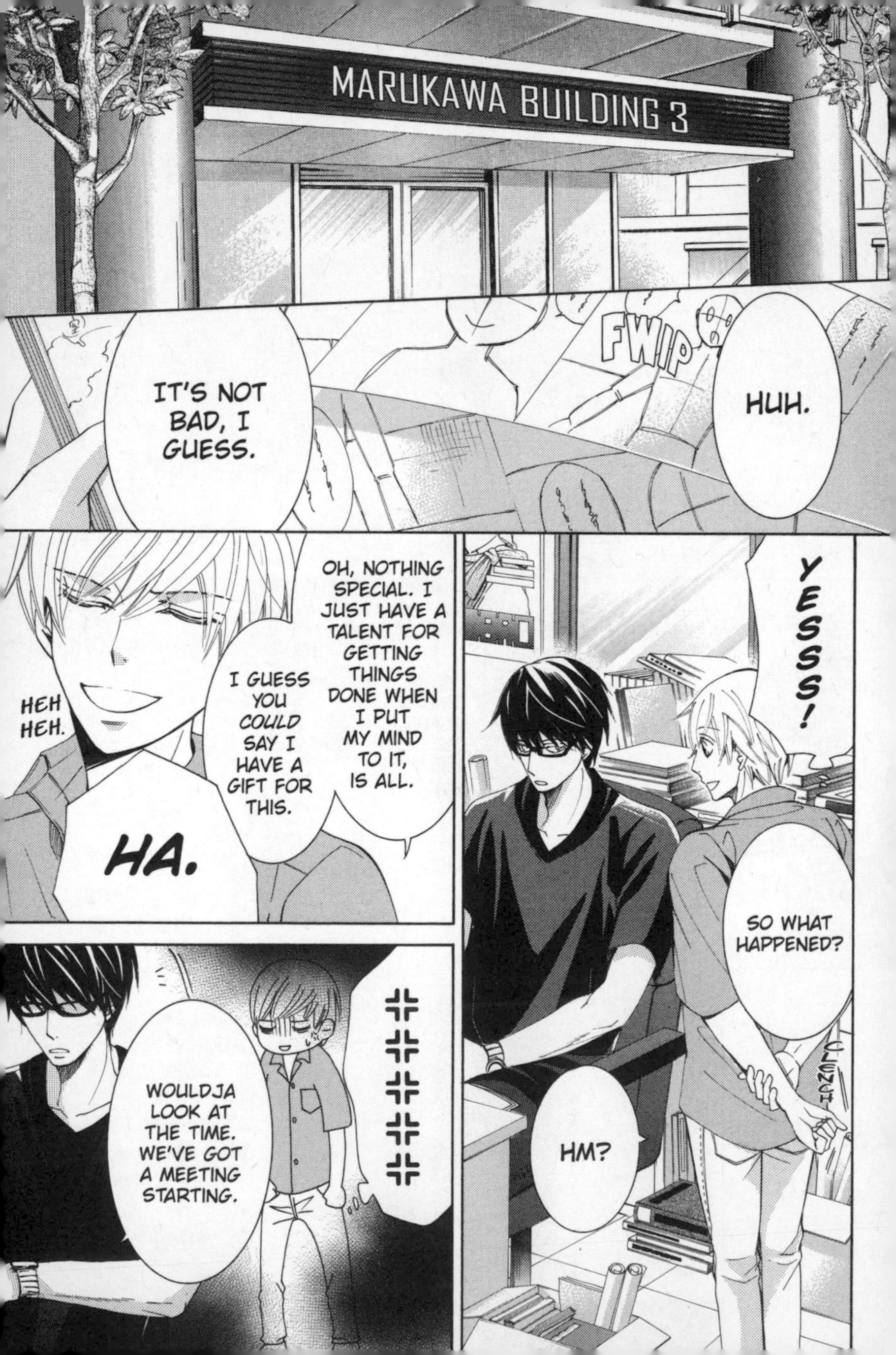

MARUKAWA BUILDING 3
HUH.
FWIP
IT'S NOT BAD, I GUESS.
YESSS!
SO WHAT HAPPENED?
CLENCH
HM?
OH, NOTHING SPECIAL. I JUST HAVE A TALENT FOR GETTING THINGS DONE WHEN I PUT MY MIND TO IT, IS ALL.
I GUESS YOU COULD SAY I HAVE A GIFT FOR THIS.
HEH HEH.
HA.
WOULDJA LOOK AT THE TIME. WE'VE GOT A MEETING STARTING.

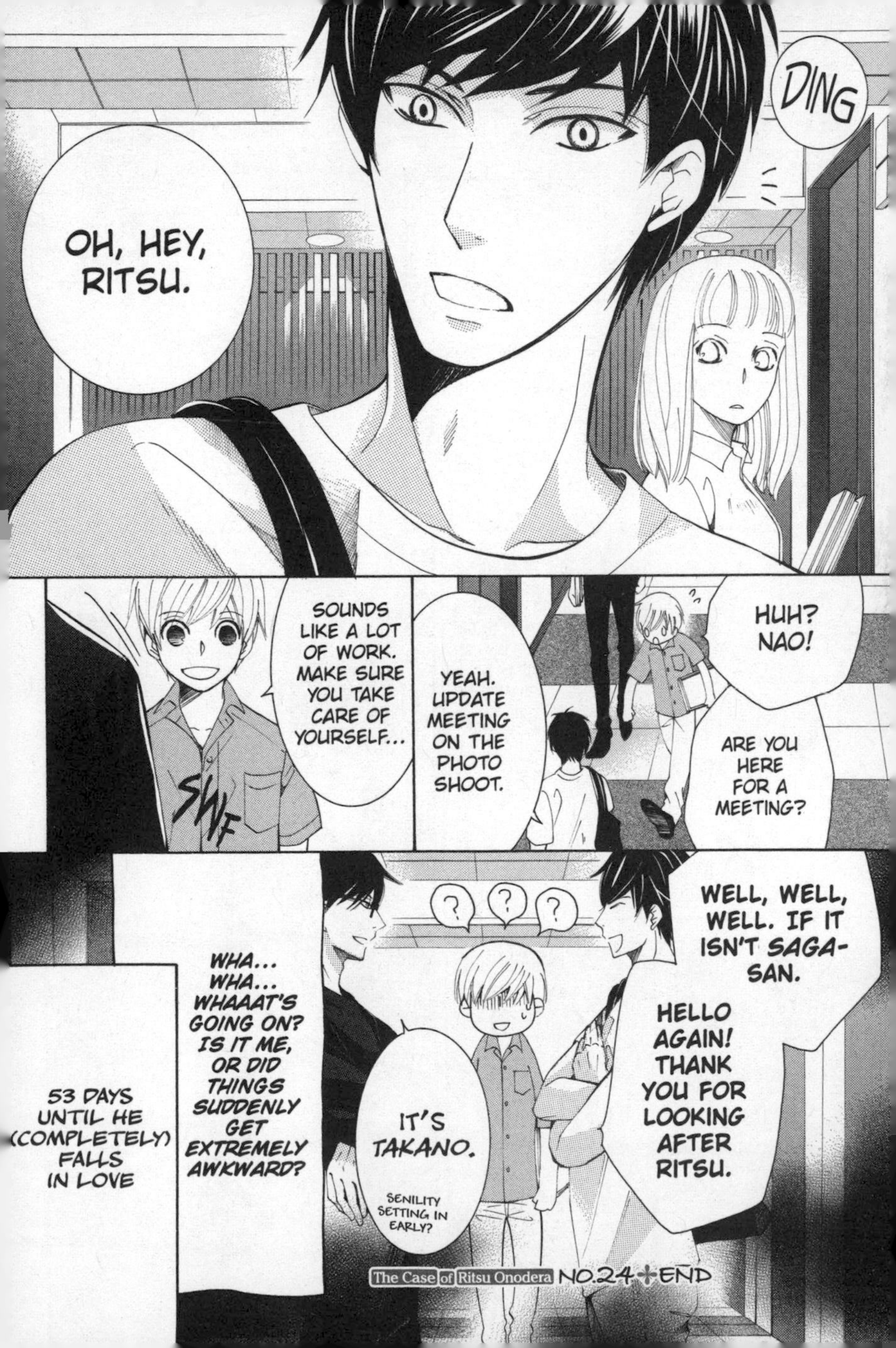
DING
OH, HEY, RITSU.
HUH? NAO!
ARE YOU HERE FOR A MEETING?
YEAH. UPDATE MEETING ON THE PHOTO SHOOT.
SOUNDS LIKE A LOT OF WORK. MAKE SURE YOU TAKE CARE OF YOURSELF...
SWF
WELL, WELL, WELL. IF IT ISN'T SAGA-SAN.
HELLO AGAIN! THANK YOU FOR LOOKING AFTER RITSU.
?
?
?
IT'S TAKANO.
SENILITY SETTING IN EARLY?
WHA... WHA... WHAAAT'S GOING ON? IS IT ME, OR DID THINGS SUDDENLY GET EXTREMELY AWKWARD?
53 DAYS UNTIL HE (COMPLETELY) FALLS IN LOVE
The Case of Ritsu Onodera NO.24 END

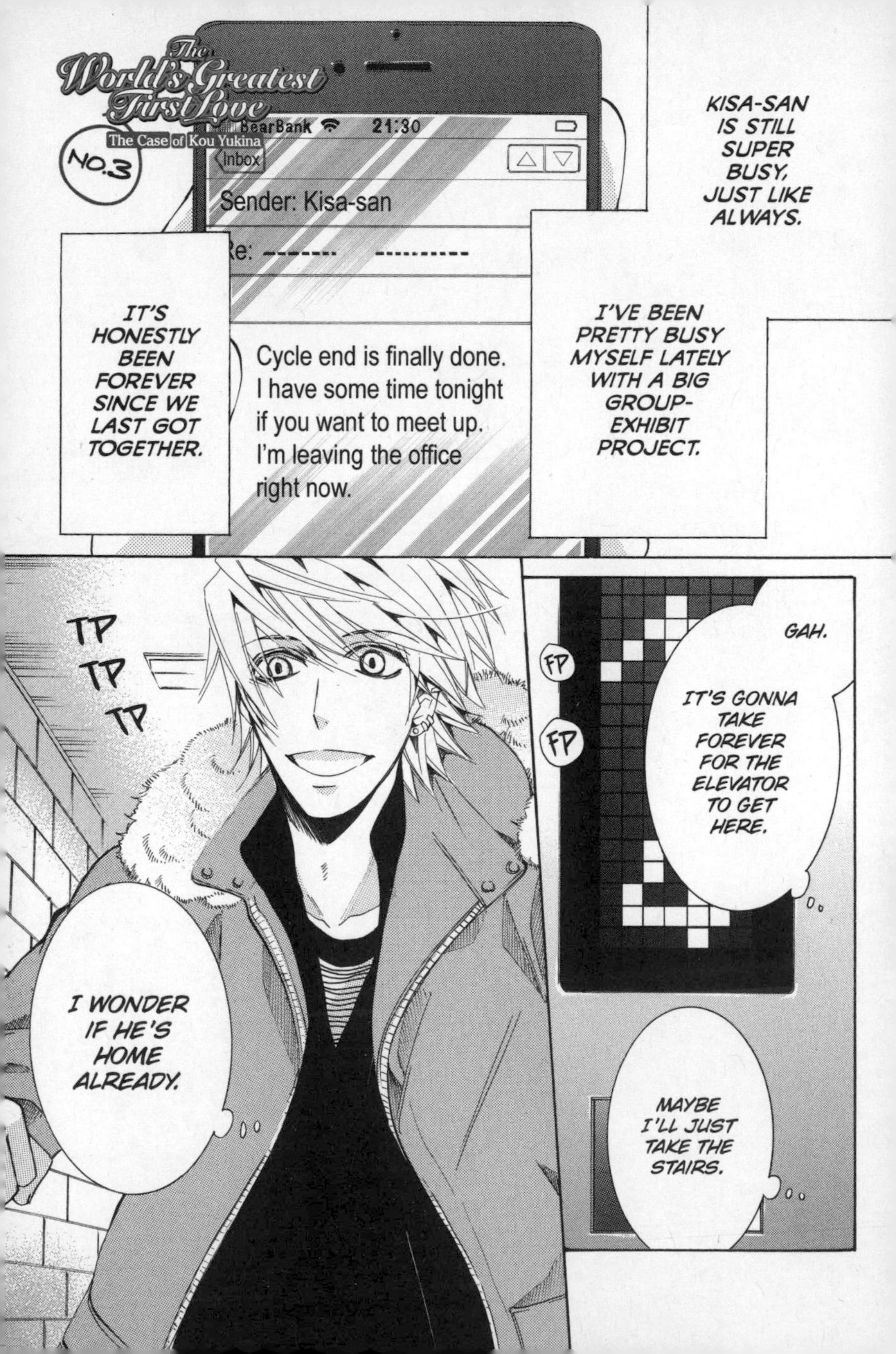
The World's Greatest First Love
The Case of Kou Yukina
NO.3
KISA-SAN IS STILL SUPER BUSY, JUST LIKE ALWAYS.
I'VE BEEN PRETTY BUSY MYSELF LATELY WITH A BIG GROUP-EXHIBIT PROJECT.
BearBank 21:30
Inbox
Sender: Kisa-san
Re:
Cycle end is finally done. I have some time tonight if you want to meet up. I'm leaving the office right now.
IT'S HONESTLY BEEN FOREVER SINCE WE LAST GOT TOGETHER.
GAH.
IT'S GONNA TAKE FOREVER FOR THE ELEVATOR TO GET HERE.
FP
FP
MAYBE I'LL JUST TAKE THE STAIRS.
TP
TP
TP
I WONDER IF HE'S HOME ALREADY.

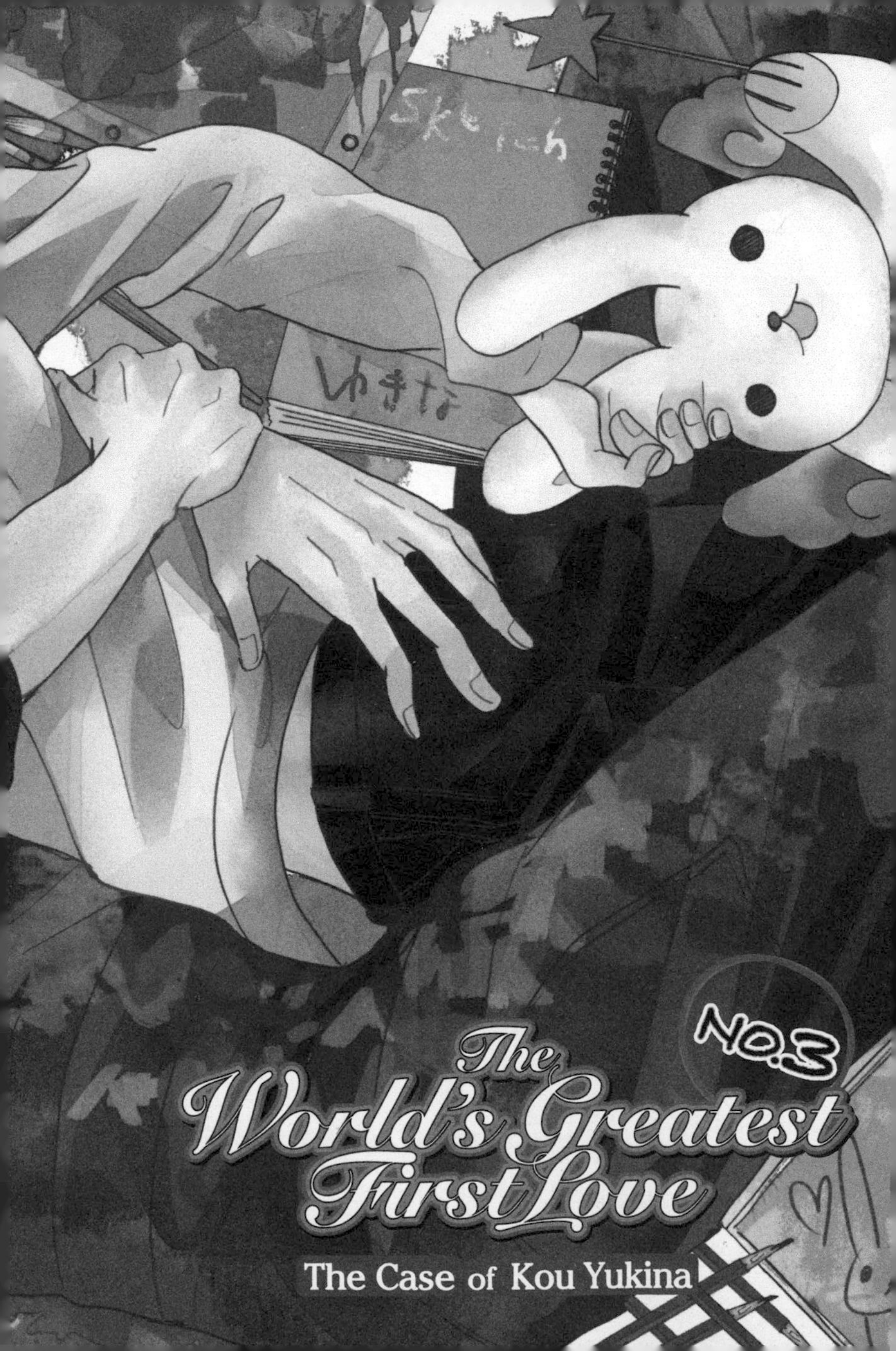
Sketch
ゆきな
NO.3
The World's Greatest First Love
The Case of Kou Yukina

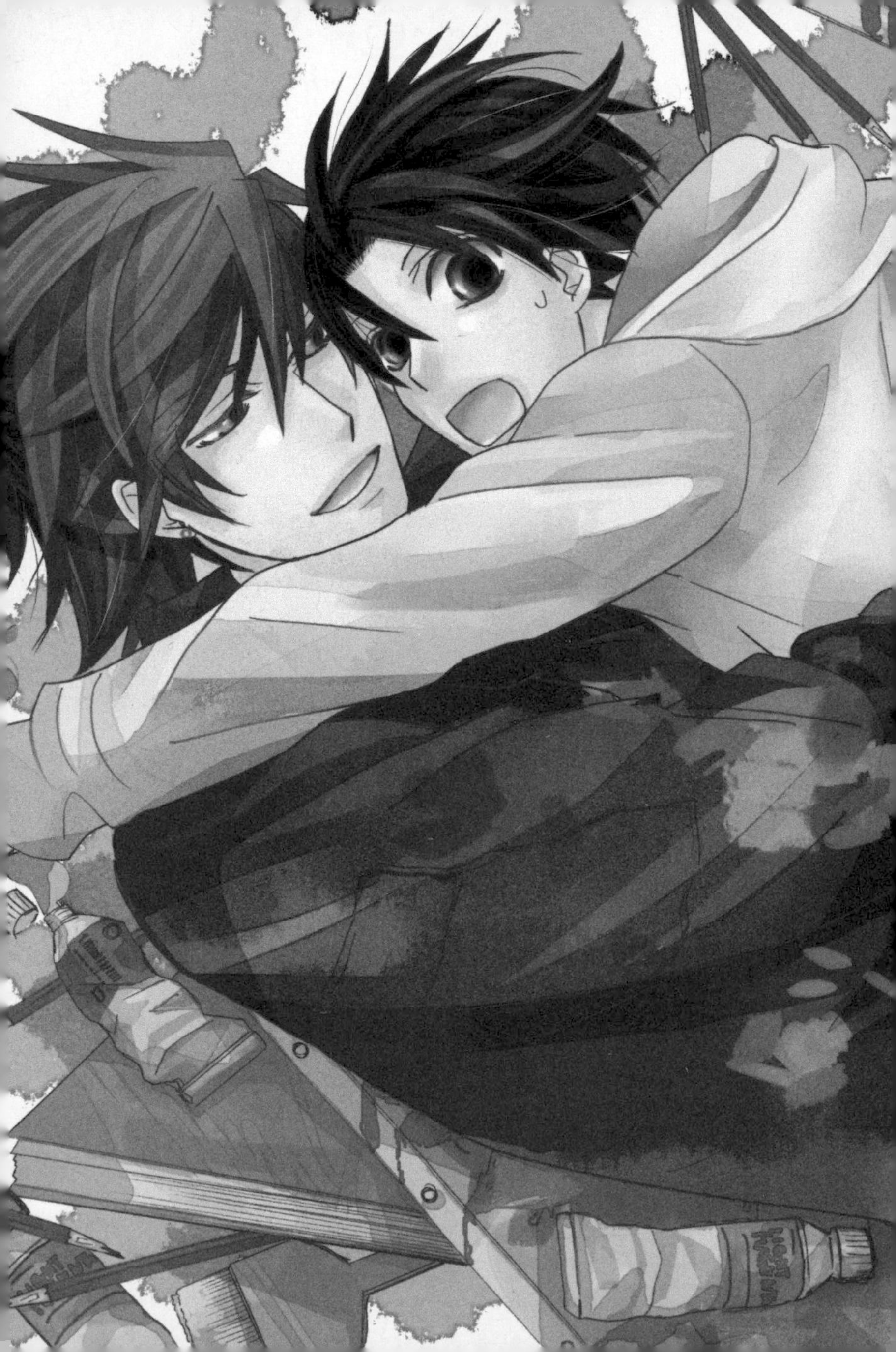

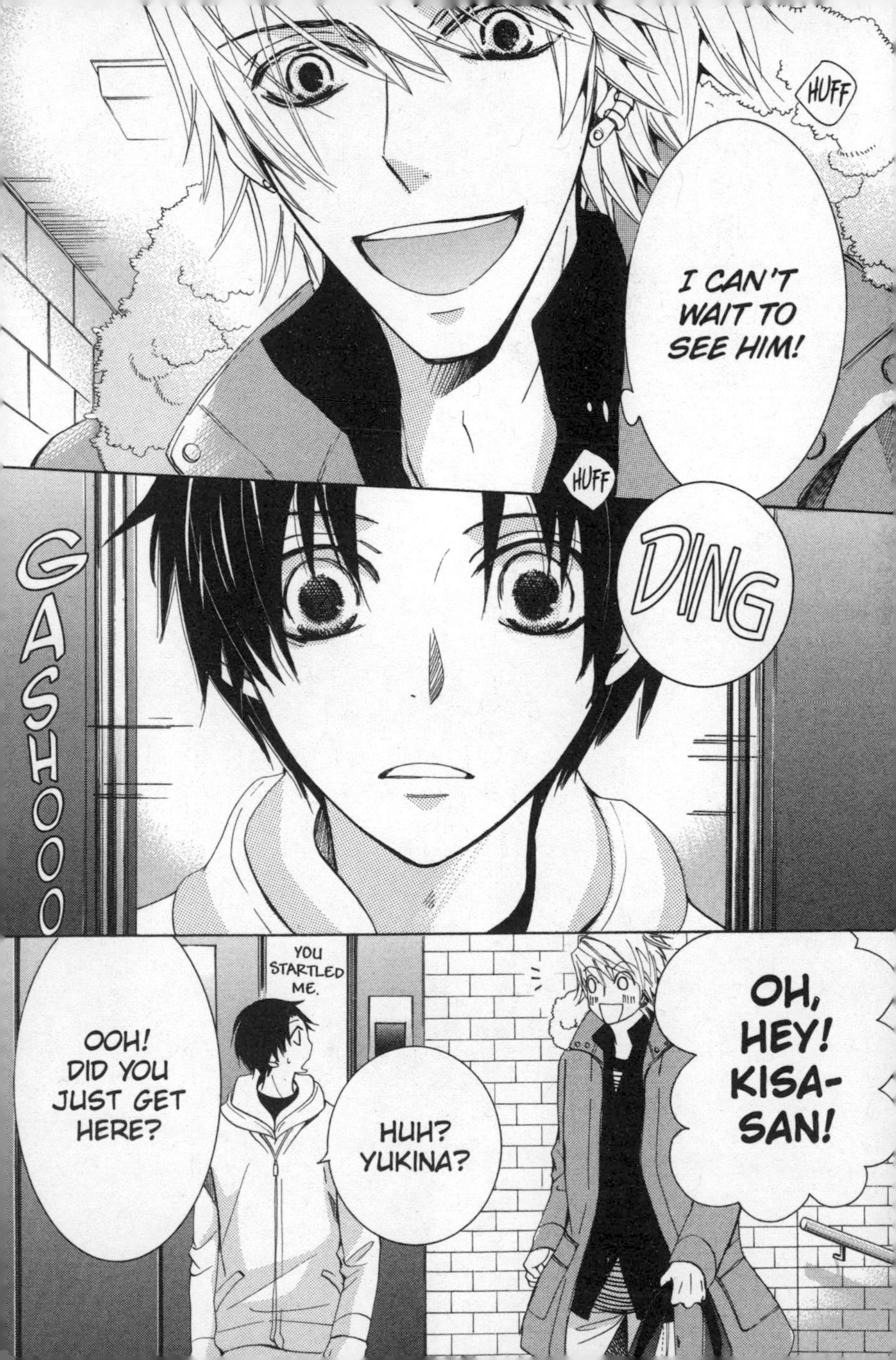
HUFF
I CAN'T WAIT TO SEE HIM!
HUFF
DING
GASHOOO
OH, HEY! KISA-SAN!
HUH? YUKINA?
YOU STARTLED ME.
OOH! DID YOU JUST GET HERE?

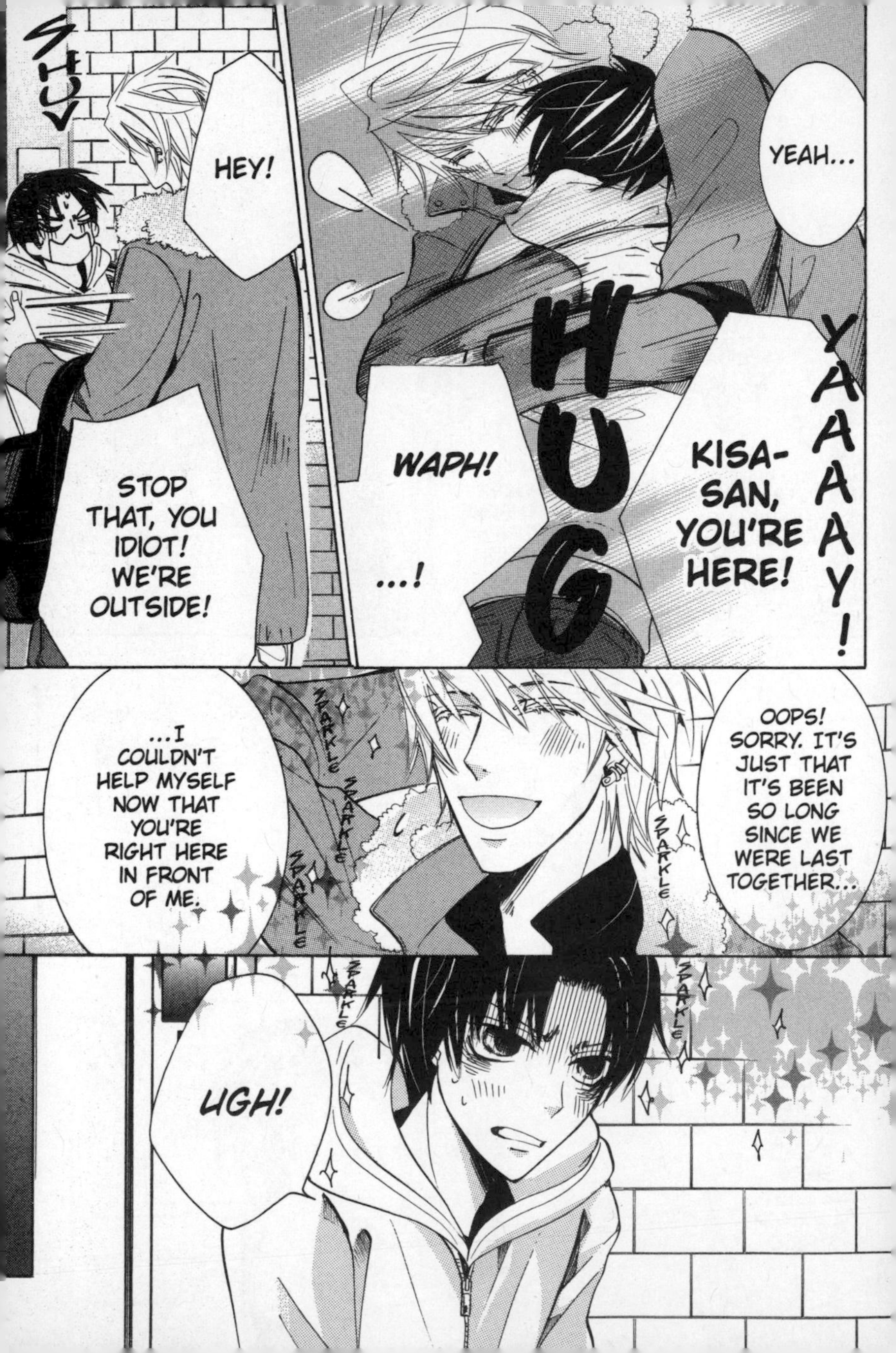
YEAH...
YAAAAY!
KISA-SAN, YOU'RE HERE!
HUG
WAPH!
...!
SHUV
HEY!
STOP THAT, YOU IDIOT! WE'RE OUTSIDE!
OOPS! SORRY. IT'S JUST THAT IT'S BEEN SO LONG SINCE WE WERE LAST TOGETHER...
SPARKLE SPARKLE SPARKLE SPARKLE
...I COULDN'T HELP MYSELF NOW THAT YOU'RE RIGHT HERE IN FRONT OF ME.
SPARKLE SPARKLE
UGH!

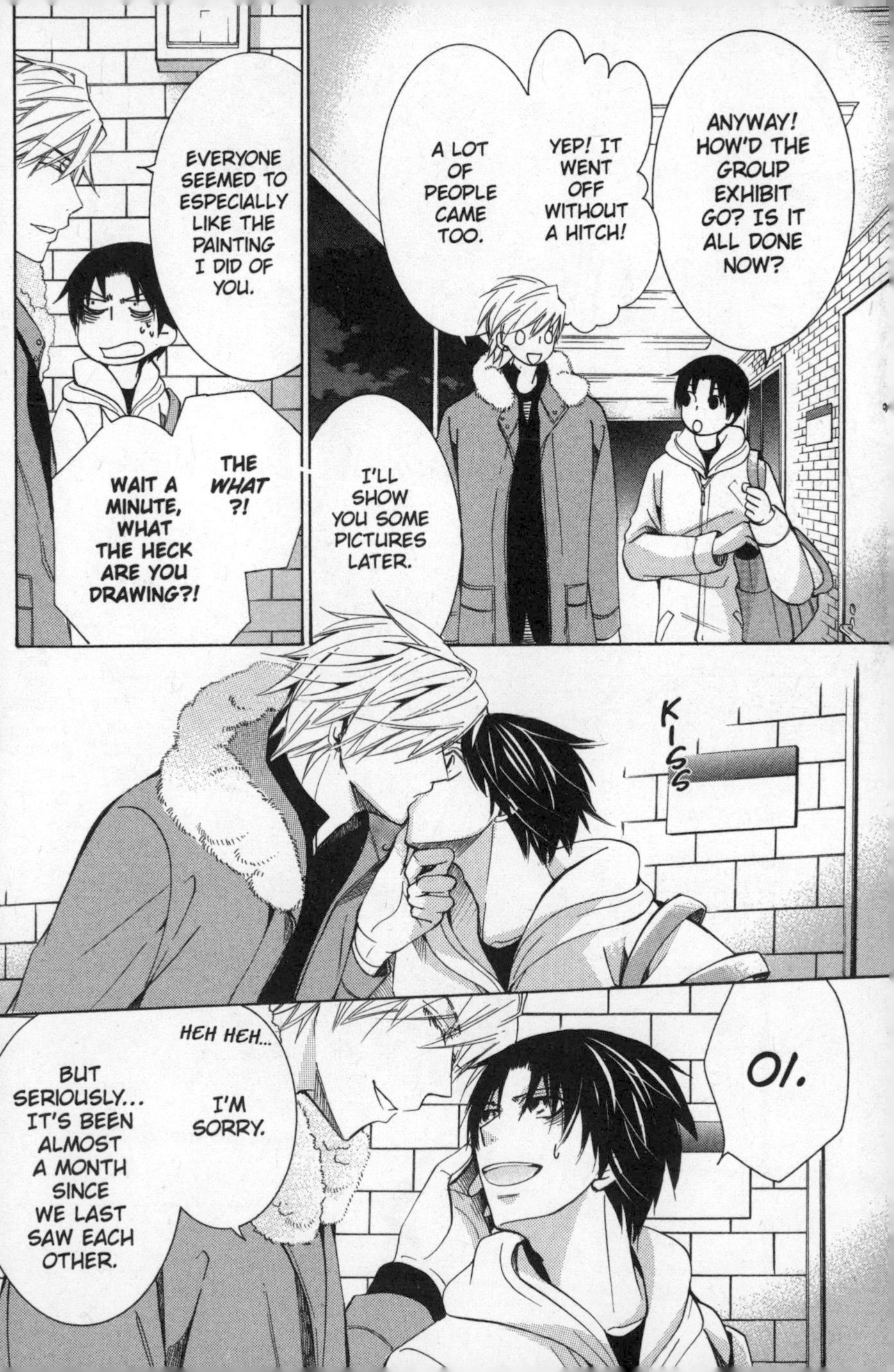
ANYWAY! HOW'D THE GROUP EXHIBIT GO? IS IT ALL DONE NOW?
YEP! IT WENT OFF WITHOUT A HITCH!
A LOT OF PEOPLE CAME TOO.
I'LL SHOW YOU SOME PICTURES LATER.
EVERYONE SEEMED TO ESPECIALLY LIKE THE PAINTING I DID OF YOU.
THE *WHAT* ?!
WAIT A MINUTE, WHAT THE HECK ARE YOU DRAWING?!
KISS
OI.
I'M SORRY.
HEH HEH...
BUT SERIOUSLY... IT'S BEEN ALMOST A MONTH SINCE WE LAST SAW EACH OTHER.

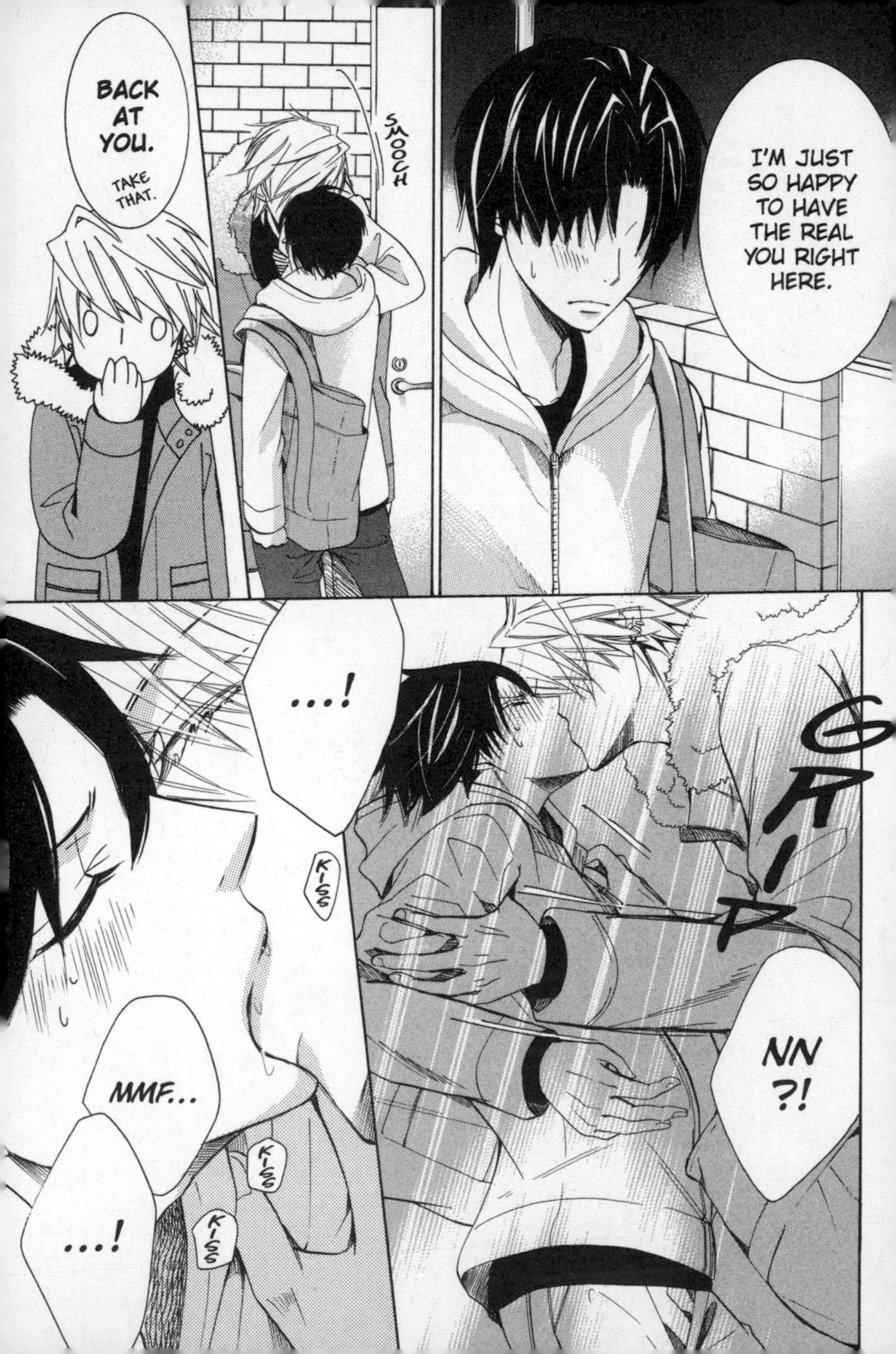
I'M JUST SO HAPPY TO HAVE THE REAL YOU RIGHT HERE.
SMOOCH
BACK AT YOU.
TAKE THAT.
GRIP
NN?!
...!
KISS
MMF...
KISS
KISS
...!

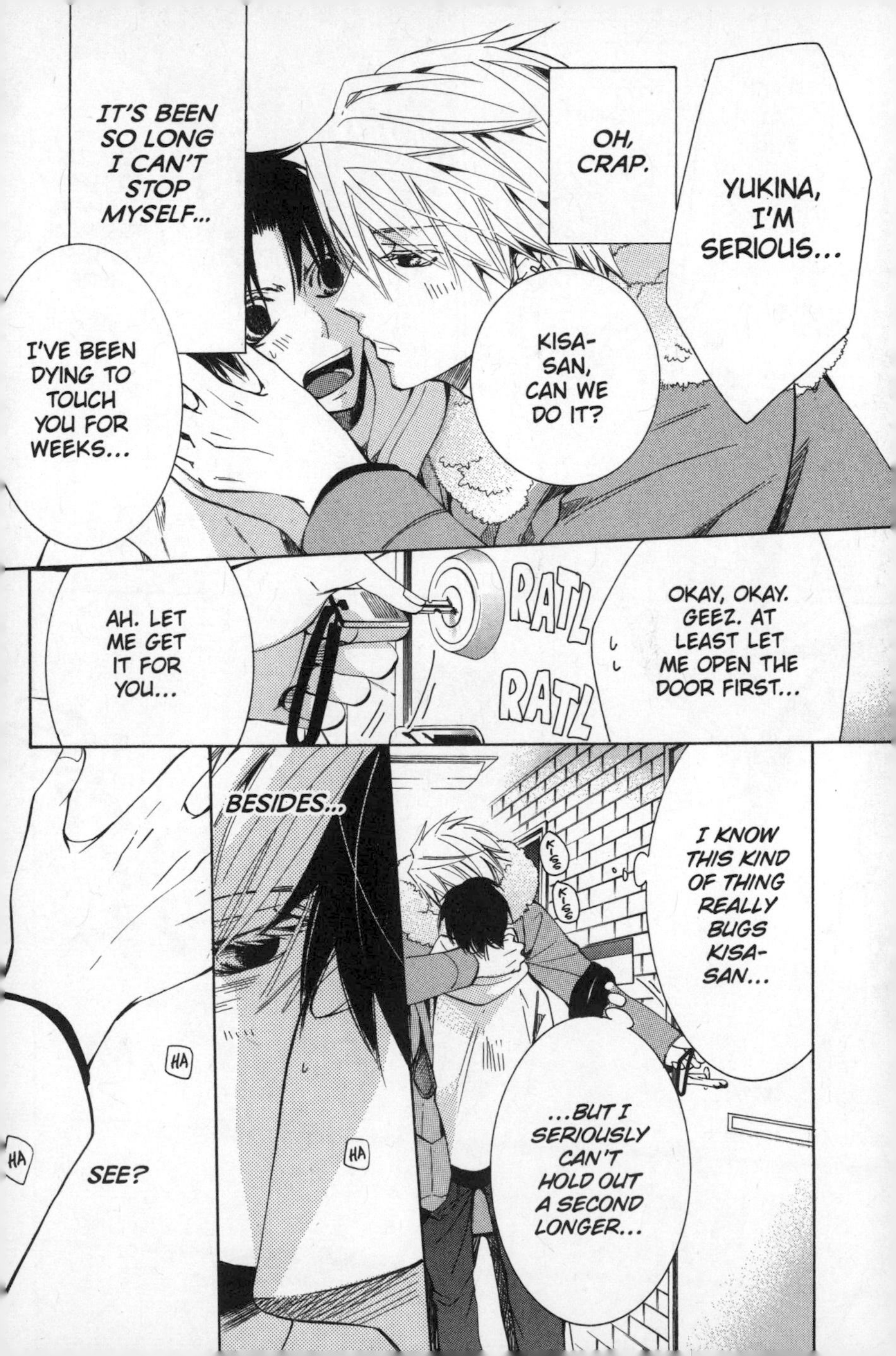
YUKINA, I'M SERIOUS...
OH, CRAP.
KISA-SAN, CAN WE DO IT?
IT'S BEEN SO LONG I CAN'T STOP MYSELF...
I'VE BEEN DYING TO TOUCH YOU FOR WEEKS...
OKAY, OKAY. GEEZ. AT LEAST LET ME OPEN THE DOOR FIRST...
RATL
RATL
AH. LET ME GET IT FOR YOU...
I KNOW THIS KIND OF THING REALLY BUGS KISA-SAN...
KISS
KISS
...BUT I SERIOUSLY CAN'T HOLD OUT A SECOND LONGER...
BESIDES...
HA
HA
HA
SEE?

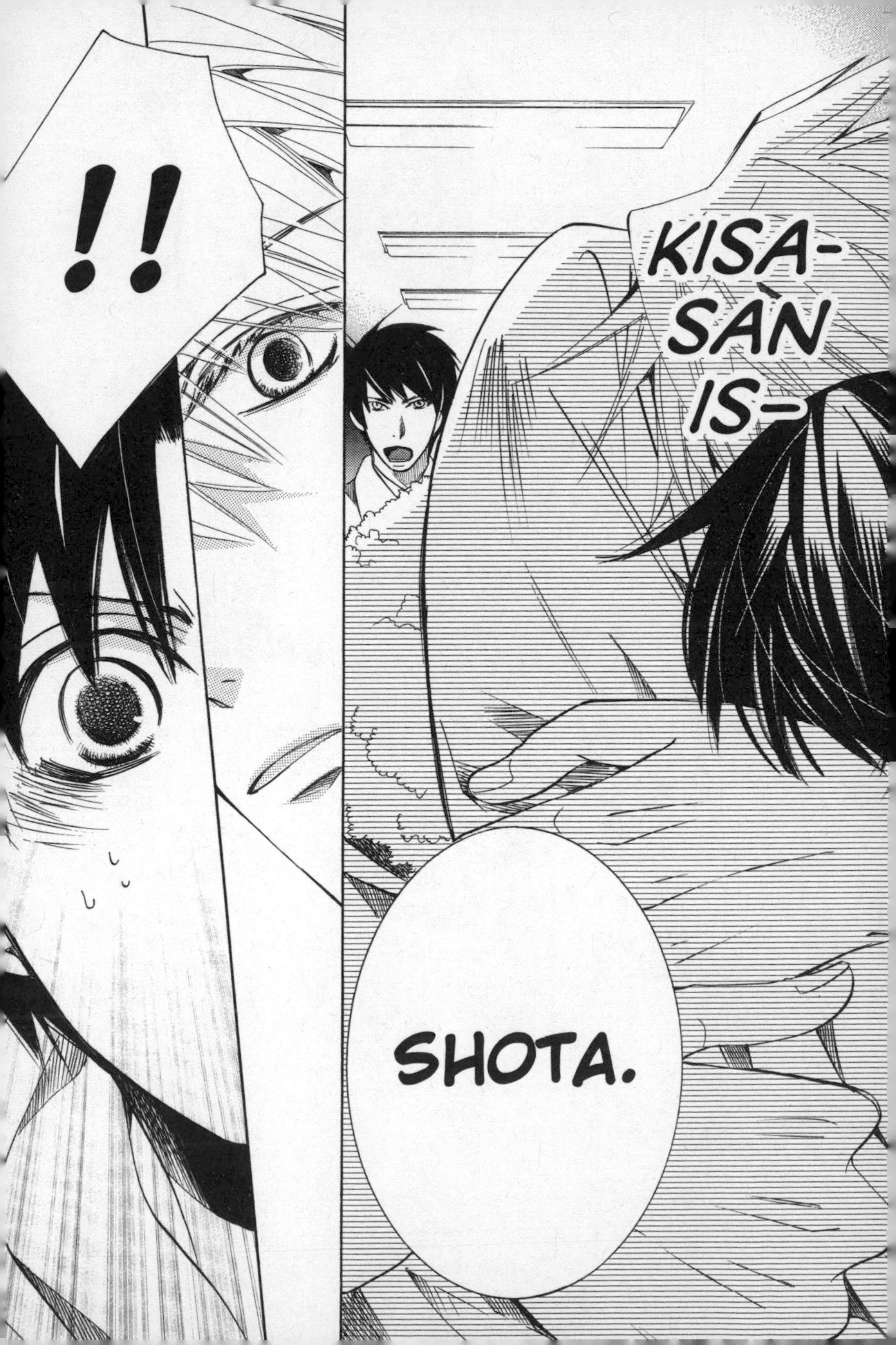
KISA-SAN IS—
SHOTA.
!!

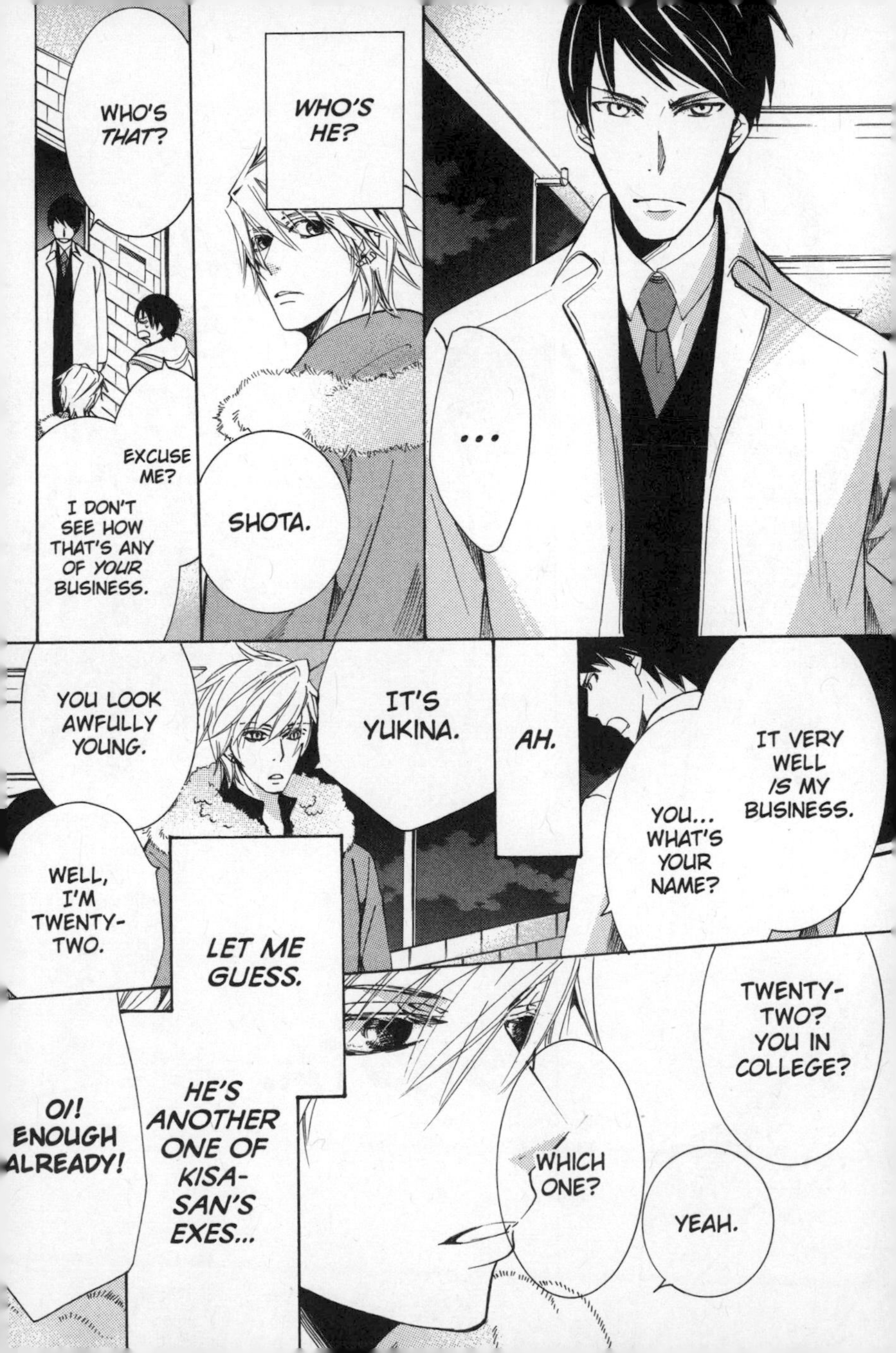

...
WHO'S HE?
SHOTA.
WHO'S THAT?
EXCUSE ME?
I DON'T SEE HOW THAT'S ANY OF YOUR BUSINESS.
IT VERY WELL IS MY BUSINESS.
YOU... WHAT'S YOUR NAME?
AH.
IT'S YUKINA.
YOU LOOK AWFULLY YOUNG.
WELL, I'M TWENTY-TWO.
LET ME GUESS.
TWENTY-TWO? YOU IN COLLEGE?
YEAH.
WHICH ONE?
HE'S ANOTHER ONE OF KISA-SAN'S EXES...
OI! ENOUGH ALREADY!

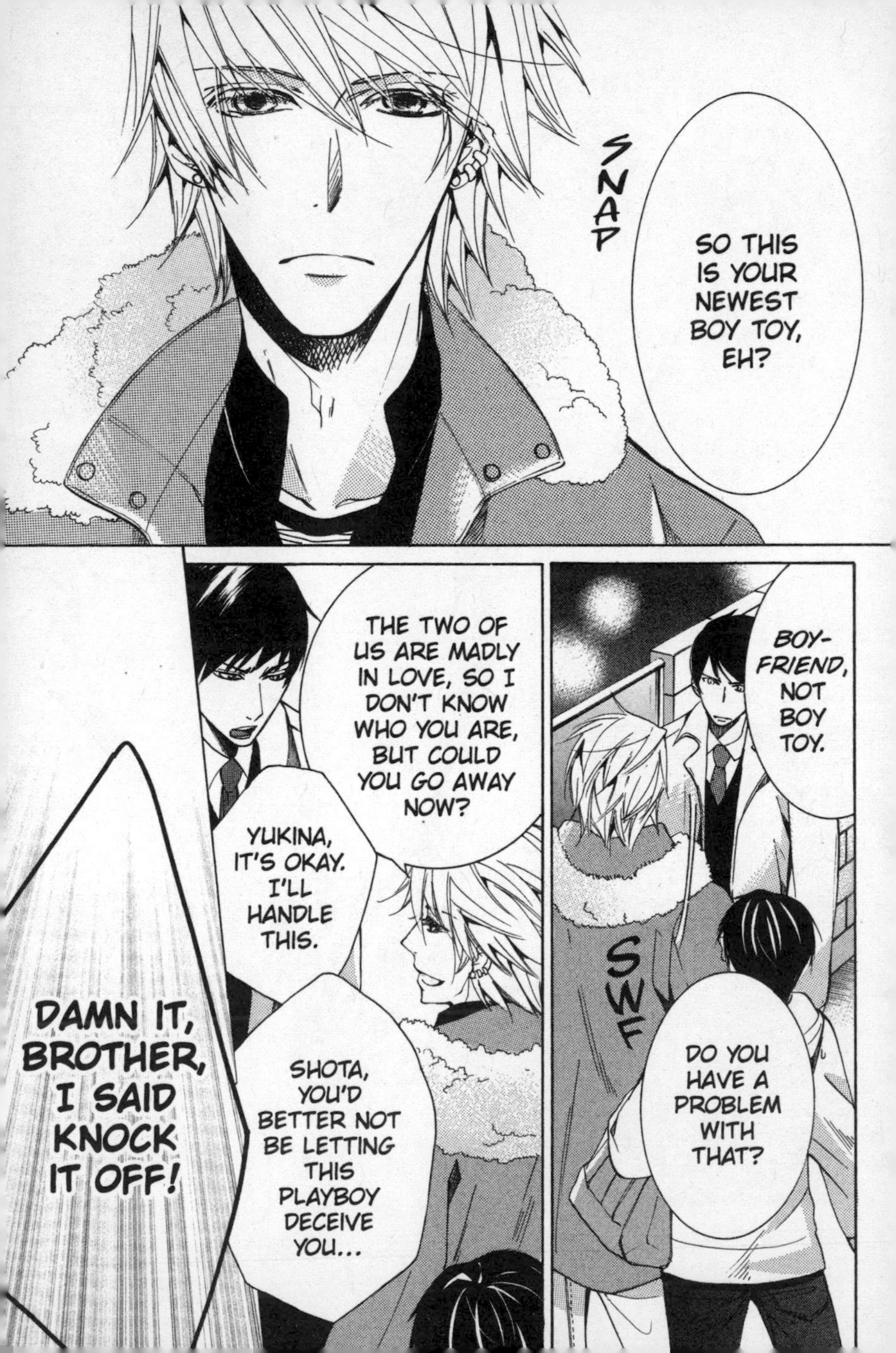
SO THIS IS YOUR NEWEST BOY TOY, EH?
SNAP
BOY-FRIEND, NOT BOY TOY.
SWF
DO YOU HAVE A PROBLEM WITH THAT?
THE TWO OF US ARE MADLY IN LOVE, SO I DON'T KNOW WHO YOU ARE, BUT COULD YOU GO AWAY NOW?
YUKINA, IT'S OKAY. I'LL HANDLE THIS.
SHOTA, YOU'D BETTER NOT BE LETTING THIS PLAYBOY DECEIVE YOU...
DAMN IT, BROTHER, I SAID KNOCK IT OFF!

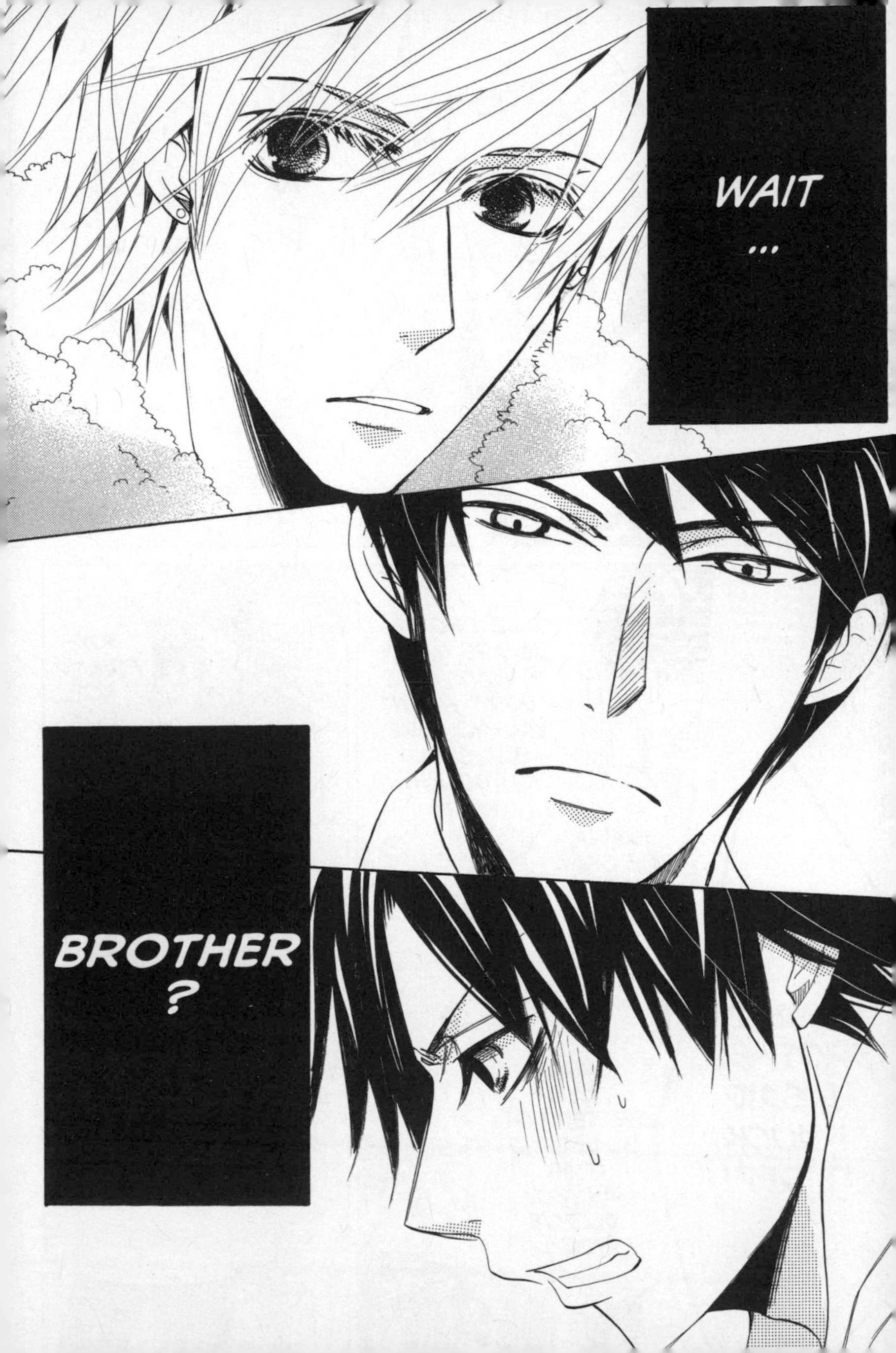
WAIT ...
BROTHER ?

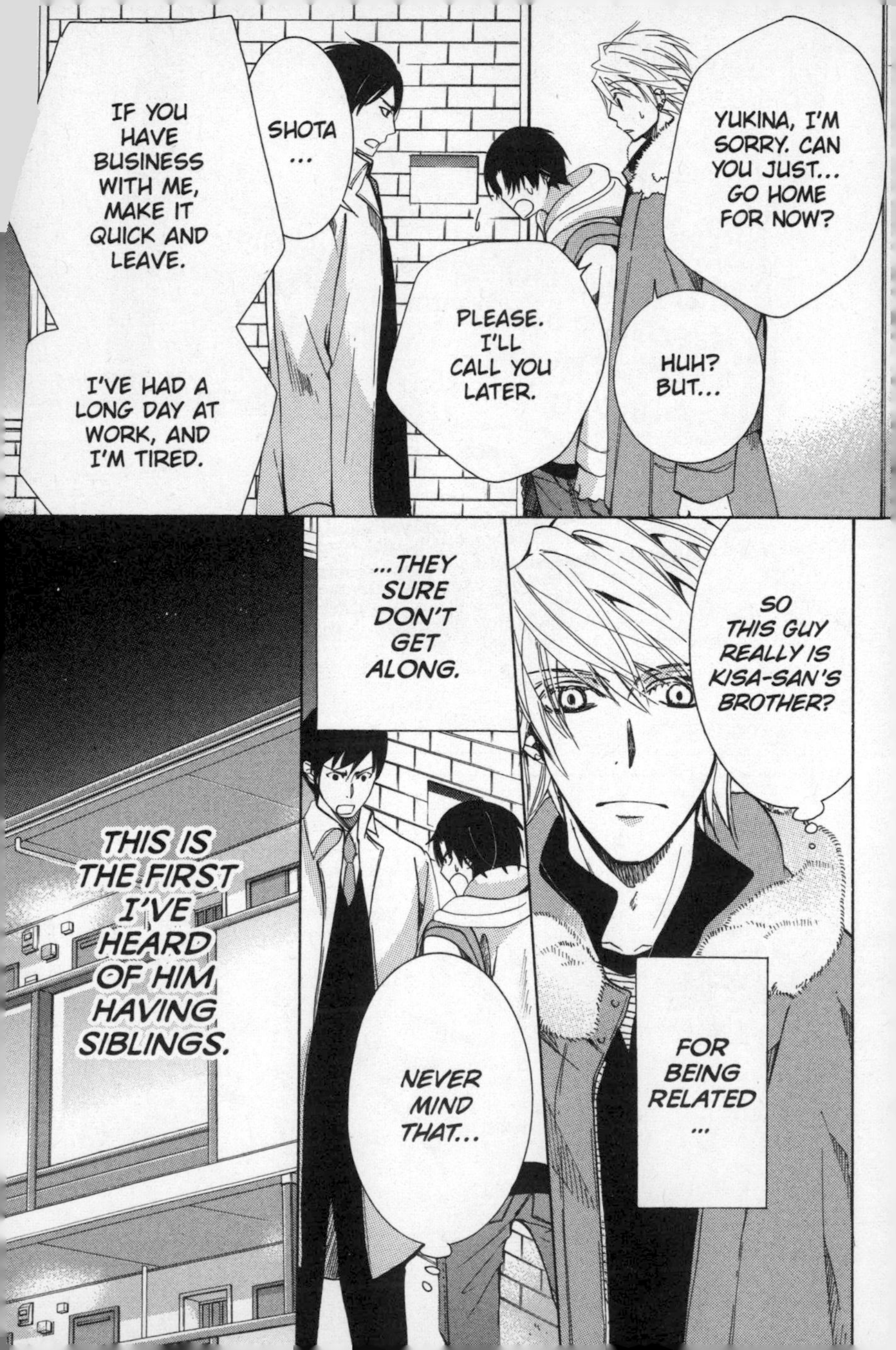
YUKINA, I'M SORRY. CAN YOU JUST... GO HOME FOR NOW?
HUH? BUT...
PLEASE. I'LL CALL YOU LATER.
SHOTA ...
IF YOU HAVE BUSINESS WITH ME, MAKE IT QUICK AND LEAVE.
I'VE HAD A LONG DAY AT WORK, AND I'M TIRED.
SO THIS GUY REALLY IS KISA-SAN'S BROTHER?
...THEY SURE DON'T GET ALONG.
FOR BEING RELATED ...
NEVER MIND THAT...
THIS IS THE FIRST I'VE HEARD OF HIM HAVING SIBLINGS.

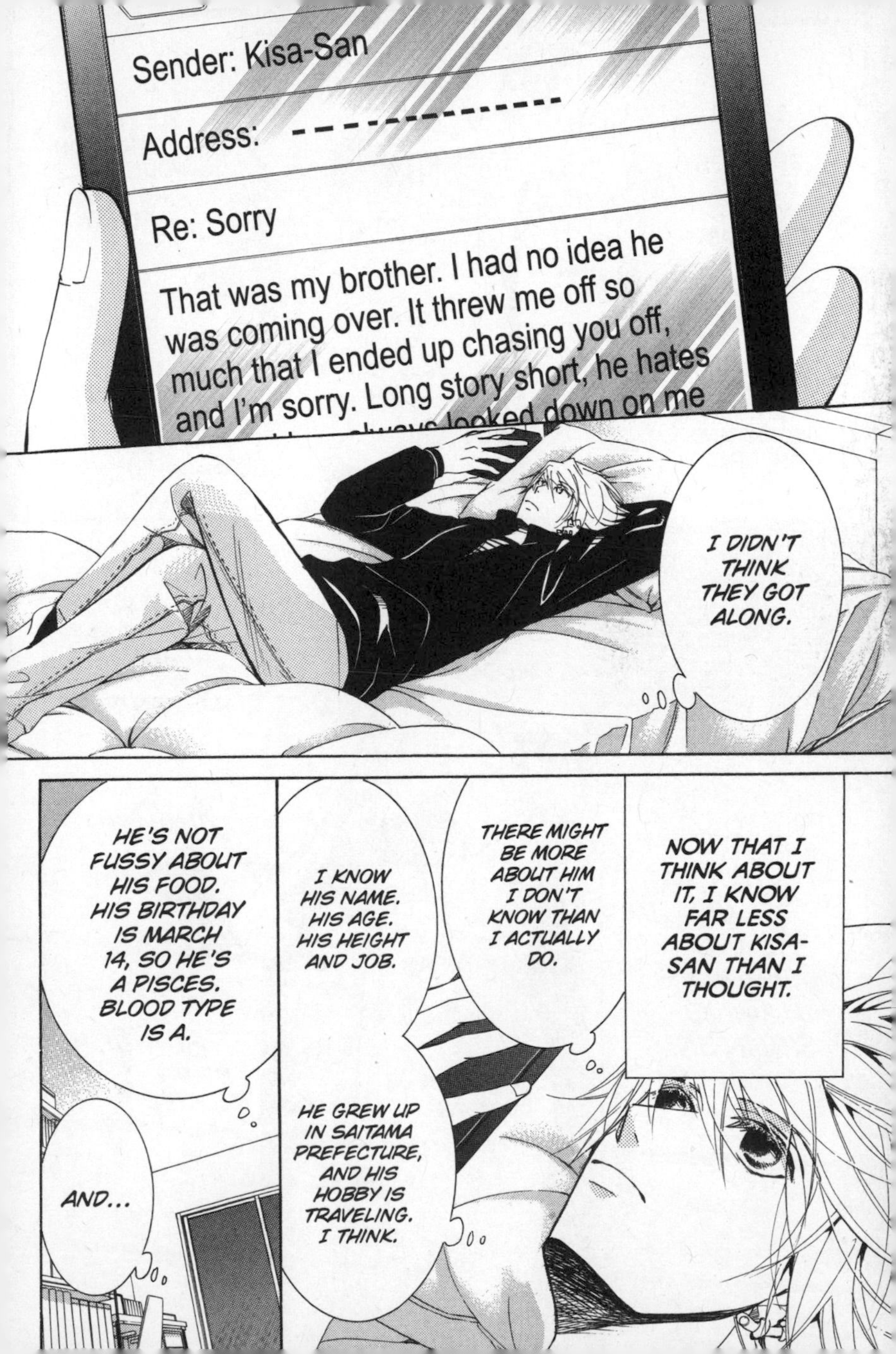
Sender: Kisa-San
Address: ----------------
Re: Sorry
That was my brother. I had no idea he was coming over. It threw me off so much that I ended up chasing you off, and I'm sorry. Long story short, he hates
I DIDN'T THINK THEY GOT ALONG.
NOW THAT I THINK ABOUT IT, I KNOW FAR LESS ABOUT KISA-SAN THAN I THOUGHT.
THERE MIGHT BE MORE ABOUT HIM I DON'T KNOW THAN I ACTUALLY DO.
I KNOW HIS NAME. HIS AGE. HIS HEIGHT AND JOB.
HE'S NOT FUSSY ABOUT HIS FOOD. HIS BIRTHDAY IS MARCH 14, SO HE'S A PISCES. BLOOD TYPE IS A.
HE GREW UP IN SAITAMA PREFECTURE, AND HIS HOBBY IS TRAVELING. I THINK.
AND...

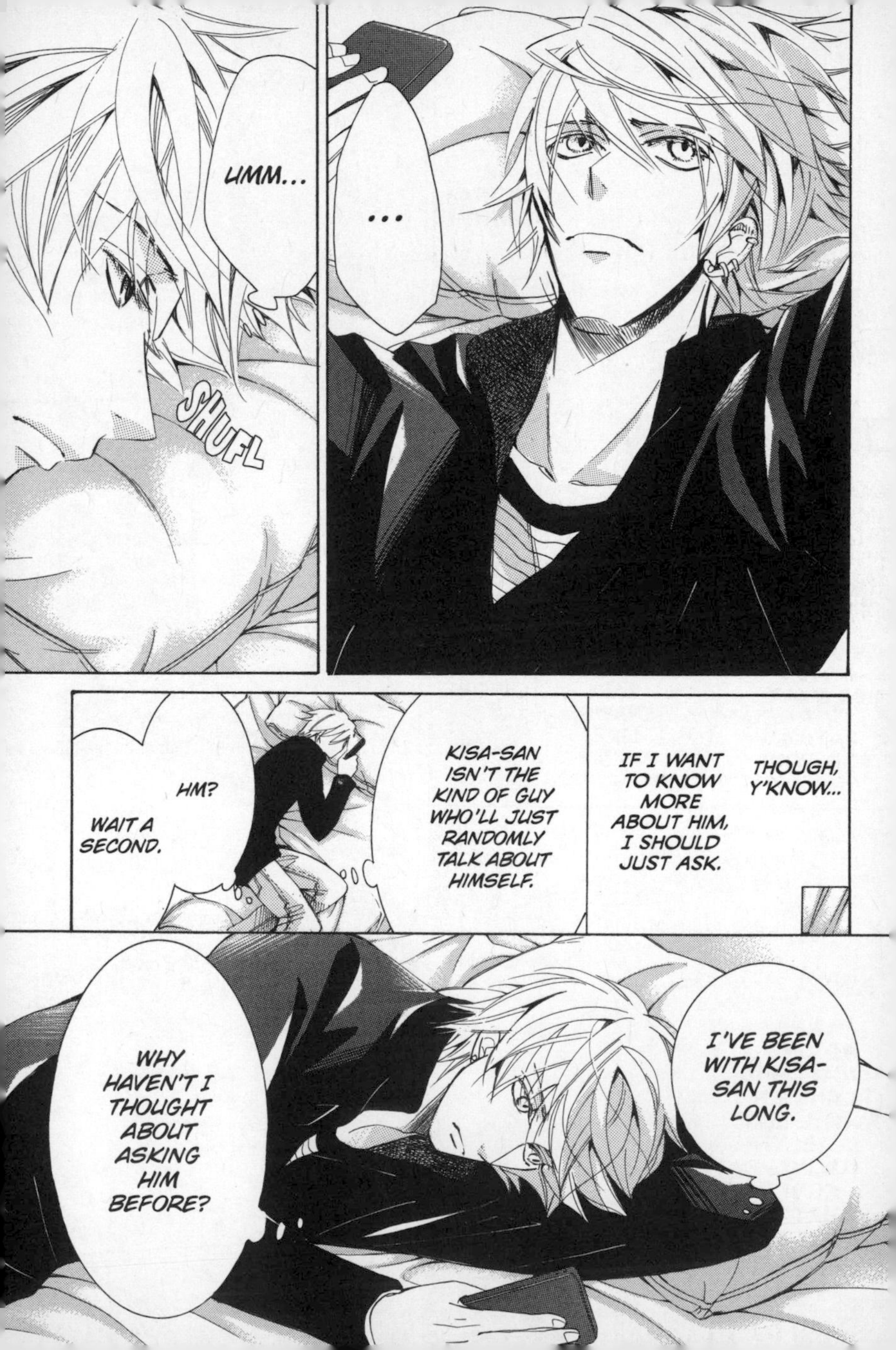
...
UMM...
SHUFL
THOUGH, Y'KNOW...
IF I WANT TO KNOW MORE ABOUT HIM, I SHOULD JUST ASK.
KISA-SAN ISN'T THE KIND OF GUY WHO'LL JUST RANDOMLY TALK ABOUT HIMSELF.
HM?
WAIT A SECOND.
I'VE BEEN WITH KISA-SAN THIS LONG.
WHY HAVEN'T I THOUGHT ABOUT ASKING HIM BEFORE?

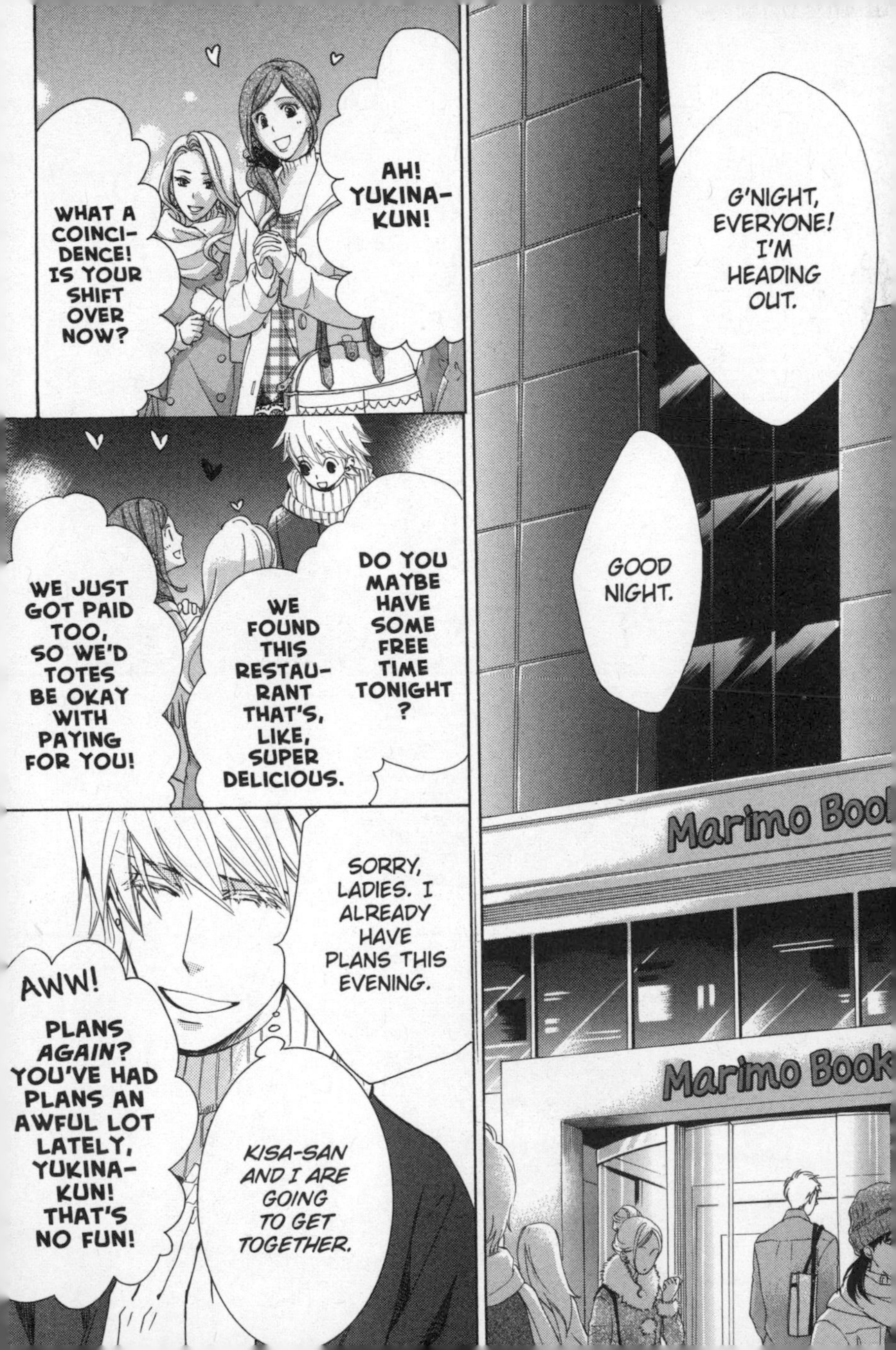
G'NIGHT, EVERYONE! I'M HEADING OUT.
GOOD NIGHT.
AH! YUKINA-KUN!
WHAT A COINCIDENCE! IS YOUR SHIFT OVER NOW?
DO YOU MAYBE HAVE SOME FREE TIME TONIGHT?
WE FOUND THIS RESTAURANT THAT'S, LIKE, SUPER DELICIOUS.
WE JUST GOT PAID TOO, SO WE'D TOTES BE OKAY WITH PAYING FOR YOU!
SORRY, LADIES. I ALREADY HAVE PLANS THIS EVENING.
KISA-SAN AND I ARE GOING TO GET TOGETHER.
AWW!
PLANS *AGAIN*? YOU'VE HAD PLANS AN AWFUL LOT LATELY, YUKINA-KUN! THAT'S NO FUN!

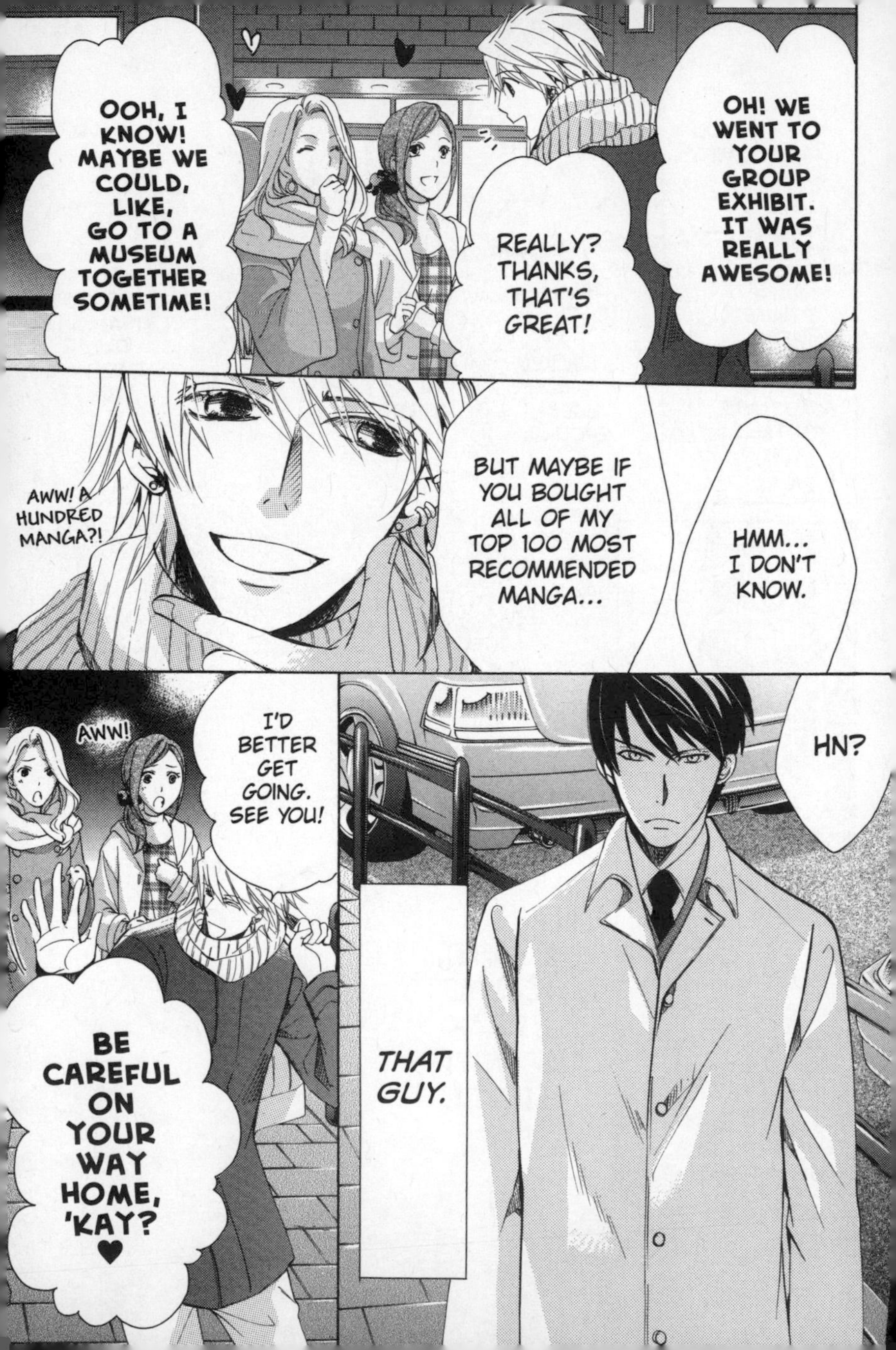
OH! WE WENT TO YOUR GROUP EXHIBIT. IT WAS REALLY AWESOME!
REALLY? THANKS, THAT'S GREAT!
OOH, I KNOW! MAYBE WE COULD, LIKE, GO TO A MUSEUM TOGETHER SOMETIME!
HMM... I DON'T KNOW.
BUT MAYBE IF YOU BOUGHT ALL OF MY TOP 100 MOST RECOMMENDED MANGA...
AWW! A HUNDRED MANGA?!
HN?
THAT GUY.
I'D BETTER GET GOING. SEE YOU!
AWW!
BE CAREFUL ON YOUR WAY HOME, 'KAY? ♥

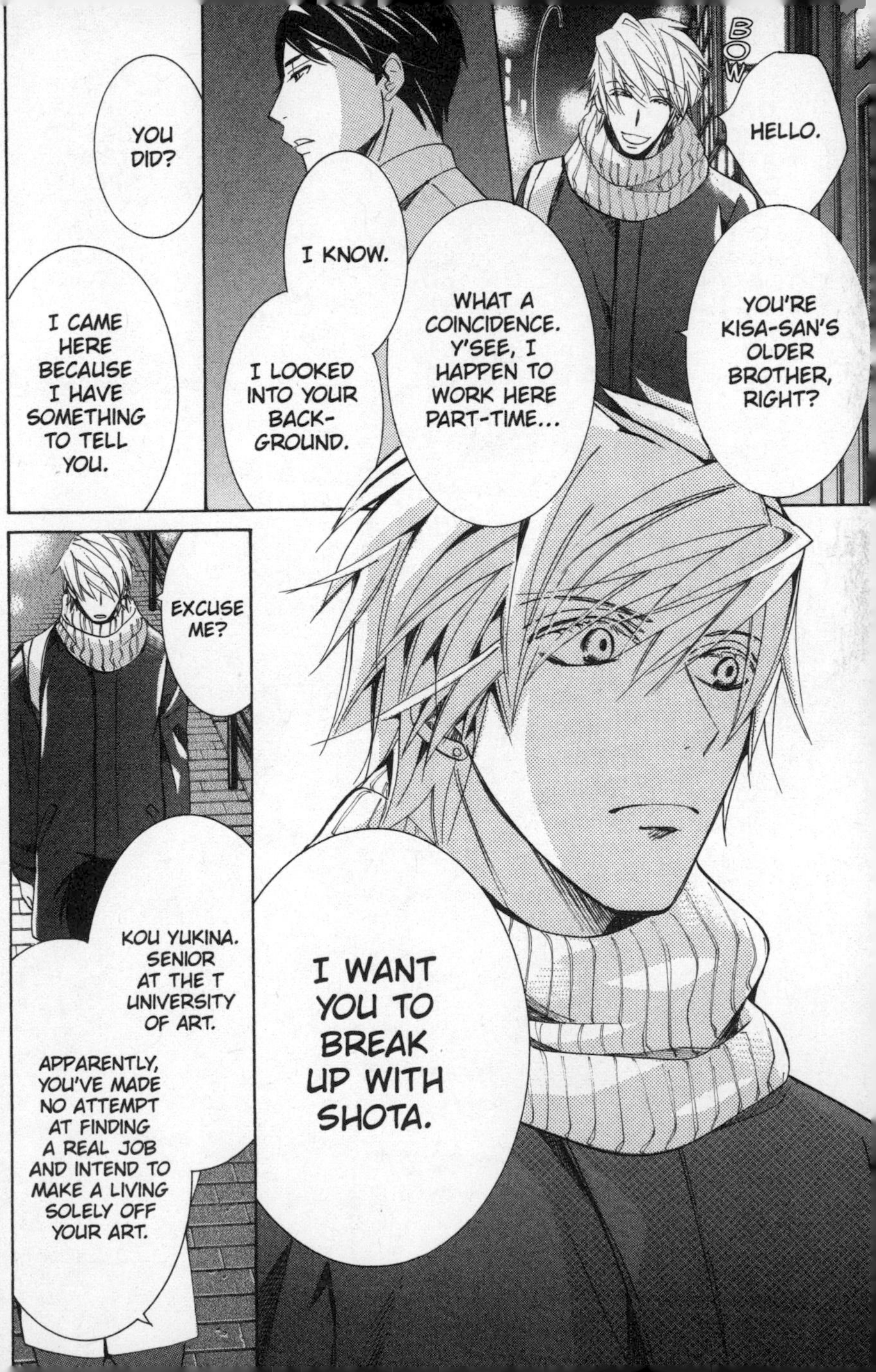
BOW
HELLO.
YOU'RE KISA-SAN'S OLDER BROTHER, RIGHT?
WHAT A COINCIDENCE. Y'SEE, I HAPPEN TO WORK HERE PART-TIME...
I KNOW.
I LOOKED INTO YOUR BACK-GROUND.
YOU DID?
I CAME HERE BECAUSE I HAVE SOMETHING TO TELL YOU.
I WANT YOU TO BREAK UP WITH SHOTA.
EXCUSE ME?
KOU YUKINA. SENIOR AT THE T UNIVERSITY OF ART.
APPARENTLY, YOU'VE MADE NO ATTEMPT AT FINDING A REAL JOB AND INTEND TO MAKE A LIVING SOLELY OFF YOUR ART.

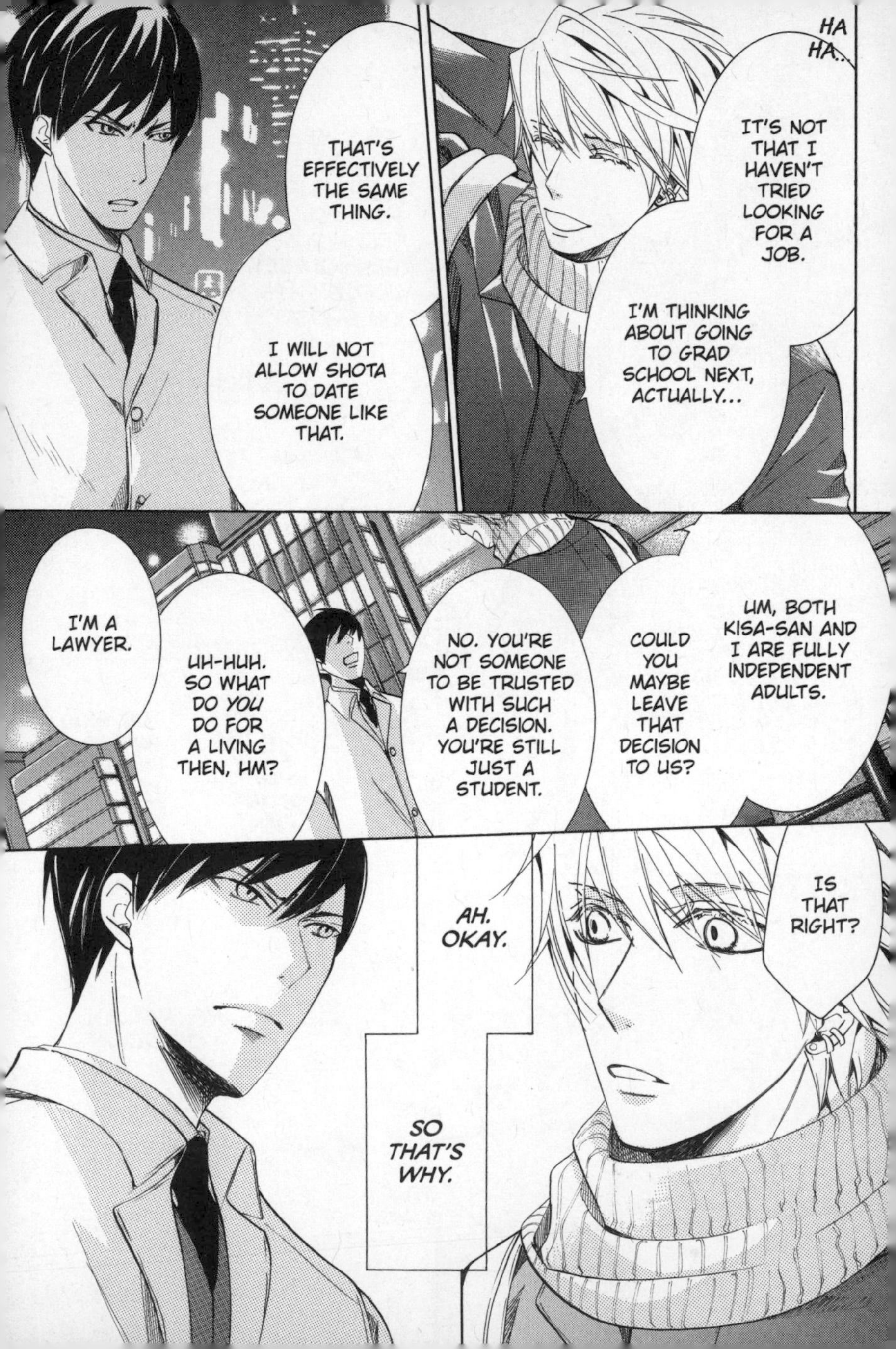
HA HA...
IT'S NOT THAT I HAVEN'T TRIED LOOKING FOR A JOB.
I'M THINKING ABOUT GOING TO GRAD SCHOOL NEXT, ACTUALLY...
THAT'S EFFECTIVELY THE SAME THING.
I WILL NOT ALLOW SHOTA TO DATE SOMEONE LIKE THAT.
UM, BOTH KISA-SAN AND I ARE FULLY INDEPENDENT ADULTS.
COULD YOU MAYBE LEAVE THAT DECISION TO US?
NO. YOU'RE NOT SOMEONE TO BE TRUSTED WITH SUCH A DECISION. YOU'RE STILL JUST A STUDENT.
UH-HUH. SO WHAT DO *YOU* DO FOR A LIVING THEN, HM?
I'M A LAWYER.
IS THAT RIGHT?
AH. OKAY.
SO THAT'S WHY.

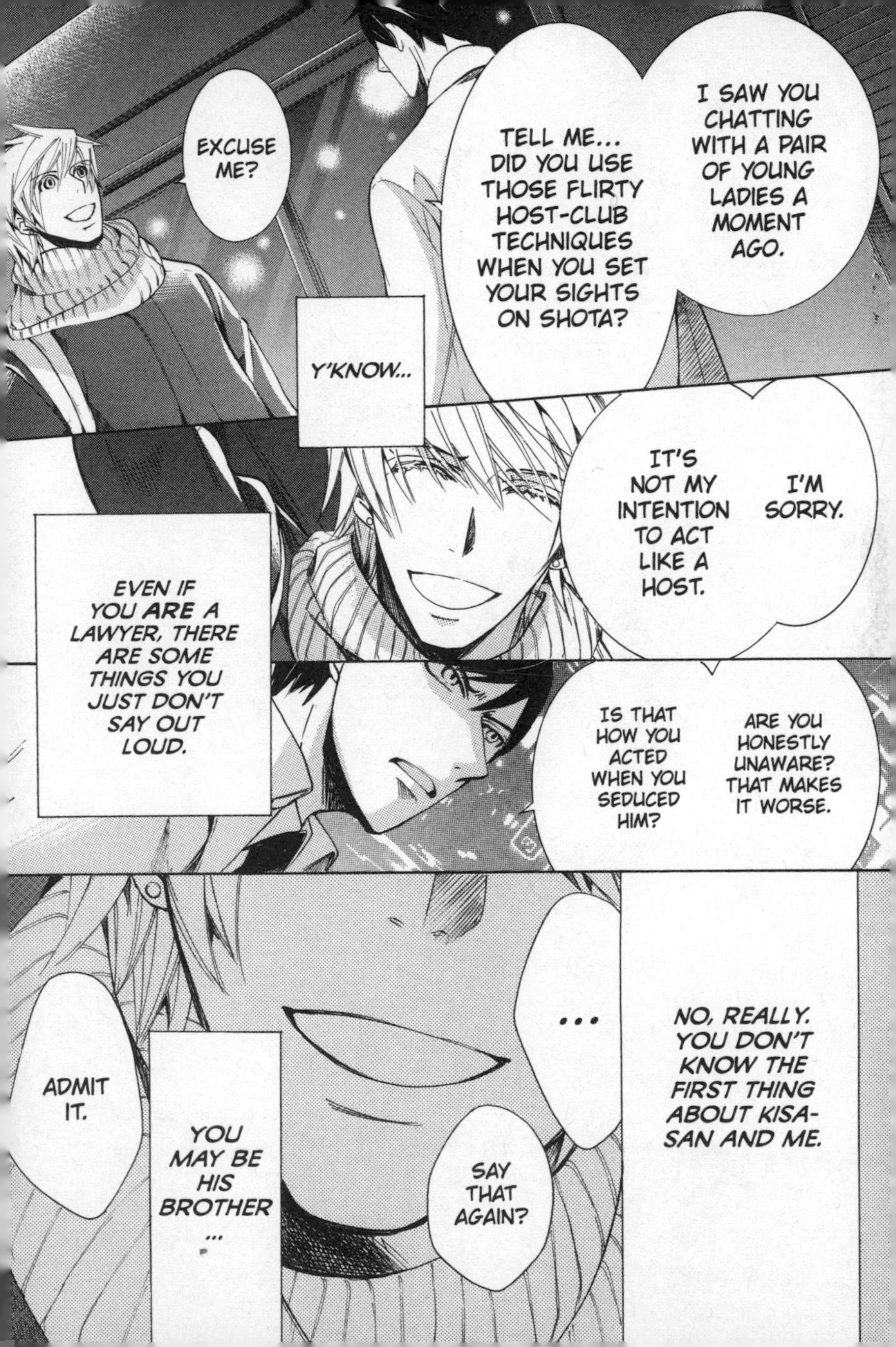
I SAW YOU CHATTING WITH A PAIR OF YOUNG LADIES A MOMENT AGO.
TELL ME... DID YOU USE THOSE FLIRTY HOST-CLUB TECHNIQUES WHEN YOU SET YOUR SIGHTS ON SHOTA?
EXCUSE ME?
Y'KNOW...
I'M SORRY.
IT'S NOT MY INTENTION TO ACT LIKE A HOST.
EVEN IF YOU ARE A LAWYER, THERE ARE SOME THINGS YOU JUST DON'T SAY OUT LOUD.
ARE YOU HONESTLY UNAWARE? THAT MAKES IT WORSE.
IS THAT HOW YOU ACTED WHEN YOU SEDUCED HIM?
NO, REALLY. YOU DON'T KNOW THE FIRST THING ABOUT KISA-SAN AND ME.
...
SAY THAT AGAIN?
YOU MAY BE HIS BROTHER...
ADMIT IT.

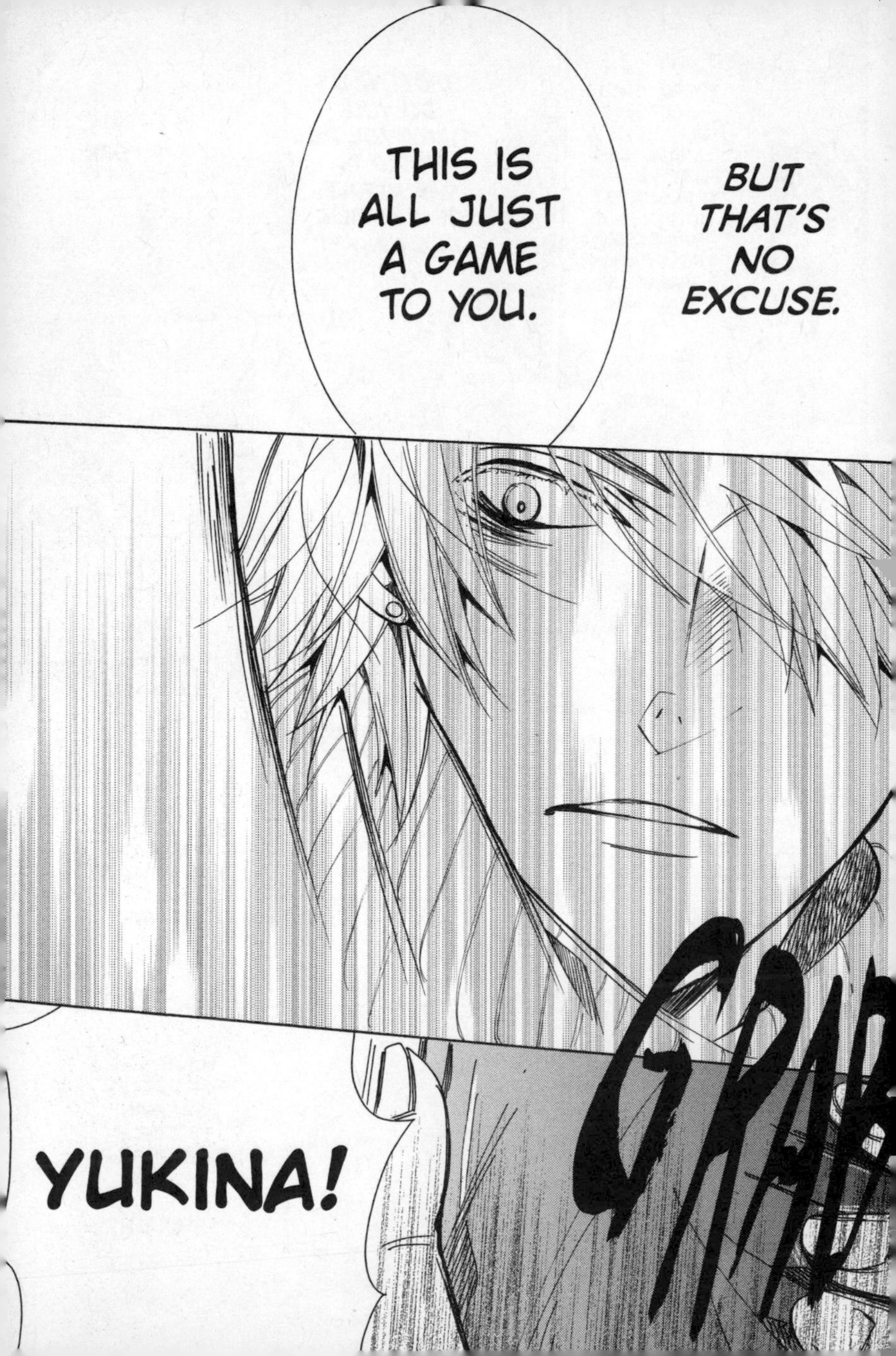
BUT THAT'S NO EXCUSE.
THIS IS ALL JUST A GAME TO YOU.
GRAB
YUKINA!

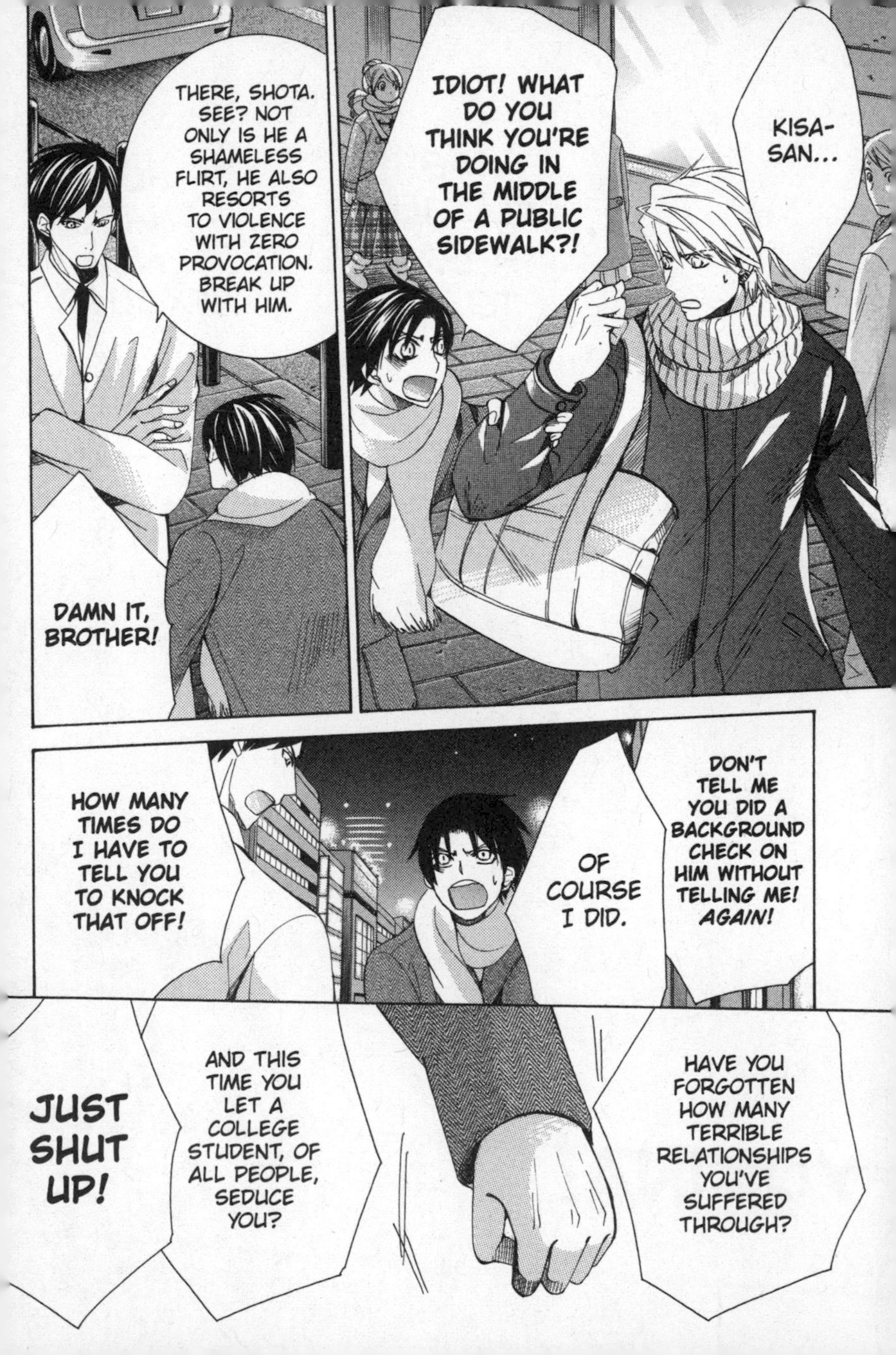
KISA-SAN...
IDIOT! WHAT DO YOU THINK YOU'RE DOING IN THE MIDDLE OF A PUBLIC SIDEWALK?!
THERE, SHOTA. SEE? NOT ONLY IS HE A SHAMELESS FLIRT, HE ALSO RESORTS TO VIOLENCE WITH ZERO PROVOCATION. BREAK UP WITH HIM.
DAMN IT, BROTHER!
DON'T TELL ME YOU DID A BACKGROUND CHECK ON HIM WITHOUT TELLING ME! *AGAIN!*
OF COURSE I DID.
HOW MANY TIMES DO I HAVE TO TELL YOU TO KNOCK THAT OFF!
HAVE YOU FORGOTTEN HOW MANY TERRIBLE RELATIONSHIPS YOU'VE SUFFERED THROUGH?
AND THIS TIME YOU LET A COLLEGE STUDENT, OF ALL PEOPLE, SEDUCE YOU?
JUST SHUT UP!

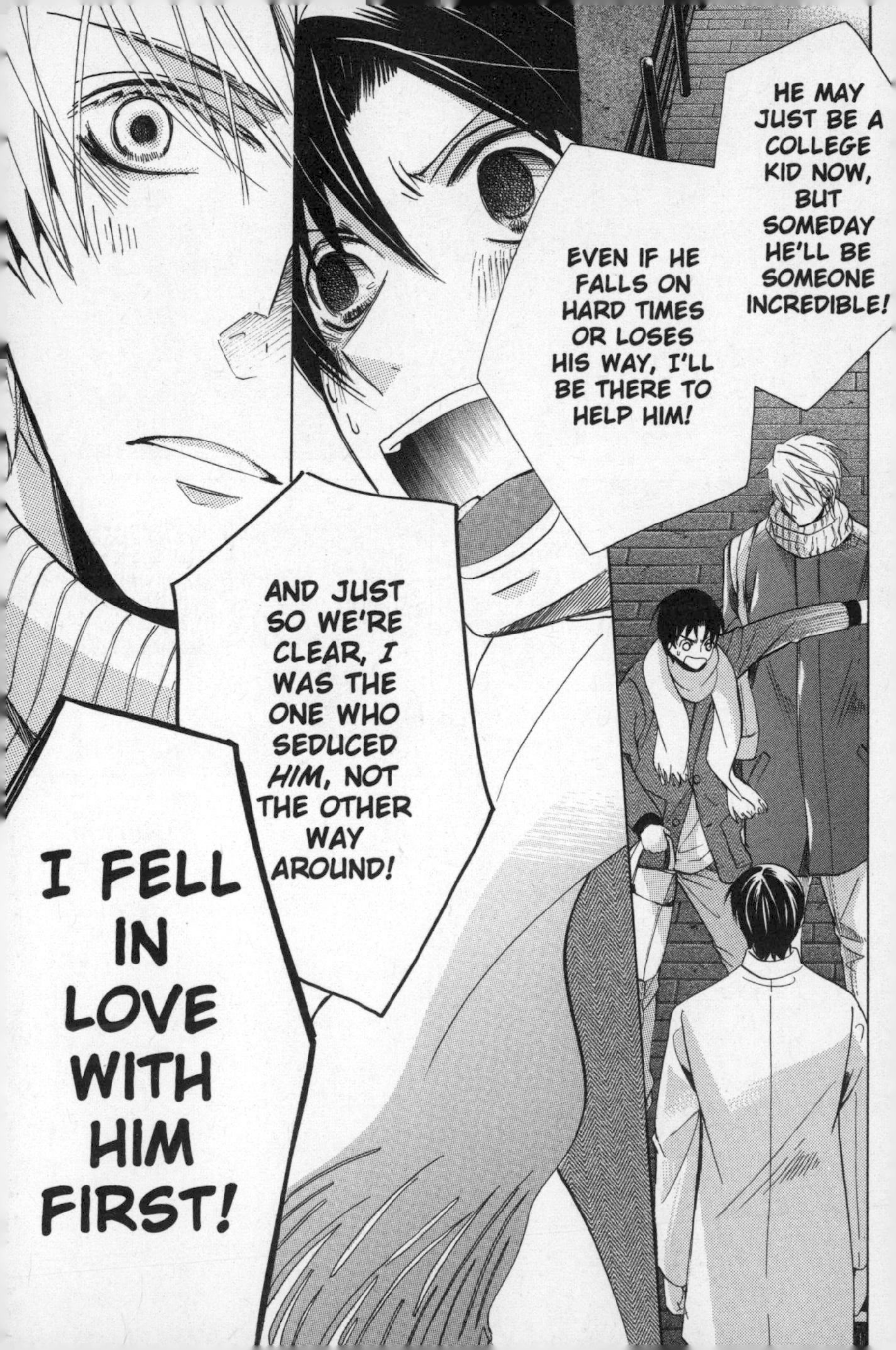
HE MAY JUST BE A COLLEGE KID NOW, BUT SOMEDAY HE'LL BE SOMEONE INCREDIBLE!
EVEN IF HE FALLS ON HARD TIMES OR LOSES HIS WAY, I'LL BE THERE TO HELP HIM!
AND JUST SO WE'RE CLEAR, *I* WAS THE ONE WHO SEDUCED *HIM*, NOT THE OTHER WAY AROUND!
I FELL IN LOVE WITH HIM FIRST!

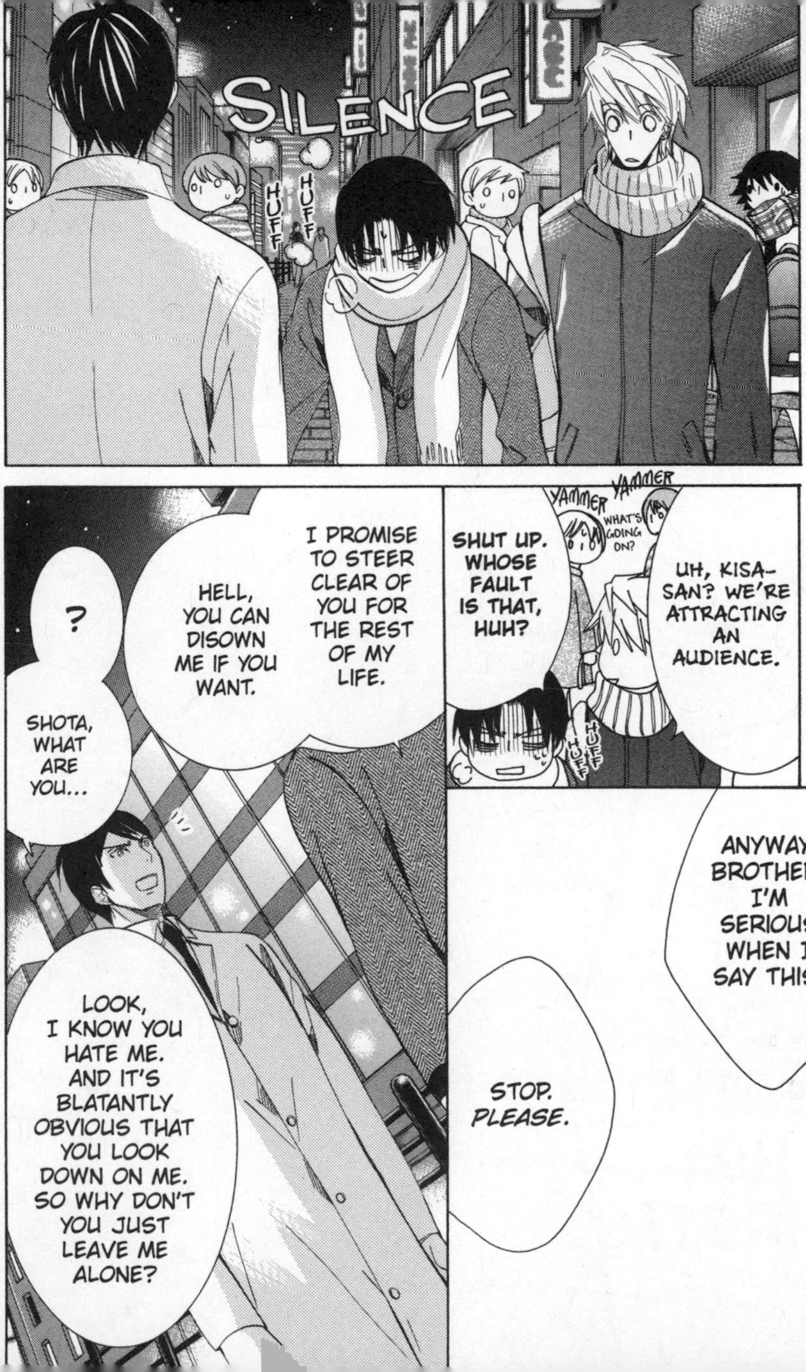
SILENCE
HUFF HUFF
YAMMER
YAMMER
WHAT'S GOING ON?
UH, KISA-SAN? WE'RE ATTRACTING AN AUDIENCE.
SHUT UP. WHOSE FAULT IS THAT, HUH?
HUFF HUFF
ANYWAY, BROTHER, I'M SERIOUS WHEN I SAY THIS.
STOP. PLEASE.
I PROMISE TO STEER CLEAR OF YOU FOR THE REST OF MY LIFE.
HELL, YOU CAN DISOWN ME IF YOU WANT.
?
SHOTA, WHAT ARE YOU...
LOOK, I KNOW YOU HATE ME. AND IT'S BLATANTLY OBVIOUS THAT YOU LOOK DOWN ON ME. SO WHY DON'T YOU JUST LEAVE ME ALONE?

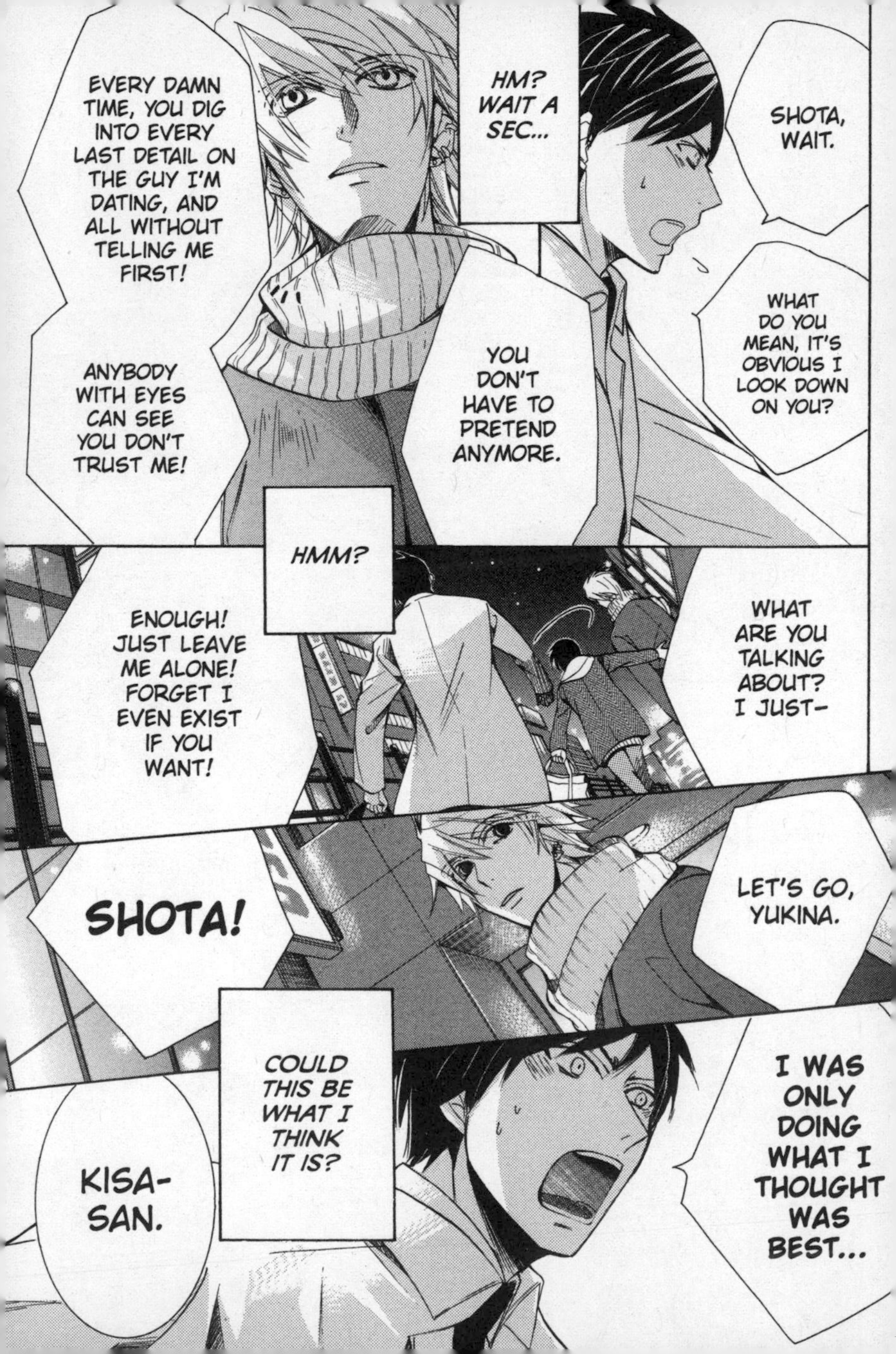
SHOTA, WAIT.
WHAT DO YOU MEAN, IT'S OBVIOUS I LOOK DOWN ON YOU?
HM? WAIT A SEC...
EVERY DAMN TIME, YOU DIG INTO EVERY LAST DETAIL ON THE GUY I'M DATING, AND ALL WITHOUT TELLING ME FIRST!
YOU DON'T HAVE TO PRETEND ANYMORE.
ANYBODY WITH EYES CAN SEE YOU DON'T TRUST ME!
WHAT ARE YOU TALKING ABOUT? I JUST-
HMM?
ENOUGH! JUST LEAVE ME ALONE! FORGET I EVEN EXIST IF YOU WANT!
LET'S GO, YUKINA.
SHOTA!
I WAS ONLY DOING WHAT I THOUGHT WAS BEST...
COULD THIS BE WHAT I THINK IT IS?
KISA-SAN.

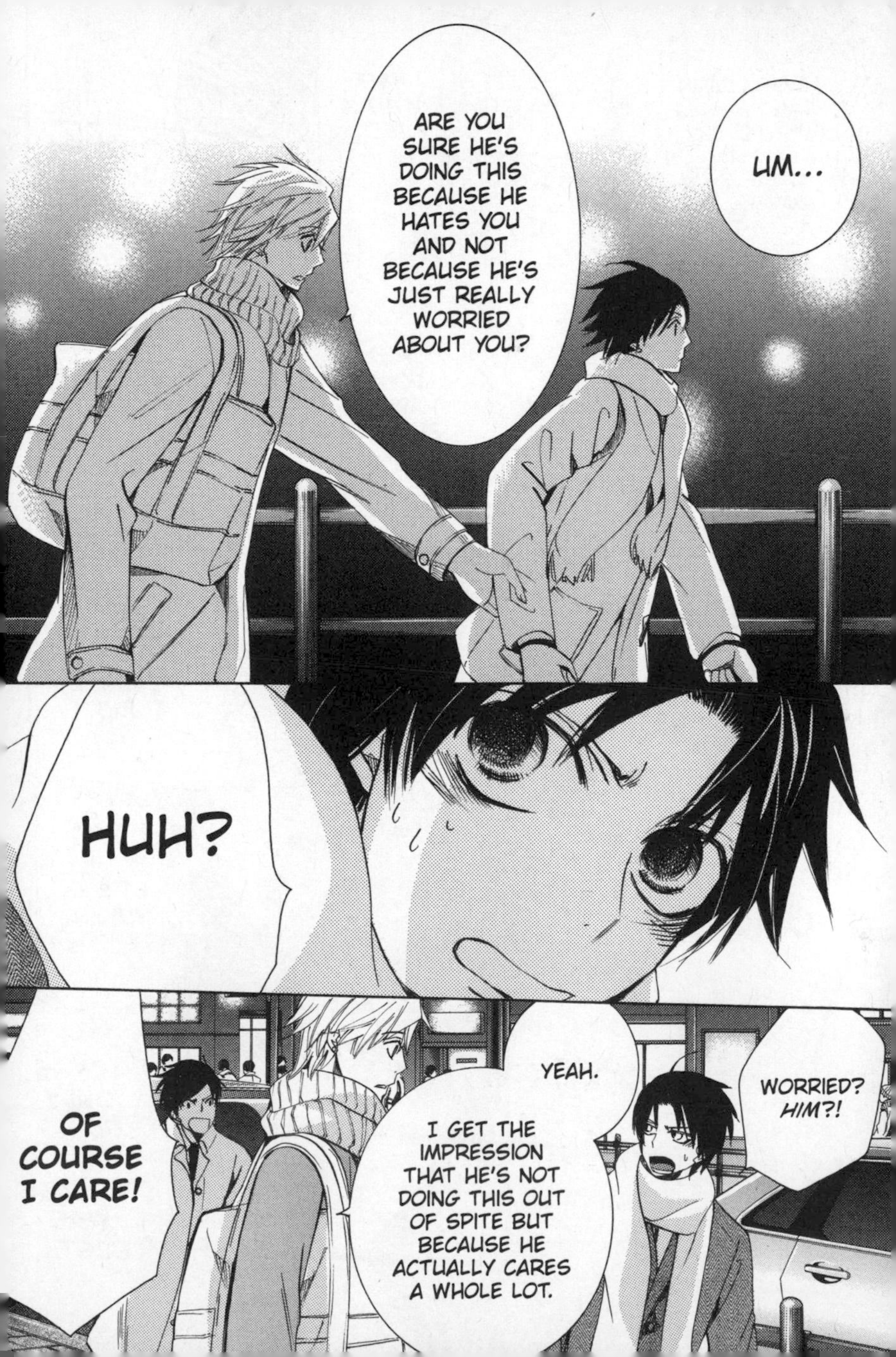
UM...
ARE YOU SURE HE'S DOING THIS BECAUSE HE HATES YOU AND NOT BECAUSE HE'S JUST REALLY WORRIED ABOUT YOU?
HUH?
WORRIED? *HIM?!*
YEAH.
I GET THE IMPRESSION THAT HE'S NOT DOING THIS OUT OF SPITE BUT BECAUSE HE ACTUALLY CARES A WHOLE LOT.
OF COURSE I CARE!

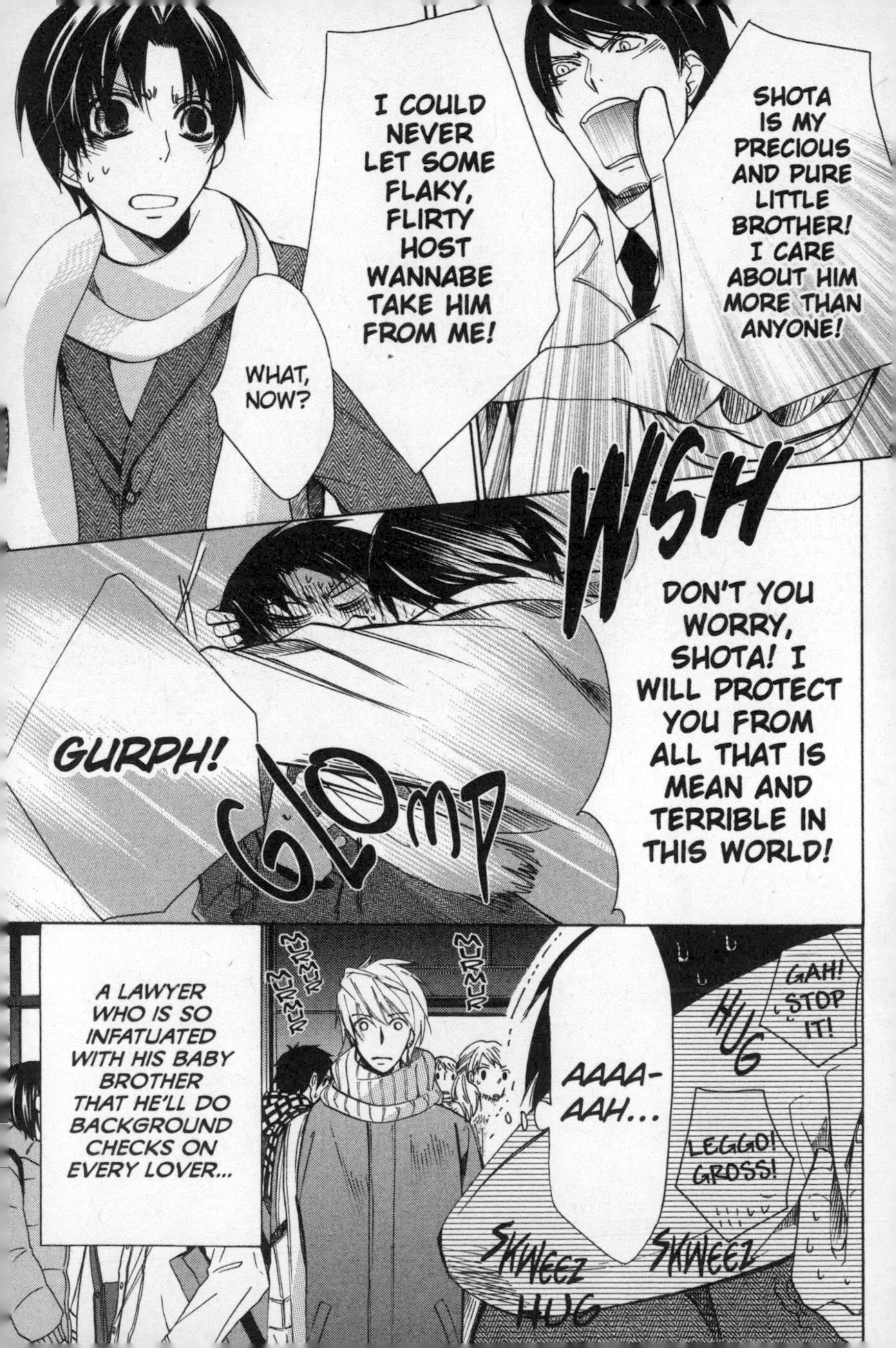
SHOTA IS MY PRECIOUS AND PURE LITTLE BROTHER! I CARE ABOUT HIM MORE THAN ANYONE!
I COULD NEVER LET SOME FLAKY, FLIRTY HOST WANNABE TAKE HIM FROM ME!
WHAT, NOW?
WSH
DON'T YOU WORRY, SHOTA! I WILL PROTECT YOU FROM ALL THAT IS MEAN AND TERRIBLE IN THIS WORLD!
GLOMP
GURPH!
GAH! STOP IT!
HUG
AAAA-AAH...
LEGGO! GROSS!
SKWEEZ
SKWEEZ
HUG
MURMUR
MURMUR
MURMUR
A LAWYER WHO IS SO INFATUATED WITH HIS BABY BROTHER THAT HE'LL DO BACKGROUND CHECKS ON EVERY LOVER...

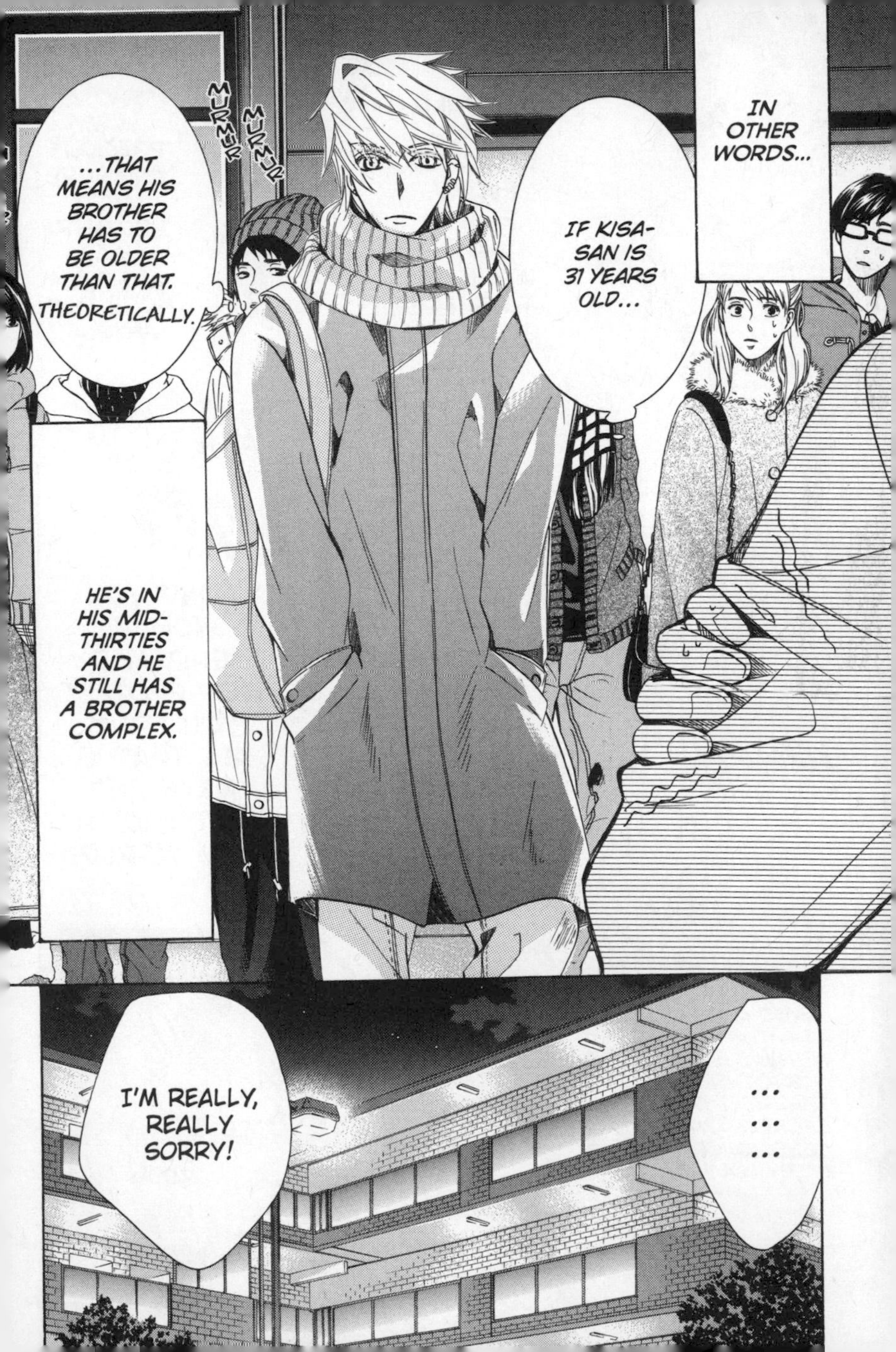
IN OTHER WORDS...
IF KISA-SAN IS 31 YEARS OLD...
MURMUR MURMUR
...THAT MEANS HIS BROTHER HAS TO BE OLDER THAN THAT. THEORETICALLY.
HE'S IN HIS MID-THIRTIES AND HE STILL HAS A BROTHER COMPLEX.
... ...
I'M REALLY, REALLY SORRY!

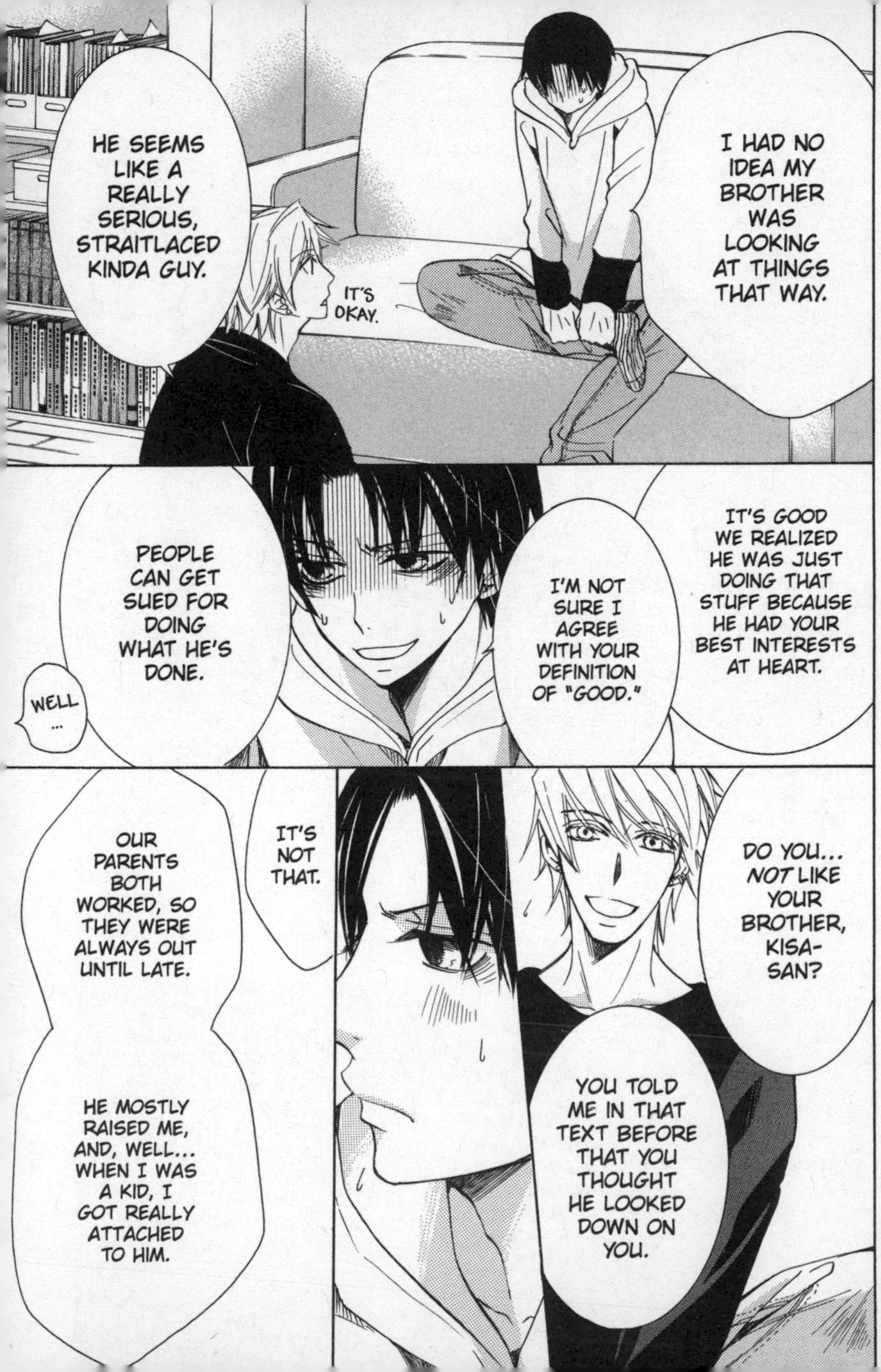
I HAD NO IDEA MY BROTHER WAS LOOKING AT THINGS THAT WAY.
IT'S OKAY.
HE SEEMS LIKE A REALLY SERIOUS, STRAITLACED KINDA GUY.
IT'S GOOD WE REALIZED HE WAS JUST DOING THAT STUFF BECAUSE HE HAD YOUR BEST INTERESTS AT HEART.
I'M NOT SURE I AGREE WITH YOUR DEFINITION OF "GOOD."
PEOPLE CAN GET SUED FOR DOING WHAT HE'S DONE.
WELL...
DO YOU... *NOT* LIKE YOUR BROTHER, KISA-SAN?
YOU TOLD ME IN THAT TEXT BEFORE THAT YOU THOUGHT HE LOOKED DOWN ON YOU.
IT'S NOT THAT.
OUR PARENTS BOTH WORKED, SO THEY WERE ALWAYS OUT UNTIL LATE.
HE MOSTLY RAISED ME, AND, WELL... WHEN I WAS A KID, I GOT REALLY ATTACHED TO HIM.

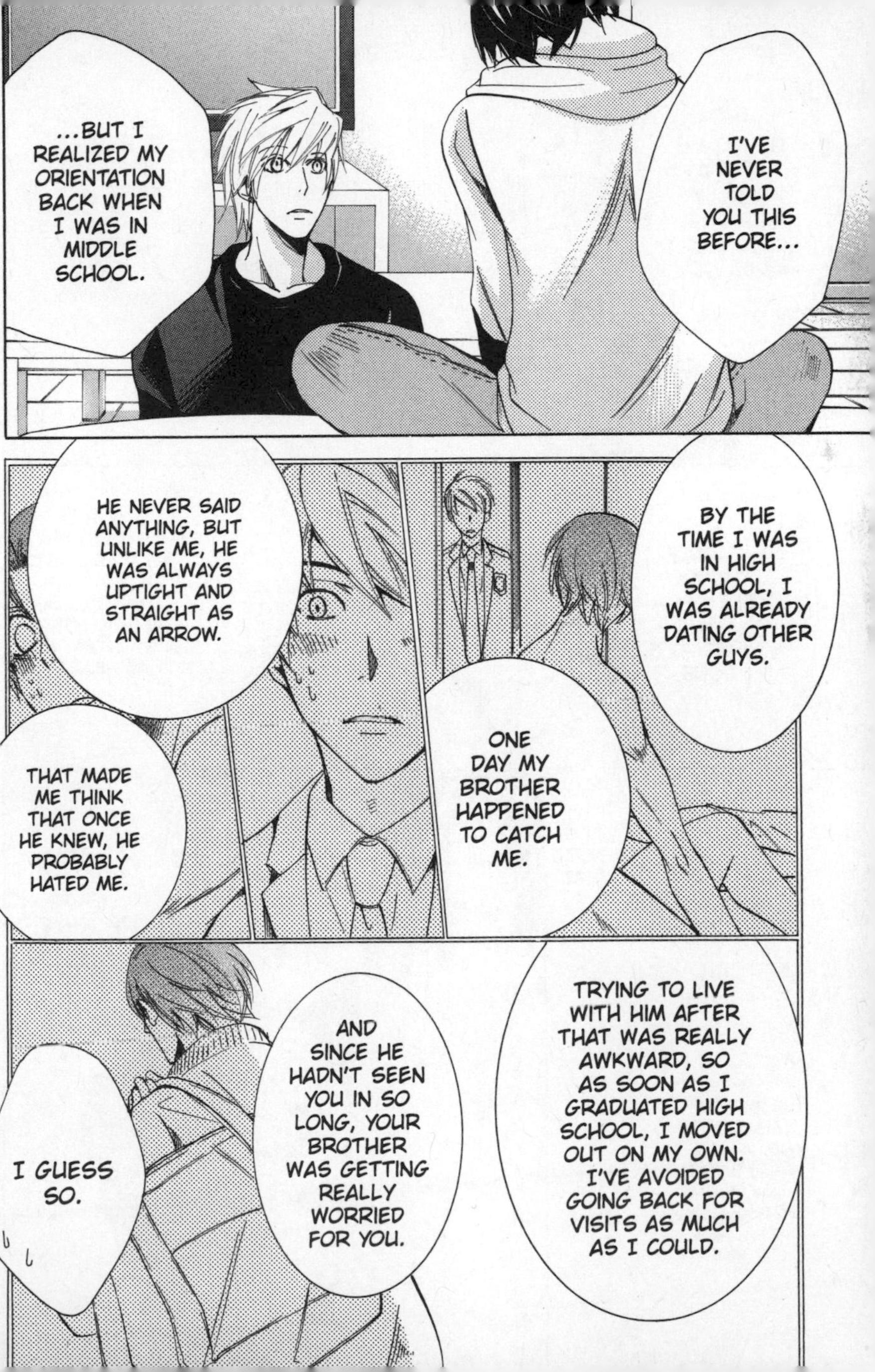
I'VE NEVER TOLD YOU THIS BEFORE...
...BUT I REALIZED MY ORIENTATION BACK WHEN I WAS IN MIDDLE SCHOOL.
BY THE TIME I WAS IN HIGH SCHOOL, I WAS ALREADY DATING OTHER GUYS.
ONE DAY MY BROTHER HAPPENED TO CATCH ME.
HE NEVER SAID ANYTHING, BUT UNLIKE ME, HE WAS ALWAYS UPTIGHT AND STRAIGHT AS AN ARROW.
THAT MADE ME THINK THAT ONCE HE KNEW, HE PROBABLY HATED ME.
TRYING TO LIVE WITH HIM AFTER THAT WAS REALLY AWKWARD, SO AS SOON AS I GRADUATED HIGH SCHOOL, I MOVED OUT ON MY OWN. I'VE AVOIDED GOING BACK FOR VISITS AS MUCH AS I COULD.
AND SINCE HE HADN'T SEEN YOU IN SO LONG, YOUR BROTHER WAS GETTING REALLY WORRIED FOR YOU.
I GUESS SO.

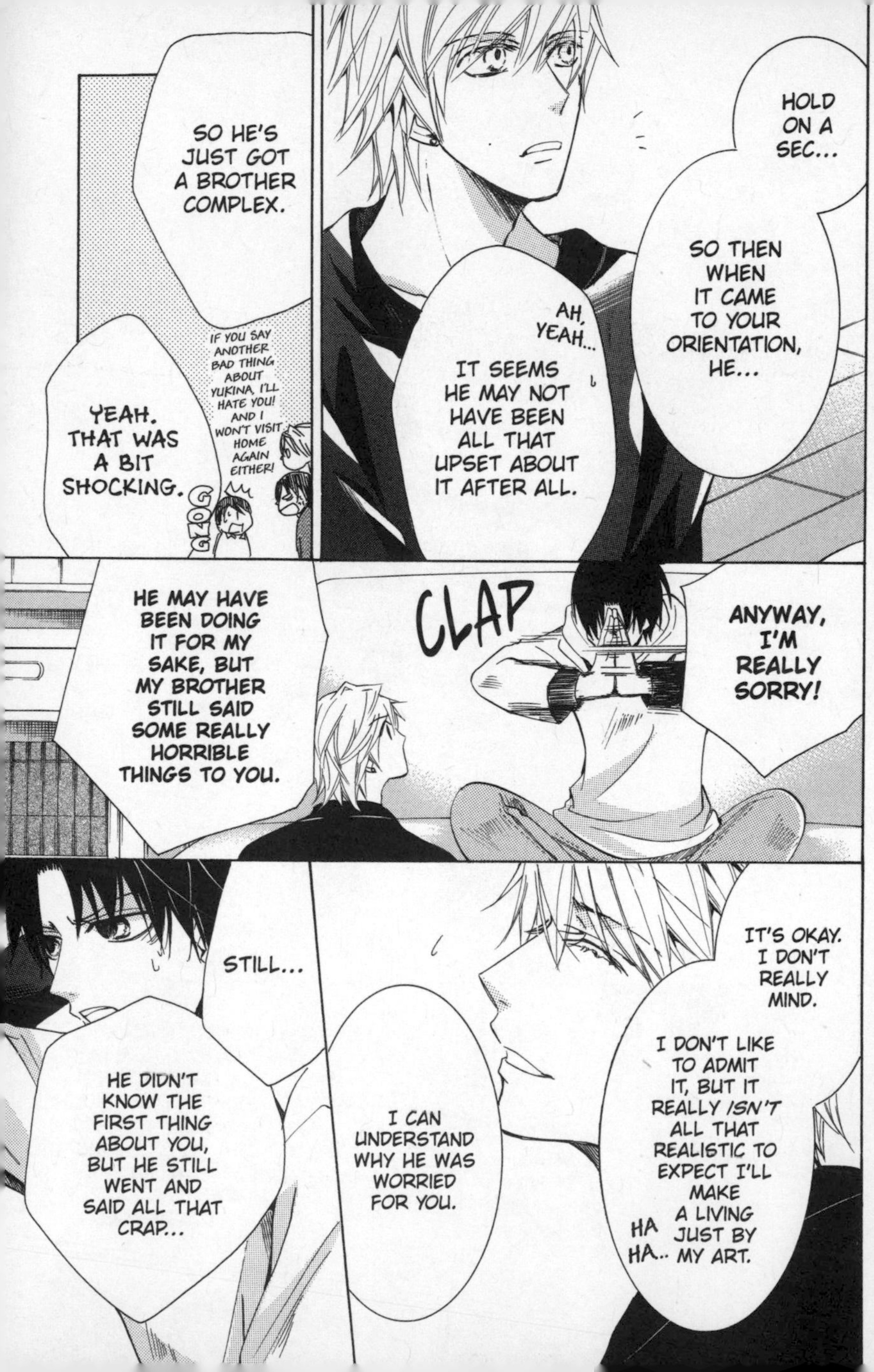
HOLD ON A SEC...
SO THEN WHEN IT CAME TO YOUR ORIENTATION, HE...
AH, YEAH...
IT SEEMS HE MAY NOT HAVE BEEN ALL THAT UPSET ABOUT IT AFTER ALL.
SO HE'S JUST GOT A BROTHER COMPLEX.
IF YOU SAY ANOTHER BAD THING ABOUT YUKINA, I'LL HATE YOU! AND I WON'T VISIT HOME AGAIN EITHER!
YEAH. THAT WAS A BIT SHOCKING.
GONG
ANYWAY, I'M REALLY SORRY!
CLAP
HE MAY HAVE BEEN DOING IT FOR MY SAKE, BUT MY BROTHER STILL SAID SOME REALLY HORRIBLE THINGS TO YOU.
IT'S OKAY. I DON'T REALLY MIND.
I DON'T LIKE TO ADMIT IT, BUT IT REALLY *ISN'T* ALL THAT REALISTIC TO EXPECT I'LL MAKE A LIVING JUST BY MY ART.
HA HA..
I CAN UNDERSTAND WHY HE WAS WORRIED FOR YOU.
STILL...
HE DIDN'T KNOW THE FIRST THING ABOUT YOU, BUT HE STILL WENT AND SAID ALL THAT CRAP...

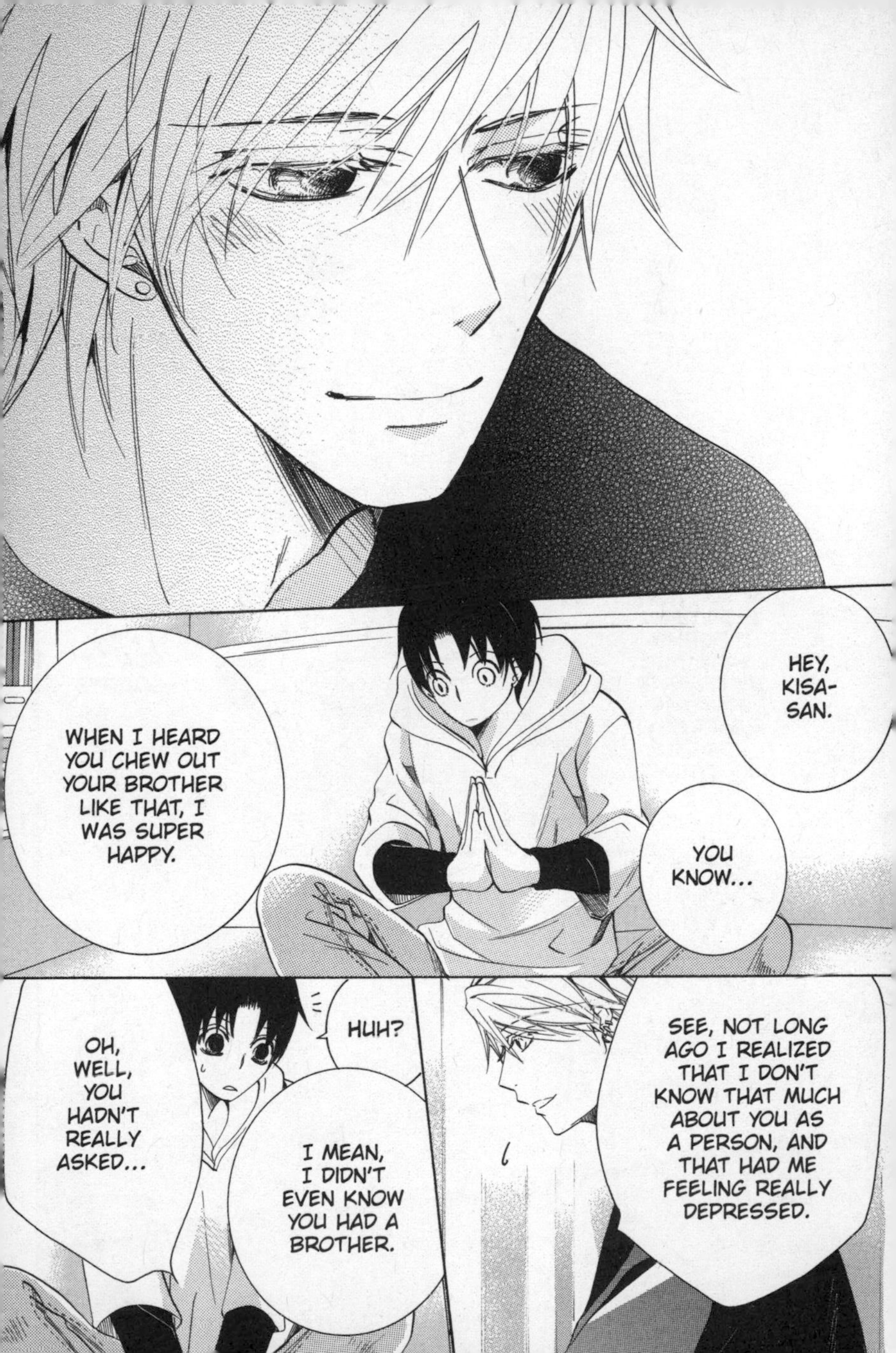
HEY, KISA-SAN.
YOU KNOW...
WHEN I HEARD YOU CHEW OUT YOUR BROTHER LIKE THAT, I WAS SUPER HAPPY.
SEE, NOT LONG AGO I REALIZED THAT I DON'T KNOW THAT MUCH ABOUT YOU AS A PERSON, AND THAT HAD ME FEELING REALLY DEPRESSED.
HUH?
I MEAN, I DIDN'T EVEN KNOW YOU HAD A BROTHER.
OH, WELL, YOU HADN'T REALLY ASKED...

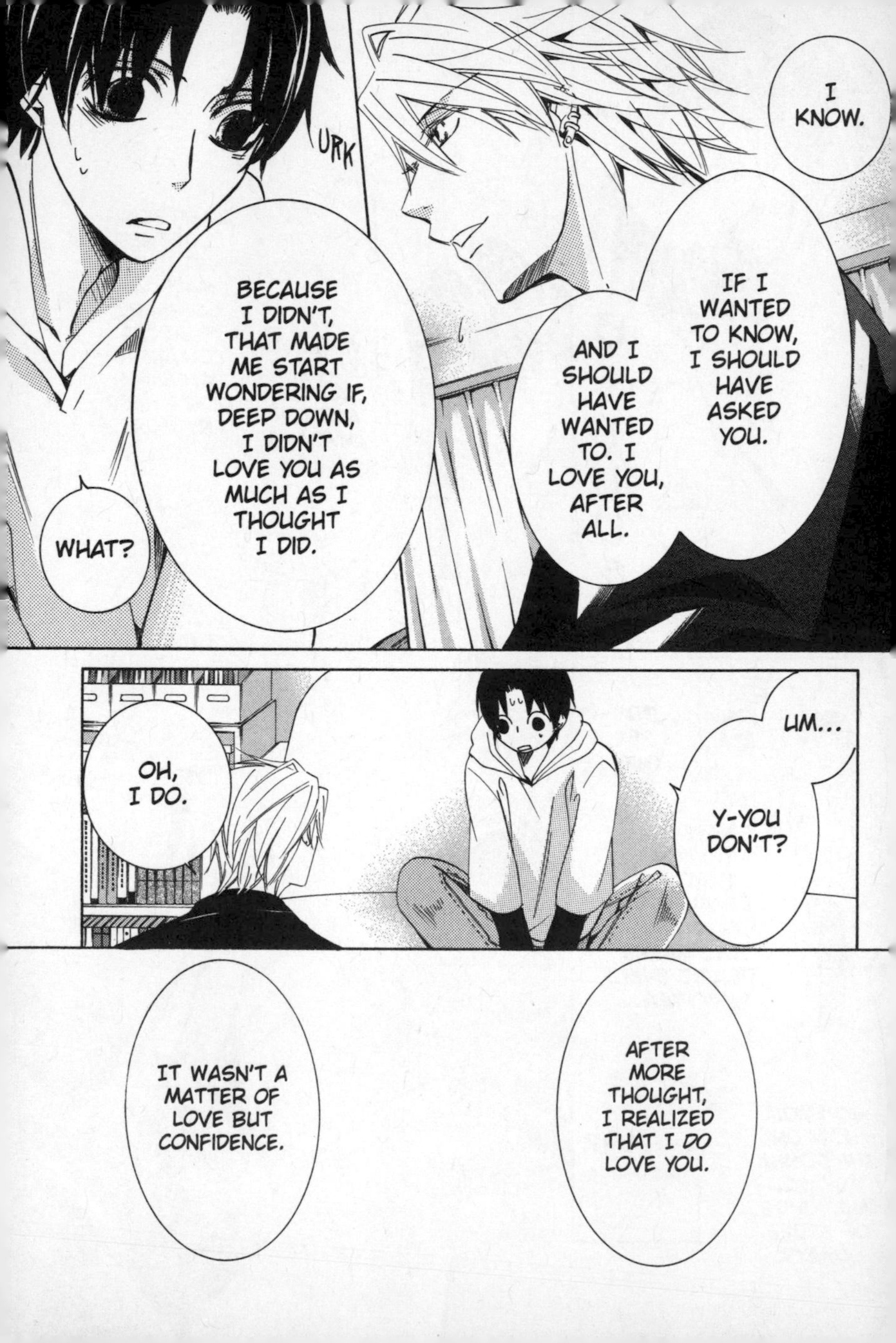
I KNOW.
IF I WANTED TO KNOW, I SHOULD HAVE ASKED YOU.
AND I SHOULD HAVE WANTED TO. I LOVE YOU, AFTER ALL.
URK
BECAUSE I DIDN'T, THAT MADE ME START WONDERING IF, DEEP DOWN, I DIDN'T LOVE YOU AS MUCH AS I THOUGHT I DID.
WHAT?
UM...
Y-YOU DON'T?
OH, I DO.
AFTER MORE THOUGHT, I REALIZED THAT I *DO* LOVE YOU.
IT WASN'T A MATTER OF LOVE BUT CONFIDENCE.

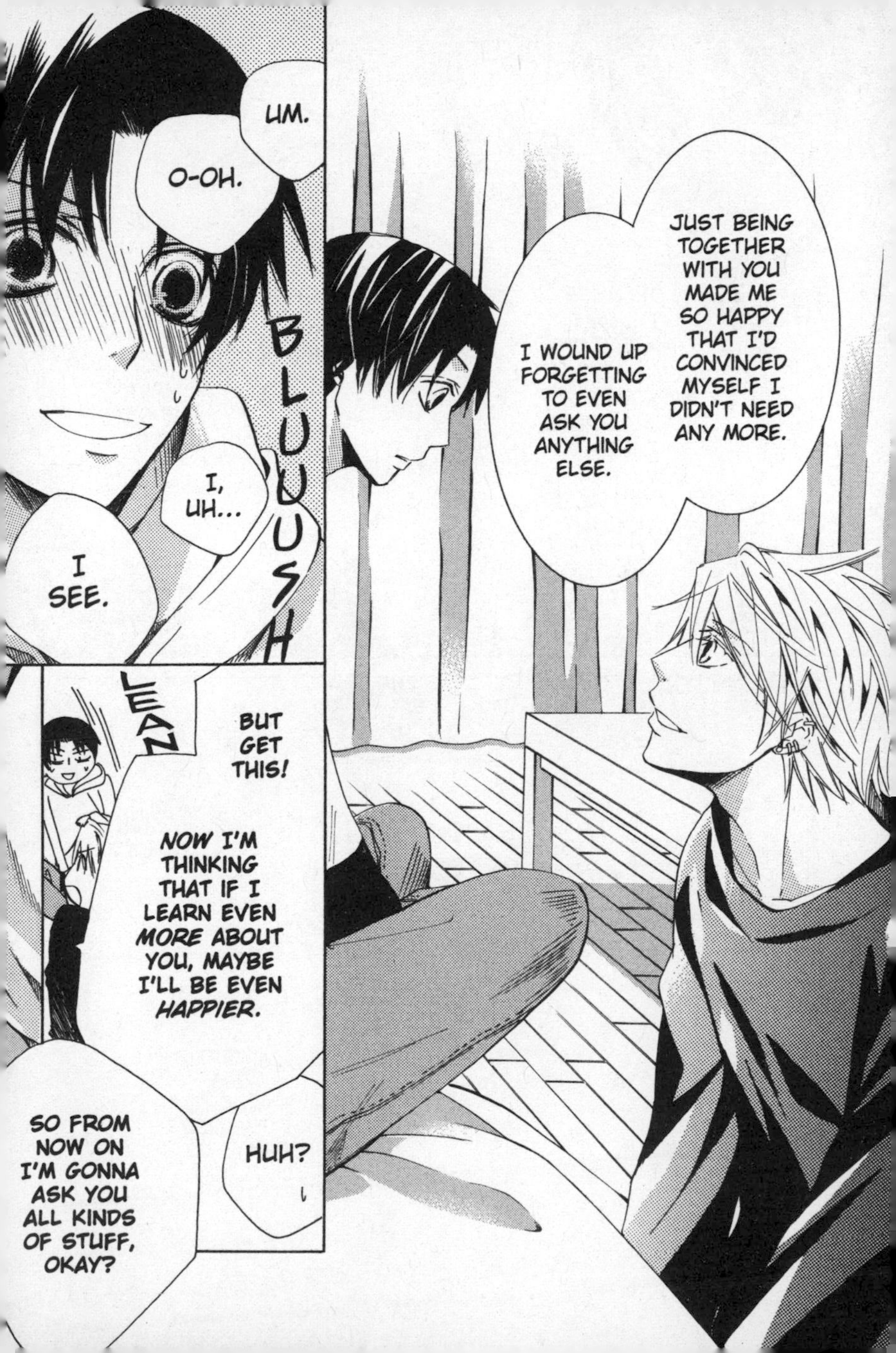
JUST BEING TOGETHER WITH YOU MADE ME SO HAPPY THAT I'D CONVINCED MYSELF I DIDN'T NEED ANY MORE.
I WOUND UP FORGETTING TO EVEN ASK YOU ANYTHING ELSE.
UM.
O-OH.
BLUUUSH
I, UH...
I SEE.
LEAN
BUT GET THIS!
NOW I'M THINKING THAT IF I LEARN EVEN *MORE* ABOUT YOU, MAYBE I'LL BE EVEN *HAPPIER*.
HUH?
SO FROM NOW ON I'M GONNA ASK YOU ALL KINDS OF STUFF, OKAY?

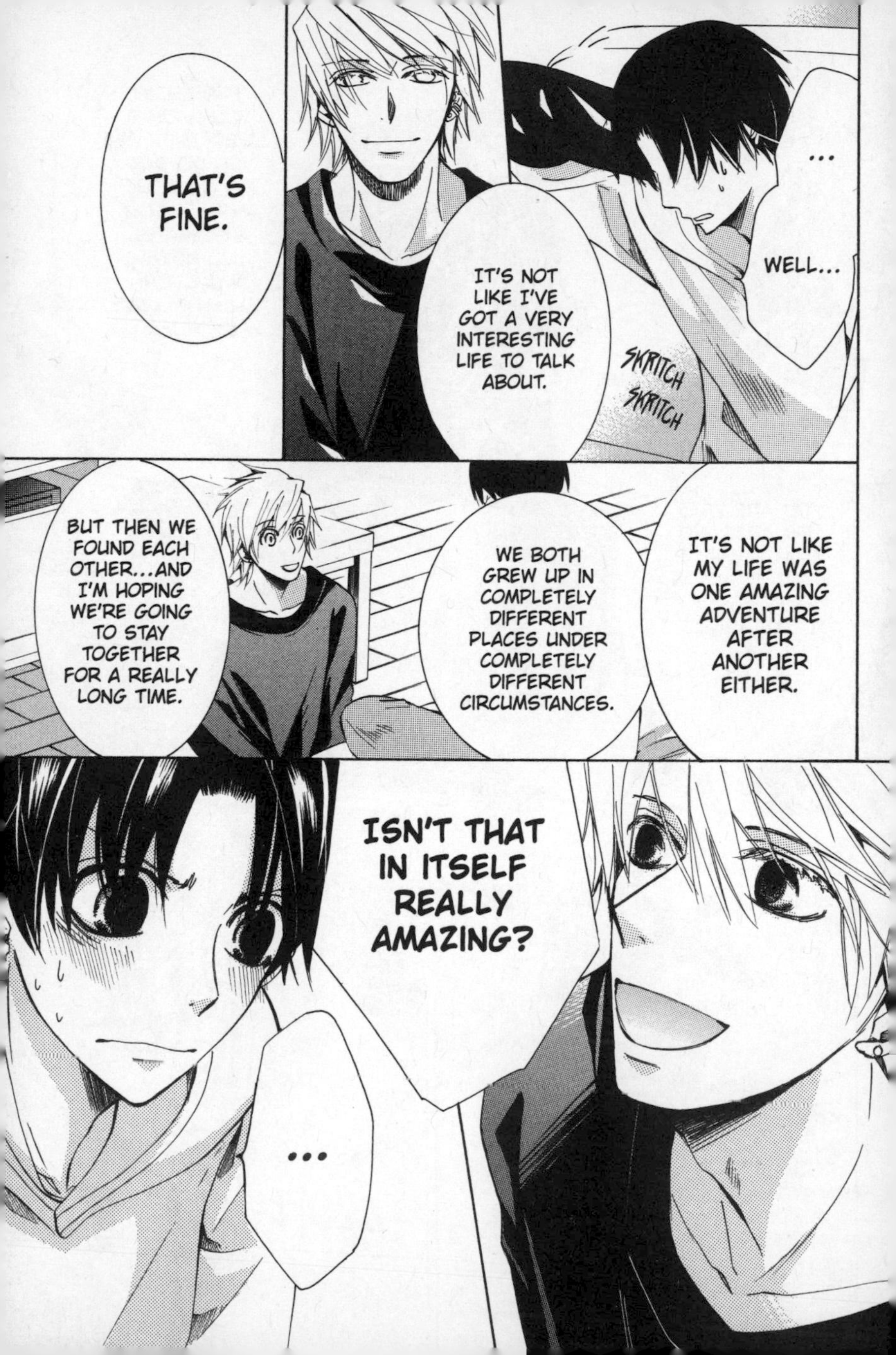
...
WELL...
IT'S NOT LIKE I'VE GOT A VERY INTERESTING LIFE TO TALK ABOUT.
SKRITCH SKRITCH
THAT'S FINE.
IT'S NOT LIKE MY LIFE WAS ONE AMAZING ADVENTURE AFTER ANOTHER EITHER.
WE BOTH GREW UP IN COMPLETELY DIFFERENT PLACES UNDER COMPLETELY DIFFERENT CIRCUMSTANCES.
BUT THEN WE FOUND EACH OTHER...AND I'M HOPING WE'RE GOING TO STAY TOGETHER FOR A REALLY LONG TIME.
ISN'T THAT IN ITSELF REALLY AMAZING?
...

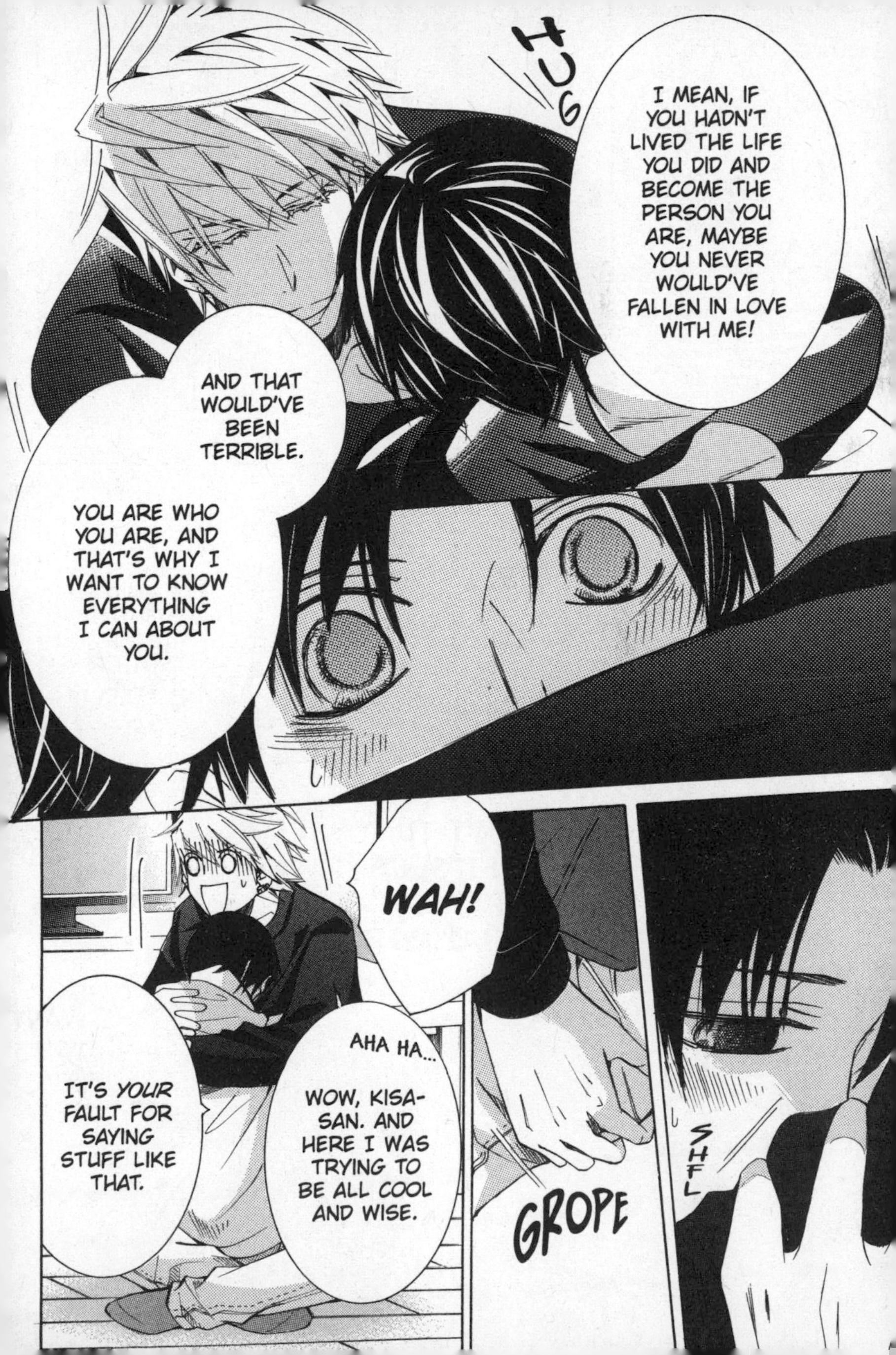
HUG
I MEAN, IF YOU HADN'T LIVED THE LIFE YOU DID AND BECOME THE PERSON YOU ARE, MAYBE YOU NEVER WOULD'VE FALLEN IN LOVE WITH ME!
AND THAT WOULD'VE BEEN TERRIBLE.
YOU ARE WHO YOU ARE, AND THAT'S WHY I WANT TO KNOW EVERYTHING I CAN ABOUT YOU.
SHFL
GROPE
WAH!
AHA HA...
WOW, KISA-SAN. AND HERE I WAS TRYING TO BE ALL COOL AND WISE.
IT'S *YOUR* FAULT FOR SAYING STUFF LIKE THAT.

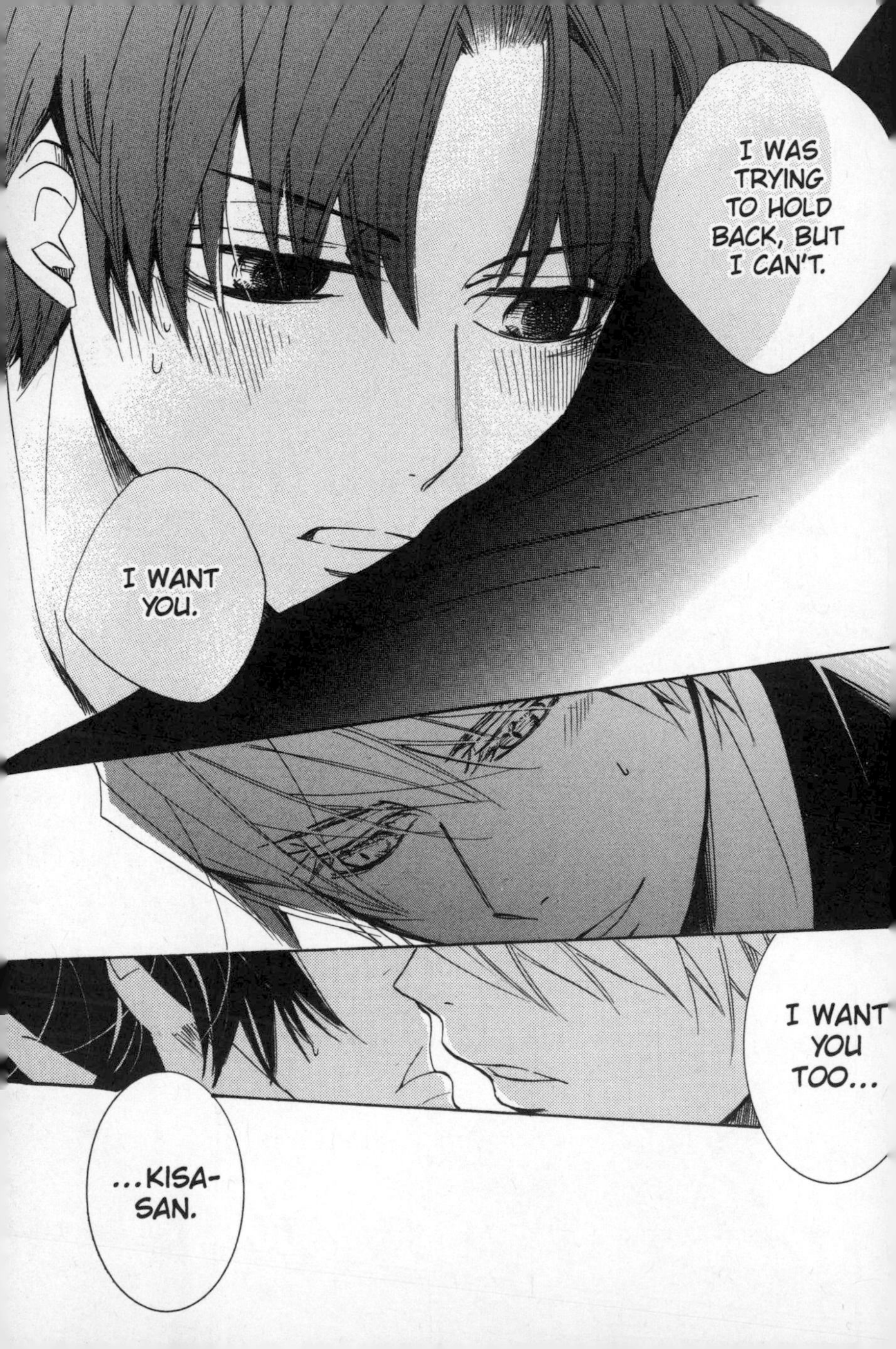
I WAS TRYING TO HOLD BACK, BUT I CAN'T.
I WANT YOU.
I WANT YOU TOO...
...KISA-SAN.

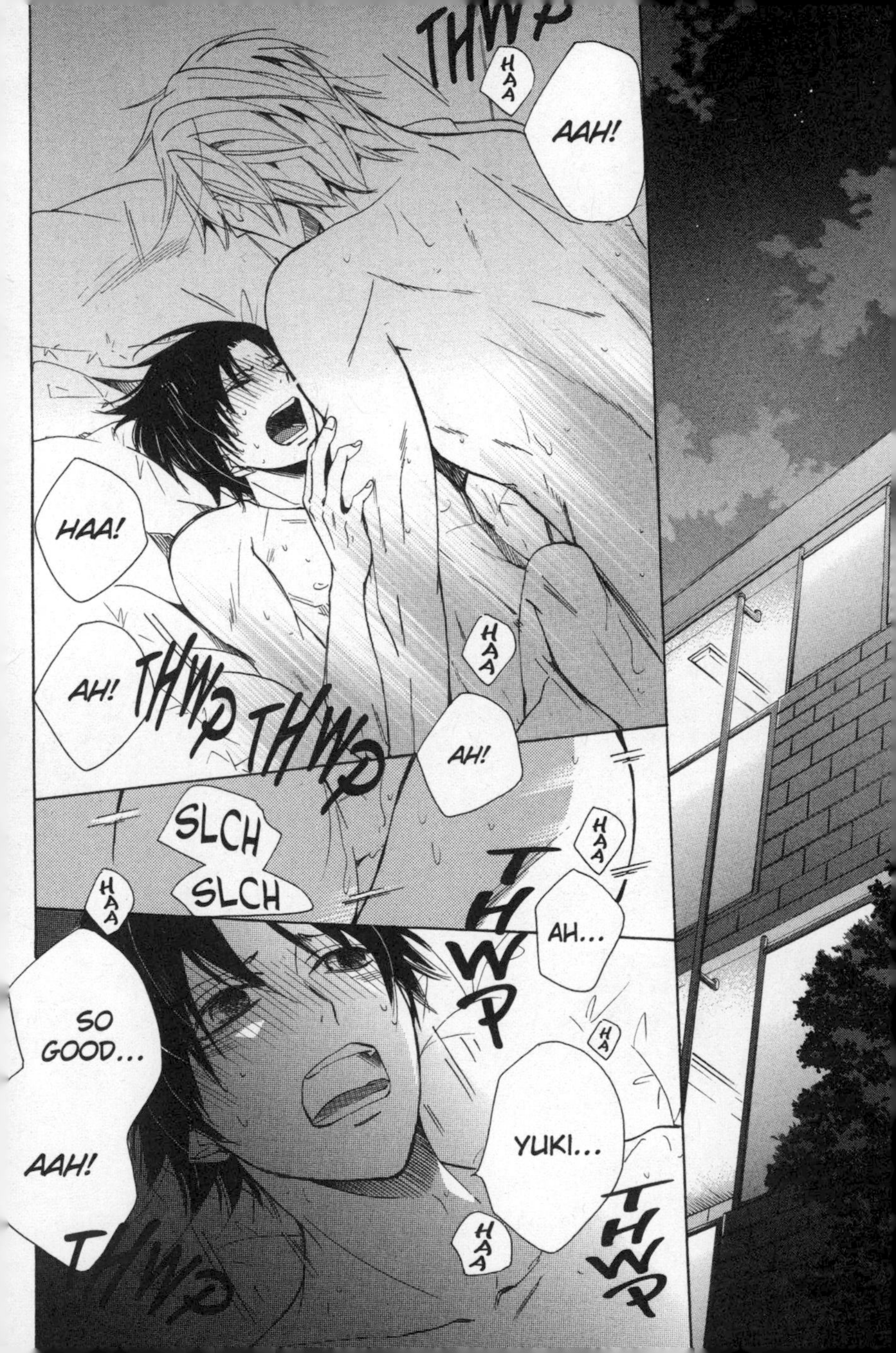
THWP
HAA
AAH!
HAA
AH!
HAA!
AH!
THWP
THWP
HAA
SLCH
SLCH
THWP
AH...
HAA
HA
YUKI...
SO GOOD...
AAH!
THWP
HAA
THWP

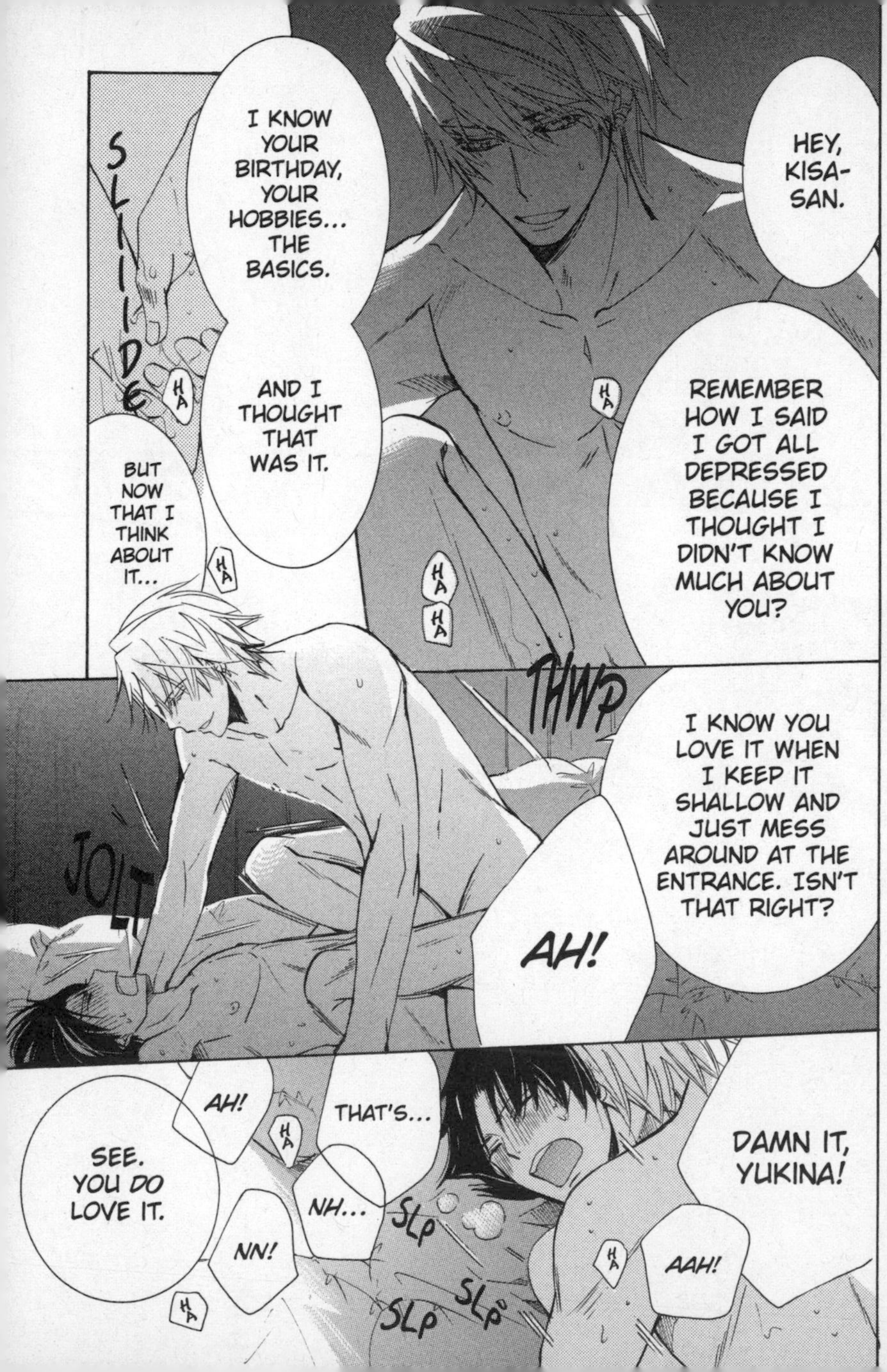
HEY, KISA-SAN.
REMEMBER HOW I SAID I GOT ALL DEPRESSED BECAUSE I THOUGHT I DIDN'T KNOW MUCH ABOUT YOU?
HA
I KNOW YOUR BIRTHDAY, YOUR HOBBIES... THE BASICS.
AND I THOUGHT THAT WAS IT.
HA HA
SLIIIDE
HA
HA
BUT NOW THAT I THINK ABOUT IT...
THWP
I KNOW YOU LOVE IT WHEN I KEEP IT SHALLOW AND JUST MESS AROUND AT THE ENTRANCE. ISN'T THAT RIGHT?
AH!
JOLT
DAMN IT, YUKINA!
AAH!
HA
THAT'S...
AH!
HA
NH...
SLP
SLP
SLP
SEE. YOU DO LOVE IT.
NN!
HA

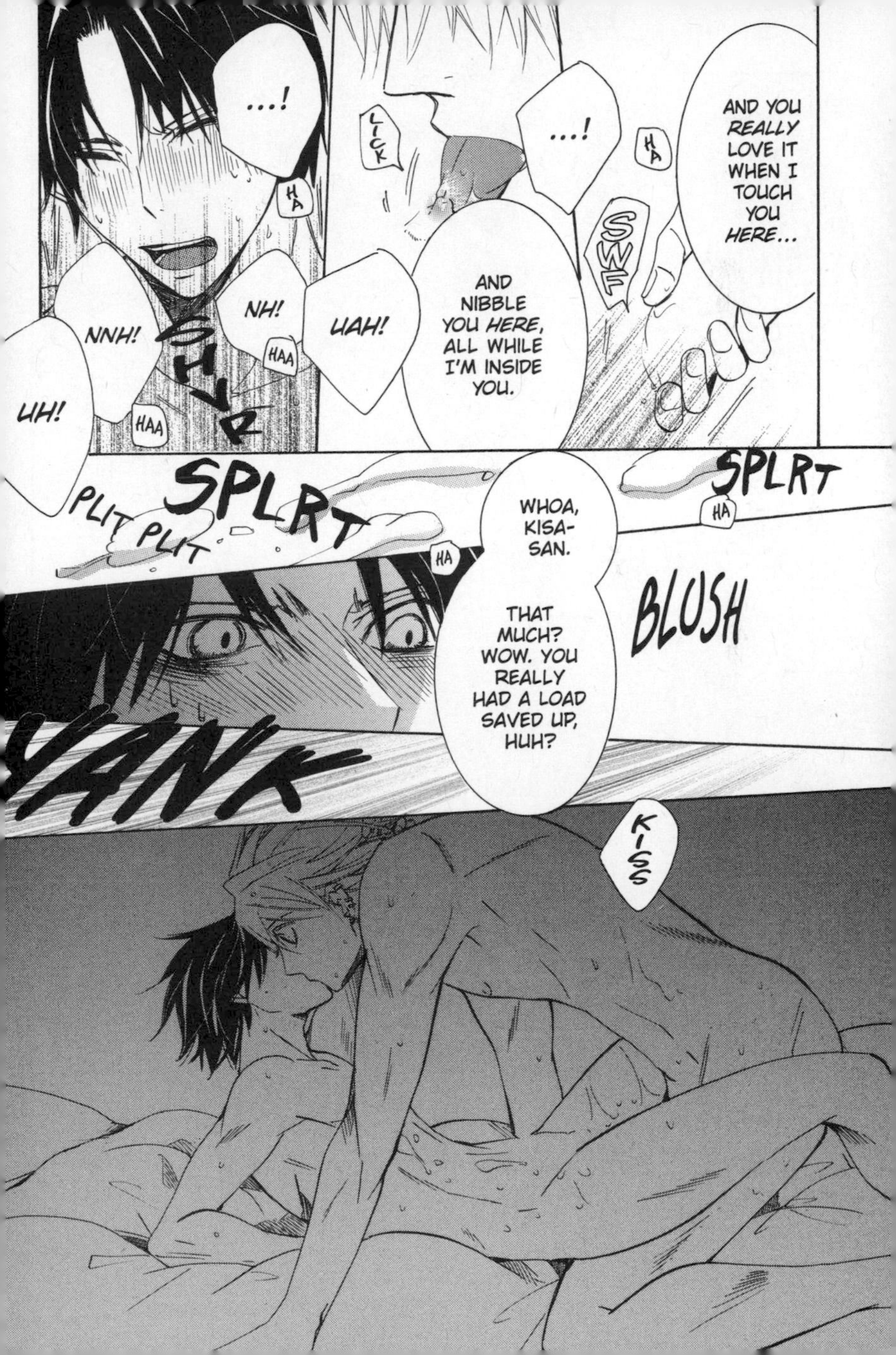
AND YOU REALLY LOVE IT WHEN I TOUCH YOU HERE...
HA
SWF
...!
LICK
AND NIBBLE YOU HERE, ALL WHILE I'M INSIDE YOU.
...!
HA
UAH!
NH!
HAA
SHVR
NNH!
HAA
UH!
SPLRT
HA
WHOA, KISA-SAN.
SPLRT
PLIT PLIT
HA
BLUSH
THAT MUCH? WOW. YOU REALLY HAD A LOAD SAVED UP, HUH?
YANK
KISS

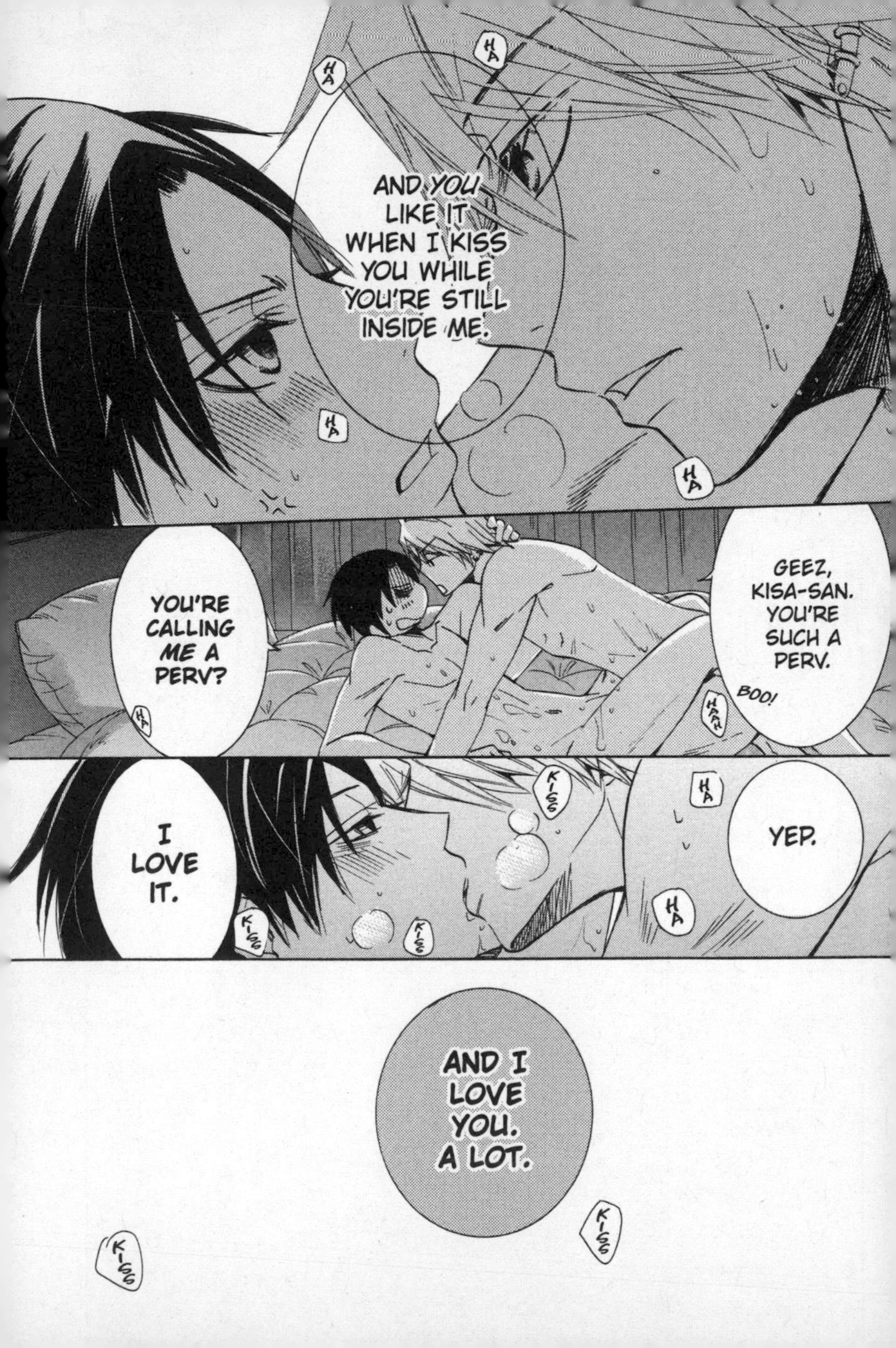
HA
HA
AND YOU LIKE IT WHEN I KISS YOU WHILE YOU'RE STILL INSIDE ME.
HA
HA
GEEZ, KISA-SAN. YOU'RE SUCH A PERV.
BOO!
HAAH
YOU'RE CALLING ME A PERV?
HA
YEP.
HA
HA
KISS
I LOVE IT.
KISS
KISS
AND I LOVE YOU. A LOT.
KISS
KISS

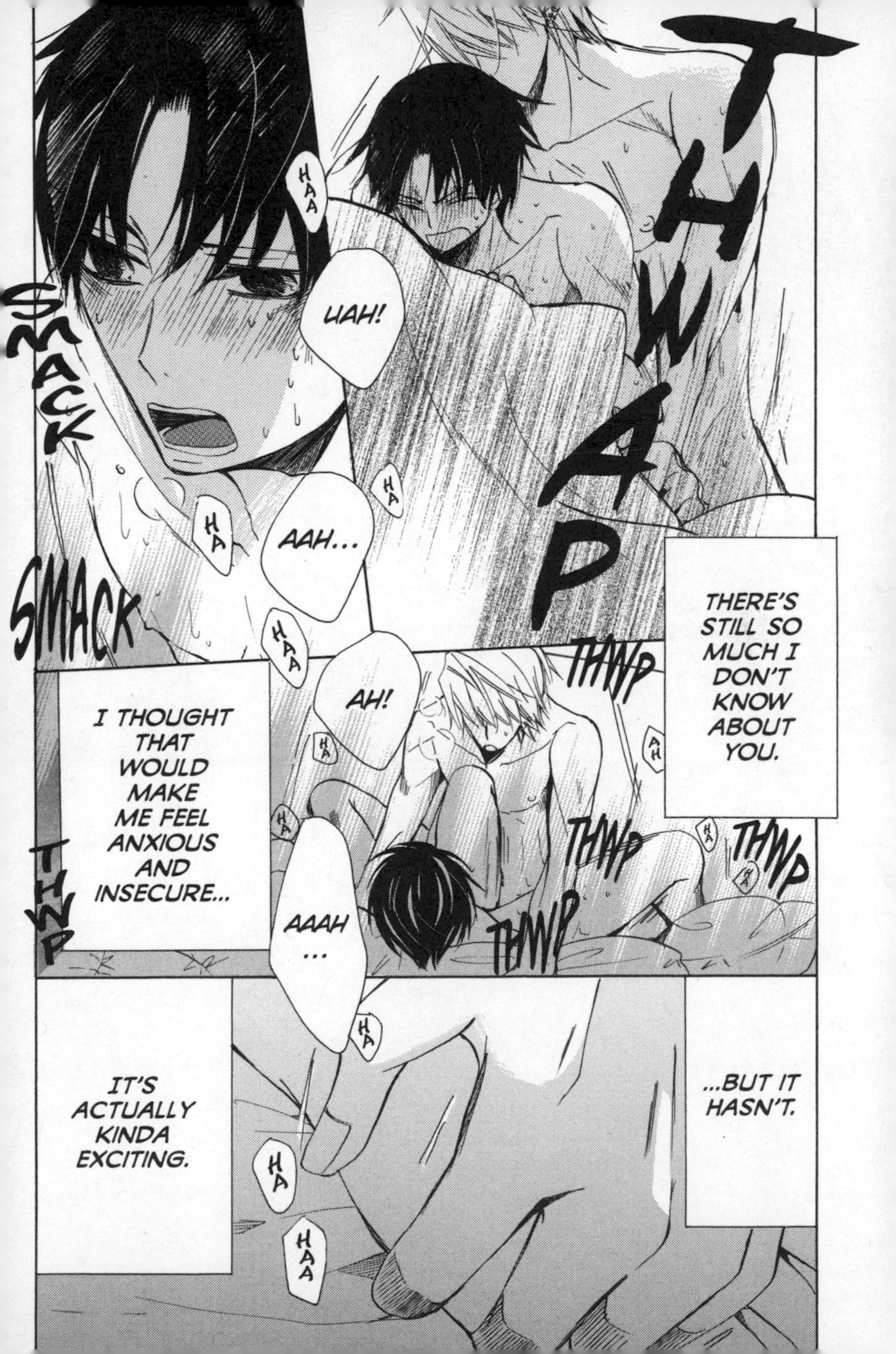
THWAP
HAA
UAH!
HA
AAH...
HA
HAA
SMACK
SMACK
THERE'S STILL SO MUCH I DON'T KNOW ABOUT YOU.
THWP
AH!
AH
HA
HA
THWP
THWP
HA
HA
THWP
AAAH ...
I THOUGHT THAT WOULD MAKE ME FEEL ANXIOUS AND INSECURE...
THWP
...BUT IT HASN'T.
HA
HA
HAA
IT'S ACTUALLY KINDA EXCITING.

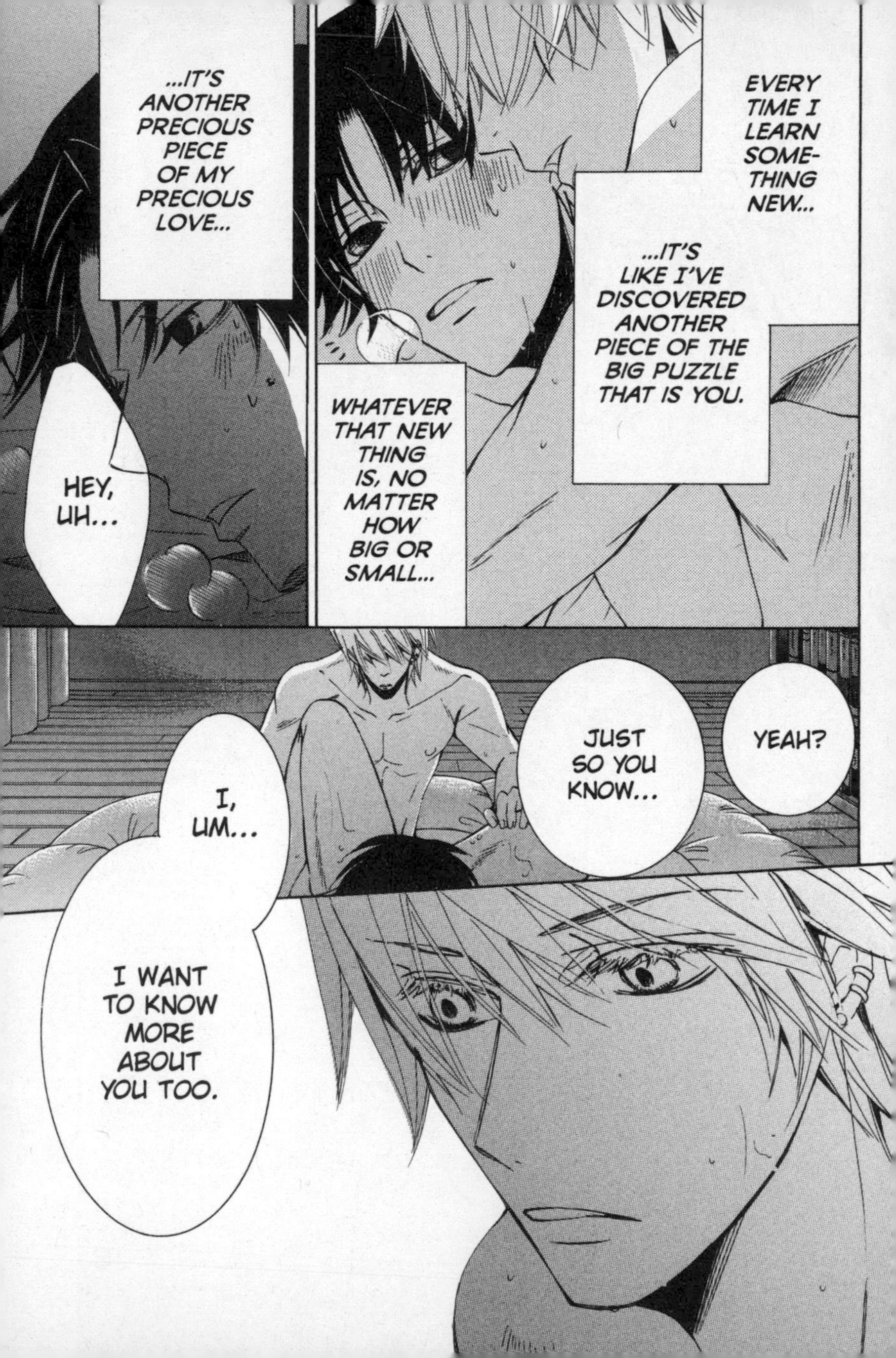
EVERY TIME I LEARN SOME-THING NEW...
...IT'S LIKE I'VE DISCOVERED ANOTHER PIECE OF THE BIG PUZZLE THAT IS YOU.
WHATEVER THAT NEW THING IS, NO MATTER HOW BIG OR SMALL...
...IT'S ANOTHER PRECIOUS PIECE OF MY PRECIOUS LOVE...
HEY, UH...
YEAH?
JUST SO YOU KNOW...
I, UM...
I WANT TO KNOW MORE ABOUT YOU TOO.

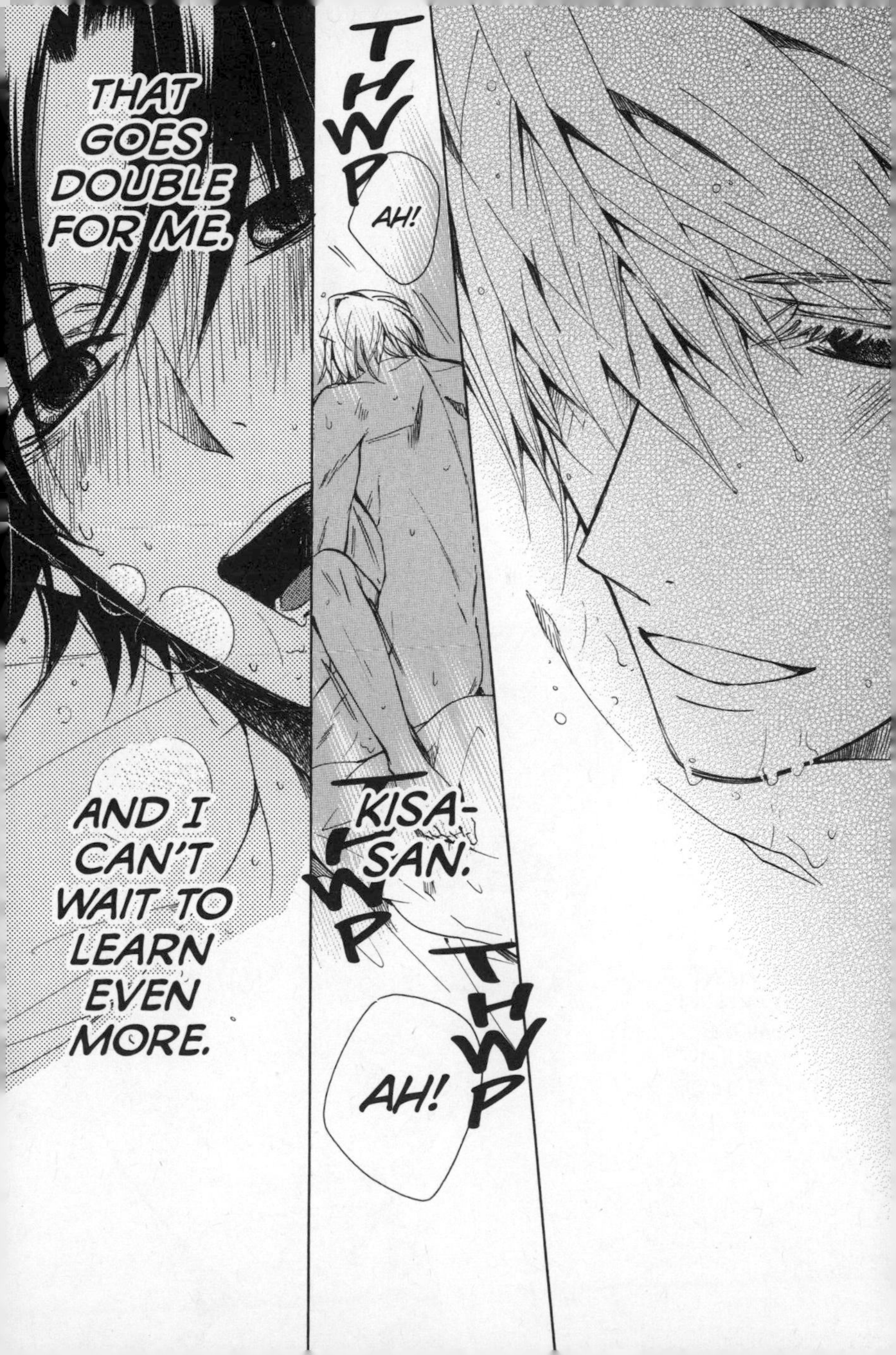
THWP
AH!
KISA-SAN.
THWP
THWP
AH!
THAT GOES DOUBLE FOR ME.
AND I CAN'T WAIT TO LEARN EVEN MORE.

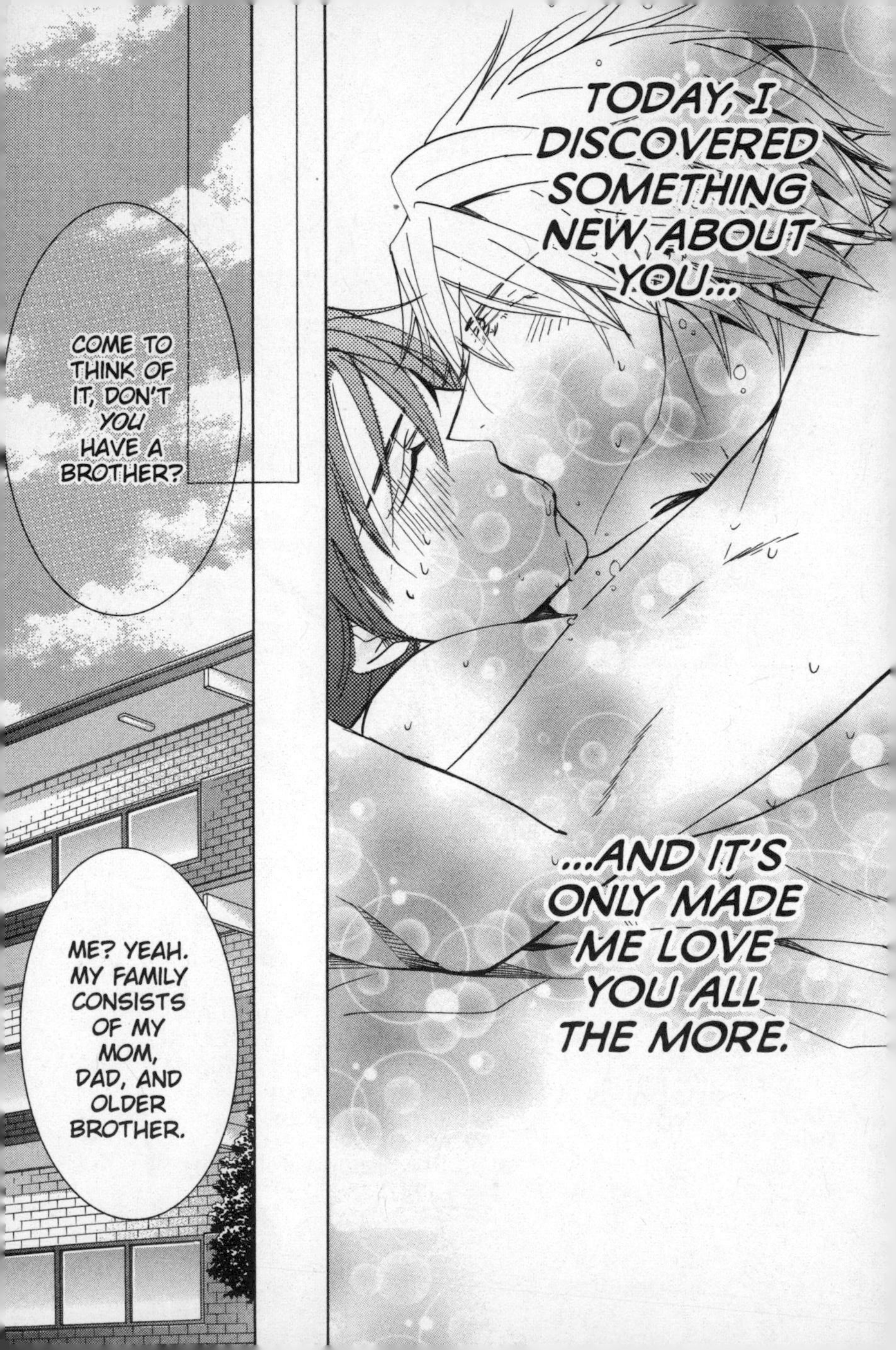
TODAY, I DISCOVERED SOMETHING NEW ABOUT YOU...
...AND IT'S ONLY MADE ME LOVE YOU ALL THE MORE.
COME TO THINK OF IT, DON'T YOU HAVE A BROTHER?
ME? YEAH. MY FAMILY CONSISTS OF MY MOM, DAD, AND OLDER BROTHER.

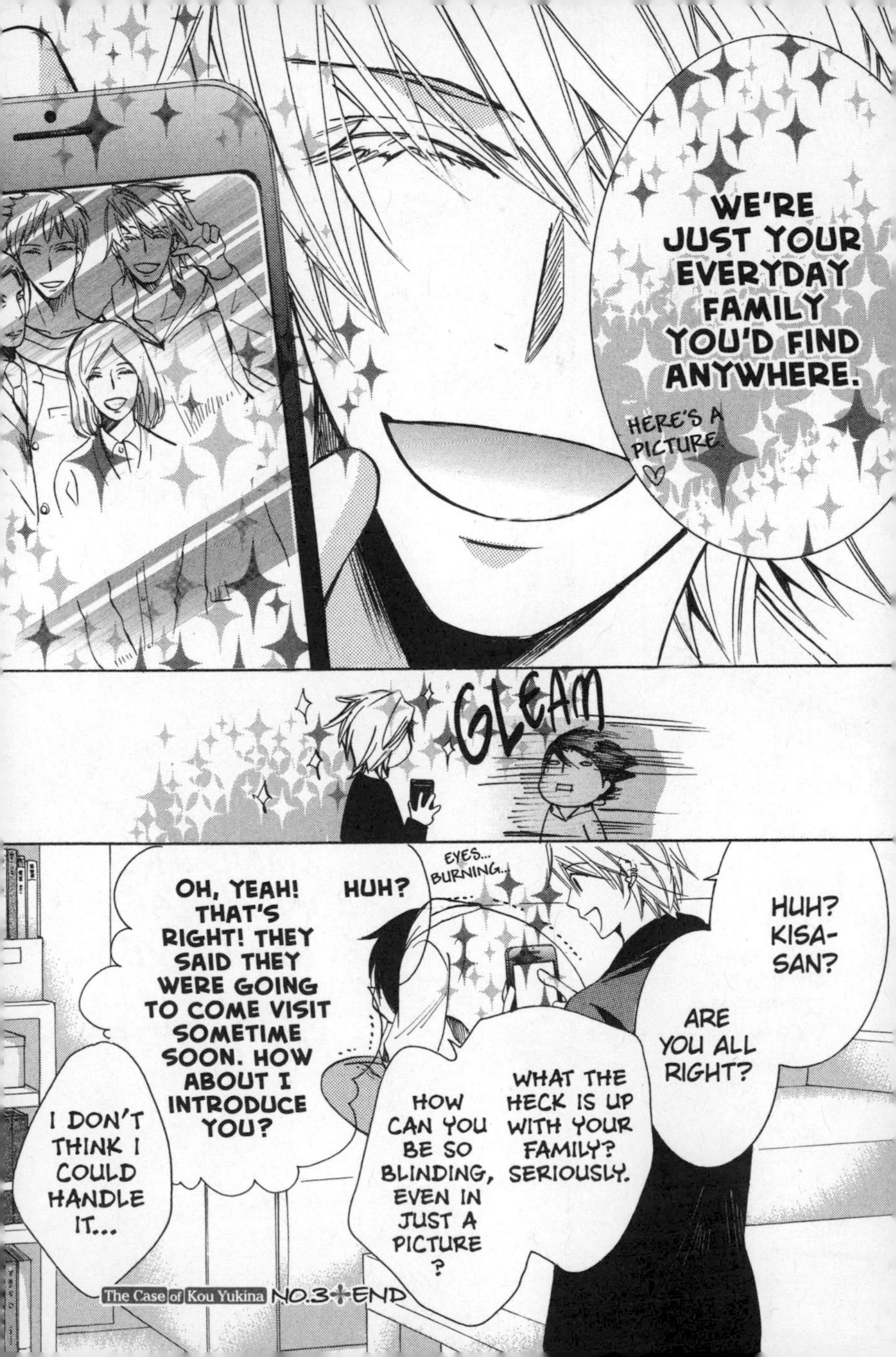
WE'RE JUST YOUR EVERYDAY FAMILY YOU'D FIND ANYWHERE.
HERE'S A PICTURE ♡
GLEAM
HUH? KISA-SAN?
ARE YOU ALL RIGHT?
EYES... BURNING...
WHAT THE HECK IS UP WITH YOUR FAMILY? SERIOUSLY.
HOW CAN YOU BE SO BLINDING, EVEN IN JUST A PICTURE?
HUH?
OH, YEAH! THAT'S RIGHT! THEY SAID THEY WERE GOING TO COME VISIT SOMETIME SOON. HOW ABOUT I INTRODUCE YOU?
I DON'T THINK I COULD HANDLE IT...
The Case of Kou Yukina NO.3 END

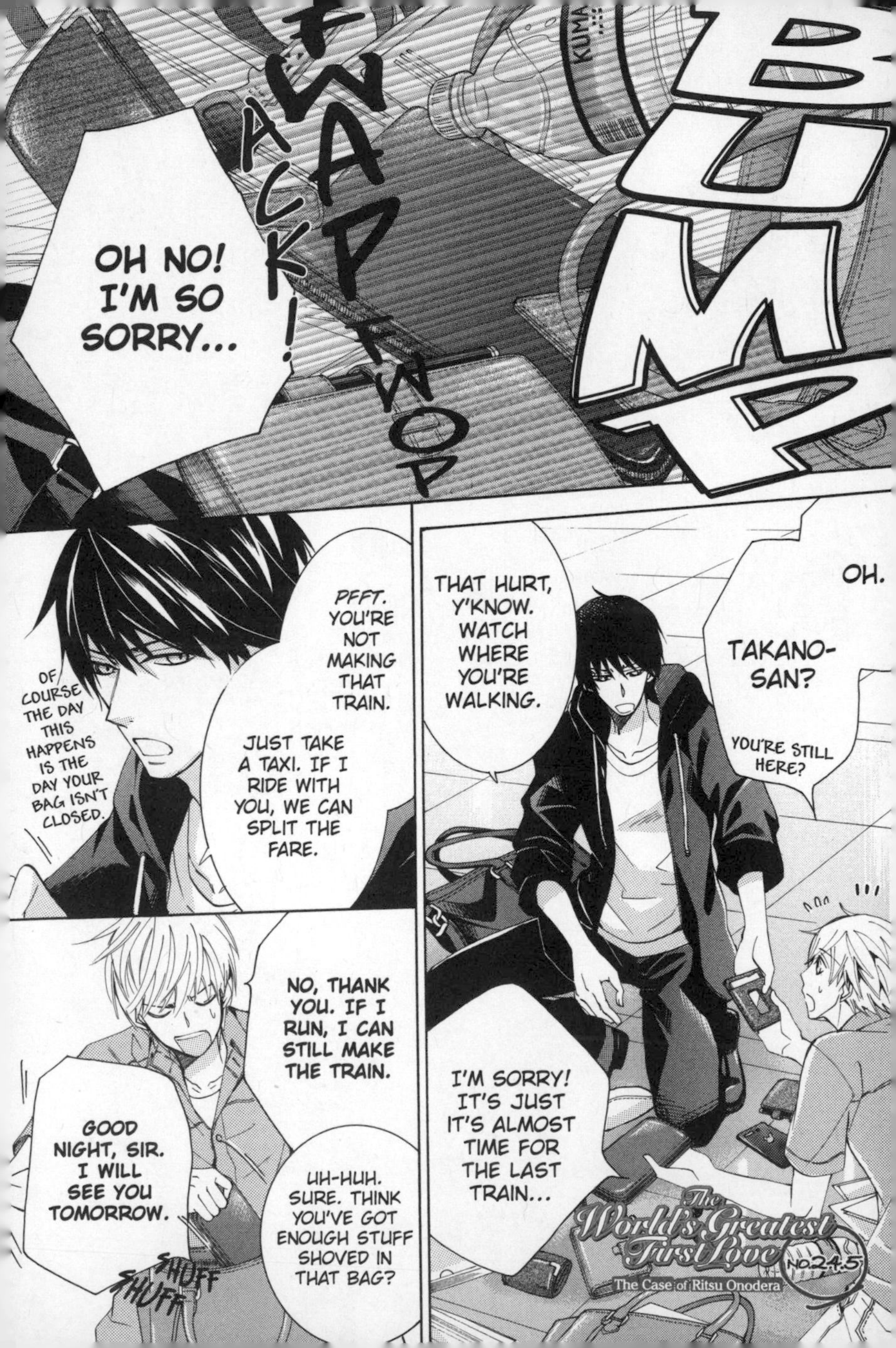
KUMA
BUMP
FWAP
FWOP
WHACK!
OH NO! I'M SO SORRY...
OH.
TAKANO-SAN?
YOU'RE STILL HERE?
THAT HURT, Y'KNOW. WATCH WHERE YOU'RE WALKING.
I'M SORRY! IT'S JUST IT'S ALMOST TIME FOR THE LAST TRAIN...
The World's Greatest First Love
No.24.5
The Case of Ritsu Onodera
PFFT. YOU'RE NOT MAKING THAT TRAIN.
JUST TAKE A TAXI. IF I RIDE WITH YOU, WE CAN SPLIT THE FARE.
OF COURSE THE DAY THIS HAPPENS IS THE DAY YOUR BAG ISN'T CLOSED.
NO, THANK YOU. IF I RUN, I CAN STILL MAKE THE TRAIN.
UH-HUH. SURE. THINK YOU'VE GOT ENOUGH STUFF SHOVED IN THAT BAG?
GOOD NIGHT, SIR. I WILL SEE YOU TOMORROW.
SHUFF
SHUFF

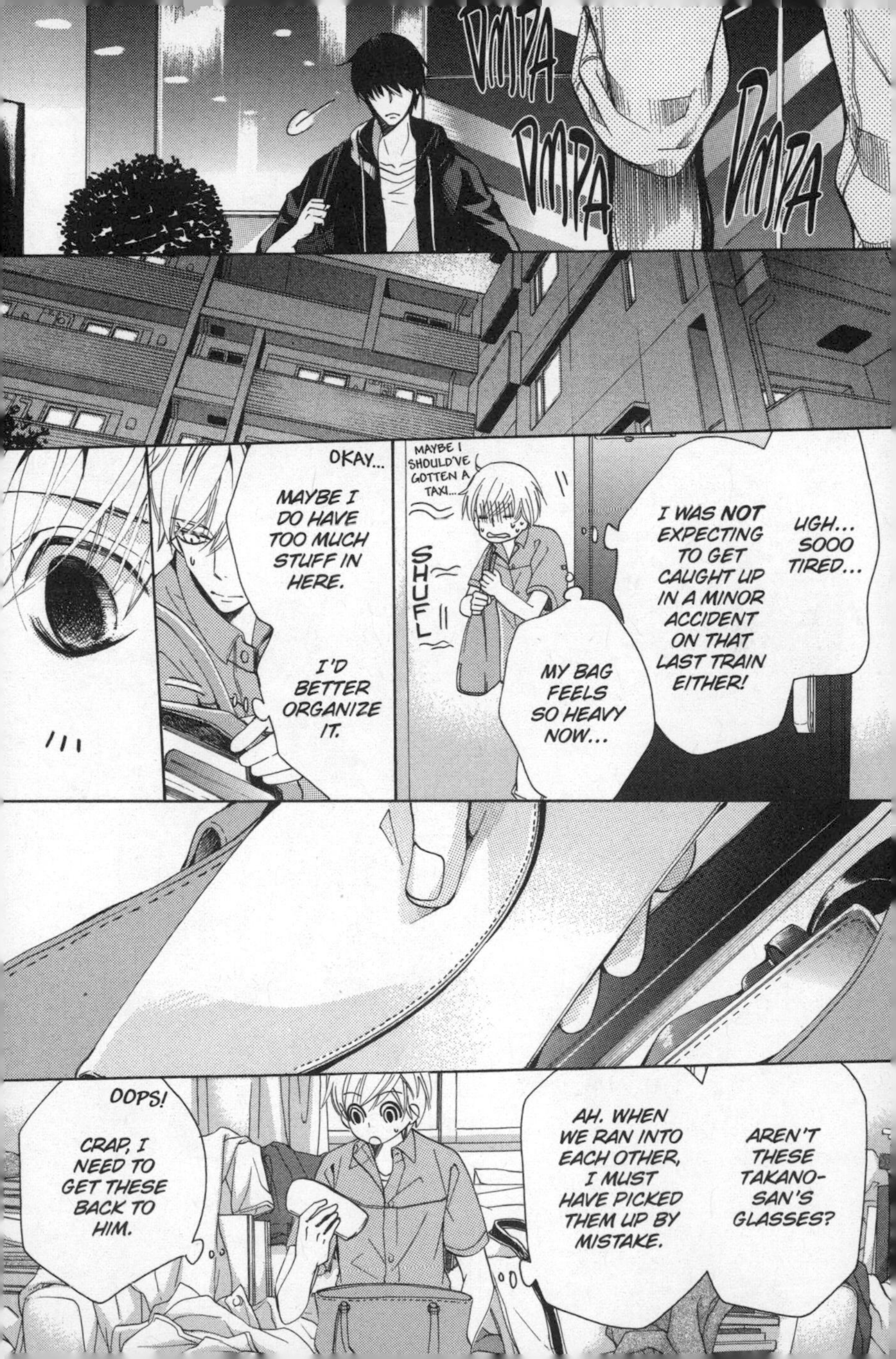
DMPA
DMPA
DMPA
UGH... SOOO TIRED...
I WAS NOT EXPECTING TO GET CAUGHT UP IN A MINOR ACCIDENT ON THAT LAST TRAIN EITHER!
MAYBE I SHOULD'VE GOTTEN A TAXI...
SHUFL
MY BAG FEELS SO HEAVY NOW...
OKAY...
MAYBE I DO HAVE TOO MUCH STUFF IN HERE.
I'D BETTER ORGANIZE IT.
AREN'T THESE TAKANO-SAN'S GLASSES?
AH. WHEN WE RAN INTO EACH OTHER, I MUST HAVE PICKED THEM UP BY MISTAKE.
OOPS!
CRAP, I NEED TO GET THESE BACK TO HIM.

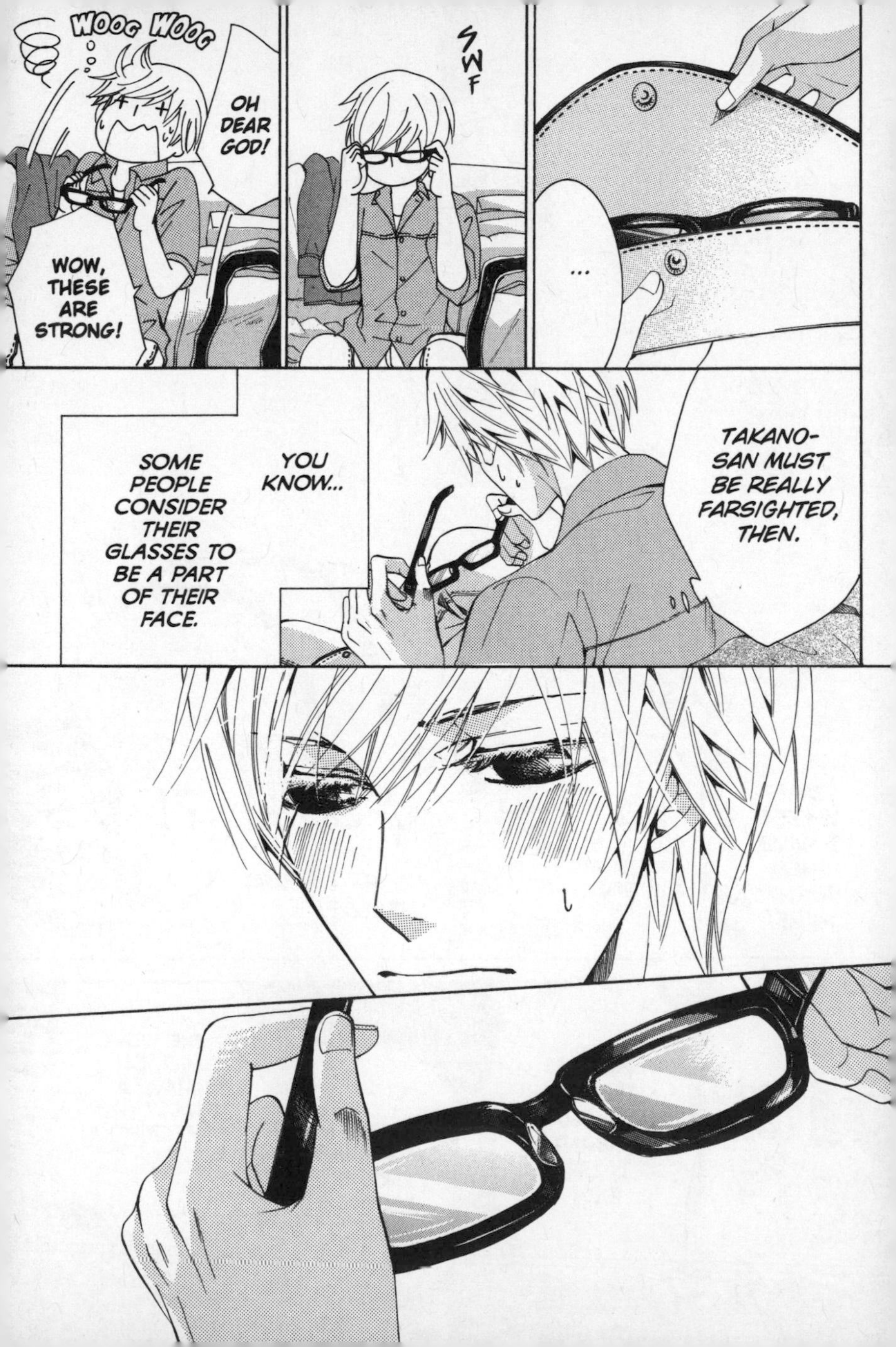
...
SWF
WOOG WOOG
OH DEAR GOD!
WOW, THESE ARE STRONG!
TAKANO-SAN MUST BE REALLY FARSIGHTED, THEN.
YOU KNOW...
SOME PEOPLE CONSIDER THEIR GLASSES TO BE A PART OF THEIR FACE.

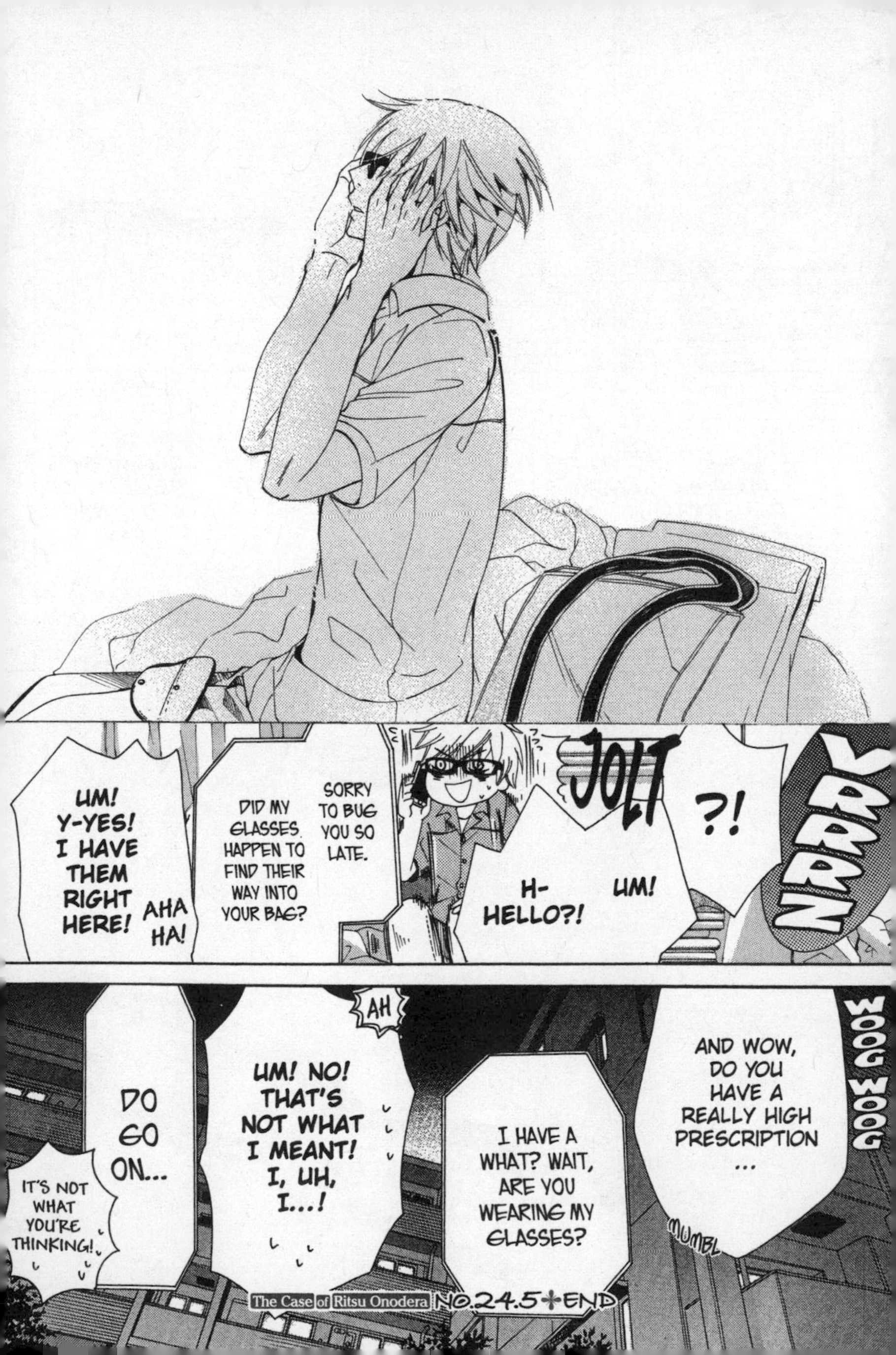
YARRN
?!
UM!
H- HELLO?!
JOLT
SORRY TO BUG YOU SO LATE.
DID MY GLASSES HAPPEN TO FIND THEIR WAY INTO YOUR BAG?
UM! Y-YES! I HAVE THEM RIGHT HERE!
AHA HA!
WOOG WOOG
AND WOW, DO YOU HAVE A REALLY HIGH PRESCRIPTION ...
MUMBL
I HAVE A WHAT? WAIT, ARE YOU WEARING MY GLASSES?
AH
UM! NO! THAT'S NOT WHAT I MEANT! I, UH, I...!
DO GO ON...
IT'S NOT WHAT YOU'RE THINKING!
The Case of Ritsu Onodera NO.24.5 END

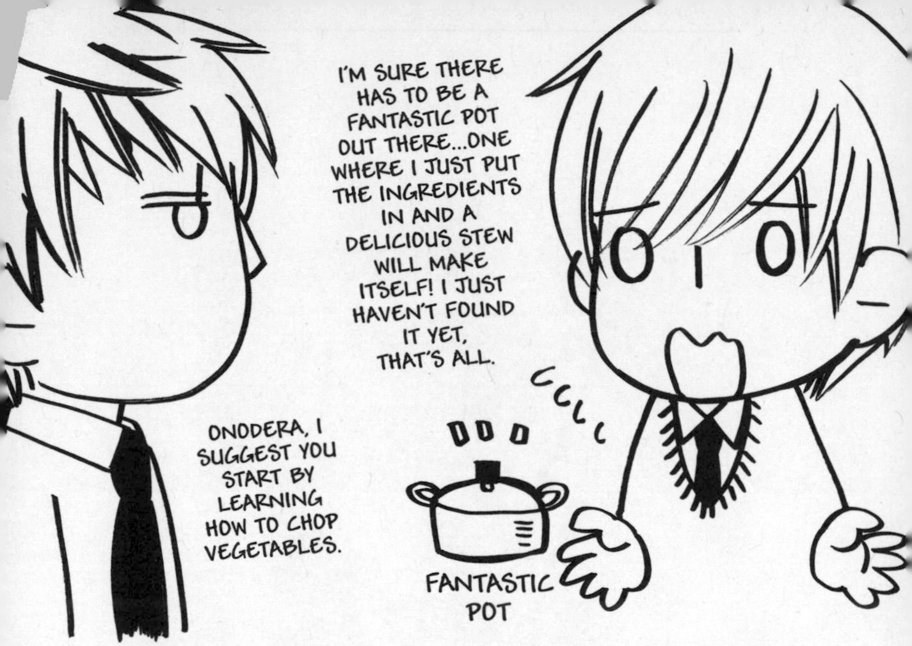
I'M SURE THERE HAS TO BE A FANTASTIC POT OUT THERE...ONE WHERE I JUST PUT THE INGREDIENTS IN AND A DELICIOUS STEW WILL MAKE ITSELF! I JUST HAVEN'T FOUND IT YET, THAT'S ALL.
FANTASTIC POT
ONODERA, I SUGGEST YOU START BY LEARNING HOW TO CHOP VEGETABLES.

HELLO. MY NAME IS SHUNGIKU NAKAMURA. THANK YOU FOR BUYING VOLUME 12 OF *THE WORLD'S GREATEST FIRST LOVE ~THE CASE OF RITSU ONODERA~*! I HOPE YOU ENJOYED IT. THE STORY WILL CONTINUE ON, SO I HOPE YOU KEEP READING. I LOOK FORWARD TO SEEING YOU NEXT VOLUME. THANK YOU VERY MUCH!

SHUNGIKU NAKAMURA

CURRENT SITUATION

I PLANTED SOME ROSES AT MY FAMILY'S HOME. THEY GET VERY NICE SUNLIGHT, SO THEY'RE GROWING MUCH, *MUCH* BETTER THAN THE ONES ON MY APARTMENT VERANDA. I'M ACTUALLY KIND OF ANNOYED, DESPITE BEING THE ONE WHO PLANTED THEM. I'M LOOKING FORWARD TO THEIR BLOOMING THIS YEAR!

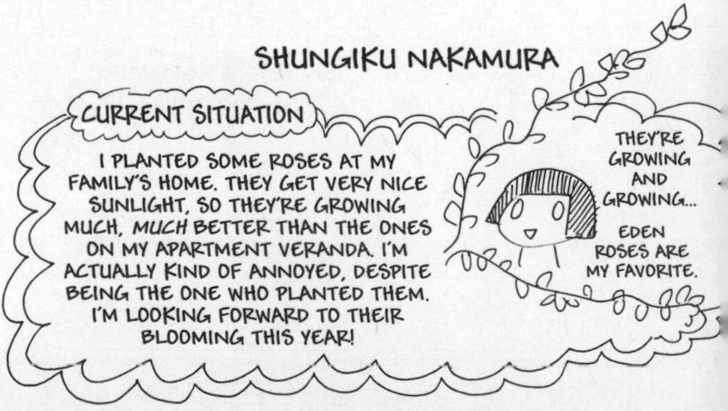
THEY'RE GROWING AND GROWING...
EDEN ROSES ARE MY FAVORITE.

My current goal is to organize
the area around my drawing
hand to make my tools
more easily accessible.

About the Author

Shungiku Nakamura
DOB December 13
Sagittarius
Blood Type O